Irish Criminal Justice:
Theory, Process and Procedure

Irish Criminal Justice:
Theory, Process and Procedure

By

Dr Vicky Conway

BCL, LLM, MSc (Criminology and Criminal Justice), PhD

Dr Yvonne Daly

BCL, PhD

Jennifer Schweppe

BCL, LLM, Grad. Dip

CLARUS
PRESS

Published by
Clarus Press Ltd,
Griffith Campus,
South Circular Road,
Dublin 8.

Typeset by
Datapage International Limited,
157 Rathmines Road Upper,
Rathmines,
Dublin 6.

Printed by
Colour Books Ltd,
Baldoyle,
Dublin 13.

ISBN
978-1-905536-32-0

For
Darren Dinsmore,
Cora and Jim Daly,
and
James Mayo

FOREWORD

The subject of Irish criminal procedure has been transformed in recent years. The greater prominence given by the Irish judiciary to constitutional requirements throughout the criminal justice system, the increasing importance attached to human rights law developed by humans rights bodies such as the European Court of Human Rights and the greater focus on pre-trial police investigation away from the courts have added considerably to the complexity of the field and to the breadth of its scope. Although the criminal trial continues to be of great symbolic importance for the criminal justice system, much of the action within the criminal justice process increasingly takes place outside trials as more and more defendants are sentenced without the benefit of a trial and increasing numbers are diverted away from criminal proceedings altogether. At the same time the focus on human rights law has broadened beyond the fair trial rights of the defendant to include rights for victims caught up in the criminal process and for prisoners at the receiving end of it. These developments have been accompanied by a maze of complex legislation and case law which makes the subject difficult for both students and practitioners to digest.

This stimulating book written by experts who have taught and researched in the field provides students and practitioners with a text which covers all these changes in an accessible and most readable way. The book has a number of strengths. It meets the extended reach of criminal procedure by including chapters on police powers and accountability, juvenile justice, victims, prisoners' rights and remedies for miscarriages of justice. It brings a critical edge to its subject matter by engaging with the theoretical literature and the policies that have shaped recent changes. Domestic legislation and case law are also placed within a comparative perspective by reference to developments in other jurisdictions. The book should appeal not only to students and practitioners of law but also to those studying courses in criminology and penology and involved in policy making.

I commend this scholarly text to all those who are looking for an accessible guide to take them through the complexities of the modern Irish criminal justice system and to direct them to the most up-to-date developments. It should be essential reading for all students of the subject.

John Jackson
10th September 2010

PREFACE

The impetus for this book came from our collective concern that students undertaking modules in criminal procedure or criminal justice in this jurisdiction did not have an Irish textbook relevant to their studies. *Irish Criminal Justice: Theory, Process and Procedure* is therefore primarily student-oriented, though we foresee that practitioners will also find it a useful resource and anyone with an interest in the functioning of the Irish criminal justice system will hopefully find its contents of value.

That said, we cannot but recognise the work done in the areas of criminal justice and criminal procedure by others in this jurisdiction. In particular, we are in awe of the seminal works of Professor Dermot Walsh and Tom O'Malley in their respective texts, *Criminal Procedure* and *The Criminal Process.*

We would like to thank a number of individuals who have supported us throughout the writing of this book. David McCartney of Clarus Press was enormously supportive and good natured throughout the writing process, and we would like to thank him for his encouragement and assistance. Many thanks also to Alma Clissman for proof-reading the text, and to Fabrice Robin for the cover design. We would also like to thank our respective institutions, the School of Law at Queen's University Belfast, the School of Law and Government at Dublin City University and the School of Law at the University of Limerick for providing space and time within which to complete this work. A special word of thanks is due to Professor John Jackson for kindly agreeing to write the Foreword to the text.

Finally, we would like to thank our respective friends and families for their support throughout the writing process. We are aware that we disappeared into this work for some time but hope you will welcome us back into your lives now that it is completed.

While the masculine pronoun is used throughout the book, in referring to offenders, members of an Garda Síochána, victims, prisoners and so on, this incorporates application to the feminine. In spite of all the assistance from colleagues, friends and families, any mistakes remain the authors' own. The law relating to criminal procedure is ever-changing and the text is correct as of 10th August 2010.

Vicky Conway
Yvonne Daly
Jennifer Schweppe

16th September 2010

CONTENTS

TABLE OF CASES

TABLE OF LEGISLATION

Acts of the Oireachtas

Secondary Irish Legislation

European Union

International Treaties and Conventions

Other Jurisdictions

Canada

England & Wales

United States

LIST OF ABBREVIATIONS

AG	–	Attorney General
CCRC	–	Criminal Case Review Commission
CPT	–	European Committee for the Prevention of Torture and Inhuman or Degrading Treatment or Punishment
CRC	–	UN Convention on the Rights of the Child
CSO	–	Community Service Order
DPP	–	Director of Public Prosecutions
EAW	–	European Arrest Warrant
ECHR	–	European Convention on Human Rights
ECtHR	–	European Court of Human Rights
EEW	–	European Evidence Warrant
HSE	–	Health Service Executive
ICCPR	–	International Covenant on Civil and Political Rights
IHRC	–	Irish Human Rights Commission
IPRT	–	Irish Penal Reform Trust
JLO	–	Juvenile Liaison Officer
MIC	–	Member in Charge
OASA	–	Offences Against the State Act
VIS	–	Victim Impact Statement(s)

CHAPTER 1
Introduction

Media reports on recent criminal events, TV programmes documenting unsolved cases or following fictitious forensic investigators, movies depicting crime gangs or terrorist plots, true crime and crime fiction novels: all seem more popular than ever before in 21st century society. Criminal behaviour is a fact of modern life and our fascination with criminal activity, policing, forensic investigations, victims and prisons is only further fuelled by the media representation of those things.[1] **[1–01]**

Away from the make-up and the cameras though, away from the imaginations of novelists and script-writers, the true world of the criminal justice system is in action every day and is, in its own way, also fascinating. This book examines the Irish criminal process, from the first potential interactions of the citizen with the criminal process through to the final step a convicted person can take, an application for a miscarriage of justice declaration. The central focus is criminal procedure, which covers the laws and regulations on the handling of criminal investigations and cases as they proceed through the system. However, the book also touches on criminal justice and criminological issues, as well as the law of evidence and the substantive criminal law. **[1–02]**

The Irish criminal process has gradually developed to its current position since the foundation of the state. The nature of that development has been shaped by the courts' interpretation of *Bunreacht na hÉireann* (the Irish Constitution), by the Acts of the Oireachtas, by the common law, by international treaties such as the European Convention on Human Rights and the UN Convention on the Rights of the Child, and by the input of bodies such as the European Court of Human Rights and the European Committee for the Prevention of Torture and Inhuman or Degrading Treatment or Punishment (CPT). This introduction outlines briefly a number of preliminary matters of note. **[1–03]**

I. The Irish Criminal Court Structure

The District Court is the lowest in the criminal court structure in Ireland. There are 24 Districts around the country, in which 63 judges preside under the leadership of the **[1–04]**

---

[1] On the interaction of crime and the media see Jewkes, *Media and Crime: A Critical Introduction* (Sage, London, 2004) and Carrabine, *Crime, Culture and the Media* (Polity, Cambridge, 2008).

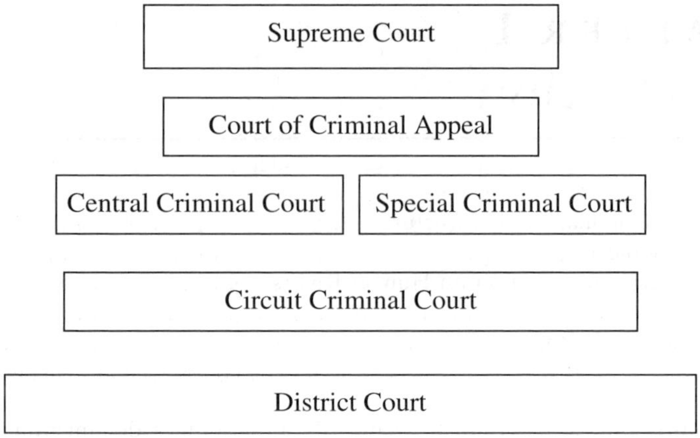

Figure 1.1 The Criminal Court Structure in Ireland

President of the District Court.[2] The District Court deals with minor offences in a summary manner, meaning that there is no jury and one judge, sitting alone, makes all decisions of law and of fact. Generally, the District Court deals with cases where a potential maximum punishment of a €5,000 fine[3] or 12 months imprisonment may be imposed.[4] On occasion, the District Court can try more serious offences, where this is provided for in legislation. These are known as indictable offences triable summarily and are further discussed in Chapter Seven. The District Court also acts as a "clearing house", sending cases forward for hearing in the higher courts. The District Court is the home of the Children Court, which deals with juvenile offenders and is examined in Chapter Eleven.

[1–05] Above the District Court is the Circuit Criminal Court. There are eight circuits around the country, with 37 ordinary judges under the leadership of the President of the Circuit Court.[5] This court can hear all indictable offences, i.e. serious offences, except "reserved offences" which can only be heard in the Central Criminal Court. The Circuit Criminal Court sits with a judge and jury.

[1–06] The Central Criminal Court is the highest court of first instance in the criminal court structure. This court, known as the High Court when addressing civil matters, sits in Dublin, though it visits the various circuits around the country at different times of the year. There are 35 judges of the Central Criminal Court under the leadership of the

---

[2] Courts and Court Officers Act 1995, s 11(1) as amended by the Civil Law (Miscellaneous Provisions) Act 2008, s 32.

[3] O'Malley, *The Criminal Process* (Round Hall, Dublin, 2009), p 257.

[4] A term of imprisonment of two years may be handed down by the District Court where consecutive sentences are being imposed: Criminal Justice Act 1984, s 12(1).

[5] Courts and Court Officers Act 1995, s 10(1) as amended by the Courts and Court Officers (Amendment) Act 2007, s 3.

President of the High Court.[6] The court sits with a judge and jury and can hear all criminal cases, with exclusive jurisdiction for the "reserved offences" of murder, rape, aggravated sexual assault, treason, piracy and related offences.

There is one more court of first instance in the Irish criminal court structure: the Special Criminal Court. This court, which is considered in detail in Chapter Eight, was legislated for by the Offences Against the State Act 1939[7] to operate when the ordinary courts are considered incapable of properly trying a particular offence. The Special Criminal Court sits as a three-judge court, with no jury, and the judges are usually selected from the benches of the Central Criminal Court, the Circuit Criminal Court and the District Court. In the past, this court, controversial for its denial of the right to a trial by jury, was most often used for the trial of those accused of paramilitary offences, related to the conflict in Northern Ireland. Nowadays, many so-called "gangland criminals" are tried in this court. **[1–07]**

In relation to appeals in the criminal court structure, a *de novo* hearing (i.e. a rehearing of the entire case) of a case originally heard in the District Court may take place in the Circuit Criminal Court. All other appeals are allowed on a point of law only. An appeal on a point of law lies from the District Court to the Central Criminal Court. An appeal on a point of law from the Circuit Court, the Central Criminal Court and the Special Criminal Court lies to the Court of Criminal Appeal, with an additional appeal on a point of law of exceptional public importance available to the Supreme Court. The Supreme Court is the highest possible court of appeal in the Irish court structure. It comprises seven judges, presided over by the Chief Justice.[8] **[1–08]**

The Court of Criminal Appeal[9] is a slightly peculiar body within the Irish criminal court structure as it has been due for abolition since the enactment of the Courts and Court Officers Act 1995.[10] Under that legislation, the functions of the Court of Criminal Appeal would transfer to the Supreme Court on its abolition. This has not occurred as yet and, given the workload of the Supreme Court, it seems unlikely to occur in the near future.[11] The Court of Criminal Appeal is an appeal court only and it sits with three judges: one from the Supreme Court and two from the Central Criminal Court.[12] Like the other appellate courts, it conducts appeals against both conviction and sentence. The appeals process in the Irish criminal justice system is discussed in Chapter Ten. **[1–09]**

---

[6] Courts and Court Officers Act 1995, s 9 as amended by the Courts and Court Officers (Amendment) Act 2007, s 2.
[7] s 35(2).
[8] Courts (Establishment and Constitution) Act 1961, s 1(2) as amended by the Courts and Court Officers Act 1995, s 6(1).
[9] Established under the Courts (Establishment and Constitution) Act 1961, s 3(1).
[10] s 4.
[11] The creation of a more permanent court of appeal within the Irish court structure was advocated in the *Report of the Working Group on a Court of Appeal* (chaired by Ms Justice Susan Denham) (Stationery Office, Dublin, May 2009).
[12] Courts (Establishment and Constitution) Act 1961, s 3(2).

II. Constitutional Rights

[1–10] At the heart of the criminal justice system are conflicts which arise between the societal need for criminal offences to be investigated and prosecuted on the one hand and the rights of the individual suspected or accused of committing a crime on the other. The Irish Constitution is a source of many rights central to the criminal process, both rights expressly set out therein, and rights which the judges of the superior courts have recognised as having constitutional protection. Express rights specifically relevant to the criminal process include

- Article 38.1 – the right to a fair trial;
- Article 38.5 – the right to trial by jury on serious criminal charges;
- Article 40.4.1 – the right to liberty; and,
- Article 40.5 – the inviolability of the dwelling.

[1–11] Many more unenumerated rights, i.e. those not expressly set out in the text of the Constitution but recognised by the judges of the superior courts, have been set out. Some of these flow from Art 38.1, more are located within the general provisions of Art 40.3 or within other provisions, while the constitutional location of some of these rights has not been clearly established.[13] What follows is an inexhaustive list of such rights:

- The presumption of innocence;
- The right to privacy;
- The right to dignity;
- The right to bodily integrity;
- The right to silence;
- The right to legal advice;
- The right to trial within a reasonable time;
- The right to bail; and,
- The right to proportionality in sentencing.

[1–12] The courts guard rights which have constitutional status with particular care and are slow to allow any practices to develop which would breach those rights. This is evidenced by the strict exclusionary rule which applies in the criminal courts to evidence obtained in breach of constitutional rights.[14] Having said that, where legislation is enacted by the Oireachtas which restricts or impinges on constitutional rights, the courts have often endorsed the legislative scheme allowing for such restrictions. Examples include provisions for detention without charge of potentially 168 hours duration in certain circumstances,[15] numerous restrictions on the right to silence[16] and mandatory sentencing.[17] Operating a presumption of constitutionality,

---

[13] For example the right to pre-trial legal advice (discussed in Chapter Three); see *People (DPP) v Healy* [1990] 2 IR 73.

[14] Discussed in Chapter Four.

[15] Under the Criminal Justice (Drug Trafficking) Act 1996, s 2 and the Criminal Justice Act 2007, s 50.

[16] For example, the Criminal Justice Act 1984. ss 18,19 and 19A as amended by the Criminal Justice Act, 2007.

[17] For example the mandatory life sentence for murder under the Criminal Justice Act 1990, s 2.

and invoking the concept of proportionality, the courts generally do not invalidate legislation where it can be read in a constitutionally-compliant manner.

III. The European Convention on Human Rights

The second important document which provides protection for the rights of the citizens of Ireland in the context of the criminal process is the European Convention on Human Rights and Fundamental Freedoms (ECHR). This international treaty, created in 1950, protects many rights, some of which are particularly relevant in the context of criminal procedure. Article 6, for example, protects the right to a fair trial, including the presumption of innocence and the right to trial with reasonable expedition. It has also been held to include other related rights such as the right to silence/privilege against self-incrimination.[18] Article 8 is of particular importance also protecting, as it does, the right to privacy. [1–13]

In 2003 the ECHR was brought within Irish domestic law by virtue of the European Convention on Human Rights Act 2003. As a result judges in the Irish courts must take "judicial notice" of the Convention and the decisions of the European Court of Human Rights (ECtHR).[19] While there is some overlap between the rights protected by the Irish Constitution and those set out or recognised within the ECHR this does not mean that the latter instrument is redundant. In fact, rights are often given a significantly different interpretation under the two documents,[20] which allows for expanded debate on the relevant issues, and increasingly Convention rights are being argued in criminal cases at a domestic level. Indeed since the passing of the Act in 2003, human rights discourse seems to be penetrating all aspects of the criminal justice system, from garda investigations[21] through to the treatment of prisoners[22]; a development which is to be warmly welcomed. [1–14]

IV. Notable Themes

A number of themes, reflecting the development of the modern criminal justice system in Ireland, are notable throughout this book. Two of most significant relate to the shifting focus of the criminal process and the manner in which change has come about therein. [1–15]

In recent years, the Oireachtas has become more involved in legislating for matters of criminal procedure than was the case in the first 50 or so years of the state. Statutes altering aspects of the criminal process have seemed to come hot on one another's heels, particularly in the past 15 years, in which more than 15 Acts have been passed, each introducing substantive reforms to the investigation, prosecution and sentencing [1–16]

---

[18] See *Funke v France* (1993) 16 EHRR 297; *Murray v United Kingdom* (1996) 22 EHRR 29; *Saunders v United Kingdom* (1996) 23 EHRR 313; *Heaney and McGuinness v Ireland* (2001) 33 EHRR 12.

[19] European Convention on Human Rights Act 2003, s 4.

[20] The right to silence (discussed in Chapter Three), for example, is protected under Art 40.6 of the Constitution, as a corollary of the right to freedom of expression; while within the ECHR system it has been recognised as an essential part of the right to a fair trial under Art 6.

[21] Discussed in Chapters Two, Three, Four and Five.

[22] Discussed in Chapter Thirteen.

of serious crimes. By the nature of their position as legislators, the members of the Oireachtas have forced new concepts on the criminal process and have, in places, removed old rules. While much of this is beneficial to the investigation, trial and punishment of offenders, which is of course the main function of the criminal process, much of it too raises concerns about the protection of important individual rights of the citizens of the state. Or, to employ the terminology adopted by Herbert L. Packer in the 1960s, it seems clear that there has been a shift in the Irish criminal process away from its due process foundations towards a crime control orientation.[23] Powers of detention,[24] covert surveillance[25] and forensic sampling[26] along with severe restrictions on the right to silence[27] and the right to bail[28] seem to shift the centre of gravity of the process ever more away from the courts and into the pre-trial period of garda investigation. Even where the courts are more central to the process, this shift can be noted in the expanding use of non-jury trials[29] and legislative provision for presumptive and mandatory sentences.[30]

[1–17] Many of the changes which have occurred in the Irish criminal process in recent years have been in reaction to crises, or perceived crises. The 1996 provisions for prolonged detention of suspected drug traffickers[31] and for alterations to the law on bail,[32] for example, were enacted in the direct aftermath of the killings of Detective Garda Jerry McCabe and investigative journalist Veronica Guerin. Ten years later, the 2006 provision for the presentation of prior inconsistent witness statements at trial[33] was a clear response to the collapse of the Liam Keane trial for murder and the shocking image of the accused on all of the national newspapers sticking his two fingers up to the camera, and, it seemed, to society. Again, in 2009, the killing of Roy Collins, a family member of a witness in a "gangland" trial five years previously, sparked a wave of legislative responses enhancing garda powers of investigation, allowing for the use of the Special Criminal Court for non-terrorist offences, and introducing tough sentences for specific offences.[34] While such provisions may be necessary within the criminal process, the manner of their enactment, often knee-jerk, in times of high tension and pressure, must raise concerns. Furthermore, a number of enactments stated to be aimed at particular issues within the criminal process, for example "gangland crime", have in

---

[23] Packer, *The Limits of the Criminal Sanction* (Stanford University Press, Stanford, 1968) and "Two Models of the Criminal Process" (1964) 113 U Pa L Rev 1.
[24] Discussed in Chapter Two.
[25] Discussed in Chapter Four.
[26] *ibid.*
[27] Discussed in Chapter Three.
[28] Discussed in Chapter Six.
[29] Discussed in Chapter Eight.
[30] Discussed in Chapter Nine.
[31] Criminal Justice (Drug Trafficking) Act 1996.
[32] Bail Act 1997 introduced following a constitutional referendum to insert Art 40.4.7.
[33] Criminal Justice Act 2006, s 16.
[34] Both the Criminal Justice (Miscellaneous Provisions) Act 2009 and the Criminal Justice (Amendment) Act 2009 were passed into legislation with alarming haste - just three weeks in the case of the latter, which creates new organised crime offences, schedules certain organised crime offences meaning they will be tried in non-jury courts, expands the use of inferences from silence and adds post-release provisions to sentences.

fact not been limited to application in such circumstances only, and provisions enacted to address specific crises have more often than not found their way into the mainstream criminal process in a short period of time.[35] A lack of strategic forward-planning has characterised the Irish criminal process to date with new legislation often being introduced before the effectiveness of existing legislation can be assessed. At the time of writing, a consultation process is taking place under the auspices of the Department of Justice through a White Paper on Crime. This may allow for greater depth of analysis prior to the enactment of legislation in the future than has been the case in the past, though its remit has to date been limited to particular matters such as crime prevention and community safety, and criminal sanctions.

V. Structure of this Book

This book engages in a processual exploration of the Irish criminal process. The first four substantive chapters are primarily concerned with pre-trial procedure and the related interaction between citizens and An Garda Síochána. Chapter Two outlines the procedure involved in garda powers of *Stop, Search, Arrest and Detention.* Chapter Three discusses *Interrogation* during pre-trial detention. Chapter Four looks at the *Collection and Admissibility of Evidence* considering the duty to preserve and seek out evidence, searches of private property, forensic sampling, covert surveillance, the European Evidence Warrant and the exclusionary rule. Chapter Five outlines the issues related to *Garda Accountability* and the manner in which errant gardaí[36] can be disciplined. **[1–18]**

Chapters Six to Ten consider the operation of the courts and court officers in the trial and appeal stages of the criminal process. Chapter Six begins this discussion with an examination of *Prosecutions,* detailing the role of the DPP amongst other matters. Chapters Seven and Eight respectively explore *Summary Trial* and *Trial on Indictment* considering the procedural elements of both and the significant differences between the two. Chapter Nine looks at *Sentencing*, detailing the various theories of sentencing and purposes of punishment before outlining the procedural aspects of sentencing hearings and the sentencing options available to the Irish courts. Chapter Ten then outlines *Appeals* procedures. **[1–19]**

In Chapters Eleven, Twelve and Thirteen the rules relating to particular groups within the criminal process are examined. These chapters focus on *Juvenile Justice, Victims,* and *Prisoners' Rights.* As distinct entities within the criminal process, specific rights are held by and specific rules apply to these groups, all of which are outlined in the relevant chapters. **[1–20]**

The book concludes with Chapter Fourteen on *Miscarriages of Justice*, the final opportunity for convicted persons to claim their innocence, or at least to assert that they ought not to have been convicted.

---

[35] A clear early example of this is the Offences Against the State Act 1939 which had a significant effect on changing the "ordinary" criminal justice landscape of Ireland: see Walsh, "The Impact of Anti-Subversive Laws on Police Powers and Practice in Ireland: The Silent Erosion of Individual Freedom" (1989) 62 *Temple Law Review* 1099.

[36] Note that throughout this work the term 'gardaí' is used to refer to members of An Garda Síochána generally and is not restrictive in terms of rank.

[1–21] At the end of this book the reader will have a thorough understanding of the Irish criminal process and the theories, processes and procedures which are in operation within the system every day. Exploration of the book should also lead to a critical understanding of developments in Irish criminal justice in recent years and generate thinking around necessary reforms, particularly if Ireland is to continue to fulfil its international human rights commitments.

CHAPTER 2
Stop, Search, Arrest and Detention

In this chapter we consider key elements of the pre-trial process and what are often the first contacts suspects have with the criminal justice system: stop and search, arrest and detention. These pre-trial powers play an important role in the detection, investigation and prevention of crime yet have the potential to conflict with personal rights such as liberty, privacy and bodily integrity. Achieving a balance between individual rights and the public interest in preventing and investigating crime creates tensions in the use of these powers. **[2–01]**

Stop and search involves stopping an individual on the street or in a vehicle or vessel to conduct a search of his person and/or property to look for evidence of a crime that has been committed, or for a weapon, drugs or firearm and so on, that it is believed will be used in the commission of an offence. This chapter explores the powers which gardaí have to conduct stops and searches under both common law and statute law and the conditions which must be adhered to in the exercise of these powers. It then sets out the powers which gardaí have to arrest suspects, critically analysing the potential infringements of the right to liberty which arise in this context. The final section of the chapter examines the procedure and safeguards applying to persons in detention in garda custody. **[2–02]**

I. Reasonable Suspicion

[2–03] In nearly all instances where a power of stop and search, arrest, or detention is afforded by legislation there is a requirement for reasonableness.[1] In the UK case of *Dallison and Caffrey*[2] Lord Diplock defined the term reasonable suspicion as

> "whether a reasonable man, assumed to know the law and possessed of the information which in fact was possessed by the defendant, would believe that there was reasonable and probable cause."[3]

[2–04] It is an objective test, unconcerned with the arresting officer's subjective belief. In *Hussein v Chong Fook Kam*[4] the House of Lords stated that a lower standard than a *prima facie* case constituted suspicion. Suspicion is the first step on the road toward building a case. This, the court held, may involve evidence which might not be admissible in a trial but which could be substantiated through further investigation prior to being presented in court. It would be prohibitive to the investigation of crime to impose a higher burden at this point. For instance, evidence such as hearsay or an individual's previous record could be used by an officer to form a reasonable suspicion to arrest an individual, even if this is not admissible evidence in court. On the other hand, some English case-law suggests that it can be possible to arrest prematurely and that further questioning may be required prior to arrest.[5]

[2–05] The Supreme Court clarified the Irish position in the case of *DPP (Walsh) v Cash*,[6] where a man was arrested for burglary following a match between fingerprints found at the scene and fingerprints on garda record, the lawful retention of which could not be assured to the trial court. This match was the sole basis for the reasonable suspicion of the investigating garda. While further aspects of this case are considered in Chapter Four,[7] one question for the Supreme Court was whether the potentially illegally or unconstitutionally retained prints could lawfully form the basis of reasonable suspicion to ground an arrest. The Supreme Court declared that it could, refusing to accept that "where a suspicion used to ground an arrest is itself based on illegality, the subsequent arrest is unlawful." Fennelly J concluded that

> "the appellant has not established that an onus rests on the prosecution to establish the lawful provenance of material relied upon by a [garda]... or that such material was obtained without breach of a constitutional right to form reasonable cause justifying an arrest."[8]

---

[1] This can be represented as 'reasonably suspects', 'with reasonable cause suspects' or 'has reasonable grounds to suspect' but the courts apply no different meaning to these terms.
[2] [1964] 2 All ER 610.
[3] *ibid.* at 619.
[4] [1970] AC 942.
[5] *ibid.*
[6] [2010] IESC 1.
[7] We will see in Chapter Four that the applicants attempted to extend the exclusionary rule of evidence to the investigatory stage of the process.
[8] [2010] IESC 1 at para 42.

The European Court of Human Rights (ECtHR) has held that reasonableness forms an "essential part of the safeguard against arbitrary arrest and detention"[9] and that reasonable suspicion

> "...presupposes the existence of facts or information which would satisfy an objective observer that the person concerned may have committed the offence. What may be regarded as 'reasonable' will however depend upon all the circumstances."[10]

II. Stop and Search

Stop and search is an important policing tool in the prevention and investigation of crime. It can assist the police in detecting prohibited items such as weapons and controlled substances in public places, and in the discovery of evidence for offences under investigation. Encounters are usually brief with no lasting consequences yet it is a controversial power due to potential invasions of privacy and discriminatory application. In England in the 1970s and 1980s it was alleged that broad powers targeted at young black men led to riots in Brixton and Toxteth.[11] While the law regulating stop and search was substantially reformed and safeguarded by the Police and Criminal Evidence Act 1984, claims of racial discrimination in the use of the powers continue.[12] In *Gillan v UK*,[13] in 2009, the ECtHR held that powers under the UK Terrorism Act 2000 were in breach of the right to liberty under Art 6 European Convention on Human Rights (ECHR) and privacy under Art 8 ECHR. While similar case law and data is not available for Ireland the European Union Minorities and Discrimination Survey 2008 found that 59 per cent of Sub-Saharan Africans had been stopped at least once by a garda in the previous year.[14] **[2–06]**

Stop and Question

In the case of *DPP (Stratford) v Fagan*[15] the Supreme Court examined whether gardaí had a common law power to stop individuals. In that case, a garda saw a man exit a public house, get into his car and begin driving. There was nothing evidentially wrong with the man's driving but the garda chose to stop the car, smelt alcohol on the man's breath, breathalysed him and arrested him. The central issue in the case was whether **[2–07]**

---

[9] *Fox v United Kingdom* (1991) 13 EHRR 157 at para 32.

[10] *ibid.*

[11] On this generally see Scarman, *Report on the Disturbances in Brixton 10th to 13th April 1981* (HMSO, London, 1981). See Bowling and Philips, "Policing Ethnic Minority Communities" in *The Handbook of Policing* (Newburn (ed.), Willan, Devon, 2003).

[12] Bowling and Philips, "Disproportionate and Discriminatory: Reviewing the Evidence on Police Stop and Search" (2007) 70(6) MLR 936 cite that black people in England were, in 2005, six times more likely to be stopped and searched than a white person. See further Miller, Quinton and Bland, *Police Stops and Searches: Lessons From a Programme of Research* (Police Research Series Papers, Home Office, London, 2000); Waddington, Stenson and Don, "In Proportion: Race and Police Stop and Search" (2004) 44(6) *British Journal of Criminology* 889; Edwards, "Stop and Search, Terrorism and the Human Rights Deficit" (2008) 37(3) CLWR 32.

[13] [2009] ECHR 28.

[14] Report available at http://fra.europa.eu/fraWebsite/eu-midis/eumidis_main_results_report_en.htm.

[15] [1994] 2 ILRM 349.

the garda had lawful authority to stop this individual or if it was an unlawful deprivation of liberty. The Supreme Court held that gardaí have a common law power to stop motorists at random for the purpose of detecting and preventing crime. This is a power to stop, which does not extend to obliging the driver or passengers to answer questions or to conducting a search. This decision relates solely to motorists and while Walsh criticised that it is at odds with the rule that the police have no power to curtail liberty short of arrest,[16] the High Court has reaffirmed the common law power in relation to stopping vehicles for the prevention and detection of drug crime, in *DPP (Higgins) v Farrell*.[17]

[2–08] Gardaí have a number of statutory powers to stop individuals. Section 30 of the Offences Against the State Act 1939 (OASA) allows gardaí to stop and question anyone suspected of being involved in or attempting an offence under that Act or carrying documents relating to offences against the State. This includes a power to interrogate, with the provision of false information constituting an offence,[18] and while negative inferences can be drawn from silence from the point of being placed in custody, this will not be done at the point of stopping. The section also provides for arrest and detention[19] but if a garda is simply stopping and questioning an individual under this provision the procedure should be brief and not of itself involve any detention of the individual.[20]

[2–09] Other statutory provisions tend to relate to very specific instances such as where a garda suspects an individual is in possession of an archaeological object and suspects there is an offence involved,[21] where people are doing house to house collections,[22] or littering.[23] There is no obligation on a person stopped by a garda in such circumstances to answer questions. This is important because detention safeguards, such as the right to legal advice,[24] do not apply in these specific instances.

Stop and Search

[2–10] While the court in *Fagan*[25] recognised a common law power to stop and question, no common law power to stop and search has been recognised in Ireland as it presents a greater intrusion on liberty and privacy. In *DPP (Higgins) v Farrell*[26] Clark J, in the High Court, stated that once a car was stopped under the common law power, a request could be made to search the car but the driver's consent would be required to conduct the search. To conduct a search, therefore, gardaí must rely either on the voluntary consent of the individual, who would need to be informed that he[27] is under

16 Walsh, *Criminal Procedure* (Round Hall, Dublin, 2002), p 362.
17 [2009] IEHC 368.
18 OASA, s 30(6).
19 See below para 2-38.
20 Walsh, above n 16, p 364.
21 National Monument (Amendment) Act 1987, s 20.
22 Street and House to House Collection Act 1962, ss 19 and 20.
23 Litter Act 1997, s 23.
24 Discussed in Chapter Three.
25 Above n 15.
26 Above n 17.
27 Throughout the book, use of the masculine pronoun does not exclude application to the feminine.

no obligation to submit to the search, or on a statutory power. In the case, a garda stopped and searched the appellant's car under the Misuse of Drugs Act 1977, which requires that the garda with reasonable cause suspects the individual is in possession of a controlled drug. In evidence at trial the garda submitted that his suspicion was based on the fact that the area had a known drugs problem. Clark J held that the requirements of the 1977 Act were not met by the fact that the area had a known drugs problem; this was not sufficient to justify the search.

It was held in *DPP v Rooney*[28] that if a garda wishes to conduct a stop and search he must inform the individual of this intention and advise him of the statute being relied upon. However, in *DPP (Higgins) v Farrell*[29] the High Court clarified that this was not an absolute requirement and that **[2–11]**

> "...there will always be occasions where the exigencies are such that they do not permit opportunities to communicate such information or where the reason is obvious or where, as happens at airports and the entrance to many public institutions, persons impliedly consent to body searches."[30]

Statute law in Ireland grants numerous powers to conduct stops and searches on a piecemeal basis, arising in relation to specific offences including environmental concerns (e.g. protection of fish,[31] wildlife,[32] and preventing the spread of animal disease[33]); immigration[34]; smuggling[35]; public order[36]; possession of a syringe or blood with intention to cause injury or intimidate[37]; possession of a stolen item[38]; drugs[39]; firearms, weapons and imitation weapons[40]; and, explosive items.[41] **[2–12]**

One of the broadest statutory provisions for stop and search is s 30 of the OASA 1939, which permits such action where the individual is suspected of having committed, being about to commit, or being involved in the commission of an offence under Part V of the Act. Unlike most other legislation, there is no stated requirement that the suspicion be reasonable in nature. The term "search" is not defined in the legislation, leaving uncertainty as to what is permissible. Walsh contends that a strip-search in **[2–13]**

---

[28] [1992] 2 IR 7.
[29] Above n 17.
[30] *ibid.* para 32.
[31] Fisheries Act 1925.
[32] Wildlife Act 1976.
[33] Diseases of Animals Act 1966 as amended by the Wildlife (Amendment) Act 2000.
[34] Aliens Order 1946.
[35] Customs Consolidation Act 1876.
[36] Criminal Justice (Public Order) Act 1994.
[37] Non-Fatal Offences Against the Person Act 1997.
[38] Dublin Police Act 1842.
[39] Misuse of Drugs Act 1977 and the Customs and Excise (Miscellaneous Provisions) Act 1988.
[40] Firearms Act 1925 and Firearms and Offensive Weapons Act 1990 as amended by the Criminal Justice (Miscellaneous Provisions) Act 2009.
[41] Explosives Substances Act 1875.

public would be indecent so could not be done.[42] The section permits extension of the search to any vehicle or vessel if the garda suspects (again, not necessarily reasonably) that it contains someone who could be arrested under that section.

[2–14] Section 8 of the Criminal Law Act 1976 applies a different formula to the stop and search powers it contains. Under this section gardaí have the power to search any car when they suspect with reasonable cause that an offence covered by the Act has been, is being or is about to be committed, to ascertain whether someone in the car was involved in the offence or there is evidence relating to the offence in the car. If, following this search, the garda "with reasonable cause" suspects that an individual in the car was involved in or has evidence relating to the offence he may search that person. The section applies to a long list of offences: OASA offences, murder, manslaughter, larceny, malicious damage, firearms, escape from custody, offensive weapons, certain road traffic offences and illegal immigration or trafficking offences.[43] This section does not extend to searches of persons, even where suspicion exists in relation to any of these offences. Reasonable force may be used to compel the individual to stop the vehicle.[44]

[2–15] No details are provided in the legislation as to what can occur during the search of the vehicle or what might contribute to the creation of a suspicion concerning the occupants of the car. Occupants can be questioned about their identities, movements, and so on, but there is no obligation on the individuals to answer questions. No time limits are provided in the legislation, and so once the garda has had reasonable time to search the vehicle he must allow the occupants to leave, unless he is taking further action.

[2–16] Section 23 of the Misuse of Drugs Act 1977 permits a garda to search any individual he believes to be in possession of a controlled drug in breach of the Act. It permits the detention of the individual for as long as is reasonably necessary to conduct the search, if such detention is considered necessary.[45] Where an internal body search is required the individual should be brought to a garda station, though in the case of *Devoy v Ireland*[46] Finnegan P in the High Court was satisfied where individuals searched in a nightclub were taken to gender specific toilets and offered the option of being searched in the cubicles. In *O'Callaghan v Ireland*[47] the applicant challenged as unconstitutional this power of detention in the absence of arrest. The Supreme Court rejected the argument, holding that the threat posed by the danger of use and distribution of drugs justified the interference. The Court noted that the power to search could potentially prevent arrests from being made, thus protecting the individual. Importantly, the Court held that this search provision had the effect of detention and so all the rights and safeguards attaching to detention should apply, given the potential intimacy of the searches and concerns for invasion of rights to liberty, privacy and bodily integrity.

[42] Walsh, above n 16, p 369. In other jurisdictions more specific detail is provided on this issue. In the UK for instance, s 45 of the Terrorism Act 2000 states that in the conduct of a search a constable may only remove outer-clothing.
[43] Criminal Law Act 1976, s 8.
[44] s 8(3).
[45] s 23(1)(a).
[46] [2004] IEHC 404.
[47] [1994] 1 IR 555.

One problem which emerges from the decision in *O'Callaghan* is the potential for gardaí to use s 23 as a substitution for arrest. In *People (DPP) v Boylan*[48] gardaí used further provisions of s 23 which state that if reasonable suspicion regarding an individual exists then the garda is permitted to search any vehicle or vessel if he suspects – not reasonably suspects – that drugs may be found in the vehicle.[49] If the garda concerned feels the location is unsuitable for a vehicle search he may require the individual to move it to an appropriate place.[50] In *Boylan*, the applicant was stopped by gardaí under s 23 in Dublin Port. His lorry was searched and cannabis was discovered. He was taken to a shed for two hours but his lorry was only searched for a short time. He was then taken to a garda station and detained under s 4 of the Criminal Justice Act 1984,[51] which applies once an individual has been arrested. The question arose as to when the applicant had been arrested. The Court of Criminal Appeal concluded that he had been arrested on being brought to the shed. Once arrested, he should have been brought to a garda station immediately. That this did not happen meant that his subsequent detention was unlawful and any evidence gathered in that time was inadmissible in court. **[2–17]**

The Firearms Act 1925 permits stop and search of any person whom a garda believes to be in possession of a firearm or ammunition. This was extended by s 16 of the Firearms and Offensive Weapons Act 1990, as amended by s 41 of the Criminal Justice (Miscellaneous Provisions) Act 2009. Section 16, as amended, provides that if a garda suspects with reasonable cause that a person has one of a number of specified items in his possession in any public place, the garda may search and detain him for as much time as is reasonably necessary to conduct the search. The specified items include a knife, or any other item which could inflict harm,[52] or a "realistic imitation firearm".[53] Notably, gardaí are provided with powers to detain the individual while conducting the search, despite the fact that the search is unlikely to be intimate in nature. **[2–18]**

Finally, under the Road Traffic Act 2006 gardaí have a power to set up check-points for random breath testing to detect drink driving.[54] Written authorisation from a garda of the rank of inspector, which specifies the date, duration and location of the check-point, is required.[55] No belief that the driver has consumed alcohol is necessary. In *DPP (Goodman) v Weir*[56] it was held that failure to secure, and produce in court, the written authorisation would mean that it could not be proven that the breath sample had been secured in accordance with law. **[2–19]**

III. Arrest

Our starting point for discussing powers of arrest is the Irish Constitution. Article 40.4.1 states that "No citizen shall be deprived of his personal liberty save in **[2–20]**

48 [1991] 1 IR 477.
49 s 23(1)(b).
50 *ibid.*
51 For further discussion, see below para 2-45.
52 Firearms and Offensive Weapons Act 1990, s 9.
53 s 9A as inserted by the Criminal Justice (Miscellaneous Provisions) Act 2009, s 40.
54 s 4.
55 s 4(3).
56 [2008] IEHC 268.

accordance with law". This means that a citizen should be free to do what he wants unless the law states otherwise. In order to arrest a citizen, thereby depriving him of that liberty, laws must be in place, whether common law or statutory, which are grounded in due process and which observe constitutional rights. Not all deprivations of liberty can be categorised as arrest.[57] One useful definition, which can aid us in determining whether an arrest is lawful or not, is provided by Kidstone:

> "Arrest, in the context of the criminal law, is more than a deprivation of liberty. It is a step in the criminal process; the apprehending or restraining of a person in order that he may be forthcoming to answer an alleged or suspected crime, made in the lawful exercise of an asserted authority with the intention to bring the person within the criminal process, this intention being communicated to the person by words or conduct together with the reasons for the arrest."[58]

In this section we will examine those laws and the powers gardaí have to arrest individuals.

Formalities

[2–21] Because of the constitutional right to liberty, individuals only have to submit themselves to arrest where it is permitted under law. Certain information will be required by the individual to know that the proposed arrest is lawful. This is similarly required under Art 5 ECHR. The arresting garda must inform the suspect that he is being arrested, though there is some case law to suggest that it may be sufficient for someone who is obviously a garda to act in a way which leads the suspect to believe he is being arrested.[59] The individual must also be told the reason for the arrest, and in this regard the Supreme Court in *Re O'Laighléis* stated:

> "Arrest must be for a lawful purpose and since no one is obliged to submit to an unlawful arrest the citizen has a right before acquiescing in his arrest to know why he is being arrested."[60]

[2–22] In light of this the garda must inform the arrested individual of the specific offence,[61] and the time and location of the commission of the offence. This is further required under Art 5(2) ECHR.[62] Failure to comply with these formalities will make the arrest and resultant detention unlawful, though it can become lawful if the requirements are subsequently satisfied.[63] Equally, the arrest must be for the stated purpose. If a person

---

[57] The detention which can be permitted for stop and search is not arrest and Ryan and Magee point out that a kidnapper does not arrest his hostage. See Ryan and Magee, *The Irish Criminal Process* (Mercier, Dublin, 1983), p 85.

[58] Cited *ibid.* p 336.

[59] *Forsyth v Gode* (1895) 32 CLJ 288.

[60] [1960] IR 93.

[61] In *People (DPP) v Quilligan* [1986] IR 495 Walsh J stated that where an individual was being arrested under s 30 of the OASA 1939 he would need to be advised of the particular offence he was suspected of committing.

[62] Everyone who is arrested shall be informed promptly, in a language which he understands, of the reasons for his arrest and the charge against him.

[63] *People v Shaw* [1982] IR 1.

is arrested in relation to the commission of a particular offence, the power of arrest can only be used for the purpose of investigating that offence. In *Oladapo v Governor of Cloverhill Prison*[64] the Supreme Court held that while the individual had been arrested on suspicion of committing offences under the Immigration Act 2004, the purpose of the arrest was in fact to deny him permission to land. Murray CJ stated that "a person may only be lawfully arrested on a criminal charge, where, apart from other criteria, there is a *bona fide* intention of charging that person with that offence." Murray CJ went so far as to say that "what occurred in this case was a fundamental breach of the due process of law."

Linked to this, resisting lawful arrest is an offence[65] but resisting an unlawful arrest is not and it is permissible to use reasonable force to resist an unlawful arrest.[66] Reasonableness will be dependent on the circumstances. If an individual uses reasonable force because he honestly believes it is an unlawful arrest, even though it is actually lawful, this is a defence.[67] That said, under the Non-Fatal Offences Against the Person Act 1997, a person cannot use force to resist an arrest if he is aware that the arresting garda is acting in the course of duty.[68] **[2–23]**

At common law, gardaí are entitled to use such force as is reasonably necessary to effect or maintain a lawful arrest or to prevent crime. This is now also provided for by the Non-Fatal Offences Against the Person Act 1997.[69] If the accused voluntarily gives himself up for arrest then any use of force will be unlawful. Even handcuffing, which is legally an assault, is unlawful unless there is a belief that the arrestee will attempt escape or be violent.[70] Force must only be used in order to secure an arrest; if it is used for any other purpose then it is unlawful.[71] The standard for determining the belief in these issues is what the garda reasonably and honestly believed, a mixture of objective and subjective.[72] Thus, a mistaken belief is acceptable once the mistake was reasonable. **[2–24]**

The arresting garda can only use the degree of force necessary to effect or maintain an arrest. Any more than that will be unlawful. The Non-Fatal Offences Against the Person Act 1997 states that the use of force will not be a criminal offence if the person believes it is reasonable force in the circumstances to, *inter alia*, effect an arrest, prevent a crime or defend oneself.[73] Even lethal force may be justifiable on the grounds of preventing crime, particularly where the suspect is armed. In *Kelly v UK*[74] soldiers in Northern Ireland shot and killed joy-riders crossing a border checkpoint who failed to slow down. Because of their behaviour the soldiers believed they were terrorists. It was **[2–25]**

---

64 [2009] IESC 42.
65 Offences Against the Person Act 1861, s 38.
66 See the case of *Christie v Leachinsky* [1947] AC 573.
67 See *Albert v Lavin* [1982] AC 546 and *R v Geen* [1982] Crim LR 604.
68 s 18(6).
69 s 19.
70 *Reed v Wastie* [1972] Crim LR 221.
71 *Dowman v Ireland* [1986] ILRM 111.
72 Walsh, above n 16, p 188.
73 s 18.
74 European Commission on Human Rights Application No. 17579/90.

held both in the UK courts,[75] and the ECtHR[76] that the soldiers had been justified in their use of force, irrespective of their mistaken belief that they were terrorists. The ECtHR stated that lethal force will only be justified in order to effect an arrest and to protect others from violence. It is no defence if there is no belief that others would be at harm if the suspect escaped. The force used must also be proportionate. Article 2 ECHR states that the right to life will not be breached where death results from the use of force which is no more than is "absolutely necessary" to effect an arrest. In all these discussions, force has a broad definition, covering any application of force, or a threat to apply force.[77]

[2–26] In the absence of a warrant the powers of a garda to enter private property to arrest a person are quite limited. Section 6 of the Criminal Law Act 1997 makes some provisions on this issue, with different powers attaching dependent on the nature of the property. If it is not a dwelling, which attracts constitutional protection,[78] the garda may enter the property without a warrant to arrest someone for an arrestable offence.[79] The garda must know or have reasonable cause to suspect that the individual is on the property. If the property is a dwelling the garda will be required to secure the consent of the occupier or may enter where specified circumstances are in existence, for example the garda witnessed the person inside or entering the dwelling, or the individual ordinarily resides at that dwelling.[80]

Grounds for Arrest

[2–27] Lawful authority must exist for an individual to be arrested. Powers of arrest arise from common law and statute and are afforded to both citizens and police, though gardaí are afforded broader powers than citizens. Under statute, arrests can be conducted on the basis of a warrant issued by a judge or, in certain circumstances, without a warrant.

[2–28] At common law anyone could arrest anyone he saw committing or attempting to commit a felony or treason.[81] The power under common law was broader for a garda, who could arrest where he suspected such an offence had been committed, or was about to be committed. The Criminal Law Act 1997 repealed these common law powers, save in relation to breaches of the peace.[82] Breach of the peace is undefined but it is known to include threats of harm to person or property, riots, fighting, unlawful assembly, and affray.[83] However, the Public Order Act 1994 provides statutory powers of arrest for these offences which are invariably relied on.

[2–29] Legislative powers of arrest are afforded on a piecemeal basis in statutory provisions regarding particular offences. There are some general powers of arrest provided for as

[75] *AG's Reference for Northern Ireland* (No 1 of 1975) [1977] AC 105.
[76] Above n 74.
[77] Non-Fatal Offences Against the Person Act 1997, s 20.
[78] Art 40.5.
[79] Discussed below para 2-32.
[80] s 6(2)(a)-(d). See Chapter Four para 4-10.
[81] Walsh, above n 16, p 157.
[82] See *R v Howell* [1981] 3 All ER 383.
[83] *ibid.*

well as specific powers for a huge list of offences including: road traffic offences,[84] organised crime,[85] misuse of drugs,[86] official secrets,[87] offences against the state,[88] intoxicating liquor,[89] vagrancy,[90] malicious damage,[91] and sexual offences.[92]

Section 4 of the Criminal Law Act 1997 provides both citizen and garda powers of arrest, though those afforded to gardaí are greater in scope. The Act creates powers of arrest for an 'arrestable offence' which is defined by s 2 as **[2–30]**

> "an offence for which a person of full capacity and not previously convicted may, under or by virtue of any enactment, be punished by imprisonment for a term of 5 years or by a more serious penalty and includes an attempt to commit any such offence."

In effect, then, the power arises where a serious offence is involved. Section 4(1) states that *any person* can arrest someone whom he suspects is in the course of committing an offence. Section 4(2) grants the power of arrest to *any person* where a serious offence has been committed and the arrestor reasonably suspects the individual has committed that offence. Two qualifications are attached to the citizen's power of arrest: the arrestor must believe that the suspect would try and avoid arrest by a garda[93] and he must transfer the arrested suspect to gardaí as soon as possible.[94] **[2–31]**

The garda powers of arrest provided in s 4(3) state that if a garda suspects that an offence has been committed, he can arrest an individual whom he reasonably suspects has committed it. This extends the power under s 4(2) to gardaí and it states that they do not need a warrant to effect such an arrest. The purpose of this arrest power is to charge the individual in relation to the offence, not for detention prior to charge. **[2–32]**

One further power of arrest which should be noted stems from the European Arrest Warrant Act 2003. This allows for the return of a person from one European state to another. Section 10 states that where a judicial authority in one state issues an European Arrest Warrant (EAW) in respect of a person that (a) the state intends to bring proceedings against for the offence named in the warrant or (b) has fled the state after sentence was passed, the state on which the EAW is served must arrest and **[2–33]**

[84] Road Traffic Act 1961, ss 19, 40(4), 49(4), 50(6), 51(4), 53(6), 55(4), 69, 82, 107(1), 107(2), 112(6) and 113(3); Road Traffic (Amendment) Act 1968, ss 16, 56 and 59; Road Traffic (Amendment) Act 1978, ss 12, 15(3), 16(4) and 17(3).

[85] Criminal Assets Bureau Act 1996, s 16.

[86] Misuse of Drugs Act 1977, s 25.

[87] Official Secrets Act 1963, ss 15 and 16(4).

[88] Offences Against the State Act 1939, s 29(3) as amended by the Criminal Law Act 1976, s 5; Offences Against the State (Amendment) Act 1940, s 4.

[89] Illicit Distillation (Ireland) Act 1831, ss 18, 25 and 30; Licensing Act 1872, s 12; Intoxicating Liquor Act 1927, s 22(2).

[90] Vagrancy Act 1874, s 4.

[91] Criminal Damage Act 1861, s 12.

[92] Criminal Law (Amendment) Act 1912, s 1; Criminal Law (Sexual Offences) Act 1993, s 13.

[93] s 4(4).

[94] s 4(5).

surrender that person. The format of the EAW is set out in the Act[95] and once the State receives the warrant it must apply to the High Court for it to be endorsed.[96] It can then be executed by a garda in any part of the country.[97] If this person consents to being surrendered, the EAW is in order, he has been afforded an opportunity for legal advice and understands the consequences of the surrender, the High Court may order that he be surrendered to the issuing State.[98] If he does not, the High Court may still order the surrender where the EAW has been endorsed and the transfer is not prohibited for any reason.[99] A garda can arrest anyone in relation to whom the garda believes an EAW has been issued[100] and must bring that person before the High Court "as soon as may be."[101] The arrestee must be released in seven days if the EAW is not produced.[102] The arrested person must be informed of his right to legal representation and an interpreter.[103] Criminality of the offence in both states is not required: the Framework Decision on which the Act is based lists a range of offences which do not need to be criminal in the State in which the EAW is to be executed.[104]

Purpose of Arrest

[2–34] Under common law, the purpose of arrest was to bring a suspect before a court for arraignment and/or formal charge.[105] Arrest for any other purpose was unlawful. Section 15 of the Criminal Justice Act 1951 requires a suspect to be brought before a judge "as soon as reasonably practicable" once charged.[106] This term is not defined by the legislation and presumably will differ on a case by case basis.[107] In *People v Shaw*[108] the suspect challenged the delay in bringing him before a judge. He was arrested on suspicion of involvement in the abduction of two young women. Investigating gardaí believed one of the women was still alive and delayed bringing him before a judge in order to continue questioning him on this matter in the hope of finding her. The

[95] s 11.

[96] s 13.

[97] s 13(3).

[98] s 15.

[99] s 16. s 37 deals with prohibited surrenders which includes grounds such as where the state believes the individual will be punished for his sex, race, sexual orientation, ethnic origin or religion, will be sentenced to death or tortured or it contravenes any obligations under the ECHR.

[100] s 14(1)(a).

[101] s 14(3).

[102] s 14(5).

[103] s 13(4).

[104] Including terrorism, trafficking, exploitation of children, fraud, corruption, xenophobia, murder, organised crime and computer or environmental crime. *Council Framework Decision on the European Arrest Warrant*, Chapter 1, Art 2(2).

[105] This common law conception of the powers of arrest was legislated for by s 15 of the Criminal Justice Act 1951, as substituted by s 18 of the Criminal Justice (Miscellaneous Provisions) Act 1997, which provides that a person arrested with or without a warrant must be brought as soon as practicable before a District Court judge.

[106] s 15(2) dealing with arrest on foot of a warrant states the suspect must be brought before a court as soon as practicable with no mention of a charge but Walsh explains that the warrant itself acts here as the charging instrument: Walsh, above n 16, p 224.

[107] A variety of factors such as the availability of a judge, consultations with solicitors, medical treatment etc. may have an impact on the length of time prior to appearing in court.

[108] [1982] IR 1.

Supreme Court held that his detention was *prima facie* unlawful; however, in this case, the constitutional right to life of the woman outweighed his constitutional right to liberty.

On the purpose of arrest Walsh J outlined that arrest is

> "simply a process of ensuring the attendance at Court of the person so arrested... No person may be arrested with or without a warrant for the purpose of interrogation or the securing of evidence from that person."[109]

It was well established in Irish case law that an individual was not to be questioned in relation to the offence following arrest.[110] Furthermore, no acceptance of a deprivation of liberty by gardaí which fell short of arrest existed in the common law.[111] This is also the position under Art 5(1) ECHR. **[2–35]**

Over time, statutory provisions have emerged which permit, in certain instances, arrest without charge i.e. for the purpose of investigation or interrogation. Prior to this however, gardaí developed means of circumventing the law, primarily through asking persons to attend at a garda station to "help/assist with enquiries". A person voluntarily attending a station to assist gardaí creates no legal difficulties unless this "helping with enquiries" in fact amounts to garda detention of a person who is suspected of involvement in the offence which is under investigation without a formal arrest. This practice was questioned by the courts in the 1930s in *Dunne v Clinton*[112] where Hanna J held that there is no halfway house between liberty and arrest.[113] However, the practice continued to be employed until the late 1970s when the courts expressly disapproved of it. **[2–36]**

In *People (DPP) v O'Loughlin*,[114] gardaí had invited a suspect to a garda station to "help with enquiries". He voluntarily accompanied gardaí and remained at the station of his own accord while the offence was investigated. Subsequently, without being charged, the suspect was taken to another garda station and questioned about different offences. A detective garda admitted at trial that had the defendant sought to leave that station at that time he would have been arrested and charged. The court held that at the point where O'Loughlin would have been arrested had he tried to leave, he ought to have in fact been arrested, charged and brought before a court. As this had not happened, the suspect's detention was unlawful and inculpatory statements made by him in the second garda station were inadmissible. O'Higgins CJ stated that **[2–37]**

> "...our law does not contemplate or permit the holding of a person for questioning ... 'Holding for questioning' and 'taking into custody' and 'detaining' are merely different ways of describing the act of depriving a man

---

[109] *ibid.* at 14.

[110] See for instance the judgment of Kennedy CJ in *AG v Cox*, unreported, Supreme Court, 19 April 1929.

[111] *Dunne v Clinton* [1930] IR 366; *People (DPP) v O'Loughlin* [1979] IR 85; *People (DPP) v Walsh* [1980] IR 294.

[112] [1930] IR 366.

[113] *ibid.* at 372.

[114] [1979] IR 85.

of his liberty. To do such without lawful authority is an open defiance of Art. 40 s.4 ss.1 of the Constitution."[115]

Arrest for Detention Without Charge

(i) Section 30 of the Offences Against the State Act 1939

[2–38] At the time of *O'Loughlin*, and indeed until 1984, there was one exception to the general rule that an arrest was not for the purpose of detention and questioning: s 30 of the Offences Against the State Act 1939. This Act was passed by the Oireachtas as a response to growing subversive activity within the State by republican paramilitaries. A significant part of the armoury of the 1939 Act was the provision of certain pre-trial, investigatory powers to gardaí which had never before been recognised under Irish law.[116] Section 30 allows for the arrest of persons suspected of committing, being about to commit, or holding information on the commission of an offence under the Act or a scheduled offence.[117] There is no requirement for this suspicion to be reasonable in nature.[118] Walsh J stated in *People (DPP) v Quilligan* that this suspicion would need to be "*bona fide* held and not unreasonable."[119]

[2–39] A person arrested under s 30 may be detained without charge for an initial period of 24 hours and this may be extended by a second 24 hour period where a garda not below the rank of Chief Superintendent directs.[120] For an extension beyond 24 hours, the officer authorising the extension will have to suspect the individual in relation to the offence in question.[121] In 1998, in the aftermath of the Omagh bombing, the legislature introduced an amending Act allowing for a third successive period of 24-hour detention to be authorised by a judge of the District Court, upon application by a garda not below the rank of Superintendent if he has reasonable grounds for believing that such further detention is necessary for the proper investigation of the offence concerned and that the investigation is being conducted diligently and expeditiously.[122] The suspect over whom the extension is sought must be produced in court and be heard.[123] If the period of detention expires during the hearing it will be deemed not to expire until the final determination of the application.[124] Under the Criminal Justice (Amendment) Act 2009 this hearing can be heard otherwise than in public if the judge thinks it desirable and, further, in certain circumstances, the judge can direct that the garda evidence be heard in the absence of all others, including the accused.[125] If

---

115 *ibid.* at 91.

116 The Act also provided for the establishment of the Special Criminal Court; see Chapter Eight.

117 With regard to the scheduling of offences see Offences Against the State Act 1939, ss 35 and 36.

118 See *People (DPP) v Tyndall* [2005] 1 IR 593.

119 [1986] IR 495 at 507, a view reasserted in *Walshe v Fennessy* [2005] IESC 51.

120 Offences Against the State Act 1939, s 30(3).

121 See *People (DPP) v Byrne* [1989] ILRM 613, discussed in Mulloy, "What suspicions justify a garda arrest under s. 30 of the Offences Against the State Act, 1939?" (1993) 3(10) ICLJ 82.

122 s 30(4) and (4A) of the OASA 1939, as inserted by the Offences Against the State (Amendment) Act 1998, s 10.

123 s 30(4B) OASA inserted by the Offences Against the State (Amendment) Act 1998, s 10.

124 s 30(4D) OASA inserted by Criminal Justice Act 2006, s 187.

125 s 21, where the evidence of the investigation if revealed could prejudice the proper conduct of an investigation.

having heard the evidence, the judge rules that it would be acceptable he will order the re-hearing of the evidence in front of all persons.[126]

Under s 30, detention flows automatically from the arrest; no belief that detention is necessary for the proper investigation of the offence is required. In *Quilligan*[127] the Court stated **[2–40]**

> "the object of the powers given by s 30 is not to permit the arrest of people simply for the purpose of subjecting them to questioning. Rather it is for the purpose of investigation... without the possibility of obstruction or other interference which might occur if the suspected person were not under arrest."[128]

In terms of the use of the time available to gardaí for questioning under s 30, time during which medical attention is received will not be included in the calculation of the period of detention. However the time involved in making a challenge to the lawfulness of the detention will not be deducted. **[2–41]**

An unusual feature of this legislation is that in order to be charged, detainees must be brought to either the District Court or the Special Criminal Court.[129] However in the case of *State (Walshe) v Maguire*[130] the court ruled that they could be charged in the station but would have to be brought to court as soon as practicable. **[2–42]**

One practice which was developed by gardaí to broaden the application of these powers of arrest without charge was the use of "holding charges": gardaí would arrest and detain a suspect for an offence under the OASA 1939 where their real investigative interest in the suspect was in relation to a wholly different offence, not covered by the Act. The courts issued conflicting judgments on these practices. In *People (DPP) v Towson*[131] the Court of Criminal Appeal did not find an arrest under "holding charges" to be unlawful as the grounds for arrest (firearms offences under the Emergency Powers Act[132]) were involved in the offence under investigation (murder). No offence had been imagined or invented for the purpose of detention and questioning. However, in *State (Bowes) v Fitzpatrick*[133] Finlay P in the High Court deemed an arrest for malicious damage to a knife, caused in the course of a murder, to be merely a "colourable device" to facilitate the investigation of the murder charge. In *State (Trimbole) v Governor of Mountjoy Prison*[134] the Supreme Court held that an arrest under s 30 for possession of a firearm was unlawful where arresting gardaí did **[2–43]**

---

126 s 21(b).
127 Above n 119.
128 *ibid.* at 509.
129 s 30(4C).
130 [1979] IR 372.
131 [1978] ILRM 122.
132 Between 1976 and 1977 the Emergency Powers Act 1976 allowed for a person to be arrested where a garda suspected with reasonable cause that he had committed or was committing or was about to commit an offence under the Offences Against the State Act 1939 or a scheduled offence. s 2(3) of the 1976 Act provided that such an arrested person could be held initially for 48 hours and thereafter for a further five days if authorised by a garda not below the rank of chief superintendent.
133 [1978] ILRM 195.
134 [1985] IR 550.

not hold a genuine suspicion in relation to that charge and were in fact taking the arrestee into custody to ensure that he was available for the execution of an extradition warrant from the Australian authorities, where he was wanted on drugs charges.

[2–44] Some support for holding charges is found in the Supreme Court case of *People (DPP) v Quilligan.*[135] There, a violent robbery at the home of two elderly gentlemen resulted in the death of one of the men. Despite no subversive connection, the two defendants were arrested under s 30 of the OASA 1939, on suspicion of malicious damage to a door and furniture. The trial judge held that the provisions of the OASA 1939 were applicable only to offences of a "subversive" nature and not to "ordinary" offences. However, this distinction was rejected by the Supreme Court, where Walsh J felt that the Act is intended to deal with "what might be generally called the internal enemies of the State"[136] but this did not limit its application to "subversive" activities which endanger the institutions and security of the State. On the use of "holding charges" the Supreme Court held, in line with *Towson*, that the crucial issue was whether or not there was a genuine case with regard to the more minor charge, a valid suspicion of the accused's involvement in that offence and *bona fides* on the part of the arresting gardaí. If this was the case then it was irrelevant that the malicious damage charge "faded into relative insignificance" in comparison to the other offence which was the primary concern of the gardaí.[137] However, if the gardaí clearly had no real interest in pursuing the investigation or prosecution in relation to a scheduled offence in a given case and were merely using the s 30 power of arrest and detention for another purpose, this would amount to an abuse of process.[138] On the facts in *Quilligan*, the arrest under s 30 was held to be a lawful exercise of that power. Walsh has suggested that this decision effected a "silent, but very significant, shift in the traditional balance built into the criminal process."[139]

(ii) Section 4 of the Criminal Justice Act 1984

[2–45] In 1984 a broader legislative power of arrest for detention without charge was enacted by the Criminal Justice Act 1984, a development Walsh describes as a "watershed".[140] Under s 4 of that Act, a garda has the power to detain persons arrested without warrant on suspicion of involvement in any arrestable offence for an initial period of up to six hours detention without charge.[141] This effectively moved such powers from the limited remit of the Offences Against the State Act 1939 into mainstream criminal justice. A second period of six hours detention may be authorised by a garda not below the rank of superintendent if he has reasonable grounds for believing that such further detention is necessary for the proper investigation of the offence.[142] Under s 9 of the

---

[135] Above n 119.

[136] *ibid.* at 510.

[137] *ibid.* at 512 *per* Walsh J.

[138] *ibid.* at 511-512 *per* Walsh J.

[139] Walsh, "The Impact of Anti-Subversive Laws on Police Powers and Practice in Ireland: The Silent Erosion of Individual Freedom" (1989) 62 *Temple Law Review* 1099, pp 1110-1111.

[140] Walsh, above n 16, p 225.

[141] Criminal Justice Act 1984, s 4(3)(a).

[142] *ibid.* s 4(3)(b). While the phrase "necessary for the proper investigation of the offence" has not been defined, in *People (DPP) v O'Toole and Hickey,* unreported, Court of Criminal Appeal, July 20, 1990, the court intimated that it referred to that which was necessary for a full and proper investigation of the offence.

Criminal Justice Act 2006, a third period of twelve hours detention has been added to this provision, meaning that any person arrested on suspicion of committing an arrestable offence may now be held for a potential maximum of twenty-four hours without charge.[143] The third period of detention may be authorised by a garda not below the rank of Chief Superintendent where he has reasonable grounds to believe that it is necessary for the proper investigation of the offence. Practically speaking, the actual length of the detention can be extended due to rest restrictions on questioning,[144] the provision of medical treatment or where the suspect is taken to court to challenge the lawfulness of his detention. None of these suspensions, of which the suspect must be notified in writing by the member in charge (MIC),[145] will be taken to count within the time-frames.

Keane J in *People (DPP) v Finnerty*[146] suggested that the legislative policy behind the provision was **[2–46]**

> "to end the dubious practice of bringing people to the station for the purpose of 'assisting the gardaí with their inquiries', or in purported reliance on the legislation directed primarily at subversive crime, and to substitute therefore an express statutory regime under which the Gardaí would have the right to detain a person in custody for a specified period."[147]

The section formally provided for gardaí arresting individuals solely to question them about suspected involved in an offence, without charging or bringing before a judge. A number of conditions for the exercise of this power exist. It cannot be utilised where there is a warrant for an arrest. Differentiating it from s 30, the offence must have been committed and the arresting member must have reasonable cause to suspect the individual of committing the offence at the time of the arrest. The arresting officer must believe that the detention of the individual is necessary for the investigation of the offence. It cannot, therefore, be used as a means to investigate other offences. The individual must be detained at a garda station, and to ensure the application of safeguards, there must be no unreasonable delay in bringing the suspect to the station.[148] **[2–47]**

Additional requirements are placed on the MIC who must also have reasonable suspicion at the time that the suspect arrives at the station.[149] The Court of Criminal Appeal in *DPP v O'Toole*[150] held that the belief of the MIC can be based on information passed to him by someone else, but the decision must be made independently. The MIC must believe that detention is necessary for the proper investigation of the offence. The purpose of the detention does not have to be to question the individual but can be for **[2–48]**

---

[143] Criminal Justice Act 1984, s 4(3)(bb), as inserted by Criminal Justice Act 2006, s 9(c). Dependent on the timing of the arrest there could be two rest periods of eight hours.
[144] Questioning is not permitted between midnight and 8am, discussed below.
[145] s 6; this notice must include the time at which the suspension will end, and be explained orally to the suspect.
[146] [1999] 4 IR 364.
[147] *ibid.* at 378.
[148] *People (DPP) v Boylan* [1991] 1 IR 477.
[149] s 4(2).
[150] Unreported, Court of Criminal Appeal, 20 July 1990.

searches or interviews elsewhere which would require the individual to be detained. In *People (DPP) v Birney*[151] the Court of Criminal Appeal confirmed that this was not merely a "rubber stamping exercise":

> "The role of the member in charge involves both a subjective and objective element and subjectively he must believe that the applicant's detention is necessary and objectively must be satisfied that there are reasonable grounds for his belief."

The MIC will be required to appear in court and testify as to his state of mind: his signature on the custody record[152] will not be sufficient evidence in this regard.

[2–49] If at any point during detention under this section, it becomes clear that the suspect is not guilty of any of the offences for which he is being held he must be released immediately.[153] One of the anomalies of this provision is that it does not appear that gardaí have to charge a detainee as soon as they are convinced of guilt, as long as the continued detention was required for the proper investigation of the offence. In practice it seems that gardaí wait until the detention period has expired before they charge the suspect.[154] Upon this action the obligation under s 15 of the 1951 Criminal Justice Act, to bring the suspect to a judge as soon as practicable, comes into play.

(iii) Section 2 of the Criminal Justice (Drug Trafficking) Act 1996

[2–50] Section 2 of the Criminal Justice (Drug Trafficking) Act 1996 created another power of arrest for detention in relation to drug trafficking offences. This legislation was enacted in the summer of 1996, following the high-profile murders of Detective Garda Jerry McCabe and investigative journalist Veronica Guerin, when public tensions were high in relation to crime, particularly organised drug crime.[155] It provides for a potential period of detention of up to 168 hours (seven days) for drug trafficking offences. The offences are defined by s 3 of the Criminal Justice Act 1994 to include, among others, manufacture, importation, exportation, supply, distribution, possession for sale or supply of a controlled drug; money laundering the proceeds of drug trafficking; and attempting, aiding or abetting any of the above.

[2–51] As with the 1984 Act, the section can come into play where the arresting garda reasonably suspects that an individual has committed a drug trafficking offence and where the MIC has reasonable grounds for believing that his detention is necessary for the proper investigation of the offence. An initial detention period of six hours can be extended by 18 hours by a garda not below the rank of Chief Superintendent where he has reasonable grounds to believe that such detention is necessary for the proper

---

[151] [2006] IECCA 58.

[152] Discussed below at para 2-61.

[153] Criminal Justice Act 1984, s 4(5) inserted by the Criminal Justice (Miscellaneous Provisions) Act 1997, s 2(b).

[154] Walsh, above n 16, p 227.

[155] See O'Donnell and O'Sullivan, *Crime Control in Ireland The Politics of Intolerance* (Cork University Press, Cork, 2001), p 2 and Hamilton, *The Presumption of Innocence in Irish Criminal Law* (Dublin, Irish Academic Press, 2007), p 156.

investigation of the offence concerned.[156] Another period of 24 hours may be added by a garda of the same status where he has reasonable grounds to believe that further detention is necessary for the proper investigation of the offence.[157]

Following this maximum period of 48 hours detention under the authority of gardaí, an application must be made to a judge of either the District or the Circuit Court for any further detention of the suspect. The application is made by a garda not below the rank of Chief Superintendent and a warrant for a further period not exceeding 72 hours may be granted where the appropriate judge has reasonable grounds to believe that such further detention is necessary for the proper investigation of the offence concerned and that the investigation is being conducted "diligently and expeditiously."[158] This phrase has not been tested before the Irish courts and it remains to be seen in what circumstances an extension sought by gardaí might be denied on the grounds of a lack of diligence or expediency in the investigation.[159] Another application can be made for a further 48 hours, under similar criteria,[160] creating a potential for seven day detention without charge. The 1996 Act is the first legislative provision to allow for detention beyond 48 hours though it insists on judicial authorisation for extended detention periods beyond that threshold. As with detentions under s 30 OASA, the judge can decide to hear evidence other than in public and to exclude all persons, even the accused, from hearing evidence as to the investigation.[161] The comments made in relation to charging a suspect following detention under s 4 of the 1984 Act equally apply here. **[2–52]**

(iv) Section 50 of the Criminal Justice Act 2007

The Criminal Justice Act 2007, aimed at tackling so-called "gangland crime", introduced seven day detention without charge for the following offences: murder involving the use of a firearm or an explosive, capital murder[162], possession of firearms and false imprisonment involving the use of a firearm.[163] The processes and stages of extension are identical to those included in the Drug Trafficking Act 1996. The requirements of suspicion and belief placed on the arresting officer and the MIC are identical to those under the 1984 Act and the 1996 Act.[164] If at any time during detention there are no longer reasonable grounds for the suspicion then the suspect should be released.[165] Again, detention beyond 48 hours can only be judicially authorised, and the authorising judge must reasonably believe that further detention is **[2–53]**

---

[156] Criminal Justice (Drug Trafficking) Act 1996, s 2(2)(b).

[157] *ibid.* s 2(2)(c).

[158] *ibid.* s 2(2)(g).

[159] Guidance on the procedure to be used in an analysis of whether the application should be granted is provided in the UK where the phrase is also used in the Police and Criminal Evidence Act 1984.

[160] Criminal Justice (Drug Trafficking) Act 1996, s 2(2)(h).

[161] Criminal Justice (Amendment) Act 2009, s 23.

[162] s 3 of the Criminal Justice Act 1997 covers murder of a garda in the course of his duty, murder of a prison officer, murder of a foreign head of state or a diplomatic officer, or a murder committed in furtherance of attempts to usurp the powers of the Government.

[163] Criminal Justice Act 2007, s 50(1).

[164] s 50(2).

[165] s 50(6).

necessary for the proper investigation of the offence, and that the investigation is being conducted "diligently and expeditiously".[166] The same provisions in relation to private hearings of evidence also apply.[167]

[2–54] The requirement for judicial authorisation from 48 hours onwards seems to reflect a legislative desire to comply with the Constitution, the ECHR and the jurisprudence of the ECtHR. In *Brogan v United Kingdom*[168] the ECtHR held that a breach of Art 5(3) ECHR[169] had occurred where the applicant and others had been detained under Northern Ireland legislation for periods ranging from four days to nearly seven days without being brought before a judge or being "promptly" released. The Court held that the scope for flexibility in interpreting and applying the notion of "promptness" is very limited and that in the circumstances of this case even the shortest of the periods of detention in question fell outside the strict time constraints permitted under Art 5(3). The Court felt that the aim of combating terrorism was not sufficient to deviate from this.[170]

[2–55] In the Response of the Irish Government to the *Report of the European Committee for the Prevention of Torture and Inhuman or Degrading Treatment or Punishment (CPT)* in 2006, statistics showed that arrested suspects in the Irish pre-trial process are rarely detained beyond 48 hours, despite legislation allowing for such detention. In the years 2005 and 2006, 23 out of 32 Garda Divisions had no detentions of persons for over 48 hours; and the average number of persons detained for more than 48 hours in any station was between one and eight.[171] The impact of the extension of such powers of detention to a broader range of offences under the 2007 Act remains to be seen.

IV. Detention

[2–56] The next chapter will deal specifically with the interrogation of individuals in custody and the right of access to legal advice, but we will consider here the treatment of a detainee while in custody. Following the introduction of the power of detention without charge under s 4 of the Criminal Justice Act 1984, the legislature introduced safeguards for suspects by means of the Criminal Justice Act 1984 (Treatment of Persons in Custody in Garda Síochána Stations) Regulations 1987 (the Custody Regulations).[172] These regulations apply to all suspects detained for questioning in garda custody but do not come into force until the suspect arrives at the station.

---

[166] Criminal Justice Act 2007, s 50(3)(g) and (3)(h).

[167] Criminal Justice (Amendment) Act 2009, s 23.

[168] (1989) EHRR 117.

[169] Art 5(3) ECHR: "Everyone arrested or detained in accordance with the provisions of ... this article shall be brought promptly before a judge or other officer authorised by law to exercise judicial power and shall be entitled to trial within a reasonable time or to release pending trial."

[170] Above n 168, para 62.

[171] Response of the Irish Government to the *Report of the European Committee for the Prevention of Torture and Inhuman or Degrading Treatment or Punishment (CPT) on its visit to Ireland from 2 to 13 October 2006* (Stationery Office, Dublin 2007), p 14.

[172] These Regulations were promulgated in April 1987 and the commencement of many of the main provisions of the 1984 Act, including s 4, was delayed until they were in place.

The potential of the Custody Regulations to impose minimum standards for the treatment of persons in custody is weakened by the fact that they were introduced by way of statutory instrument, rather than primary legislation, thereby not conferring any rights on suspects. Further, s 7(3) of their parent statute, the Criminal Justice Act, 1984, states that breach of the Regulations alone does not provide grounds for a civil or criminal action against a garda and does not of itself affect the lawfulness of the suspect's detention or the admissibility of any statement made by him.[173] The Court of Criminal Appeal has provided conflicting opinions on how to assess the impact of a breach of the Regulations. In the *DPP v Spratt*[174] it suggested that a two-step test ought to be applied: 1) determine whether a breach of the Regulations has taken place, and 2) ascertain whether the accused has suffered prejudice as a result of such breach. In the case of *DPP v McFadden*,[175] Keane CJ in the Court of Criminal Appeal identified the question as being whether the breach was "of so trivial and inconsequential a nature as not to afford a sufficient ground for treating the detention of the person as unlawful or statements made by him as inadmissible."[176] The Supreme Court in *DPP v Diver*[177] adopted the formulation of *McFadden*, with Hardiman J stating that the breaches in the case at hand, where neither recordings nor transcripts of interviews in which the accused maintained his innocence were made, could not be viewed as "trivial or inconsequential." Overall however, it seems that breach of the Regulations which is not persistent and which is not coupled with any other misconduct will not be enough to give rise to the exercise of the judicial discretion to exclude evidence so obtained.[178] **[2–57]**

Member in Charge

The MIC has a key role in the garda station in safeguarding the rights of the detainee under the Custody Regulations. The duties of the MIC include overseeing the application of the Regulations, visiting detainees and making any necessary enquiries.[179] If any officer is acting in a way which is not consistent with the Regulations, the MIC must inform that officer and report it if it is not quickly resolved.[180] He is responsible for keeping the custody record accurately,[181] authorising that the detention is necessary when the suspect arrives at the station,[182] ensuring that the detainee is informed of why he has been arrested,[183] advising the detainee of his rights to consult a solicitor,[184] and **[2–58]**

[173] s 7(4) of the 1984 Act does allow for disciplinary proceedings to be initiated against a garda for breaching the Custody Regulations.

[174] [1995] 1 IR 585, adopted by the Court in *People (DPP) v Murphy*, unreported, Court of Criminal Appeal, 12 July, 2001.

[175] [2003] 2 IR 113.

[176] *ibid.* at 120.

[177] [2005] IESC 57.

[178] See also *People (DPP) v Connell* [1995] 1 IR 244; *DPPv Spratt* [1995] 1 IR 585; *People (DPP) v Van Onzen* [1996] 2 ILRM 387; *People (DPP) v Darcy*, unreported, Court of Criminal Appeal, 29 July 1997; *People (DPP) v Smith*, unreported, Court of Criminal Appeal, 22 November 1999.

[179] reg 5.

[180] reg 5(3).

[181] reg 6(2).

[182] reg 7(2).

[183] reg 8(1)(a).

[184] reg 8(1)(b).

letting someone know the detainee has been arrested.[185] The MIC must tell a person under 18 that a parent or guardian is being requested to attend the station, and ensure that this is done.[186] The MIC will assist in efforts to secure a solicitor if the detainee so wishes.[187] The MIC must notify district headquarters where detainees are transferred between stations.[188] He must record all details pertaining to interviews and in particular must note any complaints made by the detainee.[189] The MIC must advise a detainee who is a foreign national that he may contact his consul, and do so where requested.[190] The MIC must arrange a medical examination where it has been alleged that a detainee has been ill-treated.[191] If for some other reason medical attention is required, it is the MIC's responsibility to ensure this is provided.[192] Some of these tasks, such as visiting detainees or recording certain facts in the custody record, can be delegated to another garda but it is the MIC's responsibility to make sure it is done. It is therefore a pivotal and serious role yet the definition of who holds the position is unhelpful.

[2–59] Regulation 4 states that the MIC is whoever is in charge of the station whenever the MIC is required to do anything. The district Superintendent is supposed to issue directions on who that is in each station.[193] However, in *DPP (Lenihan) v McGuire*[194] it was stated that, practically, it was whoever was in charge at the station, not necessarily abiding by the superintendent's directions. Cases such as *People (DPP) v Van Onzen*[195] show flexibility from the courts in these cases, given that it is not often easy to keep things quite so clear in stations.

[2–60] The importance of the role of MIC and the difficulties arising were considered in detail by the sixth report of the Morris Tribunal, on the arrest and detention of suspects.[196] A number of concerns arose in that report as to how the role was being used. The Tribunal was particularly troubled by the fact that an application for extension of suspect detention was made by the MIC, which was "entirely inappropriate" as the MIC should at all times remain independent of the investigation and focus on applying the Regulations.[197] Mr Justice Morris stated that the MIC should be independent of the investigation and has "a duty to ensure that the constitutional and other legal rights of the detainee are afforded to him and observed."[198] He was not satisfied from the evidence presented to him that the role was "treated with sufficient importance or that the member in charge is vested with sufficient authority to ensure compliance with

[185] reg 8(1)(c)(i).
[186] reg 8(1)(c)(ii).
[187] reg 9(2).
[188] reg 10(2).
[189] reg 12(10).
[190] reg 14.
[191] reg 20(7).
[192] reg 21.
[193] reg 4(2).
[194] [1996] 3 IR 586.
[195] [1996] 2 ILRM 387.
[196] Morris, *Report on the Detention of 'Suspects' Following the Death of the Late Richard Barron on the 14th October 1996 and Related Detentions and Issues* (Stationery Office, Dublin, 2006).
[197] *ibid.* para 4.54.
[198] *ibid.* para 16.37.

the regulations."[199] To this end he called for the position to be vested in someone of the rank of sergeant. Equally, however, he was concerned about the institutional attitude towards the role:

> "If it is to be carried out effectively and even-handedly the member in charge must have the support of the officers of An Garda Síochána and the encouragement to execute his duty fearlessly when required. The Tribunal is not satisfied that the role of the member in charge is in practice afforded the respect and authority contemplated by the legislation. The Tribunal recommends that senior officers... reinvigorate the role."[200]

As yet reforms have not been implemented to give effect to these recommendations.

Custody Record

The custody record is a record of all details of detention and everything which occurred during that time. The regulations call for the keeping of this record and give the MIC responsibility for ensuring it is kept accurately. Every entry must be signed or initialled by the garda making it. If a detainee is transferred to another station the record should be sent with him. [2–61]

The record must include:

- the date, time, place of arrest, and identity of the arresting member[201];
- time of arrival at the station[202];
- nature of the offence[203];
- any relevant details about physical or mental conditions[204];
- any decisions taken about detention and custody while in detention[205];
- information given to the detainee about rights, and response from detainee, and what happened[206];
- details of visits, telephone calls, interrogations, letters, meals, medical treatment, end of custody[207]; and,
- details of searches, taking of samples, fingerprints etc.[208]

For a child under the age of 18, or a person with a mental illness, there are additional requirements including efforts to contact a parent or guardian.[209] In particular the record must show where authority is given to question such a person without a parent [2–62]

---

[199] *ibid.*
[200] *ibid.*
[201] reg 7(1)(a).
[202] reg 7(1)(b).
[203] reg 7(1)(c).
[204] reg 7(1)(d).
[205] reg 7(2) and (3).
[206] reg 8(4).
[207] reg 23.
[208] reg 17(6).
[209] reg 22.

or guardian present. For deaf people it will show written consent from the detainee to proceed with questioning without an interpreter present, if he agrees to this.[210]

[2–63] In relation to interviews, the custody record must show all important details: outcome, co-operation, complaints, times of beginning and end, any breaks, place of interview, name and rank of gardaí involved, and any authority given for suspending an interview.[211] It must detail any complaints made about treatment in custody,[212] and the details of the charge, if pressed.[213] The custody record must be kept for at least 12 months.[214] If any action follows it must be kept until that ends, which can include the investigation of a complaint about treatment in custody. A suspect or his legal representative can request a copy of the record at any point.[215]

Conditions of Custody

[2–64] Detainees must be provided with meals where necessary (one main meal and two small meals in a 24 hour period[216]) and be given reasonable time to rest as necessary.[217] There should be breaks from midnight to 8am which should be supplemented if it is a lengthy detention. Access to toilets must be provided.[218] Not more than one person should be held in any cell, as far as practicable.[219] If this is impossible, violent prisoners should not be placed with others. People of the opposite sex should not be placed together.[220] Persons under the age of 18 should not be detained with adults, wherever possible.[221] Those in cells should be visited every half hour, reduced to 15 minutes if the detainee is under the influence of alcohol or drugs, in which case he should be roused on each visit.[222] If the detainee is of the opposite sex to the visiting garda then the garda should be accompanied. A result of these regulations is that not all stations will be in a position to facilitate all detentions, and detainees should be transferred to another station if necessary to fulfil these requirements.[223]

[2–65] Where an individual is being searched, he is to be advised of the reason for the search and should not be searched by a member of the opposite sex.[224] If the removing of clothing is required then a person of the opposite sex should not be present,[225] and underclothing should only be removed by a doctor.[226]

---

210 reg 12(8)(b).
211 reg 12(11). Discussed further in Chapter Three.
212 reg 12(10).
213 reg 15(2).
214 reg 24.
215 reg 24(1).
216 reg 19(3): additional or different meals can be arranged at his own expense, where practicable.
217 reg 19(2).
218 reg 19(4).
219 reg 19(5).
220 reg 19(7).
221 reg 19(8).
222 reg 19(6).
223 reg 19(1).
224 reg 17.
225 reg 17(3).
226 reg 17(4).

Use of Force

Ill-treatment of detainees, or threat thereof, is prohibited.[227] In certain instances, however, the use of force will be lawful and permissible: in self-defence, to secure compliance with lawful directions, to prevent escape or to prevent injury to others, damage to property or evidence.[228] The force used must be reasonably necessary. If force is used and injury of any kind results the garda concerned must make a report to the MIC, who must report it to a superintendent.[229] If a garda becomes aware that a detainee has been ill-treated he must report it to a superintendent who must investigate without delay. If ill-treatment is alleged the MIC must arrange for a medical examination.[230] **[2–66]**

Medical Treatment

If any concern as to health arises, due to injury, intoxication, failure to respond normally to questions, the detainee appearing to suffer from a mental illness or being in need of medical attention for some other reason, the MIC must arrange for a doctor to attend.[231] If the detainee needs to attend hospital this should be done immediately and a relative informed.[232] A detainee may request his own doctor at his own expense.[233] Any instructions by a doctor for medical attention must be complied with and recorded in the custody record.[234] **[2–67]**

Information

In order to ensure rights are being effectively complied with, knowledge of the rights is required by the detainee. For this reason the Regulations require that certain information be provided to detainees. A detainee must be informed about the offence, the entitlement to consult with a solicitor, and the right to have somebody informed that he is detained.[235] This information must be given orally and promptly on arrival at the station. The MIC must give written notice of these rights. There does not appear to be an obligation to ensure that the individual understands these rights. If the detainee is under 18, he must also be informed, in a way he understands, that a parent or guardian is being contacted and being asked to attend.[236] A foreign national has the right to contact his consul and he must be informed immediately of this right.[237] **[2–68]**

V. Conclusion

The powers given to gardaí to stop, search, arrest and detain individuals are highly regulated, yet have also undergone substantial expansion in recent decades. Irish law has developed from having quite limited powers of arrest and detention without **[2–69]**

---

227 reg 20.
228 reg 20(2).
229 reg 20(3).
230 reg 20(7).
231 reg 21(1).
232 reg 21(6).
233 reg 21(4).
234 reg 21(3).
235 reg 8.
236 reg 8(1)(b)(ii) as amended.
237 reg 14.

charge, save in relation to offences against the state, to permitting arrest and detention without charge for all serious offences. The most recent changes, including developments such as allowing for the exclusion of the accused during the presentation of evidence by the investigating gardaí during the detention extension hearing, pose particular challenges for due process rights.

Chapter 3
Interrogation

During the period of pre-trial detention, discussed in the previous chapter, suspects may be interrogated about their involvement in the commission of offences. Procedural rules exist to govern the interaction between gardaí and suspects in the pre-trial process in terms of interrogation. These rules, along with the related law on confessions and the constitutionally-protected pre-trial rights to silence and legal advice, are examined in this chapter. **[3–01]**

I. Rules of Interrogation

Two of the main sets of rules in relation to the pre-trial interrogation of suspects are the Criminal Justice Act 1984 (Treatment of Persons in Custody in Garda Síochána Stations) Regulations 1987 (the Custody Regulations) and the Judges' Rules. **[3–02]**

Rules of Interrogation: The Custody Regulations

The elements of these regulations relating to detention in general were discussed in Chapter Two. The aspects directed at the interrogation of suspects will now be considered. **[3–03]**

Regulation 12(2) states that interviews with detained suspects are to be conducted in a fair and humane manner.[1] Other regulations contain specifics as to interrogations including the following:

[1] reg 12(2).

- before the interview begins the garda conducting the interview must identify himself and any other garda present by name and rank to the arrested person[2];
- no more than two gardaí shall question the arrested person at any one time[3];
- no more than four gardaí shall be present at any one time during the interview[4];
- an interview must last no longer than four hours[5];
- as far as practicable interviews should take place in rooms specifically designated for that purpose[6];
- where an arrested person asks for a solicitor, he must not be asked to make a written statement in relation to an offence until a reasonable time for the attendance of the solicitor has elapsed[7];
- detained suspects should not usually be questioned between midnight and 8 am[8];
- an arrested person who is under the influence of alcohol or drugs to the extent that he is unable to appreciate the significance of questions put to him or his answers must not be questioned in relation to an offence while he is in that condition without the authority of the member in charge (MIC)[9];
- if, while being interviewed, an arrested person makes a complaint to a garda in relation to his treatment while in custody, the garda must bring it to the attention of the MIC, if the MIC is not present at the interview, and record it or cause it to be recorded in the record of the interview[10];
- a record of each interview must be kept[11];
- no garda shall submit a detained suspect to ill-treatment of any kind or the threat of ill-treatment[12]; and
- no garda shall use force against a detained suspect except such reasonable force as is necessary in self-defence, to secure compliance with lawful directions, to prevent escape, or to restrain the detainee from injuring himself or others, damaging property or destroying or interfering with evidence.[13]

[3–04] While this list of procedures and prohibitions is important, as noted in Chapter Two, s 7(3) of the Criminal Justice Act 1984 minimises its significance by providing that a breach of the regulations does not provide grounds for an action, civil or criminal, against a garda, or of itself affect the lawfulness of a suspect's detention or the admissibility of any statement made by the suspect. The courts have generally been

2 reg 12(1).
3 reg 12(3).
4 reg 12(3).
5 reg 12(4).
6 reg 12(5)
7 reg 12(6).
8 reg 12(7).
9 reg 12(9).
10 reg 12(10).
11 reg 12(11).
12 reg 20(1).
13 reg 20(2).

reluctant to exclude statements on the grounds of a breach of the regulations alone.[14] Disciplinary action is the only consequence of a breach of the Custody Regulations.[15]

Rules of Interrogation: The Judges' Rules

The Judges' Rules, a statement by the judiciary of the basic principles which needed to be upheld by police officers when dealing with suspects in custody, were introduced in England and Wales in 1912 and updated in 1918 and 1964. They have been replaced in England and Wales by the Codes of Practice accompanying the Police and Criminal Evidence Act 1984. In Ireland, the 1918 version still applies[16] though the rules are somewhat outdated given the introduction of the Custody Regulations, which are more modern, detailed and practical. In fact, the Balance in the Criminal Law Review Group recommended a modernisation of the Judges' Rules by way of legislation.[17] At present, however, the two regimes under these differing sets of rules co-exist.[18] **[3–05]**

The nine Judges' Rules, as applied in Ireland, were laid down in *People (AG) v Cummins*[19] and may be summarised as follows: **[3–06]**

> Rule I – Gardaí investigating a crime may ask anyone from whom they think useful information may be obtained to participate in voluntary questioning and put questions to them without administering a caution;
> Rule II – Once a garda has made up his mind to charge someone with a crime, he should caution him before questioning/continuing to question him;
> Rule III – Persons who are being held in garda custody should not be questioned without first being cautioned[20];
> Rule IV – If the person detained wants to make a voluntary statement he should first be cautioned;
> Rule V – When a suspect is formally charged he should be cautioned as follows – "Do you wish to say anything in answer to the charge? You are not obliged to say anything unless you wish to do so, but whatever you say may be taken down in writing and may be given in evidence" [21];

---

14 See *People (DPP) v Connell* [1995] 1 IR 244; *DPP v Spratt* [1995] 1 IR 585; *People (DPP) v Van Onzen* [1996] 2 ILRM 387; *People (DPP) v Darcy,* unreported, Court of Criminal Appeal, 29 July 1997; *People (DPP) v Smith,* unreported, Court of Criminal Appeal, 22 November 1999.

15 See Chapter Five.

16 See *McCarrick v Leavy* [1964] IR 225; *People (AG) v Cummins* [1972] IR 312; see also *People (AG) v Regan* [1975] IR 367 which held that the 1964 version is not applicable in Ireland.

17 Balance in the Criminal Law Review Group The Right to Silence, *Interim Report*, 31 January 2007, p 43 and *Final Report*, (Stationery Office, Dublin, 2007), p 97.

18 *People (DPP) v Van Onzen* [1996] 2 ILRM 387.

19 [1972] IR 312.

20 This was initially to prevent the use of detention for questioning but the Irish courts have interpreted it as meaning that questioning should not occur in detention unless the suspect has been cautioned; see *People (DPP) v Madden* [1977] IR 336; *People (DPP) v Kelly (No 2)* [1983] IR 1; *People (DPP) v Buckley* [1990] 1 IR 14.

21 The Balance in the Criminal Law Review Group recommended an amendment to the caution in light of incursions on the right to silence (discussed below in Section III) to "You do not have to say anything. But it may harm the credibility of your defence if you do not mention when questioned something which you later rely on in Court. Anything you do say may be given in evidence": *Final Report*, (Stationery Office, Dublin, 2007), p 88.

Rule VI – If a suspect makes a statement before there is time to caution him that statement need not necessarily be excluded from evidence at trial, but the suspect should be cautioned as soon as possible;
Rule VII – When a person in custody is making a voluntary statement he is not to be cross-examined on it by gardaí and may only be asked questions which are necessary to clarify details or remove ambiguity in what has been said;
Rule VIII – Where two or more suspects are charged with the same offence any statement made by one of them ought not to be read by gardaí to the other, but a copy of such statement should be provided to the other without inviting him to reply;
Rule IX – If a suspect makes a statement it should, if possible, be taken down in writing, read back to and signed by the suspect.

[3–07] The Judges' Rules are not rules of law and exist only for the guidance of persons taking statements.[22] A breach of the Judges' Rules will not result in legal sanction against a garda, give rise to grounds for a criminal or civil action against a garda, or lead to the automatic exclusion at trial of evidence obtained as a result of such breach. However, the trial judge retains a discretion to exclude any evidence obtained in breach of the rules.

II. Confessions

[3–08] A confession may be defined as an oral or written statement, adverse to his interest, made by a suspect in the criminal process, usually during pre-trial custodial detention. Confessions are usually admissible at trial as proof of the facts stated therein. Confessions may be written or oral, signed or unsigned and need not be in the exact words spoken by the accused.[23] Confessions have become so prevalent in criminal trials that it has drawn comment from judges of the superior courts[24] and led White to claim that they have become an "institutionalised . . . core element in the criminal process"[25] since the introduction of arrest for questioning. Certain rules have developed through case law on the admissibility of confessions made by suspects in pre-trial detention, affecting that stage by prohibiting the use of specific procedures at that time and by prescribing the manner in which statements should be taken. The rules may be categorised as follows: (i) the voluntariness requirement; (ii) breach of constitutional rights; and (iii) issues of fundamental fairness.

The Voluntariness Requirement

[3–09] An involuntary confession will be excluded from evidence at trial.[26] The legal definition of "voluntariness", set out by Lord Sumner in *Ibrahim v R*[27] and adopted in Ireland in *AG v McCabe*,[28] prescribes that a voluntary statement is one which "has

---

[22] *People (DPP) v Farrell* [1978] IR 13.
[23] *AG v McCabe* [1927] IR 129.
[24] For example, Kearns J in *People (DPP) v Murphy* [2005] 4 IR 504 at 514 noted that almost every criminal case necessitates a *voir dire* to consider the admissibility of confession evidence.
[25] White, "The Confessional State – Police Interrogation in the Irish Republic" Part I (2000) 10 ICLJ 17.
[26] *Ibrahim v R* [1914] AC 599; *AG v McCabe* [1927] IR 129; *People (AG) v Cummins* [1972] IR 312.
[27] [1914] AC 599.
[28] [1927] IR 129; see also *McCarrick v Leavy* [1964] IR 225.

not been obtained ... either by fear of prejudice or hope of advantage exercised or held out by a person in authority."[29]

The requirement is based on the concept that a voluntary confession will be more reliable than a coerced confession. It will, however, also deter garda misconduct, and protect suspects' rights, such as the right to silence.[30] The burden rests on the prosecution to prove beyond a reasonable doubt that it was a voluntary statement.[31] If the court finds it was obtained on the basis of either a threat or an inducement it will be seen as involuntary and inadmissible. This has since been expanded to apply in cases where a statement has been obtained in circumstances of "oppression".[32] **[3–10]**

To find that a statement was involuntary, the court would have to be of the opinion that the particular suspect understood the words to amount to a threat or inducement[33] and that it was the threat or inducement which led him to make the confession.[34] If the effect of a threat or inducement can be said to have dissipated prior to the making of a confession then no issue of involuntariness arises.[35] The threats or inducements must have emanated from a "person in authority",[36] which will invariably be the interrogating garda in terms of a confession made in detention.[37] **[3–11]**

Voluntariness has attained constitutional status within the right to a fair trial under Art 38.1. Barrington J, in the Supreme Court, stated clearly in *Re National Irish Bank Ltd. (No 1)*[38] that a trial which admitted an involuntary confession "would not be a trial in due course of law within the meaning of Art 38 of the Constitution..."[39] Unlike breaches of the Judges' Rules or the Custody Regulations, no discretion exists, accordingly, to admit a confession obtained by threat, inducement, or oppression.[40] **[3–12]**

A threat was found to have led to the making of an inculpatory statement in *People (DPP) v Hoey*[41] where a garda interviewing a suspect in relation to firearms and ammunition found at his residence said "...it must be someone in the house. Will I **[3–13]**

---

[29] *AG v McCabe* [1927] IR 129 at 134.
[30] *People (DPP) v Hoey* [1987] IR 637.
[31] *McCarrick v Leavy* [1964] IR 225; *People (DPP) v Shaw* [1982] 1 IR 1.
[32] The concept of oppression is discussed further below at 32-15–3-18.
[33] *People (DPP) v McCann* [1998] 4 IR 397.
[34] *ibid.*
[35] *People (AG) v Galvin* [1964] IR 325; *People (AG) v Pringle* (1981) 1 Frewen 57.
[36] O'Flaherty J defined it in *People (DPP) v McCann* [1998] 4 IR 397 at 412 as "someone engaged in the arrest, detention, examination or prosecution of the accused or someone acting on behalf of the prosecution."
[37] Other possibilities are a sergeant major for soldiers in *R v Smith* [1959] 2 QB 35 or a headmistress for schoolgirls in *R v McLintock* [1962] Crim LR 549. The silence of a person in authority when someone in his presence makes a threat or inducement can be interpreted as an adoption of that threat or inducement; *R v Cleary* [1963] 48 Cr App R 116.
[38] [1999] 3 IR 145.
[39] *ibid.* at 186-187.
[40] See the judgment of Walsh J in *People (AG) v Cummins* [1972] IR 312 at 322. In *DPP v O'Neill* [2007] 4 IR 564 it was held that where a statement is found to be involuntary both the incriminatory and exculpatory portions must be excluded.
[41] [1987] IR 637.

have to get members to go up to your family and see if anyone will take responsibility?" The Supreme Court ruled that a confession in response to this was involuntary and should have been excluded at trial. It was held that there is no requirement of mala fides on the part of the garda; the important matter was the effect of the words on the individual suspect.

[3–14] An inducement, which involves the creation of hope rather than fear in a suspect, was present in *People (AG) v Murphy*[42] where an arresting garda had said to the suspect "You're alright. Come along with me...". This was held to have amounted to an inducement, rendering involuntary a statement made by the suspect. Similarly, in *People (AG) v Flynn*,[43] a confession was held inadmissible as a result of an inducement where the accused, who had said nothing for two hours of questioning, confessed after a garda had brought him his lunch and had a chat. The court held that the garda must have advised him that it would be better to confess.

It has been held by the courts that an involuntary confession brought about by way of a false pretence or a trick will be inadmissible, but only where the trick or pretence led to involuntariness, due to a level of compulsion.[44]

[3–15] The definition of oppression, which can also render a statement involuntary, as "something which tends to sap and has sapped the free will which must exist before a confession is voluntary"[45] was adopted into Irish law in *People (DPP) v Breathnach*.[46] In *People (DPP) v Pringle*[47] the court opted for a more specific definition of oppressive questioning from the English case of *R v Prager*[48]:

> "questioning which by its nature, duration or other attendant circumstances (including the fact of custody) excites hopes (such as the hope of release) or fears or so affects the mind of the subject that his will crumbles and he speaks when otherwise he would have stayed silent."[49]

[3–16] In *Pringle*, the appellants had been convicted at trial of the capital murder of two gardaí. Following lengthy detention and interrogations under s 30 of the Offences Against the State Act 1939 Pringle said "I know you know that I was involved but on the advice of my solicitor I am saying nothing and you will have to prove it all the way."[50] This was admitted in evidence by the trial judge as an admission of guilt. This decision and the voluntariness of the statement were upheld in the Court of Criminal Appeal. O'Higgins CJ held on the facts that the long duration of interviews combined

---

42 [1947] IR 236.

43 [1963] IR 255.

44 McGrath, *Evidence* (Thomson Round Hall, Dublin, 2005), pp 408-409. See *People (AG) v Sherlock* (1975) 1 Frewen 383; *Allan v UK* (2003) 36 EHRR 12.

45 *R v Priestly* (1965) 50 Cr App Rep 183.

46 (1981) 2 Frewen 43, affirmed by the Supreme Court in *People (DPP) v Lynch* [1982] IR 64.

47 (1981) 2 Frewen 57.

48 [1972] 1 All ER 1114.

49 *ibid.* at 1119 *per* Edmund Davies LJ.

50 This was contested at trial but it was determined as a matter of fact that he made this statement.

with the short duration of sleep permitted did not of itself establish oppression. Oppression, the Court found, is subjective to the character of the accused and

> "what may be oppressive to a child, an invalid, or an old man or somebody inexperienced in the ways of the world may turn out not to be oppressive when one finds that the accused person is of tough character and an experienced man of the world".[51]

O'Higgins CJ found that as a 42 year old fisherman not unused to conditions of physical hardship, it was open to the trial court to find that Pringle's will would not have been undermined by the interview experienced or by lack of sleep. The fact that the accused had five visits with his solicitor who advised him to remain silent was held by O'Higgins CJ to have strengthened his resolve not to make statements and counteracted any weakness of will which the conditions and interrogation may have created.[52] **[3–17]**

On the other hand, in *People (DPP) v Lynch*[53] the Supreme Court ruled that the suspect's lack of sleep, his being in a strange environment, isolated from all he was accustomed to and being under constant garda surveillance of which he was aware led to circumstances of oppression which meant that the confession made by him was involuntary. **[3–18]**

Breach of Constitutional Rights

If a confession or inculpatory statement is found to have been obtained in deliberate and conscious breach of the constitutional rights of a suspect, and there are no extraordinary excusing circumstances, it *must* be excluded by the trial judge.[54] Again, a causative link between the breach of constitutional rights and the making of the confession or statement is required.[55] **[3–19]**

This was first applied to confession evidence in *People (DPP) v Madden*,[56] where the accused was arrested and detained under s 30 of the Offences Against the State Act 1939. He was held in custody beyond the statutorily sanctioned period of time and made a confession during the unlawful period of detention. While the Court of Criminal Appeal held that the confession was voluntary they found it had been made in circumstances which amounted to a conscious and deliberate breach of his constitutional right to liberty. In the absence of extraordinary excusing circumstances the statement had to be excluded from evidence. **[3–20]**

A number of constitutional rights are of specific importance during the pre-trial stage of the criminal process, including, amongst others, the rights to bodily integrity, privacy, dignity, and liberty. Two further rights have been subject to particular **[3–21]**

---

51 Above n 47 at 82.
52 Discussed further in Costello, "Detention for Questioning and Oppressive Interrogation" (2001) 11(1) ICLJ 12.
53 [1982] IR 64.
54 See *People (AG) v O'Brien* [1965] IR 142; *People (DPP) v Madden* [1977] IR 336; *People (DPP) v Kenny* [1990] 2 IR 110.
55 *People (DPP) v Buck* [2002] 2 IR 268; *People (DPP) v O'Brien* unreported, Court of Criminal Appeal, 17 June, 2002; [2005] 2 IR 206 (SC).
56 [1977] IR 336.

comment in Ireland in the context of pre-trial interrogation and will be discussed further below: the rights to silence and to legal advice.[57]

Fundamental Fairness

[3–22] The third issue which relates to the admissibility at trial of confessions or statements made by the suspect during the pre-trial period is fundamental fairness. In *People (DPP) v Shaw*[58] Griffin J in the Supreme Court suggested that in order to admit a confession the court must be satisfied not only that it was voluntary but also that no other circumstances existed to interfere with the fundamental fairness of the procedures adopted in the case. He proposed that a test of fundamental fairness would be fairer and more workable than a consideration of whether the statement complies with specific constitutional provisions. The courts have opted to include that as an additional test of admissibility, rather than replacing the test based on the breach of constitutional rights.[59]

[3–23] In *Shaw*, Griffin J observed that because of our accusatorial system and constitutional commitment to fair procedures

> "the judge presiding at a criminal trial should be astute to see that, although a statement may be technically voluntary, it should nevertheless be excluded if, by reason of the manner or of the circumstances in which it was obtained, it falls below the required standards of fairness. The reason for exclusion here is not so much the risk of an erroneous conviction as the recognition that the minimum of essential standards must be observed in the administration of justice."[60]

[3–24] This is connected to the concept of oppression, however, in *People (DPP) v C*[61] it was held that there may be circumstances where the causative link necessary to exclude evidence on the basis of oppression may not be present, but the behaviour and general circumstances of the case may be said to be so unfair as to necessitate the exclusion of the evidence on public policy or fair procedure grounds.[62]

[3–25] In *People (DPP) v Murphy*[63] it was made clear that even where there have been no inducements, no threats, no oppression and no breach of constitutional rights, circumstances of unfairness can lead to the exclusion of confession evidence at trial. There, in an appeal against a murder conviction, it was argued that the suspect was emotionally manipulated into making inculpatory statements by gardaí, particularly an Inspector who spent 75 minutes alone with the suspect, ostensibly to get approval for the release of his medical records. In this time the suspect was allowed to eat a take away meal outside of his cell, given a cigarette and the Inspector arranged with the

---

57 See below Sections III and IV.

58 [1982] IR 1.

59 See McGuckian, "Recent Developments in the Law Governing the Admissibility of Confessions in Ireland" (1999) 9(1) ICLJ 8.

60 [1982] IR 1 at 61.

61 [2001] 3 IR 345.

62 See also *People (DPP) v Breen,* unreported, Court of Criminal Appeal, 13 March 1995; *People (DPP) v Paul Ward,* unreported, Special Criminal Court, 27 November 1998.

63 [2005] 4 IR 504.

suspect's solicitor to make money available for the suspect's mother. Subsequently, the suspect made inculpatory statements, revealing where the clothing of the victim could be found. The defence argued that it should not have taken 75 minutes to acquire the signature and that he had been manipulated into making the admissions. The Court of Criminal Appeal held that the Inspector had not made any improper inducements or sought to manipulate the emotions of the suspect but there was substance to the suggestion that the Inspector had hoped that if he remained in the suspect's company long enough in relaxed circumstances he might say something incriminating. The Court accepted that the suspect was in a vulnerable position that day and in those circumstances the actions of the Inspector were, possibly unconsciously, tactically unfair, taking advantage of that vulnerability.[64] The Court therefore held that the statements ought to have been excluded by the trial judge.

III. The Right to Silence

The right to silence, often referred to as the "privilege against self-incrimination",[65] refers to the entitlement of a suspect within the criminal process to refuse to answer questions put to him or to provide any information to the prosecution.[66] The origins of the right go back as far as the 17th century, if not earlier.[67] It has been recognised as having constitutional status in Ireland[68] and is protected under Art 6 ECHR.[69] Despite this, the Irish legislature has substantially limited the potential exercise of the right by creating offences based on pre-trial silence and allowing for inferences to be drawn at trial from pre-trial silence in particular circumstances. [3–26]

Offences Based on Pre-Trial Silence

Section 52 of the Offences Against the State Act 1939 provides that a person arrested and detained in custody under s 30 of that Act may be required by gardaí to account for his movements and actions during a specified period and to give all the information which he possesses in regard to the commission or intended commission by another person of any offence under the Act or any scheduled offence. Failure or refusal to give the required account or information, or the provision of false or misleading information or account is an offence punishable by a term of imprisonment not exceeding six months.[70] [3–27]

---

64 *ibid.* at 519-520.

65 The Irish courts have generally used the term "right to silence" in relation to the pre-trial period of interrogation, for example *Heaney and McGuinness v Ireland* [1996] 1 IR 580; *Rock v Ireland* [1997] 3 IR 484; [1998] 2 ILRM 35.

66 See McGrath above n 44, p 623.

67 See Cross, "The Right to Silence and the Presumption of Innocence – Sacred Cows or Safeguards of Liberty?" (1970-71) 11 *Journal of the Society of Public Teachers of Law* 66; Zuckerman, "The Right Against Self-Incrimination: An Obstacle to the Supervision of Interrogation" (1986) 102 *Law Quarterly Review* 43; Langbein, "The Historical Origins of the Privilege Against Self-Incrimination at Common Law" (1994) 92 *Michigan Law Review* 1047; Easton, *The Case for the Right to Silence* (Amesbury Series in Philosophy, 1998).

68 *Heaney v Ireland* [1996] 1 IR 580; (2001) 33 EHRR 12.

69 *Funke v France* (1993) 16 EHRR 297 and *Murray v United Kingdom* (1996) 22 EHRR 29. See Jackson, "Re-conceptualizing the right to silence as an effective fair trial standard" (2009) 58 ICLQ 835.

70 s 52(2).

[3–28] A challenge to the constitutionality of the provision in *Heaney and McGuinness v Ireland*[71] resulted in the first recognition of the constitutional status of the right to silence. While the High Court situated it within the right to a fair trial in Art 38.1, the Supreme Court preferred to locate it within Art 40.6 as a corollary of the right to freedom of expression.[72] The proviso in that Article that the right to freedom of expression may be curtailed where the exigencies of public order or morality so require, allowed the Supreme Court to hold that the incursion on the right to silence contained in s 52 of the OASA 1939 was protected under this proviso and was constitutionally sound. Applying a proportionality test[73] the Court held that the State was entitled to encroach on the citizen's right to silence in pursuit of the legitimate aim of maintaining public peace and order, though the right must be affected as little as possible. Section 52 involved a proportionate incursion given the State's aim of protecting itself.[74]

[3–29] The case ultimately went before the ECtHR,[75] which located the right to silence within the "fair trial" provision of the ECHR: Art 6. As in *Murray v United Kingdom*,[76] the ECtHR stated that the right to silence is a generally recognised international standard at the heart of the notion of a fair procedure under Art 6.[77] Further, the degree of compulsion to provide information imposed on the applicants by s 52 in effect "destroyed the very essence of their privilege against self-incrimination and their right to remain silent"[78] and was in violation of Art 6.

[3–30] However, despite this judgment and the recommendation of the Committee to Review the Offences Against the State Acts 1939–1998 that s 52 be removed from the statute books,[79] the impugned provision remains in place.[80] Furthermore, a number of other provisions which create offences based on the pre-trial silence of a suspect have been introduced. Some of the provisions compel only the utterance of an individual's name and address,[81] while others require information in relation to the possession of certain items.[82]

[3–31] The Irish courts have accepted these provisions so long as the limits placed on the right to silence are proportionate to the legitimate aim sought to be achieved.[83] Greater protection of the right is apparent in terms of the use at trial of a pre-trial statement

71 [1996] 1 IR 580; (2001) 33 EHRR 334.

72 Following the reasoning in *Educational Company of Ireland Ltd. v Fitzpatrick and Others (No 2)* [1961] IR 345 wherein the constitutional right to refuse to associate was derived from the right to freedom of association.

73 As set out in the case of *Cox v Ireland* [1992] 2 IR 503.

74 [1996] 1 IR 580 at 590 *per* O'Flaherty J.

75 (2001) 33 EHRR 334.

76 (1996) 22 EHRR 29.

77 Above n 75, at para 40. See also *Saunders v United Kingdom* (1996) 23 EHRR 313.

78 *ibid.* at para 55.

79 *Report of the Committee to Review the Offences Against the State Acts 1939-1998* (Stationery Office, Dublin, 2002), para 8.57.

80 See *Quinn v O'Leary* [2004] 3 IR 128.

81 For example, Road Traffic Act 1961, s 107 and Criminal Justice Act 1984, s 4.

82 For example, Criminal Justice Act 1984, ss 15 and 16.

83 *Heaney v Ireland* [1996] 1 IR 580; *Gilligan v Criminal Assets Bureau (No 2)* [1998] 3 IR 185; *Re National Irish Bank (under investigation) (No 1)* [1999] 3 IR 145; *Dunnes Stores v Ryan* [2002] 2 IR 60; see McGuckian, "Confessions and the Constitution" (2004) 26 DULJ 272.

made by a suspect under the compulsion of a legislative provision which deems the failure or refusal to answer particular questions to be an offence. The courts have held that the use of such a statement at trial is governed by Art 38.1 of the Constitution, which provides that no person shall be tried on a criminal charge "save in due course of law". In *Re National Irish Bank (under investigation) (No 1)*[84] the Supreme Court held that a proportionality test would be inappropriate to determine whether such statements interfered with the individual's rights under Art 38.1, as a trial was either "in due course of law" as necessitated by Art 38.1 or it was not. The question was whether a trial which admitted a confession obtained from the accused by virtue of a legislative penal sanction could be a trial in due course of law. Whether or not it should be admitted should be determined on the basis of voluntariness, which was a matter for the judge to decide in the particular circumstances of the case.

Hogan argues that the judgment in *Re National Irish Bank,* as well as that in *People (DPP) v Finnerty,*[85] discussed below,[86] represents an attempt by the Supreme Court to distance itself from the reasoning employed in *Heaney* and to move "decisively to re-establish the importance of the right to silence".[87] Decisions like *Re National Irish Bank*[88] undermine the legislative intention of creating offences based on pre-trial silence, in that compelled statements will rarely pass a test of voluntariness and will therefore generally be excluded from evidence. Nonetheless, it is still possible for a suspect to be convicted of an offence of remaining silent in the pre-trial process and refusing to provide certain specified information, separate and distinct from any offence of which he was originally suspected.

Inferences Drawn from Pre-Trial Silence

In recent times, statutory restrictions on the pre-trial right to silence in Ireland have focussed on allowing inferences to be drawn at trial from pre-trial silence in certain circumstances, possibly as a result of the ECtHR's criticisms of creating silence-based offences and the Supreme Court decision in *Re National Irish Bank* which weakened the impact of such offences. [3–32]

Little guidance has been provided in this jurisdiction as to what exact inferences can be drawn where provisions permit them. An example of what inferences may be drawn by a jury where an accused fails to mention in questioning a fact which he later seeks to rely on can be found in an English list provided by a Judicial Studies Board Specimen Direction, which lists the inferences which may be drawn under one such provision.[89] Possible inferences include that the fact now relied on is true but the defendant, for reasons of his own, chose not to reveal it; the fact now relied on is irrelevant; the 'fact' now relied on is of more recent invention; the defendant's present answer to the prosecution case is fabricated; and the defendant is guilty.[90] [3–33]

---

[84] [1999] 3 IR 145.
[85] [1999] 4 IR 364.
[86] Para 3-45.
[87] Hogan, "The Right to Silence after National Irish Banks and Finnerty" (1999) 21 DULJ 176.
[88] For example, *Dunnes Stores v Ryan* [2002] 2 IR 60.
[89] Criminal Justice and Public Order Act 1994, s 34.
[90] "Crown Court Bench Book: Directing the Jury", March 2010, p 261, available at www.jsboard.co.uk.

The first inference-drawing provisions in Ireland were promulgated in the Criminal Justice Act 1984. Though redrafted and substituted by the Criminal Justice Act 2007, the basic premise and the inferences which may be drawn remain unchanged.

[3–34] Sections 18 and 19 of the 1984 Act, as substituted by the 2007 Act, provide that an adverse inference may properly be drawn at trial against a person who has been arrested without warrant by a garda, due to his failure or refusal to account, on being requested to do so by a garda, for the presence of any object, substance or mark on his person, clothing or footwear, or in his possession, or in the place where he is arrested (s 18) or for his presence at a particular place (s 19).

[3–35] Under both sections as originally formulated, the garda who requests the relevant information must hold a reasonable belief that the presence of the object, substance or mark, or the suspect's presence at a particular place, may be attributable to the suspect's participation in the commission of the offence for which he has been arrested. The garda must inform the suspect of this belief, and must tell the suspect in ordinary language what the possible consequences of failure or refusal to answer might be. Both ss 18 and 19 also provide that a person cannot be convicted solely or mainly on the basis of any inference which might be drawn from his failure or refusal to account for the relevant item; however, such failure or refusal may amount to corroboration of any other evidence in relation to which it is material. Some additional requirements and safeguards are now included in ss 18 and 19 by virtue of the 2007 Act. These are outlined below.

[3–36] The constitutionality of ss 18 and 19 was tested, prior to the addition of the new safeguards under the 2007 Act, in *Rock v Ireland*.[91] Both the High Court and the Supreme Court upheld the constitutionality of the inference-drawing provisions. As it had previously held in *Heaney*,[92] the Supreme Court restated that the pre-trial right to silence in the Irish Constitution is protected under Art 40.6 but that it may be restricted in order to serve the exigencies of public order and morality. Applying a proportionality test to ss 18 and 19 in order to assess the restriction on the right to silence, the court held that it was proportionate to the aim which was sought to be achieved. The sections represented the necessary balance between the right to silence and the duty of the state to defend and protect the life, person and property of all its citizens. It was important that limiting factors were in place: the inferences which might be drawn were evidential in nature only and could not be the sole basis for the conviction; and in deciding what inferences may be drawn from the accused's silence, the court is obliged to act in accordance with the principles of constitutional justice and, having regard to an accused's right to a fair trial, is under a constitutional obligation to ensure that no improper or unfair inferences are drawn from that silence.[93] Therefore, the Supreme Court held that ss 18 and 19 of the 1984 Act did not constitute an unjust attack on the right to silence or on the presumption of innocence.[94]

[91] [1997] 3 IR 484.

[92] [1996] 1 IR 580.

[93] Above n 91, at 501 *per* Hamilton CJ.

[94] See also the decisions of the ECtHR in *Murray v United Kingdom* (1996) 22 EHRR 29 and *Averill v United Kingdom* (2001) 31 EHRR 839.

Broadly defined inference-drawing provisions were included in both the Criminal Justice (Drug Trafficking) Act 1996[95] and the Offences Against the State (Amendment) Act 1998[96] which allowed for inferences to be drawn at trial for a suspect's failure to mention, during the pre-trial process, a fact which he later relied on in his defence, being a fact which he ought reasonably to have mentioned at the time of questioning or charging.[97] These have been repealed by the Criminal Justice Act 2007 which inserts into the Criminal Justice Act 1984 a new, broadly applicable inference-drawing provision – s 19A. **[3–37]**

Section 19A[98] applies to all arrestable offences[99] and provides that inferences may be drawn at trial from a suspect's failure in the pre-trial period to mention any fact, when he is being questioned, charged or informed that he might be charged with a particular offence, which he later relies on in his defence at trial, being a fact which in the circumstances existing at the time "clearly called for an explanation". A number of safeguards are provided for suspects under s 19A and these are also applicable to ss 18 and 19 of the 1984 Act:[100] **[3–38]**

- the inference may not be the sole or main basis for a conviction but may serve as corroboration of any evidence in relation to which the failure is material;
- the accused must be told in ordinary language that it may harm the credibility of his defence if he does not mention when questioned, charged or informed that he may be prosecuted, something which he later relies on in court;
- the accused must be afforded a reasonable opportunity to consult a solicitor prior to the relevant silence;
- the court or jury in deciding whether or not to draw inferences ought to consider when the account or fact concerned was first mentioned by the accused; and
- no inference shall be drawn in relation to a question asked in an interview unless either the interview has been electronically recorded or the detained person has consented in writing to the non-recording of the interview.

While the requirements regarding access to legal advice and electronic recording are unprecedented in the context of incursions on the right to pre-trial silence under Irish legislation, s 19A nonetheless represents the broadest restriction on the right to silence in this jurisdiction to date. Furthermore, as we will see below, access to legal advice in **[3–39]**

---

[95] s 7 for trafficking offences.

[96] s 5 for offences under the OASA 1939 or scheduled offences.

[97] See Ryan, "The Criminal Justice (Drug Trafficking) Act, 1996: Decline and Fall of the Right to Silence?" (1997) 7(1) ICLJ 22.

[98] Criminal Justice Act 1984, s 19A as inserted by the Criminal Justice Act 2007, s 30. This was proposed by the Balance in the Criminal Law Review Group, above n 21, pp 96-97.

[99] Thereby encompassing the offences covered by both the Criminal Justice (Drug Trafficking) Act 1996 and the Offences Against the State Acts and scheduled offences.

[100] The safeguards were inserted into ss 18, 19 and the new s 19A of the Criminal Justice Act 1984 by ss 28, 29 and 30 of the Criminal Justice Act 2007. They also apply under s 31 of the 2007 Act to s 2 of the Offences Against the State (Amendment) Act 1998 which provides that an inference may be drawn at trial against an accused person in relation to membership of an unlawful organisation from his failure to answer any question posed by a garda which was material to the investigation of the offence.

the pre-trial process has been given a limited definition and there have been difficulties in terms of the audio-visual recording of interviews,[101] potentially making these perceived protections shallow in effect.

[3–40] Section 19A was first applied in the murder trial of Gerard Mackin in the Special Criminal Court in 2008 where the court held that it was entitled to draw inferences under s 19A from the accused's refusal to answer questions put to him by gardaí in the pre-trial period.[102] Despite this judicial endorsement, there is some suggestion that gardaí are hesitant in employing s 19A as no regulations have been promulgated to date by the Minister for Justice on the technicalities of its application, particularly on the caution to be employed in such circumstances.[103] Regulations would provide clarity for both gardaí and suspects.

[3–41] Section 19A remains to be constitutionally tested by the courts, but it seems that in light of the Supreme Court decision in *Rock*, as well as certain *obiter dictum* comments of Fennelly J in *People (DPP) v Bowes*[104] which referred to the operation of s 7 of the 1996 Act, the incursion on the right to silence is likely to be accepted by the courts as being proportionate and constitutional.

[3–42] The ECtHR has also accepted inference-drawing provisions. In *Murray v United Kingdom*,[105] it was held that the right to silence, protected under Art 6 ECHR, is not absolute and may be interfered with by inference-drawing provisions in appropriate circumstances. The decision as to whether or not the drawing of adverse inferences was in violation of Art 6 should be determined in light of all the circumstances of a given case, having particular regard to the situations where inferences may be drawn, the weight to be attached to them by the national courts and the degree of compulsion inherent in the situation.[106]

[3–43] One further inference-drawing provision has been enacted: s 72A of the Criminal Justice Act 2006, inserted by s 9 of the Criminal Justice (Amendment) Act 2009. This operates only in the context of "organised crime"[107] and provides that an inference may be drawn at trial from the failure of a suspect to "answer a question material to the investigation of the offence".[108] A person is not to be convicted solely or mainly on an inference drawn from such a failure. Furthermore, the suspect must have been told in ordinary language when being questioned what the effect of such a failure might be, he must have been afforded a reasonable opportunity to consult a solicitor before such

[101] Discussed further below at Section VI.

[102] "Court rules for first time on new gangland laws" *The Irish Times*, 13 November 2008.

[103] On the issue of cautioning under s 19A see McGillicuddy, "Restrictions on the Right to Silence under the Criminal Justice Act 2007 – Part 2" (2008) 18(4) ICLJ 112.

[104] [2004] 4 IR 223.

[105] (1996) 22 EHRR 29.

[106] *ibid.* at para 47.

[107] A "criminal organisation" and participation in "organised crime" are defined under ss 70 and 72 of the Criminal Justice Act 2006, as amended by ss 3 and 6 of the Criminal Justice (Amendment) Act 2009.

[108] Criminal Justice Act 2006, s 72A.

a failure occurred and the relevant interview must have been recorded by electronic or similar means unless the suspect consented in writing to it not being recorded.[109]

The section defines "any question material to the investigation of the offence" as including, *inter alia*, a request that the suspect give a full account of his movements, actions, activities or associations during any specified period relevant to the offence being investigated; questions related to statements or conduct of the suspect implying or leading to a reasonable inference that he was at a material time directing the activities of a criminal organisation; and, questions relating to any benefit which the suspect may have obtained from directing a criminal organisation or committing a serious offence within a criminal organisation.[110] No question is to be regarded as being material to the investigation of the offence unless the garda concerned reasonably believed that the question related to the participation of the defendant in the commission of the offence.[111] This permits inferences to be drawn from a suspect's failure to assist in the garda investigation of the commission of an offence. The focus of previous inference-drawing provisions has been either on pre-trial failure to account for a specific matter or reliance on a fact at trial which was not mentioned during pre-trial questioning. Section 72A involves a different concept which raises issues in relation to the presumption of innocence and the burden of proof in a criminal trial. The provision places a heavy onus on the suspect to provide gardaí with information on which to base their further investigations. An inference, it seems, may be drawn whether or not the failure to answer the particular question is a specifically relevant matter in the later trial: failure alone gives rise to the inference. The use and interpretation of this section is likely to give rise to constitutional challenges which will need to be addressed by the superior courts. Such matters may arise before the courts for decision given that the President declined to refer the 2009 Act as a Bill to the Supreme Court under Art 26, following consultation with the Council of State in July 2009.[112] **[3–44]**

The Supreme Court has ruled that inferences from silence may only be drawn against an accused person where there is specific legislative provision to that end. In *People (DPP) v Finnerty*,[113] the accused had been convicted of rape and appealed because the trial judge had allowed counsel for the prosecution to present evidence that during the pre-trial period the accused had not provided the account of events in relation to his interaction with the complainant which was being presented by his lawyer at trial and had allowed prosecuting counsel to question the accused about his reasons for maintaining silence in this regard during pre-trial interrogation. The Supreme Court noted, on appeal, that the legislature had made special provision under the Criminal Justice Act 1984 for the drawing of inferences in certain delineated circumstances but, at that time, no broader powers had been introduced and "[t]he absence of any such provision in the Act of 1984 speaks for itself."[114] Any restriction of the right to silence **[3–45]**

109 *ibid.*
110 *ibid.*
111 *ibid.*
112 "President signs gang crime and defamation Bills", *The Irish Times*, 24 July 2009.
113 [1999] 4 IR 364.
114 *ibid.* at 380.

must be specifically set out by the Oireachtas.[115] In *People (DPP) v Bowes*[116] it was held that the prosecution could not mention a pre-trial failure to account for objects found during opening statements as it could not be known at that stage whether the accused intended to rely on a fact which he could reasonably have been expected to mention when questioned in the pre-trial period. This principle presumably applies to s 19A of the Criminal Justice Act 1984.

IV. The Right to Pre-Trial Legal Advice

[3–46] In England and Wales a suspect in detention has a right to consult privately with a solicitor at any time, on request[117]; to free legal advice through a duty solicitor scheme[118]; to be informed of his right to access such advice[119]; and to have a lawyer present during interrogation if he wishes.[120] Solicitors and other pre-trial legal advisers[121] in England and Wales are entitled to remain in the interview room throughout interrogation so long as their conduct is not such that the interviewer is unable properly to put questions to the suspect.[122]

[3–47] In the United States, following the seminal Supreme Court case of *Miranda v Arizona*,[123] a suspect in the pre-trial process is entitled to legal representation which may be provided free of charge to impecunious suspects; a suspect is entitled to be informed of the right to legal representation and the possibility of a legal adviser being appointed if he cannot afford to retain one; a suspect is entitled also to remain silent and to be informed of his right to remain silent. No questioning should proceed without legal representation where the suspect indicates that he will not speak without legal representation. If the suspect indicates that he does not wish to speak at all, then there ought to be no interrogation.[124] In *Miranda* Warren CJ explained,

> "the circumstances surrounding in-custody interrogation can operate very quickly to overbear the will of one merely made aware of his privilege [against self-incrimination] by his interrogators".[125]

[3–48] The right of access to pre-trial legal advice is seen as necessary to ensure the effectiveness of the pre-trial privilege against self-incrimination, or right to silence.

---

[115] *Finnerty* was followed and applied in *People (DPP) v Coddington,* unreported, Court of Criminal Appeal, 31 May 2001 and *People (DPP) v McCowan* [2003] 4 IR 349.
[116] [2004] 4 IR 223.
[117] Police and Criminal Evidence Act 1984, s 58.
[118] Provided under s 59 of the Police and Criminal Evidence Act 1984 and the Legal Aid Act 1988.
[119] Police and Criminal Evidence Act 1984, Code of Practice for the Detention, Treatment and Questioning of Persons by Police Officers (Code of Practice C), para 3.1.
[120] *ibid.* para 6.6.
[121] Provision is made in England and Wales for an individual to be accredited by the Legal Aid Board as a non-solicitor police station adviser.
[122] Above n 119, paras 6.8–6.11.
[123] 384 US 436 (1966); see also *Dickerson v United States* 530 US 428 (2000).
[124] *ibid.* at 445 per Warren CJ.
[125] *ibid.* at 469.

A lawyer is therefore entitled to be present throughout interrogation in the United States,[126] as in England and Wales.

The Right of Access to Pre-Trial Legal Advice in Ireland

In Ireland, the right of access to pre-trial legal advice has been partly legislated for but has also been recognised by the courts as a right of constitutional status. Section 5 of the Criminal Justice Act 1984 specified the right to be informed of the right of access to legal advice in the pre-trial period, but not the right to legal advice itself. Under s 5, a person detained pursuant to s 4 of the 1984 Act shall be informed by the MIC that he is entitled to consult a solicitor. On request being made by the suspect for a particular solicitor the MIC must cause that solicitor to be notified accordingly as soon as practicable.[127] While s 5 applies only to detention under the 1984 Act, reference is also made in the Custody Regulations to the possibility of consulting with a solicitor in the pre-trial period. These regulations apply to all suspects held in garda custody, thus applying to persons detained under s 30 of the 1939 Act, s 4 of the 1984 Act, s 2 of the Criminal Justice (Drug Trafficking) Act 1996 and s 50 of the Criminal Justice Act 2007. The Custody Regulations provide the following: **[3–49]**

- an arrested person shall have reasonable access to a solicitor of his choice and be enabled to communicate with the solicitor privately[128];
- an arrested person must be informed of his right to consult with a solicitor and if the arrested person does not wish to exercise this right immediately he must be informed that he can invoke it at a later time[129];
- the right of access to legal advice must be explained orally to the detained suspect and written notice must also be provided[130];
- where an arrested person does request a solicitor the MIC must notify the solicitor as soon as practicable and if the solicitor cannot be contacted within a reasonable time or is unable or unwilling to attend the garda station the suspect must be asked to supply the name of an alternative solicitor to be contacted, who should then be notified by the MIC as soon as practicable[131];
- a suspect's consultation with a solicitor may take place in the sight but out of hearing of a garda[132]; and
- where a detained suspect has requested a consultation with a solicitor he is not to be asked to make a written statement until a reasonable time for the attendance of the solicitor has elapsed.[133]

---

[126] *ibid.* at 470.

[127] s 5 also allows for a person reasonably named by the detained suspect to be notified of his detention and of the station where he is being detained.

[128] reg 11(1).

[129] reg 8(1).

[130] regs 8(1) and 8(2).

[131] reg 9(2).

[132] reg 11(3).

[133] reg 11(6).

Breaches of these regulations do not, of course, render a garda liable to any criminal or civil proceedings or of itself affect the lawfulness of the custody of the detained person or the admissibility of any statement made by him.[134]

[3–50] The new provisions on the drawing of inferences from silence under ss 18, 19 and 19A of the Criminal Justice Act 1984 specifically provide that inferences may not be drawn unless a suspect in the pre-trial period has been afforded a reasonable opportunity to consult with a solicitor. This is an interesting recognition of the link between the right to silence and the right of access to pre-trial legal advice.[135]

[3–51] The Irish courts adverted to the existence of a right of access to pre-trial legal advice in cases such as *In Re Article 26 and the Emergency Powers Bill, 1976*,[136] *People (DPP) v Madden*,[137] *People (DPP) v Farrell*[138] and *People (DPP) v Conroy*.[139] It was not, however, until the 1990 case of *People (DPP) v Healy*[140] that the Supreme Court held that the right was of constitutional status.

[3–52] In *Healy*, the suspect had been arrested and detained for questioning under s 30 of the OASA 1939 on suspicion of being in possession of unlawful firearms. He was questioned by gardaí for a number of hours in regard to an attempted armed robbery and eventually began to make an inculpatory statement. As he was making this statement, a solicitor who had been retained by the suspect's family arrived at the garda station and was refused immediate access to the suspect as the MIC considered that it would be "bad manners" to interrupt the ongoing garda interview. At trial, the only evidence against him was the inculpatory statement which he had made to gardaí. He was convicted and appealed on grounds of a breach of his right of access to legal advice.

[3–53] The Supreme Court held that the right of reasonable access to a solicitor was derived from and protected by the Constitution. This right encompassed a right to be immediately informed of the arrival of one's solicitor at the place of detention and given immediate access to him if requested. If the denial of this right to a solicitor could be said to be the result of a deliberate and conscious act by gardaí, then any admissions later obtained from the accused would be inadmissible against him at trial. The motives of the gardaí were irrelevant, so long as the act or acts which brought about the breach of the accused's constitutional right could be said to be deliberate and conscious. On the facts, the inculpatory statements made by the suspect following the breach of his constitutional right of access to pre-trial legal advice had been correctly excluded from evidence at trial.

---

[134] Criminal Justice Act 1984, s 7(3).

[135] The ECtHR has also noted a link between the right to silence and the right of access to pre-trial legal advice in cases such as *Murray v United Kingdom* (1996) 22 EHRR 29 and *Averill v United Kingdom* (2001) 31 EHRR 839.

[136] [1977] IR 159.

[137] [1977] IR 336.

[138] [1978] IR 13.

[139] [1986] IR 460.

[140] [1990] 2 IR 73.

Finlay CJ did not specify the particular constitutional provision in which the court was locating the right[141]; however, he appeared to recognise a two-fold *raison d'être* for the right. The Chief Justice suggested that the right is necessary so that a suspect is fully aware of all his legal rights, allowing for any decision as to whether or not to make a statement to be freely reached and therefore voluntary.[142] The right would also redress the imbalance which exists in the pre-trial period between the power and position of the detained suspect and that of the gardaí; advice from a solicitor would contribute to some measure of equality of arms between these participants in the process.[143] **[3–54]**

The decision in *Healy* left a number of matters relating to the ambit of the right to pre-trial legal advice unresolved. These will now be examined.

Definitional Ambit of the Right to Pre-Trial Legal Advice

The Supreme Court in *Healy* failed to resolve whether a constitutional right to be informed of the right of access to pre-trial legal advice existed.[144] McGrath suggests that O'Higgins CJ's reasoning on an accused's right to be informed of his right to legal aid in the trial period in *State (Healy) v Donoghue*[145] is equally applicable to the pre-trial stage.[146] In that case, O'Higgins CJ stated that "[i]f the person charged does not know of his right, he cannot exercise it; if he cannot exercise it, his right is violated".[147] While this reasoning may indeed be applicable, to date no constitutional right to be informed of the right of access to pre-trial legal advice has been declared by the Irish courts. A legal right to be informed of the right of access to pre-trial legal advice is, as noted above, provided for under legislation. **[3–55]**

Healy also did not clarify whether or not the recognised constitutional right of "reasonable access" to pre-trial legal advice encompassed the broader right to have a solicitor present throughout garda interrogation. The Court expressly reserved judgment on this matter[148]; however, later courts have, rather bluntly, concluded that there is no such right. **[3–56]**

In *Lavery v Member-in-Charge, Carrickmacross Garda Station*,[149] the accused had been arrested under s 30 of the OASA 1939 on suspicion of membership of an unlawful **[3–57]**

---

[141] Walsh J (dissenting) in *People (DPP) v Conroy* [1986] IR 460 had suggested that the right was located in Art 40.3, though Finlay CJ's judgment in *Healy* could also be read as including elements of Art 38.1 protections for the rights of the accused. White has argued that both Arts 38.1 and 40.3 mandate the recognition of the right, "The Confessional State – Police Interrogation in the Irish Republic" Part I (2000) 10(1) ICLJ 17 and Part II (2000) 10(2) ICLJ 2.

[142] [1990] 2 IR 73 at 81.

[143] *ibid.*

[144] *ibid.* at 78.

[145] [1976] IR 325.

[146] McGrath above n 44, p 375; see also Butler, "The Right to be Informed of the Right to a Lawyer—The Constitutional Dimension" (1993) 3(2) ICLJ 173.

[147] [1976] IR 325 at 352.

[148] [1990] 2 IR 73 at 78. Prior to that decision it had been suggested in a number of cases that the right of access to pre-trial legal advice, whether constitutional or otherwise, was a right of reasonable access only and there was no entitlement for a suspect to have his solicitor present throughout interrogation: e.g. *People (DPP) v Pringle* (1981) 2 Frewen 57.

[149] [1999] 2 IR 390.

organisation and was detained for questioning at Carrickmacross Garda Station. One hour after his arrest, the detained suspect spoke with his solicitor on the telephone and received general advice from him in relation to ss 2 and 5 of the 1998 Act, which allowed for inferences to be drawn at trial from the failure, in the pre-trial process, to mention particular facts or give particular information. Requests from the solicitor for gardaí to audio-visually record the interview or to take a complete set of notes and to provide them to the suspect and his solicitor before the end of the detention period were refused.

[3–58] In the High Court, McGuinness J granted an order of *habeus corpus*, holding that in light of the inference-drawing provisions of the 1998 Act, persons in custody whom that Act affects ought to have access to legal advice and to notes taken during garda interviews. On appeal to the Supreme Court, however, this ruling was overturned. O'Flaherty J held that while blanket denial of access to legal advice would render detention unlawful, there was no need for gardaí to give solicitors updates on the progress of their investigations. Gardaí must be allowed to exercise their powers of interrogation as they see fit, provided they act reasonably. O'Flaherty J bluntly stated that "[t]he solicitor is not entitled to be present at the interviews".[150] No Irish case has arisen since *Lavery* to challenge the decision given therein and, accordingly, there is no right to have one's solicitor present throughout interrogation by gardaí.

[3–59] The ECtHR has not insisted on the adoption by member states of a broad definition of the right of access to pre-trial legal advice so as to encompass a right to have one's legal adviser present throughout interrogation. Early cases suggested that in order to satisfy the requirements of the ECHR all that was necessary was that the suspect was not denied access to some legal advice in the early stages of his detention, which was particularly important where inferences from silence might later be drawn.[151] More recently in *Salduz v Turkey*,[152] the ECtHR suggested that where a suspect is interviewed by police in connection with a serious criminal matter he must first be given access to legal advice, unless there are compelling reasons to justify the denial of such advice. A failure to allow this access would deprive the suspect of an effective right to a fair trial under Art 6 ECHR.

[3–60] In Ireland it is a matter of constitutional uncertainty as to whether or not the questioning of a suspect must be suspended pending the arrival of a solicitor requested by him. The Custody Regulations provide only that a suspect should not be asked to complete a written statement until a reasonable time has elapsed for the arrival of a requested solicitor, but provide no legal obligation to refrain from questioning a suspect in such circumstances.[153] Walsh J suggested in a dissenting Supreme Court

---

[150] *ibid*. See also *Barry v Waldron* Unreported, High Court, *ex tempore*, 23 May, 1996 and McGrath, "Evidence" in *Annual Review of Irish Law 1999* (Byrne and Binchy (eds.), Thomson Round Hall, Dublin, 2000), pp 233-235.

[151] *Murray v United Kingdom* (1996) 22 EHRR 29; *Averill v United Kingdom* (2001) 31 EHRR 839; *Condron v United Kingdom* (2001) 31 EHRR 1; and *Beckles v United Kingdom* (2003) 36 EHRR 13.

[152] [2008] ECHR 36391/02 [Grand Chamber] (27 November 2008). See also *Panovits v Cyprus* [2008] ECHR 36391/02 [First Section] (27 November 2008).

[153] reg 11(6).

judgment in *People (DPP) v Conroy*[154] that the interrogation of a suspect by gardaí after he had requested a solicitor but before the solicitor's arrival was a "constitutionally forbidden procedure".[155] However, the Court of Criminal Appeal was concerned in *People (DPP) v Cullen*[156] that such an obligation to suspend questioning until after a consultation between solicitor and client would place a duty on the State to provide a panel of solicitors who would always be available to attend at any Garda station where persons might be held if their presence was requested. This duty did not exist and so there was no obligation on gardaí to cease questioning a detained suspect prior to the arrival of a requested solicitor.[157] Cases such as *People (DPP) v Buck*[158] and *People (DPP) v O'Brien*[159] seem to confirm this.

In *Buck*, gardaí had particular difficulty in locating a solicitor who was willing to attend at the station to advise the suspect, as requested by him. Gardaí, it was found, had at all times acted bona fide in their efforts to secure a solicitor for the suspect. While they questioned the suspect prior to the arrival of his solicitor, he made no statement until after he had in fact consulted with him. In the absence of a conscious and deliberate breach of the suspect's rights the statements were admissible. It was suggested that even if there had been such a breach, a causative link between the breach and the making of the statement would have to be shown before the statement would be excluded from evidence at trial.[160] **[3–61]**

In *O'Brien* gardaí were found to have acted mala fides in their efforts to secure a solicitor to the extent that they had consciously and deliberately breached the accused's constitutional right of access to legal advice. The trial judge held they had chosen a solicitor they knew to be a busy, sole practitioner whose court commitments would usually be far away from the location of the garda station. The suspect made statements to gardaí before and after eventual consultation with his solicitor. It was held by the Supreme Court that the first set of statements made by the suspect while the breach of his right to pre-trial legal advice was ongoing had to be excluded from evidence at trial due to that breach. The second set of statements could be admitted in evidence as the breach was no longer ongoing.[161] **[3–62]**

It is clear from these cases that there is no constitutional prohibition on questioning a suspect prior to the arrival of his requested solicitor as long as genuine attempts to contact the solicitor have been made and there must be a causative link between any conscious and deliberate breach of this right and the making of any statement in order for such statement to be excluded from evidence at trial. The former issue may require further consideration given the above-outlined case-law of the ECtHR. **[3–63]**

154 [1986] IR 460.
155 *ibid.* at 479.
156 Unreported, Court of Criminal Appeal, 30 March 1993.
157 See also *DPP v Gormley* [2010] IECCA 22.
158 [2002] 2 IR 260.
159 Unreported, Court of Criminal Appeal, 17 June 2002; [2005] 2 IR 206.
160 See further Ryan, "Avoiding the Hard Question: *DPP v Buck* and the Constitutional Right of Access to Legal Advice" (2003) 25 DULJ 257.
161 See further Daly, "Does the Buck Stop Here?: An Examination of the Pre-Trial Right to Legal Advice in light of *O'Brien v DPP*" (2006) 28 DULJ 345.

Accessibility of the Right to Pre-Trial Legal Advice

[3–64] As noted in *People (DPP) v Cullen,*[162] there is no duty solicitor scheme in Ireland.[163] Relatively recently, the Criminal Legal Aid Review Committee examined the matter and concluded that a Duty Solicitor Scheme ought not to be established in Ireland as it would lead to a lack of continuity for clients.[164]

[3–65] The only scheme which does exist in Ireland to facilitate the provision of legal advice to detained suspects who cannot afford to retain their own solicitor is the Garda Station Legal Advice Scheme. This administrative, non-statutory scheme was established in February 2002. Only persons in receipt of Social Welfare payments or earning less than €20,316 per annum are entitled to free legal advice. As an administrative scheme it, as such, creates no right to free legal advice for a detained suspect and places no specific obligation on gardaí to inform the detained suspect of the existence of the scheme or the possibility that he may be able to obtain legal advice free of charge if eligible under its terms.[165]

V. Reliance on Legal Advice to Remain Silent

[3–66] A concern which may arise in Ireland in the future relates to the interaction between the pre-trial rights to silence and legal advice, a link which has now been statutorily recognised in Ireland within inference-drawing provisions. In England problems have arisen with the operation of a similar provision,[166] when suspects assert that they have remained silent on the advice of a solicitor.

[3–67] Such suspects have claimed that no inference should be drawn against them at trial due to their pre-trial failure to mention a particular fact now relied upon, as they could not reasonably have been expected to mention that fact having received legal advice to remain silent. Permitting an accused person to avoid the drawing of inferences on this basis could enable legal advice to be used to circumvent the relevant legislation. On the other hand it would appear unfair to draw inferences where a suspect truly does rely on legal advice.

[3–68] Through a serious of somewhat complex cases before both the English courts and the ECtHR,[167] it has been held that in circumstances such as these a jury must consider both the genuineness of the suspect's reliance on legal advice and the reasonableness of

---

[162] Unreported, Court of Criminal Appeal, 30 March 1993; Butler and Ong, "Breach of the Constitutional Right of Access to a Lawyer and the Exclusion of Evidence – The Causative Link" (1995) 5(2) ICLJ 156.

[163] For debates on this see the *Report the Committee to Recommend Certain Safeguards for Persons in Custody and for Members of an Garda Síochána* (Stationery Office, Dublin, 1978), para 62 and *First Interim Report of the "Tormey" Committee* (Stationery Office, Dublin, 1977).

[164] Criminal Legal Aid Review Committee *Final Report* (Stationery Office, Dublin, 2002), Chapter 3. The Committee thought it better that a suspect would be able to choose his own solicitor as he could be represented at trial by the same solicitor who would better understand the circumstances of the case.

[165] See further Daly, above n 161.

[166] Criminal Justice and Public Order Act 1984, s 34.

[167] These cases included *Condron v UK* (2001) 31 EHRR 1; *R v Betts* [2001] 2 Cr App R 257; *R v Howell* [2005] 1 Cr App R 1; *R v Hoare* [2005] 1 WLR 1804; and *R v Beckles* [2005] 1 WLR 2829.

that reliance.[168] Thus, a suspect in the pre-trial period of investigative detention who is advised by his solicitor to remain silent cannot blindly take that advice and rely upon it. The suspect is expected to consider the reasonableness of that advice for himself, and if the suspect considers it unreasonable then he should not remain silent.

Many of the defences to criminal charges, such as provocation or duress, may not be readily apparent to the layman and it is somewhat harsh to place a burden upon a suspect in the police station to mention at that point any fact which he thinks may be of relevance to a later defence. This is especially true when, as in Ireland, the detained suspect is entitled only to a "reasonable opportunity" to consult with his solicitor at this point. If questioning in the absence of the solicitor takes a direction not anticipated or foreseen during the consultation, the suspect would again be burdened with the need to consider what facts might form part of a defence, the important legal elements of which are unknown to him. **[3–69]**

The need to examine whether the accused's reliance on the legal advice received was both reasonable and genuine could create concerns for the operation of legal professional privilege, as it operates between an accused and his lawyer.[169] To assist the court in making such a decision, it might be necessary for the solicitor, in order to prove the genuineness and reasonableness of the accused's reliance on his advice, to clarify the reasons for this advice, and thus privilege would be waived. Once privilege is waived, the prosecution are free to ask questions on all of the communications between the suspect and his solicitor. Knowledge that this situation could arise could have an impact on the legal advice given to a suspect detained for questioning by gardaí. **[3–70]**

Whether or not the employment of s 19A will give rise to these issues remains to be seen, but it should at least be clear from the English experience that the alteration of the law in one area can have significant secondary effects in others. In this context, the curtailment of the right to silence under s 19A, and indeed under s 72A of the Criminal Justice Act 2006, may require the Irish courts to engage in difficult balancing exercises in order to ensure the protection and effectiveness of the pre-trial right to legal advice and the overall fairness of a suspect's trial. **[3–71]**

VI. Audio-Visual Recording of Garda Interviews

Under the Criminal Justice Act 1984 (Electronic Recording of Interviews) Regulations 1997 interviews with persons arrested and detained under s 30 of the Offences Against the State Act 1939, s 4 of the Criminal Justice Act 1984, s 2 of the Criminal Justice (Drug Trafficking) Act 1996 or s 50 of the Criminal Justice Act 2007[170] shall be electronically recorded, except where **[3–72]**

---

168 This is now set out in a specimen direction issued by the Judicial Studies Board: "Defendant's Failure to Mention Facts when Questioned or Charged" in *Crown Court Bench Book: Directing the Jury*, March 2010, pp 259-260, available at www.jsboard.co.uk.

169 On legal professional privilege see Fennell, *The Law of Evidence in Ireland*, (3rd ed, Bloomsbury Professional, Dublin, 2010), p 320.

170 The applicability of the Electronic Recording Regulations to s 50 of the Criminal Justice Act 2007 was ensured by an amendment to reg 2 of the Criminal Justice Act 1984 (Electronic Recording of Interviews)(Amendment) Regulations 2009.

> "(i) the equipment is unavailable due to a functional fault, or
> (ii) the equipment is already in use at the time the interview is to commence, and the member in charge considers on reasonable grounds that the interview should not be delayed until the fault is rectified or the equipment becomes available; or
> (iii) where otherwise the electronic recording of the interview is not practicable."[171]

Breach of these Electronic Recording Regulations does not of itself render a garda liable to civil or criminal proceedings or render inadmissible in evidence anything said during questioning, though a court may exclude evidence at its discretion.[172]

[3–73] In interpreting and applying the Electronic Recording Regulations, the courts were originally somewhat lenient in relation to the absence of audio-visual recording,[173] but more recently they have become stricter in their approach, especially where inferences may later be drawn from the silence of a suspect during pre-trial garda interviews. In cases such as *People (DPP) v Connolly*,[174] *People (DPP) v Kelly*[175] and *People (DPP) v Diver*,[176] for example, the superior courts observed the routine nature of audio-visual recording of pre-trial interrogations in most first world common law countries and criticised the failure of the Irish criminal justice system to bring the procedure to a similarly routine standing in this jurisdiction. In *Kelly*, the members of the Special Criminal Court questioned, in particular, the fairness of interrogating a suspect under inference-drawing provisions without audio-visually recording that interrogation. This has, as noted above, recently been addressed by the amendment of ss 18 and 19 of the Criminal Justice Act 1984 and the insertion of s 19A, whereby no inferences can be drawn unless the interview has been electronically recorded or the detained suspect has consented in writing to the non-recording of the interview.

[3–74] In *People (DPP) v Cunningham*,[177] the Court of Criminal Appeal considered a claim that a trial judge erred in refusing to exclude evidence of garda interviews which were not audio-visually recorded. On the facts it was held that the interview evidence had been properly admitted, but O'Malley has observed that there is nothing in the judgment to suggest that the court would routinely stand over the admission of unrecorded evidence.[178]

[3–75] There is some suggestion that the audio-visual recording of interviews in Ireland has been adopted as an alternative to the recognition of a more expansive right of access to pre-trial legal advice; however this is not fully clear. The European Committee for the

[171] reg 4.
[172] Criminal Justice Act 1984, s 27.
[173] For example, *People (DPP) v Holland,* unreported, Court of Criminal Appeal, 15 June 1998.
[174] [2003] 2 IR 1.
[175] Unreported, Special Criminal Court, 26 November 2004—see *The Irish Times*, "Basic fairness dictates that, where possible, interview of accused on IRA charge should be video-recorded" Monday 17 January 2005.
[176] [2005] 3 IR 270.
[177] [2007] IECCA 49.
[178] O'Malley, *The Criminal Process* (Round Hall, Dublin, 2009), p 776.

Prevention of Torture and Inhuman or Degrading Treatment or Punishment (CPT), in 1998, invited the Irish authorities to take appropriate action with a view to introducing a right for arrested persons to have a lawyer present during interrogation.[179] The response of the Irish government seemed to suggest that it had decided, in the alternative, to provide for audio-visual recording of garda interviews.[180]

VII. Conclusion

This chapter has examined the rules which govern the interrogation of suspects within the pre-trial period of custodial detention in the Irish criminal justice system. This stage of the investigation of criminal offences is usually crucial for gardaí in terms of evidence-gathering; however, it is also arguably the context in which suspects' rights are most vulnerable to neglect or interference. While provisions such as the Custody Regulations and the Judges' Rules aim to set a framework for the interrogation of offenders, they are limited in their capacity to ensure the protection of suspects' rights given the rather weak consequences of a breach thereof. The rules on confession evidence, constructed within the common law but having a constitutional value also, are stricter and more likely to lead to the exclusion of probative evidence at trial. Furthermore, the recognition of certain constitutional rights within the pre-trial period, along with protection for those rights under the ECHR, strengthens the position of the suspect. **[3–76]**

However, as noted throughout this chapter, even those rights which have been recognised as having both constitutional and ECHR status have been curtailed so that their strength is, perhaps, more illusory than it may first appear.

The right to silence, in particular, has been so curtailed by legislative enactments in recent times that it can no longer truly be claimed that a suspect is free to rely upon it within the Irish pre-trial process. Although certain safeguards have been included within these provisions, their true worth is somewhat illusory also, given the narrowly-defined protection of the pre-trial right to legal advice and the potential avoidance of electronic recording. Furthermore, the introduction of s 72A in the context of "organised crime" appears to suggest that despite the broad ambit of s 19A, the Irish legislature is not yet finished with its efforts to curtail the pre-trial right to silence. **[3–77]**

To date the courts have accepted legislative curtailment of pre-trial rights based on the provision of certain safeguards and the general concept of proportionality. The courts **[3–78]**

---

[179] *Report to the Irish Government on the visit to Ireland carried out by the European Committee for the Prevention of Torture and Inhuman or Degrading Treatment or Punishment (CPT) from 31 August to 9 September 1998,* at para 22.

[180] *ibid.* paras 47-48. It is also notable that in the *Report of the Committee to enquire into Certain Aspects of Criminal Procedure* (Stationery Office, Dublin, 1990) in March 1990, the Martin Committee, concluded that there was no need for a suspect to be entitled to have his legal representative present if garda interrogations of suspects were to be the subject of audio-visual recording. The CPT in 2002 stated that while it was pleased that recording had been introduced it was not satisfied as regards the denial of lawyers during the interview. *Report to the Irish Government on the visit to Ireland carried out by the European Committee for the Prevention of Torture and Inhuman or Degrading Treatment or Punishment (CPT) from 20 to 28 May 2002,* para 22.

are constitutionally obliged to respect the role of the legislature in this regard and will only reject legislation where no other course is possible. The nature of interrogation has changed over the years since the introduction of the concept of arrest for detention and questioning. This has largely been brought about by increased involvement of the legislature in the criminal process, and the acquiescence of the courts in the legislative changes.[181] A number of constitutional issues still remain to be clarified, however, and the law on interrogation in the Irish pre-trial process may well be further altered in the future.

[181] See further Daly, "Is Silence Golden?: The Legislative and Judicial Treatment of Pre-Trial Silence in Ireland" (2009) 31 DULJ 35.

CHAPTER 4
Collection and Admissibility of Evidence

I. Introduction

This chapter will examine a number of issues relevant to the collection and admissibility of evidence. Specifically, the following matters will be outlined: the duty to seek out and preserve evidence; forensic sampling; covert surveillance; the European Evidence Warrant; and, the exclusionary rule. Like many other criminal procedure issues in Ireland, there have been some notable changes in relation to these matters in recent times and the possibility of further change is not remote. [4–01]

II. Duty to Seek Out and Preserve Evidence

In the course of their investigations into alleged criminal activity, gardaí are obliged to seek out and preserve all relevant evidence,[1] both that which implicates and that which might exonerate a suspect. In the 1989 High Court case of *Murphy v DPP*,[2] Lynch J held that evidence relevant to guilt or innocence must, so far as is necessary and practicable, be kept until the conclusion of a trial, and that articles which may give rise to the reasonable possibility of securing relevant evidence must also be preserved.[3] Although [4–02]

---

1 *Dillon v O'Brien and Davis* (1887) 20 LRIR 300.

2 [1989] ILRM 71.

3 For a discussion of this case see O'Connor, "The Duty to Preserve Evidence in Irish and American Criminal Law" (1989) 7 ILT 158.

the courts are generally reluctant to prohibit a trial on grounds of a failure to preserve evidence, in recent years a significant number of injunctions against prosecution have been sought on that basis and the courts have outlined a number of core principles.

[4–03] In *Braddish v DPP*,[4] which concerned a failure to preserve CCTV footage of a robbery in a shop, Hardiman J, in the Supreme Court, set out the general rule in the following terms:

> "It is the duty of the Gardaí, arising from their unique investigative role, to seek out and preserve all evidence having a bearing or potential bearing on the issue of guilt or innocence. This is so whether the prosecution propose to rely on the evidence or not, and regardless of whether it assists the case the prosecution is advancing or not".[5]

[4–04] Drawing on a number of superior court cases, Heffernan[6] lists some characteristics of the duty to preserve evidence:

- The duty does not lend itself to a precise, exhaustive definition; it must be interpreted realistically on the facts of each individual case[7];
- The prosecution is obliged to disclose all relevant evidence within its possession to the defence. Therefore, evidence relevant to guilt or innocence must be kept until the conclusion of the trial, so far as that is necessary and practicable;
- Relevant evidence includes material which might reasonably lead to other information which may prove or disprove the accused's involvement in the relevant offence[8];
- The obligation on gardaí may go beyond simply preserving evidence and include a duty to seek out evidence that may assist the defence[9];
- The duty is not absolute and must be tempered by considerations of necessity and practicality in contemporary policing[10];
- The defence are under an onus to act promptly in requesting material considered to be relevant[11];
- In seeking to obtain an order prohibiting the progression of a trial due to the absence of evidence which ought to have been preserved, the accused must show that there is a real risk that his trial would be unfair and that directions or rulings by the trial judge would be insufficient to avoid such unfairness[12];

---

4 [2001] 3 IR 127.

5 *ibid.* at 133.

6 Heffernan, "The Duty to Preserve Evidence" in *Criminal Law and Procedures: Current Issues and Emerging Trends* (Bacik and Heffernan (eds.), FirstLaw, Dublin, 2009), pp 55-56.

7 *Braddish v DPP* [2001] 3 IR 127.

8 *People (DPP) v Meleady* [1995] 2 IR 517; *Dunne v DPP* [2002] 2 IR 25.

9 *Dunne v DPP* [2002] 2 IR 25 (Fennelly J dissenting).

10 *Braddish v DPP* [2001] 3 IR 127; *Mitchell v DPP* [2000] 2 ILRM 396; *Scully v DPP* [2005] 1 IR 242; *Connolly v DPP* [2003] 4 IR 121.

11 *Rogers v DPP* [1992] 2 ILRM 695; *Mitchell v DPP* [2000] 2 ILRM 396; *McKeown v DPP*, unreported, Supreme Court, 9 April 2003; *Scully v DPP* [2005] 1 IR 242.

12 *Z v DPP* [1994] 2 IR 476 at 506-507 (*per* Finlay CJ); *Bowes v DPP* [2003] 2 IR 25.

- Where the relevant evidence belongs to a third party, some consideration should be given to the need to return the property to its rightful owner at the earliest opportunity.[13]

The reluctance of the courts to prohibit a trial on the basis of a failure by gardaí to preserve evidence has been particularly true where alternative relevant evidence is still available to the defence. In *Savage v DPP*,[14] for example, the Supreme Court refused to grant an order prohibiting a trial on charges of using a vehicle without the consent of the owner and dangerous driving causing serious injury. The vehicle in question had been destroyed before the defence had sought to carry out its own inspection thereof. However, a Public Service Vehicle (PSV) Inspector had examined the vehicle and his report was made available to the defence. The prosecution indicated that it did not intend to raise the condition of the vehicle or the PSV inspector's report at trial, however, the defence still sought to have the trial prohibited on grounds that the failure to preserve the vehicle led to a real risk of unfairness. The Supreme Court held that there was not a real risk of unfairness in this case due to the failure to preserve the vehicle itself and therefore refused to prohibit the trial.[15] **[4–05]**

By contrast, an order prohibiting a trial was granted in *Ludlow v DPP*.[16] The applicant, a truck driver, was involved in a road traffic accident where his truck collided with a car. This resulted in the death of the car driver. The truck, driving on a wet surface in the rain, had allegedly slid from one side of the road to the other, colliding with the car. At the scene, a PSV Inspector carried out an examination of the truck and noted in his report that some of the tyres were excessively worn. This, he suggested, would have contributed to a loss of control in wet conditions. The truck was returned to its owner, the applicant's employer, who disposed of the tyres, not having been told to retain them. The Supreme Court recognised in *Ludlow*, that the missing evidence had huge evidential significance as the condition of the tyres was central to the prosecution's case against the applicant. Thus, the fact that the defence did not now have access to the tyres and had not been able to carry out their own examination was seriously detrimental to the fairness of the trial. Hardiman J noted that in this case "a fraction of a millimetre may be the difference between guilt and innocence" and between liberty and a potential 10 year sentence. On the facts of this case it was held that there was a real risk of an unfair trial and therefore any further prosecution by the DPP was precluded by way of injunction. **[4–06]**

Looking at *Savage* and *Ludlow* together, Heffernan suggests that:

> "...the prosecution's case plays an influential part in the potential nexus between missing evidence and unfairness at trial. In particular, the viability of the alternative evidence (as a substitute for evidence lost through a breach of the duty to preserve) turns in no small measure on the nature of the allegations levelled against the applicant".[17]

---

[13] *Rogers v DPP* [1992] 2 ILRM 695; *McKeown v DPP*, unreported, Supreme Court, 9 April 2003; *Connolly v DPP* [2003] 4 IR 121.

[14] [2009] 1 IR 185.

[15] See also *Byrne v Judges of the Circuit Court* [2007] IEHC 266.

[16] [2009] 1 IR 640.

[17] Heffernan above n 6, p 59. See also *Toohey v DPP* [2008] IESC 64.

[4–07] Although the courts generally do not issue injunctions prohibiting prosecution, this ought not to be seen as legitimating the actions of gardaí in particular cases.[18] On the facts it may be held that the fairness of a trial is unaffected by the garda failure to preserve relevant evidence, but this does not mean that there has not been such a failure in garda duty. Nonetheless, the fairness of the trial is the sole concern of the courts in this regard, rather than any disciplinary role in relation to the gardaí.

Denham J, in *Savage*, did provide some specific advice on how to proceed in such cases, which involved providing the accused with notice of the intention to destroy evidence and providing time to request that the evidence not be destroyed.[19]

Similar words of advice for the gardaí were proffered by the same judge in *Ludlow*:

> "Just as it would not be appropriate to return a bloody knife at a scene of an assault to its owner, until DNA and other forensic evidence is taken, so too would it be best practice not to return defective tyres to their owner at the scene of a serious road traffic accident, or to enable them to be destroyed, until an accused or relevant party has had the opportunity to have them analysed".[20]

[4–08] In *RC v DPP*[21] the appellant had been charged with sexual assault of a minor and a central element of the investigation and the prosecution case related to telephone communications between the appellant and the complainant. The gardaí, in their investigations, had accessed the mobile phone records of the appellant, showing only the outgoing calls from his phone. The appellant claimed that calls incoming to his phone from the complainant's phone were of central importance as proof that he had only responded to communication she initiated, supporting his denial of all allegations against him.

[4–09] Denham J, in the Supreme Court, noted that an order to prohibit prosecution should only be given in exceptional circumstances.[22] She further noted that while, in general, the absence of phone records is not a reason to prohibit a trial, in the specific circumstances of this case the absence of the relevant records created circumstances where there was a real risk of an unfair trial and an order for prohibition was appropriate.[23]

It is clear from the foregoing that, while there is a general duty on gardaí to seek out and preserve all relevant evidence in a criminal case, decisions on the prohibition or otherwise of a prosecution due to a failure in this duty turn on the specific circumstances of a given case and the risk of an unfair trial in those specific circumstances.

---

18 *Savage v DPP* [2009] 1 IR 185 at 206 *per* Hardiman J.

19 *ibid.* at 205 *per* Denham J.

20 [2009] 1 IR 640 at 652 *per* Denham J.

21 [2009] IESC 32. See also *McHugh v DPP* [2009] IESC 15. Recent examples of cases where applicants unsuccessfully sought to prohibit prosecutions include *Kearney v DPP* [2009] IEHC 347 and *CD v DPP* [2009] IESC 70.

22 [2009] IESC 32 at para 10.

23 *ibid.* at para 30.

III. Search of Private Property

In order to enter private property to search for evidence gardaí must act under specific legal authority. The protection afforded to private dwellings is particularly strong and entry into a dwelling without lawful authority would amount to a breach not only of legal rights, but also of the constitutional right to the inviolability of the dwelling set out in Art 40.5 of the Irish Constitution. [4–10]

There are four main situations in which a garda will be lawfully admitted to enter, or remain within, a private premises and carry out a search:

- With consent;
- Under specific statutory authority[24];
- On arrest; or,
- Under a search warrant.

In relation to arrest, s 6 of the Criminal Law Act 1997 provides a general power of entry, without a warrant, for the purpose of arrest and search in relation to all arrestable offences.[25] Under s 6, in order to effect an arrest a garda may enter and search any premises (including a dwelling) where the person to be arrested is or where the garda, with reasonable cause, suspects that person to be. Where the premises is a dwelling the garda shall not enter, unless acting with the consent of an occupier or other person who appears to the garda to be in charge of the dwelling, unless: [4–11]

a. he, or another garda, has observed the person within or entering the dwelling, or
b. he, with reasonable cause, suspects that before a warrant of arrest could be obtained the person will either abscond for the purpose of avoiding justice or will obstruct the course of justice, or
c. he, with reasonable cause, suspects that before a warrant of arrest could be obtained the person would commit an arrestable offence, or
d. the person ordinarily resides at that dwelling.[26]

Despite the existence of these other powers of entry for search, Bacik suggests that the usual way for gardaí to enter and search premises, particularly private homes, is under the authority of a search warrant.[27]

Search Warrants

A search warrant may be described as a written authorisation to search a premises, which usually includes permission to seize goods found. Warrants must be strictly construed because they potentially have far-reaching effects for important individual [4–12]

---

[24] For example, under the Housing (Miscellaneous Provisions) Act 1997, s 12, a garda investigating the unlawful occupation of a dwelling may enter premises in order to arrest an individual and carry out a search.

[25] Any offence which is potentially punishable by at least five years imprisonment: Criminal Law Act 1997, s 2(1), as amended by the Criminal Justice Act 2006, s 8.

[26] In relation to the operation of s 6 see *People (DPP) v Laide and Ryan* [2005] 1 IR 209.

[27] Bacik, "Recent Development in the Law on Search Warrants" in *Criminal Law and Procedures: Current Issues and Emerging Trends* (Bacik and Heffernan (eds.), FirstLaw, Dublin, 2009), p 36.

rights such as the rights to liberty, privacy and property.[28] Resultantly, where there is any dispute about the lawfulness of a search warrant, it must be read in the manner most favourable to the individual whose premises is to be searched and against the interests of the State.

[4–13] The power to issue a search warrant is often set out in legislation relating to specific offences, which allocates the issuing power to a designated entity (usually a District Court judge, a Peace Commissioner, or a garda not below the rank of Superintendent in certain cases). The legislation also sets out the person(s) who may apply for a warrant: the kind of evidence necessary to ground the warrant; whether that evidence must be sworn; the duration of the warrant; the actions which may be taken on foot of it; and, the person(s) who may execute it.[29] A general power to issue search warrants in respect of evidence relating to the commission of an arrestable offence is set out in s 10 of the Criminal Justice (Miscellaneous Provisions) Act 1997.[30] This provision allows for a District Judge to issue a search warrant in respect of a specifically named place, which may include a dwelling, on hearing evidence on oath from a garda not below the rank of sergeant, if the judge is satisfied that there are reasonable grounds for suspecting that evidence relating to an arrestable offence is to be found at that place. The name of a specific garda will be placed on the warrant and he will have the power to enter the premises in order to effect a search within one week of the date of issue and to seize anything found at that place, or anything found in the possession of a person present at that place at the time of the search, which he reasonably believes to be evidence of or relating to an arrestable offence.[31] It is an offence to obstruct a garda acting under the authority of a search warrant issued under this provision.[32]

[4–14] It has been held by the courts that the issuance of search warrants is an executive, rather than a judicial, function, but in considering whether or not to issue a warrant the issuing person must act judicially.[33] O'Malley considers that this means, at a minimum, that the person must "consider the sworn evidence or information carefully, satisfy himself as best he can that the furnished information is accurate, and make a considered judgment on whether to issue a warrant".[34]

[4–15] A number of preliminary matters of procedure are notable. First, s 26 of the Criminal Justice (Amendment) Act 2009 provides that applications for the issuance of search warrants to a court, or a judge of a court, are to be heard "otherwise than in public".

---

[28] See, for example, *Byrne v Grey* [1988] IR 31; *DPP v McGoldrick* [2005] 3 IR 123.

[29] O'Malley, *The Criminal Process* (Round Hall, Dublin, 2009), pp 351-352. Examples of legislation providing for the issuance of search warrants include the Offences Against the State Act 1939, s 29, as amended; the Misuse of Drugs Act 1977, s 26, as amended; the Criminal Justice (Theft and Fraud Offences) Act 2001, s 48.

[30] As amended by the Criminal Justice Act 2006, s 6.

[31] Criminal Justice (Miscellaneous Provisions) Act 1997, s 10(2) as amended by s 6 of the Criminal Justice Act 2006.

[32] Criminal Justice (Miscellaneous Provisions) Act 1997, s 10(4) as amended by s 6 of the Criminal Justice Act 2006.

[33] *Creaven v Criminal Assets Bureau* [2004] 2 IR 434.

[34] O'Malley, above n 29, p 354.

Although contained in legislation said to be aimed at tackling organised crime,[35] s 26 expressly states that it applies to search warrant applications "under any enactment". The breadth of this provision for privacy in the issuing of search warrants raises some concerns about transparency in the criminal process and fairness to criminal suspects.

Secondly, though less controversially, following a number of cases in which evidence obtained under a search warrant issued by a District Judge had to be excluded at trial due to the fact that it had been executed for a district in which the relevant judge had no jurisdiction,[36] s 32A of the Court (Supplemental Provisions) Act 1961 was inserted by s 180 of the Criminal Justice Act 2006 in order to provide that search warrants issued by District Judges may apply in districts outside of that to which they are specifically assigned. **[4–16]**

When the information seeking to ground the warrant is being presented to the District Judge, or other person with power to issue a search warrant, legislation usually provides that the information ought to be sworn. In *DPP v Yamanoha*[37] the Court of Criminal Appeal quashed the conviction of the accused which had been based on evidence obtained on foot of a warrant as it was found that the applicant garda had only sworn an oath *after* providing relevant information to the District Judge. **[4–17]**

Different statutory provisions allowing for the issuance of search warrants make reference to either "reasonable belief" or "reasonable suspicion" on the part of the issuer in relation to a particular state of affairs. In examining any distinction between the concepts, O'Malley states that "[t]here is an accepted distinction between suspicion and belief, to the extent that belief imports a greater degree of certainty."[38] **[4–18]**

Certain statutes give the power to issue search warrants to Peace Commissioners and/ or District Court judges. Although the power of Peace Commissioners to issue search warrants has been upheld by the courts,[39] O'Malley suggests that the modern tendency is to confine the power to judges only.[40]

Peace Commissioners are appointed by the Minister for Justice under s 88 of the Courts of Justice Act 1924 and, in the context of search warrants, must act independently and must be satisfied of the necessary matters on the information of the applicant. At any subsequent trial the Peace Commissioner who issued the relevant warrant must attend court to prove that he was personally satisfied to the required extent at the time when he issued the warrant.[41] He must be available for cross-examination at trial. The stringency of this requirement has caused some difficulties in the courts where the Peace Commissioner has become seriously ill or has passed away **[4–19]**

---

35 See the Second Stage speech of Minister for Justice Dermot Ahern TD: 687 *Dáil Debates* Col 2.

36 *Creaven v Criminal Assets Bureau* [2004] 2 IR 434; *People (DPP) v Joyce* [2008] IECCA 1.

37 [1994] 1 IR 565.

38 O'Malley above n 29, p 362. See further Chapter Two.

39 *Ryan v O'Callaghan,* unreported, High Court, 22 July 1987.

40 O'Malley above n 29, p 363.

41 O'Malley above n 29, p 364.

between the issuance of the warrant and the trial date.[42] The requirement to attend a later trial does not apply to District Judges.

[4–20] Certain legislative provisions allow for search warrants to be issued by gardaí of prescribed ranks. Section 29 of the Offences Against the State Act 1939,[43] for example, allows for a garda of superintendent rank or above to issue a search warrant where he has reasonable grounds to believe that evidence of or relating to the commission or intended commission of, *inter alia*, an offence under the OASA 939 or a scheduled offence is to be found in any particular place. This warrant may be issued to a garda not below the rank of sergeant and must be executed within one week. This provision has been criticised and the Committee to Review the Offences Against the State Acts recommended that warrants issued thereunder ought to last only for 24 hours, not one week.[44] This would limit the use of warrants issued by the gardaí essentially to circumstances of urgency.

[4–21] Other provisions which allow for garda issuance of search warrants include s 14 of the Criminal Assets Bureau Act 1996 and s 26(1) of the Misuse of Drugs Act 1977.[45] Under these statutes, a search warrant may be issued in relation to the investigation of relevant offences by a garda not below the rank of superintendent.[46] A warrant is not to be so issued unless there are "circumstances of urgency giving rise to the need for the immediate issue" of the warrant which would make it impracticable to apply to a District Judge, or a peace commissioner in the case of the Misuse of Drugs Act.[47] The warrant issued under either statute must be executed within 24 hours.

[4–22] Considering the garda issuance of warrants under s 29 of the OASA 1939, the Morris Tribunal recommended that only judges should be allowed to issue warrants, noting that in the modern age of communications, it should be possible to contact a District Judge in a very short space of time if a warrant is urgently required.[48] Furthermore, the Morris Tribunal report suggests that s 29 warrants are "not only open to abuse but have been abused in the past" and that "[t]here is a danger that the power to issue a section 29 warrant becomes a mere formality in which the investigating sergeant might as well be empowered to issue a search warrant to himself".[49] This is particularly true as it has been held that there is no requirement under s 29 for the issuing superintendent to be one who is not directly involved in the relevant investigation.[50]

---

[42] See *People (DPP) v Owens* [1999] 2 IR 16.

[43] As substituted by the Criminal Law Act 1976 s 5.

[44] *Report of the Committee to Review the Offences Against the State Acts 1939-1998* (Stationery Office, Dublin, 2002), p 142.

[45] As amended by the Criminal Justice (Drug Trafficking) Act 1996, s 8.

[46] The relevant garda must be a member of the Criminal Assets Bureau (CAB) in order to issue a warrant under the Criminal Assets Bureau Act 1996.

[47] The circumstances of urgency must be demonstrated to exist: *People (DPP) v Peter Byrne* [2003] 4 IR 423.

[48] *Report on the Detention of "Suspects" following the death of the late Richard Barron Volume 3*, Morris Tribunal, (Stationery Office, Dublin, 2008), Recommendations 6.23 and 6.24, pp 1255-1257.

[49] *ibid.* p 1256.

[50] *People (DPP) v Birney and Others* [2007] 1 IR 337.

The consequences of invalidly issued or executed search warrants are explored below in the context of the exclusionary rule.[51]

IV. Forensic Sampling

Advances in science and technology have meant that much information can be obtained from a small amount of bodily material taken from an individual and this may be matched with matter taken from the scene of a crime in order to connect that individual with an offence which has been committed. Forensic evidence and, more particularly, DNA evidence, can provide very specific information about an individual and can scientifically prove to a high degree of probability that a sample obtained from an individual matches a sample taken from the scene of a crime. Forensic sampling has become increasingly important within the Irish criminal justice system. The following sections outline the law on fingerprinting and the taking of bodily samples in Ireland. Current legislation in this area is likely to be repealed in the near future and replaced under the terms of the Criminal Justice (Forensic Evidence and DNA Database System) Bill 2010. The general provisions of this Bill are also discussed below.[52] **[4–23]**

The Current Regime

Fingerprints and bodily samples may be taken from individuals, either with their consent, or under the specifics of a number of statutes, most significantly the Criminal Justice (Forensic Evidence) Act 1990. Legislation provides for the taking of fingerprints[53] and/or bodily samples[54] from persons arrested and detained on suspicion of involvement in the commission of a particular offence covered by s 30 of the Offences Against the State Act 1939, s 4 of the Criminal Justice Act 1984, s 2 of the Criminal Justice (Drug Trafficking) Act 1996, or s 50 of the Criminal Justice Act 2007.[55] Most of the relevant offences carry potential sentences of five years or more. **[4–24]**

Fingerprints and "non-intimate" samples may be taken without consent from detained suspects once authorised by a garda not below the rank of superintendent.[56] No grounds for such authorisation are provided in terms of fingerprints, but the legislation governing bodily samples states that authorisation is only to be given where the garda has reasonable grounds for suspecting the involvement of the person, from whom the sample is to be taken, in the offence in respect of which he is in custody and for believing that the sample will tend to confirm or disprove his involvement in that **[4–25]**

[51] Para 4–49.

[52] Para 4–29.

[53] Hereafter the term "fingerprints" is used to encompass both fingerprints and palm prints.

[54] As defined in s 2 of the Criminal Justice (Forensic Evidence) Act 1990.

[55] See the Offences Against the State Act 1939, s 30(5); the Criminal Law Act 1976, s 7; the Criminal Justice Act 1984, s 6, as amended by the Criminal Justice (Drug Trafficking) Act 1996, s 5; and the Criminal Justice (Forensic Evidence) Act 1990, s 2, as amended by the Criminal Justice Act 2007.

[56] Criminal Justice Act 1984, s 6(2) and Criminal Justice (Forensic Evidence) Act 1990, ss 2(4)(a) and 5. See also O'Donnell, "Legal Situation of forensic DNA analysis in the Republic of Ireland" (1997) 88 *Forensic Science International* 63. In terms of fingerprint evidence, the requirement of prior authorisation does not apply to persons detained under the OASA 1939.

offence.[57] Therefore, unless there is some forensic evidence available from the scene of the crime which would be likely to connect the offender with the scene, or there is a likelihood that such scene-of-crime forensic evidence will come to light, no authorisation for the taking of a bodily sample from a suspect detained in garda custody ought to be granted.[58]

"Non-intimate" samples include:

- samples of saliva, hair other than pubic hair, a nail, any material found under a nail[59];
- a swab from any part of the body including the mouth but not from any other body orifice or a genital region[60]; and
- a footprint or similar impression of any part of the person's body other than a part of his hand.[61]

So-called "intimate" samples, which may not be taken without consent, include:

- samples of blood,[62] pubic hair,[63] or urine;
- a swab from a body orifice, other than the mouth, or a genital region[64]; and
- a dental impression.[65]

[4–26] Adverse inferences may be drawn at trial from the failure of a suspect to consent to the taking of an "intimate" sample "without good cause".[66] Refusal to consent may, on the basis of inferences drawn, act as corroboration of any evidence in relation to which the refusal is material but cannot be the sole basis for conviction. No inferences are to be drawn unless the suspect was told, in ordinary language by a garda when seeking his consent, that the sample was required for the purpose of forensic testing, that his consent was necessary and, if his consent was not given, what the effect of a refusal by him of such consent could be.[67] As with "non-intimate" samples, prior authorisation for requesting the consent of the suspect to provide an "intimate" sample is necessary and such authorisation is only to be granted by a garda not below the rank of superintendent where he has reasonable grounds for suspecting the involvement of the suspect in the offence in respect of which he is in custody and for believing that the sample will tend to confirm or disprove his involvement in that offence.[68]

---

[57] Criminal Justice (Forensic Evidence) Act 1990, ss 2(4)(a) and 5.
[58] See Heffernan, "The Taking of Forensic Samples: A Review of Proposed Reforms" (2006) 16 (2) ICLJ 2, p 3.
[59] Criminal Justice (Forensic Evidence) Act 1990, s 2.
[60] *ibid.* Until the Criminal Justice Act 2006 mouth swabs and saliva samples were considered intimate samples.
[61] *ibid.* Criminal Justice (Forensic Evidence) Act 1990, s 2.
[62] May only be taken by a registered medical practitioner under s 2(8).
[63] May only be taken by a registered medical practitioner under s 2(8).
[64] A genital swab may only be taken by a registered medical practitioner under s 2(8).
[65] *ibid.*
[66] s 3.
[67] s 3(3).
[68] s 2(5).

Fingerprints and bodily samples (or the information taken from such samples, including DNA profiles) obtained from persons who are thereafter convicted may be retained indefinitely, while those obtained from persons who are ultimately acquitted or against whom no proceedings are initiated must be destroyed within a prescribed period. Section 8 of the Criminal Justice Act 1984 provides that fingerprints taken from suspects who have been arrested and detained under either the 1984 or the 1996 Acts and any copies thereof must be destroyed at the expiration of 12 months from the taking of such prints if proceedings are not instituted against the relevant suspect and the failure to institute the proceedings within that period is not due to the fact that he has absconded or cannot be found. If proceedings are instituted within 12 months and the suspect is, thereafter, acquitted or discharged or the proceedings are discontinued, the relevant fingerprints or copies of fingerprints must be destroyed within 21 days.[69] Section 4 of the Criminal Justice (Forensic Evidence) Act 1990 makes similar provisions for the destruction of bodily samples taken from persons who are not later convicted.[70] This is in line with the jurisprudence of the ECtHR, which has disapproved of the practice of indefinitely retaining forensic material obtained from non-convicted suspects.[71] Somewhat controversially, however, the Irish Supreme Court in *People (DPP) v Cash*[72] refused to exclude fingerprint evidence obtained from the accused following his arrest which was based on a scene of crime match with stored fingerprints, which the prosecution could not prove to have been lawfully retained. This case is discussed further below.[73] **[4–27]**

An electronic database of fingerprints exists by virtue of s 11 of the Criminal Justice (Miscellaneous Provisions) Act 1997. Plans for the creation of a DNA database are now well advanced and this, along with changes to the law in relation to the taking and destruction of bodily samples, are provided for in the Criminal Justice (Forensic Evidence and DNA Database System) Bill 2010. **[4–28]**

Criminal Justice (Forensic Evidence and DNA Database System) Bill 2010

This Bill was published in January 2010 following a Consultation Paper and Report from the Law Reform Commission[74] and the General Scheme of a Bill in 2007.[75] The **[4–29]**

[69] Criminal Justice Act 1984, s 8, as amended by the Criminal Justice Act 2006. Retention of fingerprints may be authorised in certain specified circumstances. Legislative provision is made for the destruction of bodily samples, but not fingerprints, obtained from suspects detained under the Offences Against the State Act 1939. Nor is the destruction of fingerprints provided on a voluntary basis provided for.

[70] Criminal Justice (Forensic Evidence) Act 1990, s 4, as amended by the Criminal Justice Act 2006. Retention of bodily samples (and any record of information drawn therefrom) may be authorised in certain specified circumstances. See *McGinley v Judge Michael Reilly* [2006] IEHC 357.

[71] *S and Marper v UK*, 4 December 2008.

[72] [2010] IESC 1.

[73] Para 4–67.

[74] *Law Reform Commission Consultation Paper on the Establishment of a DNA Database* March 2004 (LRC CP29-2004); *Law Reform Commission Report on the Establishment of a DNA Database* November 2005 (LRC 78-2005).

[75] Criminal Justice (Forensic Sampling and Evidence) Bill 2007.

2010 Bill provides for the creation of a DNA database — referred to as the DNA Database System — to be used for two purposes: (i) in the investigation of criminal offences; and (ii) in the search for missing or unknown persons.

[4–30] In the context of forensic sampling, the Bill purports to entirely repeal and replace the Criminal Justice (Forensic Evidence) Act 1990[76] and make new provision for the taking of bodily samples from detained suspects, although the list of relevant detention provisions remains the same.[77] A most welcome element in the Bill is what appears to be a reversal of the Supreme Court decision in *DPP v Boyce*,[78] where it had been decided that the statutory regime created under the 1990 Act for the taking of bodily samples did not displace the garda power at common law to take such samples with the consent of an individual. This had meant that even in the case of detained suspects the statutory safeguards applicable to the taking of bodily samples could be avoided by obtaining the consent of the suspect.

Section 26 of the Bill provides that a garda:

> "… shall not … take, or cause to be taken, a bodily sample for forensic testing from a person who is detained under [the specified legislative provisions] other than in accordance with this Part".

This appears to ensure that the safeguards specifically built into the legislation apply whenever a sample is taken from a detained suspect.

[4–31] There are three possible situations in which a sample may be taken from a detained suspect under the proposed legislation:

i. a sample, authorised by a garda not below the rank of sergeant, may be taken in order to generate a DNA profile which will be added to the DNA Database System (s 11)[79];
ii. an intimate sample, authorised by a garda not below the rank of inspector, may be taken for the purposes of forensic testing, and may also generate a DNA profile to be added to the DNA Database System (s 12); and,
iii. a non-intimate sample, authorised by a garda not below the rank of inspector, may be taken for the purposes of forensic testing, and may also generate a DNA profile to be added to the DNA Database System (s 13).[80]

A sample taken under s 11 on the authorisation of a sergeant for the purposes of creating a DNA profile to enter on the DNA Database System, can be used for evidential purposes in the instant investigation if authorised by an inspector or garda of more senior rank.

[76] Criminal Justice (Forensic Evidence and DNA Database System) Bill 2010, s 6.
[77] s 9.
[78] [2009] 2 IR 124.
[79] "Samples" under s 11 refer to samples of hair, other than pubic hair, or a swab from the mouth.
[80] s 2 states that "Intimate" and "non-intimate" samples have the same meaning under the Bill as under current legislation.

Some of the safeguards provided within the Bill are as follows: **[4–32]**

- samples are only to be taken under the authorisation of a garda of the rank of sergeant or above (under s 11) or a garda of the rank of inspector or above (under ss 12 and 13);
- where a sample is to be used for forensic analysis in a specific case, it is only to be taken where the authorising garda suspects, on reasonable grounds, that the person from whom the sample is to be taken has been involved in the commission of the offence in respect of which he or she is detained and that the sample will tend to confirm or disprove such involvement[81]; and,
- no inference is to be drawn from refusal to consent to provide an intimate sample unless the detained suspect was given a reasonable opportunity to consult with a solicitor prior to such refusal and, unless the seeking of such consent by a garda is video-recorded or the person consents in writing to it not being so recorded.[82]

The default destruction time for samples taken under the proposed legislation is three years[83] while the default destruction time for profiles generated from such samples is 10 years.[84] The ECtHR has held that indefinite retention of forensic material gathered from suspects who are not later convicted is in breach of Art 8.[85] Whether retention of DNA profiles for up to 10 years might also be seen as a disproportionate interference with the right to privacy remains to be seen. Arguably, proportionality may be achieved by provision for a person from whom a sample has been taken to apply in writing to the Commissioner of An Garda Síochána prior to the expiration of the delineated time limits, requesting destruction of the sample and removal of the related profile from the DNA Database System.[86] Such an application will only be considered where no proceedings have been instituted against the person within 12 months of the taking of the relevant sample, or that person has been acquitted at trial, had the charges dismissed or the proceedings discontinued, or, in certain circumstances, been given probation.[87] An appeal to the District Court is available against any decision of the Commissioner.[88] **[4–33]**

It seems almost certain that a DNA database will soon form part of the criminal justice landscape in this jurisdiction, however, there are a number of matters of concern within the Bill. One of which, already noted, is the lengthy default retention periods for samples and profiles obtained from non-convicted suspects. Section 11 allows for the taking of samples from suspects in order to generate a profile for the DNA Database System without having any specific investigative or evidential purpose in the case then under investigation. This appears to allow for something of a fishing expedition and the Irish Human Rights Commission (IHRC) has recommended the removal of s 11 from the Bill, arguing that it may be in breach of the privacy protections contained **[4–34]**

---

81 Criminal Justice (Forensic Evidence and DNA Database System) Bill 2010, ss 12(3) and 13(3).
82 s 19.
83 s 77.
84 s 78.
85 *S and Marper v UK*, 4 December 2008.
86 Criminal Justice (Forensic Evidence and DNA Database System) Bill 2010, s 74.
87 s 72.
88 s 74(10).

within Art 8 ECHR.[89] Further, this could lead to a situation whereby gardaí arrest individuals solely in order to operate its provisions and fill up the DNA Database System with profiles. This is not a fanciful notion as allegations such as this have been levelled against the police in England and Wales.[90]

[4–35] The 2010 Bill also provides for cross-border co-operation within the police forces of the European Union. The "Prum Council Decision"[91] allows for the exchange of information between EU Member States in the area of criminal justice by granting access to, amongst other things, the DNA databases of other Member States. Searches of the Irish DNA Database System, in order to find a match with an unidentified DNA profile gathered in another Member State, will be allowed in accordance with the Council Decision and the terms of the 2010 Bill,[92] and a reciprocal arrangement will exist with other Member States. The newly named Eolaíocht Fhóiréinseach Éireann (EFÉ) (formerly the Forensic Science Laboratory) will be the national contact point for this exchange.

While it seems necessary in an ever more open European Union that mutual co-operation and assistance between Member States on matters of policing and criminal justice should be fostered, some caution in this regard has been urged by the IHRC, which has pointed to the fact that there is a lack of protection in place for personal data in the area of police and judicial co-operation in criminal matters.[93]

V. Covert Surveillance

[4–36] In 2009, the Oireachtas introduced legislation allowing for covert surveillance to be carried out by gardaí (or members of the defence forces or the revenue commissioners in certain circumstances) and for the evidence gathered in that manner to be admitted at trial: the Criminal Justice (Surveillance) Act 2009. "Surveillance" according to the Act, includes monitoring, observing, listening to or making a recording of a particular person or group of persons or their movements, activities and communications; or monitoring or making a recording of places or things, by or with the assistance of surveillance devices.[94]

[4–37] Generally, under the legislation, a judge of the District Court may grant an authorisation for surveillance on the application of a superior officer (a garda, member of the defence forces or officer of the revenue commissioners of appropriate rank). In the context of the criminal justice system, an applicant garda (not below the rank of superintendent) must have reasonable grounds to believe that:

---

[89] Irish Human Rights Commission, *Observations on the Criminal Justice (Forensic Evidence and DNA Database System) Bill 2010* (IHRC, Dublin, 2010), Part IV.

[90] Human Genetics Commission Report, *Nothing to Hide, Nothing to Fear?* (HGC, London, 2009), para 1.19.

[91] European Council Decision 2008/615/JHA.

[92] Criminal Justice (Forensic Evidence and DNA Database System) Bill 2010 Part 11.

[93] Irish Human Rights Commission, above n 89, Part IX.

[94] Criminal Justice (Surveillance) Act 2009, s 1.

a. as part of an operation or investigation being conducted by the gardaí concerning an arrestable offence, the requested surveillance is necessary for the purposes of obtaining information as to whether the offence has been committed or as to the circumstances relating to the commission of the offence, or obtaining evidence for the purposes of proceedings in relation to the offence;
b. the requested surveillance is necessary for the purpose of preventing the commission of arrestable offences; or
c. the requested surveillance is necessary for the purpose of maintaining the security of the State.[95]

Once in possession of an authorisation, the applicant garda named therein or other gardaí designated by him may enter, if necessary by the use of reasonable force, any place for the purposes of initiating or carrying out the authorised surveillance and withdrawing the authorised surveillance device without the consent of a person who owns or is in charge of that place. The authorisation is to last no longer than three months.[96] **[4–38]**

In circumstances of urgency, provision is made for a garda to carry out surveillance under the approval of a superior officer, rather than having judicial authorisation. Such approval is only to be issued by a superior officer on application from a garda where: (i) the conditions for the grant of a judicial authorisation are in place; and (ii) before judicial authorisation could be obtained one or more of a number of specifically listed difficulties exist, e.g. it is likely that a person would abscond for the purpose of avoiding justice. An urgent approval will last for a maximum of 72 hours.[97] Tracking devices may be utilised by gardaí under the Act without any recourse to the courts, under the approval of a superior garda alone.[98] **[4–39]**

The Act provides that evidence obtained as a result of authorised or approved surveillance may be admitted as evidence in criminal proceedings.[99] Notably, the Act provides that information or documents obtained as a result of an authorised or approved surveillance may be admitted as evidence notwithstanding any error or omission on the face of the relevant authorisation or written record of approval if the court decides that: (a) the error or omission concerned was inadvertent; and (b) the information or document ought to be admitted in the interests of justice. In making this decision the court should take the following into account: **[4–40]**

i. whether the error or omission concerned was serious or merely technical in nature;
ii. the nature of any right infringed by the obtaining of the information or document concerned;
iii. whether there were circumstances of urgency;
iv. the possible prejudicial effect of the information or document concerned;
v. the probative value of the information or document concerned.[100]

95 s 4.
96 ss 4 and 5.
97 s 7.
98 s 8.
99 s 14.
100 *ibid.*

[4–41] Furthermore, the Act suggests that information or documents obtained as a result of authorised or approved surveillance may be admitted as evidence in criminal proceedings, notwithstanding any failure by a garda to comply with a requirement of the relevant authorisation or approval if the court decides that: (a) the garda or officer concerned acted in good faith and that the failure was inadvertent; and (b) the information or document ought to be admitted in the interests of justice, again taking the above list into consideration.[101]

[4–42] It is notable that the legislature made specific provision within this Act for the carrying out of a balancing test in relation to the admissibility of relevant evidence. Given that important constitutional rights including privacy and the inviolability of the dwelling will surely be affected by the provisions of this Act, the suggestion that evidence improperly obtained thereunder, which is obtained nonetheless in "good faith" by gardaí, seems to undermine the strict exclusionary rule set out in *People (DPP) v Kenny*[102] and applied in Ireland for the past 20 years.[103] It remains to be seen whether any constitutional challenge to this or other elements of the Act might arise in the future.

VI. European Evidence Warrant (EEW)

[4–43] In its efforts to create a genuine area of freedom, security and justice, where cooperation between authorities is quick and effective and judicial protection of individual rights is granted,[104] the European Union has recently provided for the introduction of a European Evidence Warrant (EEW).

[4–44] The EEW will allow for authorities in Member States to request and receive certain evidential material for use in criminal investigations or proceedings from other Member States. While previous framework decisions, such as the 2003 Framework Decision on the execution of orders freezing property or evidence, allowed for the transfer of evidentiary material in particular criminal matters under *mutual assistance* procedures, the EEW will apply the principle of *mutual legal recognition*.[105] Therefore, a judicial decision to request objects, documents or data for use in criminal proceedings issued by a competent authority in one Member State (the issuing State) will be directly recognised and enforced by a competent authority in another Member State (the executing State). The executing authority shall recognise an EEW without any further formality and take the necessary measures for its execution.

[4–45] The EEW will only allow for the gathering of evidence which is already in existence in another Member State.[106] The Framework Decision provides a list of examples of material that can be requested under the EEW including: objects, documents or data from a third party; objects, documents or data from a search of premises including the private premises of the suspect; historical data on the use of any services including

---

[101] *ibid.*

[102] [1990] 2 IR 110.

[103] Discussed at para 4–49.

[104] Tampere European Council *Presidency Conclusions 15 and 16 October 1999* available at http://www.europarl.europa.eu/summits/tam_en.htm.

[105] Mutual legal recognition is also the basis of the European Arrest Warrant, which is discussed in Chapter Two.

[106] Framework Decision on the European Arrest Warrant, Art 4, para 1.

financial transactions; historical records of statements, interviews and hearings; and, other records, including the results of special investigative techniques.[107] The EEW will not allow for the questioning of suspects, the obtaining of new witness statements, the use of covert surveillance, bodily examinations or other material which is not already in existence.[108]

The EEW will specifically refer to the requested object, document or data. However, any other object, document or data which the executing authority discovers during the execution of the EEW and without further enquiries considers to be relevant to the proceedings at the centre of the EEW may also be obtained if indicated by the issuing authority.[109] **[4–46]**

An executing authority may only refuse to act on an EEW by invoking one of the grounds for non-recognition or non-execution, or one of the grounds for postponement, as foreseen in the Framework Decision.[110] The grounds for non-recognition or non-execution include, *inter alia*, situations where: execution of the EEW would infringe the rule against double jeopardy; the EEW has not been validated by a judicial authority when this is expressly requested; or, execution of the EEW would harm essential national security interests, jeopardise the source of the information or involve the use of classified information relating to specific intelligence activities.[111] **[4–47]**

It seems that the admissibility at trial of the evidence gathered under the EEW will still be an issue for the court of the issuing State. Given varying police powers, suspect rights and procedural rules throughout the Member States of the EU, the question of admissibility of evidence is a hurdle yet to be climbed by mutual assistance or mutual recognition provisions. This may be a particularly thorny issue for the Irish courts given their strict approach to unconstitutionally obtained evidence.[112] **[4–48]**

Implementing legislation is to be promulgated in member states by January 2011.[113]

VII. The Exclusionary Rule

In this section the consequences of breaches of the rules on gathering evidence will be examined. When evidence has been improperly obtained, in that the manner in which it was found or collected breached the rights of a particular suspect, the courts may refuse to allow that evidence to be put forward in a criminal trial. The Irish courts have adopted a two-tiered approach to the so-called "exclusionary rule": evidence obtained in breach of the *legal* rights of a suspect may or may not be excluded from trial, at the discretion of the trial judge, while evidence obtained in breach of the *constitutional* **[4–49]**

[107] Point 7 of the Consideranda.
[108] Above n 106, Art 4, para 2.
[109] Art 4 para 5.
[110] Art 11 para 1.
[111] Art 13.
[112] Discussed below at para 4–60.
[113] For further discussion of the EEW see Belfiore, "Movement of Evidence in the EU: The Present Scenario and Possible Future Developments" (2009) 17(1) *European Journal of Crime, Criminal Law and Criminal Justice* 1.

rights of a suspect must be automatically excluded. There are some qualifications to this which will be discussed below. Evidence will only be excluded where there is a causative link between the breach of rights and the gathering of the impugned evidence.[114]

Different jurisdictions take differing approaches to the admission or exclusion of improperly obtained evidence.

In England and Wales, for example, the courts traditionally admitted all relevant evidence, no matter how it was obtained.[115] Section 78 of the Police and Criminal Evidence Act 1984 now provides that evidence may be excluded at the discretion of the trial judge if its admission would adversely affect the fairness of the proceedings, with the courts tending to be inclusionary rather than exclusionary.[116]

[4–50] In the US, a deterrent rationale applies to the exclusion (or "suppression") of improperly obtained evidence.[117] Where deterrence is not a factor the courts will allow the evidence to be admitted, even though it may have been obtained improperly.[118] Recently, the US Supreme Court has suggested that modern police training, discipline and accountability has reduced the occasions on which it is likely that the exclusion of evidence would have a deterrent value.[119] The Court suggested that a balancing test is required contrasting the social costs of excluding evidence — including the potential that a guilty person would go free — with the value of excluding the evidence, mainly in terms of the deterrent effect of such a ruling.

[4–51] The ECtHR has not set out any particular response which States ought to adopt in relation to improperly obtained evidence under the ECHR. In cases such as *Schenk v Switzerland*,[120] *Teixeira de Castro v Portugal*[121] and *Khan v United Kingdom*,[122] it has been held that while Art 6 ECHR guarantees the right to a fair trial, it does not lay down any rules on the admissibility of evidence and such rules, therefore, are primarily a matter for domestic regulation.

Formulating the Irish Rule

[4–52] The seminal case in relation to the exclusion of improperly obtained evidence in Ireland is *People (AG) v O'Brien*.[123] Here, a search warrant was issued by the District Court for a search of the suspects' dwelling which was at 118 Captain's Road, Crumlin

---

114 See *People (DPP) v Healy* [1990] 2 IR 73; *Walsh v O Buachalla* [1991] 1 IR 56; *People (DPP) v O'Donnell* [1995] 3 IR 551; *People (DPP) v Buck* [2002] 2 IR 269; *People (DPP) v Laide and Ryan* [2005] 1 IR 209; *People (DPP) v O'Brien* [2005] 2 IR 206.

115 *R v Leatham* (1861) 8 Cox CC 498; *Kuruma v The Queen* [1955] AC 197; *R v Sang* [1980] AC 402.

116 See *Attorney General's Reference (No. 3 of 1999)* [2001] 2 AC 91; [2001] 1 All ER 577.

117 *Boyd v United States* 116 US 616 (1866); *Wolf v Colorado* 338 US 25 (1949); *Mapp v Ohio* 367 US 643 (1961); *US v Calandra* 414 US 338 (1974).

118 *US v Leon* 468 US 897 (1983).

119 *Hudson v Michigan* 547 US 586 (2006).

120 (1988) 13 EHRR 242.

121 (1998) 28 EHRR 101.

122 (2000) 31 EHRR 1016.

123 [1965] IR 142.

in Dublin. However, the search warrant had been, innocently but erroneously, issued for "118 Cashel Road, Crumlin". The defendants argued that the search of their dwelling, in the absence of a valid warrant, was both illegal (as it amounted to a trespass) and unconstitutional (as it breached Art 40.5 of the Constitution which guarantees the inviolability of the dwelling) and that the evidence obtained as a result ought not to be admitted at trial.

The Court of Criminal Appeal included the evidence on the basis that, although improperly obtained, the evidence had been correctly admitted at trial as it was relevant to the charge against the accused. The Supreme Court, however, adopted a different approach, setting out separate rules in relation to illegally obtained and unconstitutionally obtained evidence. Illegally obtained evidence may be excluded at the discretion of the trial judge, considering all the circumstances of the case, including: the nature and extent of the illegality; whether it was intentional or unintentional; whether it was an illegality of a trivial nature or otherwise; whether it was the result of an *ad hoc* decision or represented deliberate, settled policy; and whether the public interest would be best served by the admission or exclusion of the evidence in question.[124] **[4–53]**

Unconstitutionally obtained evidence, on the other hand, must be automatically excluded where there has been a "deliberate and conscious violation" of the constitutional rights of the accused.[125] The only occasion on which evidence so obtained could be admitted, at the discretion of the trial judge, is if extraordinary excusing circumstances were in existence, such as the imminent destruction of vital evidence; the need to rescue a victim in peril; or a search without warrant which was incidental to and contemporaneous with a lawful arrest.[126] **[4–54]**

On the facts of *O'Brien*, the Supreme Court unanimously held that the mistaken address on the warrant was a pure oversight; there was nothing to suggest deliberate treachery, imposition, deceit or illegality; there was no apparent policy to disregard the Constitution or to conduct searches without a warrant[127]; and, there was clearly no deliberate and conscious violation of the rights of the accused on the part of gardaí.[128] The trial judge had correctly exercised his discretion to admit the evidence in the circumstances of this case. **[4–55]**

Illegally Obtained Evidence

In relation to illegally—though not unconstitutionally—obtained evidence, the Irish courts have adopted a rather inclusionary approach.[129] Hogan has suggested that, in **[4–56]**

124 *ibid.* at 160.
125 *ibid.* at 170.
126 *ibid.* at 170 *per* Walsh J.
127 *ibid.* at 161 *per* Kingmill Moore J.
128 *ibid.* at 170 *per* Walsh J.
129 See *People (DPP) v Lawless,* unreported, Court of Criminal Appeal, 28 November 1985; *People (DPP) v McMahon, McMeel and Wright* [1987] ILRM 87; *People (DPP) v Connell* [1995] 1 IR 244; *DPP v Spratt* [1995] 1 IR 585; *People (DPP) v Van Onzen* [1996] 2 ILRM 387; *People (DPP) v Darcy,* unreported, Court of Criminal Appeal, 29 July 1997; *DPP v Diver* [2005] 3 IR 270.

practice, the courts almost never exclude *illegally* obtained evidence as there is usually a reason why it should be admitted in the overall public interest.[130]

[4–57] In *People (DPP) v McMahon, McMeel and Wright*[131] the Supreme Court held that a trial judge's decision, as to whether or not to exercise his discretion to exclude illegally obtained evidence, would involve a balancing of the competing public interest in the solving of crime on the one hand, as against the public interest in the fair trial of the accused on the other.

[4–58] In the context of confession evidence, a judge's discretion to exclude illegally obtained evidence arises in relation to breaches of the Criminal Justice Act 1984 (Treatment of Persons in Custody in Garda Síochána Stations) Regulations 1987 and the Criminal Justice Act 1984 (Electronic Recording of Interviews) Regulations 1997. As noted in Chapter Three, the parent statute of both of these Regulations states that a breach of the Regulations alone will not of itself affect the admissibility in evidence at trial of any statement made by a suspect in the pre-trial process.[132]

[4–59] As the interaction between a criminal suspect and gardaí affects so many important constitutional rights, e.g. the right to liberty, the inviolability of the dwelling, the right to silence, the right of access to pre-trial legal advice and the right to bodily integrity, the threshold for a breach of rights to be considered a breach of constitutional, rather than mere legal, rights is quite low in practice. Therefore, the rules on unconstitutionally obtained evidence are arguably more significant.

Unconstitutionally Obtained Evidence

[4–60] The application of the rule on unconstitutionally obtained evidence, which was formulated in *O'Brien,* has been the subject of much discussion in the Irish courts. Throughout the case law the central stumbling block has been the meaning of the phrase "deliberate and conscious violation" of constitutional rights, and the underlying rationale of the rule. In a series of cases[133] culminating in *People (DPP) v Kenny*[134] it has been held that the rationale is one of protectionism and that the knowledge of the violator is irrelevant.[135]

[4–61] *Kenny,* somewhat like *O'Brien*, involved the purported execution of a defective search warrant. In *Kenny,* however, the search warrant was found to be invalid because it had been issued by a Peace Commissioner without any evidence that he was satisfied that there were reasonable grounds for the suspicion held by the garda who swore

[130] Hogan, "Note of Dissent on Exclusionary Rule by the Chairman" in Balance in the Criminal Law Review Group, *Final Report* (Stationery Office, Dublin, 2007), p 289.

[131] [1987] ILRM 87.

[132] Criminal Justice Act 1984, ss 7(3) and 27.

[133] See for example, *People (DPP) v Madden* [1977] IR 336; *People (DPP) v Shaw* [1982] IR 1.

[134] [1990] 2 IR 110.

[135] For more see Martin, "The rationale of the exclusionary rule of evidence revisited" (1992) 2(1) ICLJ 1; McGrath, "The Exclusionary Rule in Respect of Unconstitutionally Obtained Evidence" (2004) 11(1) DULJ 108; Daly, "Unconstitutionally Obtained Evidence in Ireland: Protectionism, Deterrence and the Winds of Change" (2009) 19(2) ICLJ 40.

information before him.[136] That meant that the search warrant had been issued without lawful authority. Unlike the situation in *O'Brien*, the defects on the warrant in *Kenny* were not apparent on the face of the warrant and there was no way that the gardaí could have known that the warrant was invalid and that in executing it they were breaching the suspect's constitutional rights under Art 40.5.

Adopting the US deterrence approach, the Court of Criminal Appeal held that there had been no "deliberate and conscious violation" of the constitutional rights as the relevant garda had done all that he thought necessary to obtain the search warrant and he was entirely unaware of its inherent defect. However, the Supreme Court adopted a different standpoint holding that evidence obtained from the search ought to have been excluded as the search had breached the accused's constitutional right to the inviolability of his dwelling, whether or not the relevant garda knew that to be the case. The majority of the Court expressly denounced the deterrence principle as a rationale for the exclusion of unconstitutionally obtained evidence in the Irish context, favouring the protection of rights as the basis for the operation of the rule.[137] Finlay CJ stated that: **[4–62]**

> "as between two alternative rules or principles governing the exclusion of evidence obtained as a result of the invasion of the personal rights of a citizen, the Court has . . . an obligation to choose the principle which is likely to provide a stronger and more effective defence and vindication of the right concerned".[138]

A rule of absolute protection would provide far more security for the personal constitutional rights of citizens than would an exclusionary rule based solely on the concept of deterrence.[139] Finlay CJ acknowledged that such a rule could create problems in criminal trials given its propensity to exclude from evidence items of immense probative value. However, he was of the opinion that the detection of crime and the conviction of guilty persons, although important, could not outweigh the constitutional requirement on the courts to protect and vindicate rights.[140] **[4–63]**

He then set out the exclusionary rule in relation to unconstitutionally obtained evidence in the following terms: **[4–64]**

> ". . . evidence obtained by invasion of the constitutional personal rights of a citizen must be excluded unless a court is satisfied that either the act constituting the breach of constitutional rights was committed unintentionally or accidentally, or is satisfied that there are extraordinary excusing circumstances which justify the admission of the evidence in [the court's] discretion".[141]

---

136 As is required under the provisions of the Misuse of Drugs Act 1977.
137 Strong dissents were issued by Griffin and Lynch JJ.
138 [1990] 2 IR 110 at 133.
139 *ibid.* at 133.
140 *ibid.* at 134 quoting Art 40.3.1 of the Constitution.
141 *ibid.* at 134.

On the facts of *Kenny*, it was held that the actions of the gardaí in obtaining the warrant and later forcibly entering the dwelling could not be said to be unintentional or accidental and, although the gardaí concerned had no knowledge that they were invading the constitutional rights of the appellant, the evidence ought not to have been admitted at trial.

[4–65] The protectionist stance adopted in *Kenny* has been generally applied by the Irish courts.[142] In *People (DPP) v Laide and Ryan*,[143] for example, it was held that the second defendant had been unlawfully arrested and therefore all statements made by him, while in unlawful detention, had to be excluded. The unlawful arrest arose when the gardaí entered his dwelling place under the authority of a search warrant, and then arrested him within that place. It was held that the search warrant was defective as its real purpose was to allow for the arrest of the defendant, rather than to carry out a search.

[4–66] However, the rule has not found favour in all cases or with all members of the bench. In *People (DPP) v Balfe*,[144] the Court of Criminal Appeal viewed the *O'Brien* and *Kenny* formulations of the exclusionary rule as alternatives, rather than viewing *Kenny* as a restatement of *O'Brien*, and chose to rely on *O'Brien* rather than *Kenny*. In *DPP (Walsh) v Cash*,[145] Charleton J in the High Court accepted that he was bound by *Kenny*, but he expressed his dislike for that rule, claiming that:

> "[a] rule which remorselessly excludes evidence obtained through an illegality occurring by a mistake does not commend itself to the proper ordering of society which is the purpose of the criminal law".[146]

Outside of the courts there have been calls for change in relation to the exclusion of unconstitutionally obtained evidence too. Most notably, the majority of the Balance in the Criminal Law Review Group recommended that trial courts ought not to be under a duty to automatically exclude evidence obtained in breach of the constitutional rights of a suspect, but should have a discretion to admit such evidence or not, having regard to the totality of the circumstances with particular regard to the rights of the victim.[147]

DPP (Walsh) v Cash[148]

[4–67] The recent Supreme Court decision in *DPP (Walsh) v Cash* addressed the operation of the exclusionary rule. Defence counsel in *Cash* sought to have a set of fingerprints taken from the accused following his arrest on a burglary charge excluded from evidence. He had been arrested on the basis of a match between fingerprints taken

---

142 For example, in *DPP v Yamanoha* [1994] 1 IR 565; *DPP v Connell* [1995] 1 IR 244; *People (DPP) v Dillon* [2002] 4 IR 50.
143 [2005] 1 IR 209.
144 [1998] 4 IR 50.
145 [2007] IEHC 108
146 *ibid.* at para 65 *per* Charleton J.
147 Balance in the Criminal Law Review Group, *Final Report* (Stationery Office, Dublin, 2007), p 166.
148 [2010] IESC 1.

from the scene and prints previously taken from the accused in relation to another matter some years previously which were held on file in the Garda Technical Bureau. The prosecution had been unable to clearly state the legal position of the retained prints: whether they had been taken with consent or otherwise; whether or not they ought to have been destroyed following the passage of some time and the fact that no proceedings had been instituted in relation to the earlier matter.

The main question for consideration by the Supreme Court was whether the strict exclusionary rule laid down in *Kenny* should be extended to cover facts which gave rise to a suspicion grounding an arrest, rather than facts being offered as part of the evidence at a criminal trial. Fennelly J held that the rule from *Kenny* is only relevant to the exclusion of evidence proffered at a criminal trial and is not concerned with the lawful provenance of evidence used to ground a suspicion. He suggested that the appellant in this case was seeking to extend the exclusionary rule beyond its correct boundaries and that doing so would blur the distinction between the arrest and the trial. **[4–68]**

Quoting from Charleton J in the High Court, Fennelly J observed that it has never been held that:

> "what would found a reasonable suspicion in law, requires to be based on the kind of evidence that would be admissible under the rules of evidence during the hearing of a criminal trial".

If the earlier-obtained fingerprints in this case ought to have been destroyed then their retention could be seen as breaching the appellant's right to privacy, both under the Constitution and the ECHR,[149] and their use to ground an arrest could be seen as a breach of the right to liberty. It might have been thought, on the basis of previous case-law, that these matters would be of interest to the Irish courts, in order to ensure the protection of suspects' rights in the pre-trial period of the criminal process. It seems not. **[4–69]**

While it is correct to suggest that evidence which might ground an arrest would not always be acceptable under the evidentiary rules of the courts,[150] it is arguable that a more stringent rule applies, or should apply, in the context of evidence unlawfully or unconstitutionally obtained prior to arrest. One example of the type of evidence which might ground arrest but would not be admissible in evidence at trial is hearsay evidence. The rationale for the exclusion of hearsay evidence at trial centres on the reliability of such evidence and the dangers inherent in not being able to adequately test it in the courtroom. However, the rationale for the exclusion of unconstitutionally obtained evidence from trials in Ireland, as discussed above, is the protection of constitutional rights. **[4–70]**

While the *Kenny* rule and its protectionist rationale continue to regulate the exclusion of unconstitutionally obtained evidence proffered at trial, the Supreme Court in *Cash* appears to have set pre-arrest investigative methods beyond its reach.

---

[149] See *S and Marper v UK*, 4 December 2008 and discussion above at paras 4–27 and 4–33.

[150] As discussed in Chapter Two.

VIII. Conclusion

[4–71] There are now a vast amount of powers at the disposal of gardaí in their investigation of crime. Many of these powers interfere with individual rights and a proportionate balance needs to be struck between the competing interests of the investigation of offences and the protection of rights. In recent years, increases in policing powers seem to have drawn the criminal process into the private confines of the garda station and away from the public domain of the courts more than ever before. If fairness is to be ensured in the prosecution of crime then it is essential that effective means of protecting individual rights in the pre-trial stage of the criminal process are in place, and that there is transparency in investigative techniques, bearing in mind operational concerns. All of this becomes even more important as the European Union increases its interest and involvement in the sphere of criminal law and procedure.

Chapter 5
Garda Accountability

Building on the discussion of garda powers in previous chapters, we now consider how the gardaí can be held to account when these powers are improperly used. As the previous chapters have shown there is a great deal of discretion involved in police work: although the gardaí are under a duty to seek out and preserve evidence, for example, it is at their discretion when to seek search warrants, when to stop and search an individual, when to arrest and so on. This makes attempts to control policing difficult.[1] We have also seen that gardaí are given powers to do certain things, which if done by an ordinary citizen would be considered criminal, such as to detain people or use force when necessary.[2] These powers enable the gardaí to safeguard the rights of citizens, and citizens are entitled to ensure that any interference with their rights is for that stated purpose. In his report on the Brixton riots in England in the early 1980s, Lord Scarman wrote: [5–01]

> "Accountability... renders the police answerable for what they do. Thereby it prevents them from slipping into an enclosed fortress of inward thinking and social isolation which would in the long term result in a siege mentality – the police in their fortress (happy as long as it is secure) and the rest of us outside, unhappy, uncertain and insecure (for we do not know what they will do or how they will do it)."[3]

[1] On discretion see Newburn, and Jones, "Police Accountability" in Salusbury, Mott, and Newburn, *Themes in Contemporary Policing* (PSI, London, 1996) and Scraton, *The Police State We Are In* (Pluto Press, London, 1985).
[2] See Reiner, *The Politics of the Police* (2nd ed, OUP, Oxford, 2000).
[3] *Report on the Disturbances in Brixton 10th to 13th April 1981* (HMSO, London, 1981), para 5.58.

[5–02] In this sense, accountability contributes to the concept of policing by consent, whereby the public support the police in their efforts because they believe in what they do, making it easier for the police to carry out their functions.[4]

[5–03] The Patten Commission,[5] which examined policing in Northern Ireland at the end of the conflict, identified five forms of police accountability: internal, legal, democratic, financial and transparency. For our purposes internal and legal are perhaps the most relevant. In this chapter an overview of the "architecture of police accountability" as it exists in Ireland, following substantial reform in 2005, will be provided.[6] Judicial oversight of policing through the exclusionary rule is discussed in Chapter Four.

I. Context of Reform

[5–04] It had long been argued that garda accountability in Ireland was weak, primarily, according to Walsh, due to a reliance on a complaints procedure which involved gardaí investigating allegations against gardaí.[7] This came to a head in the Morris Tribunal, established in 2002 to investigate allegations of corruption in Donegal.[8] The fact that a tribunal was necessary exposed the inability of existing mechanisms to respond appropriately when problems arose. The Tribunal exposed corruption, misconduct and supervisory negligence in the Donegal district and documented a lack of adherence to the concept of accountability. The Tribunal also documented an unwillingness of gardaí to speak out against other officers and a willingness to lie, even in evidence to the Tribunal.[9] While not specifically mandated to advise on accountability structures, the Tribunal inevitably made related recommendations. It called for the imposition of a duty to account — whereby a garda would be obliged to account to a superior for his actions — in the disciplinary code, an expansion of the powers of the Garda Commissioner for summary dismissals, enhanced supervision of officers, reforms to the conduct and recording of interrogations, and greater reporting obligations when dealing with informants. It also concluded that the Garda Complaints Board, as existed at the time, was thoroughly incapable of dealing with complaints on the scale and of the nature emanating from Donegal.[10]

[5–05] While the Tribunal was ongoing, the Garda Síochána Act 2005 was passed, introducing a wide range of new reforms, including establishment of the Garda Ombudsman Commission, Joint Policing Committees, a Garda Inspectorate and

---

[4] Reiner, above n 2, Scraton, above n 1, and Loader, "Plural Policing and Democratic Governance" (2000) 9(3) *Social and Legal Studies* 323.

[5] Patten, *The Report of the Independent Commission on Policing for Northern Ireland* (HMSO, London, 1999).

[6] Mulcahy, *Policing Northern Ireland: Conflict, Legitimacy and Reform* (Willan Publishing, Devon, 2006).

[7] Walsh, *The Irish Police: A Legal and Constitutional Perspective* (Round Hall, Dublin, 1998).

[8] For terms of reference of the Tribunal see 551 *Dáil Debates* Col 19.

[9] For example see Morris, *Report on Explosives Finds in Donegal* (Stationery Office, Dublin, 2004), para 1.08. See further, Conway, *The Blue Wall of Silence: The Morris Tribunal and Police Accountability in Ireland* (IPA, Dublin, 2010).

[10] Morris, *Report into Effectiveness of Garda Síochána Complaints Board Inquiry* (Stationery Office, Dublin, 2008).

Whistleblower's Charter as well as significant reforms to the disciplinary procedures. The mechanisms of accountability will now be discussed, incorporating these reforms.

II. Internal Accountability

Internal accountability within An Garda Síochána is built around enforcing the Disciplinary Code, most recently revised in 2007.[11] The Code categorises breaches of discipline as disobedience, neglect of duty, corruption, abuse of authority, intoxication while on duty, disreputable conduct, failure to co-operate with a disciplinary investigation, discourtesy, failure to account for actions taken on duty, making false allegations of improper practice within An Garda Síochána, and harassing a garda who makes such allegations. Breaches of the regulations can result in sanctions ranging from being docked pay to demotion or even dismissal.[12] Actions which have been prosecuted and resulted in either a conviction or an acquittal cannot be the subject of disciplinary action.[13] In all decisions on breaches of discipline the civil standard of proof, the balance of probabilities, is to be applied.[14] The Code applies to all members of the force, save for the Garda Commissioner.[15] **[5–06]**

Disciplinary Procedure

The regulations provide for informal resolution of minor breaches where advice, caution or warning can be given.[16] For "less serious breaches", which attract less serious sanctions, a garda, referred to as a Deciding Officer, may be appointed to conduct an investigation and interview the garda concerned.[17] A more serious breach, meriting at least four weeks pay deduction or a greater sanction, results in an investigation conducted by an Investigating Officer of the rank of Inspector or above.[18] If a garda admits the breach at this stage disciplinary action could involve deduction of pay, a reprimand, a warning, a caution or advice.[19] If the breach is not admitted, and the initial investigation suggests a breach may have been committed, the Garda Commissioner must establish a Board of Inquiry composed of three people[20]: the Presiding Officer selected by the Commissioner from a panel created by the Minister for Justice, either a District Court judge, a barrister or solicitor of ten years standing;[21] and two gardaí ranking Chief Superintendent and Superintendent.[22] Prior to the 2005 **[5–07]**

---

[11] Garda Síochána Discipline (Regulations) 2007.

[12] ss 14 and 22.

[13] Not a *nolle prosequi*; reg 38(1). In *McGrath v Commissioner of an Garda Síochána* [1999] ILRM 817 at 824 proceedings could be held where "the nature of the disciplinary charge becomes of a wholly different character to the criminal charge." In *Farrelly v Commissioner of an Garda Síochána* [2007] IEHC 84 a criminal charge of handling stolen goods followed by a disciplinary charge of discreditable conduct was not acceptable.

[14] reg 9.

[15] reg 3.

[16] Pt 2.

[17] reg 12.

[18] reg 24.

[19] reg 16.

[20] reg 25.

[21] reg 25(5).

[22] reg 25(6).

Act all members of the board were gardaí. The garda accused may object to any member of the Board and the individual will be replaced.[23]

[5–08] In *Noonan v Commissioner of an Garda Síochána*[24] the High Court affirmed the decision of *Hughes v Commissioner of an Garda Síochána*,[25] which held that at the end of the investigation stage, prior to the submission of the report to the Board, it was not within the power of the investigator to add additional charges. Should new breaches come to light, fair procedures and constitutional justice demand that a fresh investigation be conducted which complies with the disciplinary procedures.

[5–09] The regulations outline the procedure for the inquiry, where the accused will be given an opportunity to be heard and to question anyone giving evidence.[26] The inquiry is heard in private and can proceed in the absence of the garda.[27] The board presents a report to the Commissioner, including its decision on the allegation and recommendations for action.[28] The Commissioner decides on action/sanctions within two weeks.[29] For dismissal, recommendations of a requirement to resign or a reduction in rank for a garda above the rank of Inspector are submitted to the Government which decides.[30] If the Commissioner recommends a sanction more severe than that proposed by the board, then the garda must be given a chance to respond prior to the decision.[31] There is a right of appeal before a fresh board comprising a District Court judge or lawyer, the Commissioner or his representative, and a member of the representative association.[32]

If a garda resigns before proceedings against him are completed, then he cannot be disciplined. Walsh has called for the regulations to be tightened up "specifically to permit a disciplinary case to proceed against a member irrespective of his premature resignation"[33] and Conway has argued for a hearing to be held, even if no sanction could be imposed.[34]

Delay

[5–10] Numerous challenges, by way of judicial review seeking prohibition of proceedings, have raised the issue of delay in instigating disciplinary investigations.[35] The regulations repeatedly refer to the need to initiate the process "as soon as practicable", defined in *Ruigrok v Commissioner of An Garda Síochána* as "as soon as feasible, capable of being done."[36]

---

[23] reg 26.
[24] [2007] IEHC 354.
[25] Unreported, High Court, 23 July 1996.
[26] reg 29.
[27] reg 29.
[28] reg 30.
[29] reg 31.
[30] reg 31(2).
[31] reg 32.
[32] reg 33.
[33] Walsh above n 7, p 250.
[34] Conway above n 9, p 139.
[35] For a discussion of delay in criminal proceedings see Chapter Six.
[36] [2005] IEHC 439.

In the Supreme Court case of *McNeill v Commissioner of An Garda Síochána*[37] a failure to initiate proceedings for two to three years after it would have been feasible equated to a failure in the mandatory obligation to act as soon as practicable. The Supreme Court clarified that neither civil nor criminal standards relating to delay were applicable in these cases, which should be considered in terms of the regulations. In *Kennedy v Commissioner of An Garda Síochána*[38] the High Court stated that "the duty to proceed with expedition is to be determined in accordance with what was practicable at the time." It was accepted in *Kneafsey v Commissioner of An Garda Síochána*[39] that it may be necessary, once a complaint has been made, for a few weeks to be taken to make preliminary inquiries prior to engaging in the formal process. A failure to take action for over two years was described as "grossly excessive" and in breach of the regulations. A three month delay, during which time a background report is compiled, will not constitute delay.[40] Nor should proceedings be delayed to await the outcome of a Tribunal of Inquiry as this "would not adequately protect the rule of law."[41] [5–11]

To prohibit the inquiry the courts will seek proof of some prejudice resulting from the delay.[42] In *Ryan v Commissioner of An Garda Síochána*,[43] the delay related primarily to the furnishing of documents under discovery. The High Court accepted that the refusal to comply with the order of discovery was unlawful and "wholly inconsistent with the obligation of expediency imposed on the respondent." The Court then, however, held that delay did not automatically result in prohibition of the proceedings and that in making that decision the court must have regard to the public interest in "ensuring members do not have their reputation in the community they serve tarnished for a lengthy period while the disciplinary process unfolds" as well as "the effect of the delay on the capacity of the member to defend himself." Further, where the allegations are of a serious nature, which may tarnish the reputation of the force as a whole, and the garda is to remain in the force while proceedings are ongoing, the proceedings must be adjudicated "expeditiously". Having considered these factors in the case at hand the Court refused the relief sought, despite having found an unlawful refusal to comply with the discovery order, given both the potential impact on the reputation of the force and that the delay had not unfairly impaired the ability of the accused to defend himself. [5–12]

Dismissal of a Garda

The capacity of the Commissioner to dismiss a garda was upheld in *Keady v Commissioner of An Garda Síochána*[44] where it had been argued that, given the nature of the job, a dismissal was really an administration of justice which could only be performed by the Courts.[45] More contentious has been the power of the Commissioner [5–13]

[37] [1997] 1 IR 479.
[38] [2008] IEHC 72.
[39] [2009] IEHC 89.
[40] *Harrington v Commissioner of An Garda Síochána* [2009] IEHC 425.
[41] *O'Dowd v Commission of An Garda Síochána*, unreported, High Court, 19 May 2004.
[42] *Farrelly v Commissioner of An Garda Síochána* [2007] IEHC 84.
[43] [2009] IEHC 424.
[44] [1991] ILRM 312.
[45] Art 34, Constitution of Ireland; *In Re Solicitors Act 1954* [1960] IR 239.

to dismiss gardaí summarily and in the case of *Jordan*[46] O'Hanlon J determined that the requirements of natural justice would have to be satisfied in the exercise of the power. Regulation 39 of the Disciplinary Regulations, inserted pursuant to the Garda Síochána Act 2005, specifies three instances in which this power can be used:

- where the gravity of the offence is such that holding a board of inquiry could not affect his decision;
- where disclosure of the facts would breach state security or be "a serious and unjustifiable infringement of the rights of another person"; and,
- where the garda displays an intention to abandon membership.

[5–14] The exercise of the summary power requires the consent of the Minister for Justice and it cannot be used for a garda above the rank of Inspector, where the Government makes the decision to dismiss.[47] While the garda is given the opportunity in such instances to make submissions to the Commissioner in advance of such a decision there is no appeal process provided for in the regulations.[48]

III. Legal Accountability

[5–15] Legal accountability within An Garda Síochána takes a number of forms: citizen complaints, civil actions, judicial review, criminal actions and recently in Ireland, the Coroner's Court has played a role. Our focus will be on civil and criminal actions.

Citizen Complaints

[5–16] The Garda Síochána Ombudsman Commission (the Commission) was established under Part 3 of the Garda Síochána Act 2005 and began its work in May 2007. It replaced the Garda Complaints Board which since 1986 had handled complaints against gardaí.[49] This body had been set up partly as a response to the introduction of the detention without charge provisions in the Criminal Justice Act 1984, but was highly criticised as complaints were investigated by gardaí, and decisions in relation to more serious allegations were taken by a tribunal which had Garda representation.[50] Its replacement, the Garda Ombudsman Commission, is a three person Commission.[51] Appointments are made by the President, on the nomination of the Government.[52] Appointees must have appropriate experience, qualifications, training or expertise and the legislation states that a judge of a superior court may be appointed.[53] A

---

[46] *State (Jordan) v Commission of the Garda Síochána* [1987] ILRM 107.

[47] Discussed in para 15-13.

[48] reg 39.

[49] Prior to that, complaints by the public were dealt with internally under the disciplinary procedure outlined above. See Walsh, above n 7.

[50] Garda Síochána Complaints Act 1986, s 8. See Walsh, "Twenty Years of Police Complaints in Ireland: A Critical Assessment of the Review Board Model" (2009) 29(2) *Legal Studies* 305.

[51] Garda Síochána Act 2005, s 65.

[52] s 65(1). This has been criticised by the Irish Human Rights Commission, *Observations on the Garda Bill 2004* (IHRC, Dublin, 2005) and the Irish Council for Civil Liberties, *Submission on the Garda Síochána Bill* (ICCL, Dublin, 2005) as a missed opportunity to establish an independent appointments panel.

[53] s 65(5).

Commissioner cannot have been a garda, a member of either House of the Oireachtas, the European Parliament or a local authority.[54]

The objectives of the Commission are to perform its functions efficiently, effectively and fairly while promoting public confidence in the complaints process.[55] The functions of the Commission are, among others, to: [5–17]

- receive complaints from the public about the conduct of gardaí;
- use its powers and perform its duties with regard to those complaints;
- issue guidelines for informal resolution and set out procedures for investigations;
- report on its investigations to the Garda Commissioner and possibly the DPP;
- conduct other investigations into conduct of gardaí where necessary; and
- examine the practices, policies and procedures of An Garda Síochána.[56]

A complaint about any behaviour of a garda may be made to the Commission by a person directly affected, someone on their behalf, or someone who witnessed the incident.[57] It can be given or sent to the Garda Commissioner, any garda in any station, someone above the rank of Chief Superintendent not in a garda station, or directly to the Commission.[58] Whoever receives it must forward the complaint to the Commission and the Garda Commissioner. Complaints must be made within six months though the Commission may extend this if it believes it is justified.[59] [5–18]

The Commission first determines if the complaint is admissible, dependent on whether it is made by an authorised person, concerns conduct which would be considered misbehaviour,[60] is submitted on time,[61] and is not frivolous or vexatious.[62] There are no age restrictions on who can make a complaint. If the garda in question is no longer a garda or retires or resigns after the complaint is made, then it is inadmissible.[63] If it is inadmissible the Commission will notify all concerned of this decision.[64] If admissible, the Garda Commissioner will notify the garda concerned, providing details.[65] The Garda Commissioner is under a duty at this point to preserve all relevant evidence and [5–19]

---

54 s 5(7).
55 s 67(1).
56 s 67(2).
57 s 83(1).
58 s 83(2).
59 The Commission proved itself willing to extend the time limit for complaints over the fatal shooting of two armed raiders in Lusk, Co. Dublin, which occurred two years before the Commission began receiving complaints ("Lusk Inquest Adjourned as Ombudsman Steps In" *The Irish Times*, 26 September 2007).
60 s 82. The conduct complained of must constitute an offence or a breach of discipline.
61 In *Walsh v Garda Complaints Board* [2010] IESC 2, the Supreme Court interpreted the six month deadline as commencing on the day of the action in question. In that case, the acts complained of occurred on 5 March 2003 and a complaint received at 00.49 on 5 September was 50 minutes late.
62 For judicial consideration of the meaning of 'vexatious' see *Kelly v The Garda Síochána Complaints Board,* unreported, High Court, 15 February 2002.
63 s 87(4)(a).
64 s 88(1).
65 s 88(2).

may delay notifying the garda concerned until this has been achieved.[66] The Commission can discontinue a complaint at any point if it later appears to have been vexatious or frivolous, was made knowing that it was false or misleading, or, if the Commission considers that further investigation is unnecessary or not practicable.[67]

[5–20] Under the legislation there are a number of different ways in which a complaint can be dealt with: informal resolution or mediation (s 90), investigation by gardaí, supervised or not (s 94), or investigation by the Commission (s 95 or s 98).

[5–21] For either informal resolution or mediation to be used the consent of both the complainant and the relevant garda must be obtained.[68] To encourage garda participation, if either process is successful then the record of the complaint will be expunged from the garda's file. The Act outlines complaints of specific actions which cannot be sent for resolution in this manner,[69] restricting this option to serious offences. Both processes are confidential and nothing said can be used in either civil or criminal proceedings.[70]

[5–22] Informal resolution will involve either a Case Officer of the Commission or a garda of a more senior rank, contacting both parties in an effort to reach an agreement which is amenable to both. The emphasis is on oral communication, which is "informal… flexible… and proportionate."[71] Mediation will involve a member of the Mediation Unit within the Ombudsman Commission or an independent mediator holding separate meetings with each party, and a meeting of all three,[72] to reach consensus and satisfaction. An apology from either side is not necessary, but an acceptance of the impact of the behaviour is required.[73] If mediation is successful then the matter ends there and the record is expunged from the garda's file. If not, any of the alternative methods for dealing with a complaint remain open to the Commission.[74]

[5–23] The next step on the ladder is for the Commission to refer a complaint to the Garda Commissioner for an internal investigation under s 94. The Garda Commissioner will appoint a garda to investigate the complaint in line with disciplinary regulations.[75] The Commission may opt to supervise such an investigation.[76] This investigation may

[66] s 89.
[67] s 93.
[68] s 90(3), Garda Síochána Ombudsman Commission, *Guidelines on Informal Resolution and Mediation*, 2007.
[69] s 90(1) specifies (a) complaints to which s 91 applies, (b) complaints about conduct which appears to constitute an offence, and (c) complaints determined in accordance with the guidelines not to be suitable for resolution by mediation or other informal means. Commission guidelines, above n 68, p 3 also specify ill-treatment in custody, mistreatment resulting in assault or financial gain, engaging in prohibited or incompatible business, abuse of office, a trend of misbehaviour or behaviour discrediting the force.
[70] s 90(5).
[71] Above n 68, p 6.
[72] *ibid.* p 8.
[73] *ibid.* p 9.
[74] *ibid.*
[75] s 94(1)(a).
[76] s 94(3).

result in disciplinary action being taken or if the conduct appears to involve an offence then a subsequent s 98 investigation may take place.[77] A review will be held if the complainant is dissatisfied with the outcome and this may lead to another s 94 investigation or an investigation under either s 95 or s 98.[78]

The Commission can conduct two types of investigations dependent on whether the conduct appears not to involve an offence (s 95) or appears to involve an offence (s 98). In s 95 investigations, the Commission will give the complainant and the garda concerned an opportunity to be heard in person, present evidence and make submissions to the Commission. The Commission has the power to require someone who has information or documents relevant to the investigation to provide it to the Commission and to require him to attend in person.[79] However, the Minister can determine that a matter relates to the security of the State in which case it cannot be disclosed, unless instructed by the Minister.[80] Following the investigation, a report will be made to the Garda Commissioner who decides on sanctions.[81] A s 98 investigation is not precluded by this investigation. **[5–24]**

If the conduct appears to involve an offence it is dealt with under s 98. A designated officer investigating such an offence has all the powers, immunities, privileges, and duties of a garda,[82] including the power to: **[5–25]**

- enter and search any place pursuant to a warrant, and seize items authorised by the warrant;
- arrest, with or without a warrant, the garda under investigation;
- bring a charge against a garda;
- issue a summons to a garda;
- search a garda and take photographs, fingerprints and palm prints;
- detain and question a garda; and,
- take bodily samples or other items from the garda for the purpose of forensic testing.

Further, and perhaps most importantly, a search of a garda station may be conducted once authorised by the Commission.[83] There must be reasonable cause to suspect the relevant garda is guilty of an offence and that there is evidence in the station. The Commission must notify the Garda Commissioner and the Minister for Justice of an intention to conduct a search.[84] If the Garda Commissioner objects for reasons of the security of the State then he may ask the Minister to consider the objection.[85] The Minister can direct that the station be searched in part.[86] Any matters pertaining to **[5–26]**

---

[77] s 94(8).
[78] s 94(10).
[79] s 91(1).
[80] s 96(6).
[81] s 97.
[82] s 98(1).
[83] s 99.
[84] s 99(3).
[85] s 99(4).
[86] s 99(5).

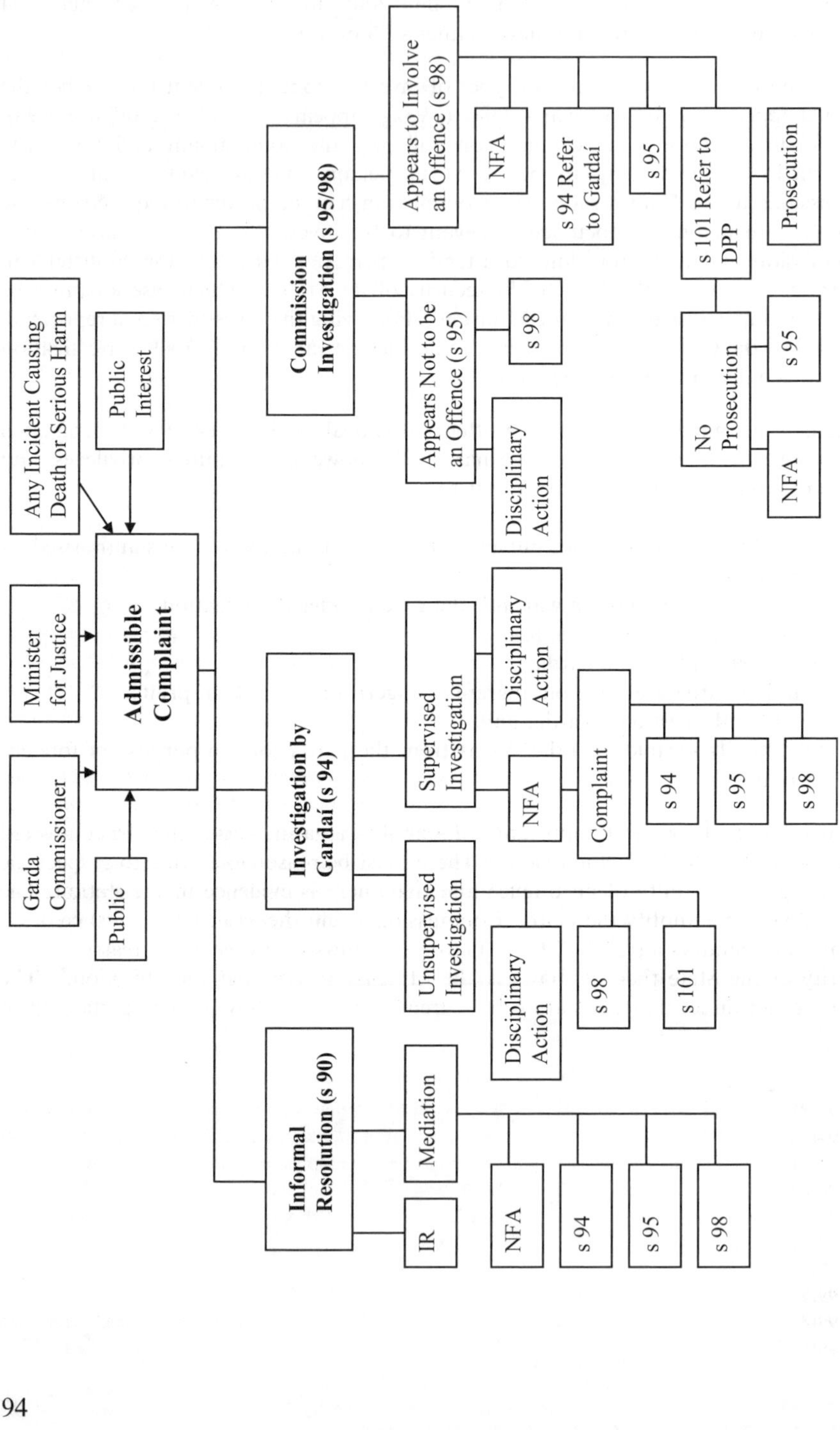

Figure 5.1 Process for complaints under Garda Síochána Ombudsman Commission

the security of the State will be considered by a High Court judge and reported to An Taoiseach.[87]

The designated officer reports to the Commission at the end of this s 98 investigation.[88] If the Commission determines at this stage that there was no offence, it can conduct a s 95 investigation. If the investigation disclosed no misconduct then it may decide to take no further action.[89] If the Commission believes it involves an offence then it sends a report to the DPP.[90] If the DPP does nothing then the Commission can conduct a s 94 (referral to Commissioner) or s 95 (conduct not involving an offence) investigation. **[5–27]**

In *McCarthy v Garda Complaints Tribunal*[91] the Supreme Court expressed its concern with delay in investigating citizen complaints in the clearest terms, citing the English case of *R v Chief Constable of Merseyside Police, ex p Merrill*[92] where it was outlined that "the public interest in complaints against police officers being fully investigated and adjudicated is undoubted, but it must be done speedily."[93] The High Court in *Boland v Garda Síochána Complaints Board*[94] equated the need for speed here with the need for complaints to be submitted in a relatively short period. This judgment was quoted with approval in *Molloy v Garda Síochána Complaints Tribunal*[95] where a hearing was postponed on four occasions over a three year period. In finding the delay to be "so inordinate and inexcusable as to amount to a violation of his basic right to natural and constitutional justice", the Court outlined that the problems in scheduling hearings were inexcusable: "the responsibility to keep things moving and to apply pressure on parties to make themselves available... can only be attributed to the [Complaints Board]." This case law is presumably applicable to the Commission. **[5–28]**

Section 91 deals with complaints of death or serious harm to a person pursuant to garda operations. When this situation arises, whether by a public complaint, an obligatory referral from the Garda Commission,[96] or where the Commission of its own accord suspects this has occurred,[97] the Commission must immediately direct a designated officer to determine what kind of investigation should occur.[98] This will depend on whether s 95 or s 98 applies. Also, without complaint, the Commission may instigate an investigation if it appears a garda has committed an offence or behaved in a manner meriting disciplinary proceedings.[99] The Minister may request the Commission to look into any matter if it appears a garda has committed an offence or behaved in a manner meriting disciplinary proceedings.[100] The Minister may also direct the **[5–29]**

---

[87] s 100.
[88] s 101.
[89] s 101(7).
[90] s 101(2)(a).
[91] [2002] 2 ILRM 341.
[92] [1989] 1 WLR 1077.
[93] *ibid.* at 1091. See also *Kenny v Garda Síochána Complaints Board* [2006] IEHC 224.
[94] Unreported, High Court, 28 November 2003.
[95] [2009] IEHC 197.
[96] s 102(1).
[97] s 102(2)(b).
[98] s 91(1).
[99] s 102(4).
[100] s 102(5).

Commission to examine the practice, policy and procedure of An Garda Síochána for which the Garda Commissioner must provide the Commission with any information or documents required.[101] However, the Minister may decide that such disclosure may prejudice a criminal investigation, the security of the State or the safety of a person and so not authorise its disclosure.[102]

[5–30] The ECtHR has found in *Govell v UK*[103] that police investigating complaints against themselves, where the complaint suggests a breach of a right under the ECHR, is a breach of Art 13 ECHR. This could be of concern in the Irish context if cases which involved allegations which amounted to breaches of rights were transferred from the Commission to gardaí to investigate. The statistics at present indicate that the Commission is restricting independent investigations to cases appearing to involve criminal offences with all others investigated by gardaí.[104] The Commission has also sought powers to 'lease back' minor criminal offences for investigation by gardaí.[105] There is potential within the ECHR for rights to be breached in ways which might not be considered criminal. Indeed in *Govell* the UK courts found that the police had acted legally but the ECtHR found that the right to respect for family life had been breached.

Criminal Actions

[5–31] Gardaí are subject to the criminal law just as members of the public are; however the nature of their powers has the effect that they can perform acts legally, which might otherwise be considered criminal.[106] The procedure where an officer is being investigated for a criminal offence is different to that applied to a citizen.[107]

[5–32] The criminal investigation itself tends to be more favourable to a garda suspected of a criminal offence then to a citizen. A garda will not be arrested; he will be informed of the complaint, then cautioned and interviewed.[108] The interview will most commonly take place while the garda is at work and he will be free to resume his duties after the interview unless suspended immediately.[109] The garda's knowledge of how interviews are conducted will stand him in good stead, as will the support of garda representative association.[110]

[5–33] The next stage is the decision to prosecute and it would again seem that this stage will favour a garda.[111] If the initial investigation indicates that a criminal offence may have

---

[101] s 106.

[102] s 106(5).

[103] *Govell v UK* [1997] 4 EHRR 438 and *Khan v UK* [2001] 31 EHRR 1016.

[104] See Conway, "A Wolf in Sheep's Clothing? Evaluating the Impact of the Garda Ombudsman Commission" [2009] *Irish Jurist* 109.

[105] Garda Síochána Ombudsman Commission, *Annual Report 2008* (Dublin, 2009).

[106] For instance it is permissible for the gardaí to use force to effect an arrest if necessary and proportionate where a citizen using the same force may be guilty of assault.

[107] Beyond this Walsh has asked "Will the force apply the same resources, effort and commitment to the investigation of the criminal allegation against the Garda as it will to the allegation against the citizen?", above n 7, p 348.

[108] Walsh, above n 7, pp 349-350

[109] *ibid.*

[110] *ibid.*

[111] *ibid.* p 351. See Chapter Six.

been committed then the case must be referred to the DPP to determine whether to proceed with a prosecution.[112] While this may provide external scrutiny it must be remembered that the decision of the DPP will be based entirely on the investigation conducted by gardaí. Also, Walsh points out that there exists a close relationship between gardaí and the DPP which would be hard to avoid taking into consideration.[113]

Should the case reach the courtroom, juries have significant reluctance in finding police officers guilty. Indeed Conor Brady of the Ombudsman Commission has stated that "the difficulty of getting convictions from a jury is clear... Juries are very reluctant. You saw it in the May Day protests, people were seen on television doing unspeakable things, and they were acquitted by a jury."[114] Often other gardaí may be required to speak as witnesses and difficulties can arise in terms of gardaí testifying against each other, as evidenced by the Morris Tribunal.[115] [5–34]

Alternative Legal Actions

A number of other legal mechanisms can be used to hold gardaí to account. Civil actions took a more prominent role over the last decade due to a perceived weakness in the Complaints Board and a growing litigiousness in Irish society generally. A garda can be sued where harm can be proven to have resulted from the unlawful act or omission of a garda.[116] Mostly commonly this will involve actions for trespass (including assault, unlawful detention or unlawful entry, search and seizure), negligence, defamation, or breach of constitutional rights, as developed in the case of *Byrne v Ireland.*[117] The lower burden of proof which applies in civil cases can be more appealing but finance can be an obstacle as unsuccessful complainants may have costs awarded against them. Legal aid is available for those who satisfy a means test and the case must be one which the Legal Aid Board is satisfied has a reasonable chance of being successful. The Garda Commissioner or the State can be sued[118] under the doctrine of vicarious liability, which was established for police officers in the case of *Fisher v Oldham Coporation.*[119] A civil action is a weak form of accountability for as Walsh notes: [5–35]

> "Its capacity to function as a catalyst for improved police practices for the benefit of all will be retarded by the law and practice governing the identity of the defendant and the source of the funds needed to meet awards."[120]

---

[112] Garda Síochána (Complaints) Act 1986, s 7(1).
[113] Walsh, above n 7, pp 351-352.
[114] "Juries Very Reluctant When Gardaí on Trial" *Irish Examiner*, 25 August 2006.
[115] At the Tribunal, one officer infamously stated 'You don't hang your own'. The solidarity between officers often leads to an unwillingness to disclose the wrongdoing of colleagues. Conway, above n 9.
[116] McMahon and Binchy, *The Irish Law of Torts* (Butterworths, Dublin, 2000).
[117] [1972] IR 241.
[118] See *Byrne v Ireland* [1972] IR 241. This is now specifically provided for under the Garda Síochána Act 2005, s 48.
[119] [1930] 2 KB 364.
[120] Walsh, above n 7, p 336.

[5–36] The defendant will be the State or the Attorney General acting in his capacity as legal representative of the State, neither of whom can have any impact on garda practice or policy. Equally the payment of damages does not come from the garda budget. Further, it is not desirable for the policing of the state to have citizens resorting to suing gardaí. Nonetheless over €32 million has been paid out in cases against gardaí between 2003 and 2009.[121]

[5–37] Judicial review can be used to challenge policy decisions as to how to enforce certain pieces of legislation[122] or the legality of decisions made by a garda in the exercise of his duties. Remedies under judicial review can include a declaration that the decision or action taken was unlawful, an order quashing the decision, an order to cease the unlawful action, an order to adopt some other course of action or the potential to combine these and order damages. Courts in this jurisdiction have declared themselves willing to review the use of discretionary powers but they have expressed an unwillingness to interfere with internal garda decisions.[123]

[5–38] In cases where it is alleged that the actions of gardaí have resulted in the death of a citizen the Coroner's Court may have a role to play, as it determines the cause of death in any instance where the death appears to be from unnatural causes.[124] While this is traditionally focused on the medical cause of death there is an understanding that it often provides much more information. On a number of occasions the Coroner's Court has been pivotal in the investigation of cases in which families, who allege garda involvement in the death, were dissatisfied with internal inquiries.[125]

IV. Other Means of Accountability

[5–39] Democratic accountability, whereby citizens can question police, was traditionally achieved in Ireland through the Minister for Justice answering questions on policing in the State to both the Dáil and the Seanad.[126] As Walsh's study reveals this was a weak system as the Minister had control of finances, internal regulations, the appointment and removal of senior officers, but not the day to day operation of the force.[127] Walsh's survey of questioning in the Dáil on policing matters from 1985–87 revealed that a substantial proportion related to operational matters, in relation to which the Minister will only be able to relay what the Commissioner tells him.[128] The Minister will invariably not have any further information to supply in supplementary questions. Additionally the Minister can refuse to answer certain questions on the grounds of

---

121 Figures available at www.justice.ie. Accessed on 10 May 2010.

122 Dixon and Smith, "Laying Down the Law: the Police, the Courts and Legal Accountability" (1998) 26 *International Journal of the Sociology of Law* 419.

123 *Garda Representative Association v Ireland* [1994] ILRM 81; *Aughey v Ireland* [1986] ILRM 206; *Stroker v Doherty* [1991] IR 21.

124 Farrell, *Coroners: Practice and Procedure* (Round Hall, Dublin, 2000).

125 As per the Coroner's decisions in the cases of Terrence Wheelock and in the case of the killing of two raiders of a post office in Lusk Co. Dublin in 2005.

126 Walsh, above n 7, and Connolly "Do we need Patten-type Reforms in the Republic?" (2000) *James Connolly Education Trust*. Available at http://www.iol.ie/~sob/jcet/2000-10-24-jc.html. Accessed 19 May 2010.

127 Walsh, above n 7, p 376.

128 *ibid.*

national security or the complexity of the matter. Overall Walsh found that the Minister tended to be highly defensive of the gardaí and that their role "could be interpreted as being designed to protect the Garda against the full rigours of democratic accountability."[129]

The 2005 Act introduced Joint Policing Committees (JPCs), which are to be established by local authorities with the Garda Commissioner.[130] JPCs are a forum for consultation, discussion and recommendations on policing matters affecting the local authority's administrative area. They are to: [5–40]

- consider levels and patterns of crime and anti social behaviour and contributing factors;
- advise the local authority and the Gardaí on how best to perform its functions;
- arrange public meetings on these matters; and
- establish, as necessary, local policing fora for discussion of such matters.[131]

Guidelines set out details such as composition of the Committees and their meetings. Still in the pilot phase, JPCs have been established in 29 of the 114 local authority areas. A review is being held in 2010, but it is expected that JPCs will be introduced to every local authority area subsequently. Each JPC must hold at least one public meeting a year, though it is difficult to imagine that one meeting a year can lead to real and effective consultation between the community and the police. The Northern Irish counterpart, the District Policing Partnership Boards, meet six times a year,[132] which seems a viable way of forming solid communication and relationships between those involved. [5–41]

V. Conclusion

As can be seen a variety of mechanisms exist for holding the gardaí to account for their use of powers. Some of these are internal to the force, some are through independent bodies while the courts also have a key role to play in the prosecution of gardaí. The accountability mechanisms in Ireland have been vastly reformed in recent years, yet problems remain in their operation. It still is the case that all proceedings, bar criminal, can be avoided through retirement or resignation. Securing convictions of gardaí proves difficult in Ireland. Ultimately the complaints system has not attained the level of independence which is desirable and may, in fact, be in contravention of the ECHR. [5–42]

---

[129] *ibid.* p 402.

[130] Garda Síochána Act 2005, s 35.

[131] *ibid.*

[132] Northern Ireland Police Board, *Code of Practice on Functions and Responsibilities of District Policing Partnerships* (January 2006).

CHAPTER 6
Prosecutions

The decision to prosecute an individual involves an assessment of the evidence to determine whether it merits the commitment of resources, the trial of the individual and the raising of hopes for a victim. The importance of this decision cannot be underestimated given the potential impact for the accused and the victim, not to mention society as a whole. As the Director of Public Prosecutions (DPP) stated in his Annual Report of 1998: **[6–01]**

> "Many observers regard it as by far the most important stage in the criminal process, involving as it does serious and far reaching consequences for those affected by it… [I]t is essential that every effort humanly possible be made to get this decision right… In all cases, irrespective of gravity or otherwise, the

greatest care must be taken to ensure that all who should be prosecuted are prosecuted and that those who should not be prosecuted are not."[1]

[6–02] As well as examining the basis for the decision to prosecute, this chapter will be concerned with who can take a prosecution. The impact of delay and the thorny question of whether the DPP should publish reasons for non-prosecution will also be discussed. Finally, the chapter will look at the initial hearings which occur prior to the trial, including the bail hearing.

I. Who Can Prosecute?

[6–03] Historically the decision to prosecute was often taken by the victim but during the 18th century, as structured police forces emerged, the offices of the DPP in the United Kingdom and the Attorney General (AG) in Ireland were created. The DPP is now responsible for most prosecutions in Ireland, though the AG, An Garda Síochána, some statutory agencies and citizens retain a right to prosecute in various circumstances.

Attorney General

[6–04] Article 30.1 of the Constitution outlines the function of the AG as "the adviser of the Government in matters of law and legal opinion". Article 30.3 states that all prosecutions shall be prosecuted on behalf of the people by the AG or some other authorised person. The Criminal Justice (Administration) Act 1924 specifically stated that charges on indictment were to be prosecuted by the AG, removing the powers of others to do so, while he *could* prosecute for summary offences.[2] The powers of the AG to prosecute were transferred to the DPP in 1974 though the AG retains prosecutorial functions in relation to offences of sea pollution and fisheries, which may have a political element.[3] Certain offences require his consent before prosecutions can proceed.[4] The Government can transfer certain prosecutorial powers back to the AG, for a limited time in relation to particular offences (rather than individual cases),[5] where it feels it is "expedient in the interests of national security."[6] This has not been done to date.

Director of Public Prosecutions

[6–05] The Prosecution of Offences Act 1974 created the office of the DPP, in part to reduce the demands made on the AG, whose role had become more demanding since Ireland joined the European Economic Community (EEC) in 1972, but also for independence from Government in the prosecution of offences. Unlike the AG who is a political

---

[1] Office of the Director of Public Prosecutions, *Annual Report 1998* (Dublin, 1998), p 14.

[2] s 9(2) specifically states that save where a prosecution is taken by the Minister for Justice, the Department or a person authorised by law all summary prosecutions shall be taken by the AG (now the DPP). In *AG v Healy* [1928] IR 460 the court stated that the AG could prosecute for summary cases where others authorised had not done so.

[3] This is stated in the Prosecution of Offences Act 1974, s 3(5) and concerns offences relating to official secrets, under the Official Secrets Act 1963, and acts of genocide, under the Geneva Convention 1962 and the Genocide Act 1973.

[4] Dumping at Sea Act 1996, Sea Pollution Act 1991 and the Fisheries (Amendment) Act 1978.

[5] As above n 3.

[6] Prosecution of Offences Act 1974, s 5(1).

appointee, the DPP is a civil servant, "independent in the performance of his functions."[7] Neither Government nor the AG can question him on the exercise of the office's functions, which the DPP has stated is essential to safeguard citizens against unjust or improperly motivated prosecutions.[8] The DPP is appointed by Government and can be removed on grounds of health or conduct following the report of a committee set up under the 1974 Act.[9] To be appointed, a person must be a barrister or solicitor of 10 years standing. Within the Office is a Chief Prosecution Solicitor, who heads the Solicitors' division of the Office, which provides the solicitor service for the Dublin area. Outside of Dublin there are 32 local State Solicitors who perform this function on a contract basis in conjunction with their private practices.

Communication with the DPP, his agent, a garda or a solicitor acting on behalf of the DPP in an official capacity, in relation to decisions to prosecute or related decisions, is unlawful.[10] Excluded from this are defendants, complainants, or communications from those acting as a medical or legal advisor, social worker or family members.[11] A politician cannot engage in any discussions with the DPP about the prosecution of a case which affects a constituent, either as defendant or victim. This issue arose as recently as 2010 when a government minister was forced to resign following the revelation that he had contacted the gardaí in relation to a prosecution.[12]

No mechanism exists to hold the DPP to account for the exercise of his powers, whereas independent bodies have been tasked with this function in other countries.[13] In England, for instance, an Inspectorate exists to examine the work of the Crown Prosecution Service.[14]

Section 3 of the 1974 Act states that the Office of the DPP must perform those functions in relation to criminal matters which were held by the AG prior to the commencement of the Act. The DPP thereby assumes the criminal prosecution functions and all related powers of the AG. The DPP is responsible for prosecutions in cases on indictment and is authorised to prosecute in summary cases. The work of the Office includes: **[6–06]**

- considering files received from gardaí;
- deciding on initiating prosecutions;
- determining if further investigation is needed;

---

[7] *ibid.* s 2(5).

[8] Office of the Director of Public Prosecutions, *Annual Report 2008* (Dublin, 2009), p 61.

[9] Comprised of the Chief Justice, a judge of the High Court and the Attorney General, s 2(9).

[10] s 6.

[11] s 6(2)(a).

[12] In February 2010 Trevor Sargent, Minister of State for Food and Horticulture, contacted gardaí on behalf of a constituent who was a victim in an assault case and dissatisfied with the slow progress. "Sargent Resigns Ministry over 'Error of Judgment'" *The Irish Times*, 23 February 2010.

[13] For a detailed analysis see Jackson, Langers, and Tillers, *Crime Evidence and Procedure in a Comparative and International Context* (Hart Publishing, Oxford, 2008).

[14] The stated purpose of Her Majesty's Inspectorate for the CPS is "to enhance the quality of justice through independent inspection and assessment of prosecution services, and in so doing improve their effectiveness and efficiency." Stated on website www.hmcpsi.gov.uk.

- determining charges to be preferred;
- considering charges preferred by gardaí;
- presenting indictable prosecutions in Dublin;
- deciding whether to transfer non-scheduled offences to the Special Criminal Court;
- instructing counsel on the conduct of the case;
- deciding whether to bring or contest appeals;
- bringing and defending judicial review, bail and habeas corpus proceedings;
- appealing against unduly lenient sentences;
- dealing with applications for extradition and international mutual assistance in criminal matters; and
- working with other agencies involved in criminal justice.[15]

The Common Informer

[6–07] The common informer is a technical term given in common law to someone who can provide information about the commission of an offence, usually the victim, a witness, or someone else who has been given reliable information about the offence, invariably a garda. The Supreme Court confirmed in *People (DPP) v Roddy*[16] that gardaí prosecuted in this role, as informer, though this has now been discontinued by the Garda Síochána Act 2005, discussed below. The Criminal Justice (Administration) Act 1924 limited the right of prosecuting trials on indictment to the AG (now the DPP), meaning that common informers now only have powers to prosecute in summary trials.[17] The Supreme Court ruled in *State (DPP) v District Justice Ruane*[18] that the DPP cannot intervene in a prosecution taken by a garda as common informer.

Gardaí

[6–08] In addition to powers to prosecute as common informers, in 1975 the DPP granted gardaí the power to institute proceedings in the District Court in his name. The Garda Síochána Act 2005 regulated this further to state that a garda can prosecute a summary case but in the name of the DPP.[19] The DPP may also issue directions for gardaí conducting prosecutions which can include preventing the gardaí from prosecuting certain offences. The DPP can assume control of the case at any point. Gardaí, therefore, no longer have independent powers of prosecution.[20]

When it comes to indictable offences gardaí must send a file to the DPP who takes the decision on whether or not to prosecute, and on what charges should be brought. Often the individual will have been charged before that happens but the advice of the DPP as to the charges should be sought before it goes to trial to ensure the charges are appropriate.

---

[15] For a detailed list see Office of the Director of Public Prosecutions, *Annual Report 2007* (Dublin, 2008), p 5.
[16] [1977] IR 177.
[17] *Wedick v Osmond* [1935] IR 820.
[18] [1985] ILRM 349.
[19] s 6.
[20] As specifically stated in the Explanatory Memorandum of the Garda Síochána Act 2005.

Other Prosecutors

Certain statutory bodies and government bodies are on occasion given powers to take prosecutions, often where they are obliged to enforce certain statutory schemes. Government Ministers are often given prosecutorial powers for summary cases in relation to offences under a particular Act relevant to their Department. For instance, s 272 of the Social Welfare (Consolidation) Act 2005 provides that proceedings for a relevant offence will only be instituted by or with the consent of the Minister for Social Welfare or an officer authorised by the Minister. **[6–09]**

II. Decision to Prosecute

A decision to prosecute could be taken in every case where a criminal complaint is made, though this is neither practically feasible nor desirable. The criminal justice system would collapse under the weight of prosecutions and resources could be wasted on cases with little chance of a conviction. There is discretion as regards this decision. When and how that is used are difficult questions. There is a need for consistency as both victims and offenders are entitled to know when it is likely that a prosecution will occur. The DPP has issued guidelines on how the decision to prosecute should be taken for anyone so tasked,[21] which should ensure some uniformity and consistency in the Irish system. **[6–10]**

The DPP has indicated that there are two stages to this decision in Ireland.[22] First, it should be ascertained if there is enough evidence to support a prima facie case of guilt for a criminal offence. This will require sufficient evidence of an admissible nature which *could* satisfy a jury beyond all reasonable doubt that the accused is guilty. The second stage is to determine whether the evidence on which the case is based is credible and reliable, which is difficult at this point given that it is unknown who is on the jury or how the evidence will be tested during the trial. A number of questions may be asked to assist in determining this issue[23]: do any of the witnesses appear to be exaggerating? Are any witnesses hostile or inconsistent? Do they have motives for telling untruths? Is there some other factor that could affect the reliability of any evidence, particularly with regard to confessions? The strength of any potential defences must also be borne in mind. Every case must be decided on its own basis. At no time is the prosecutor deciding on the guilt of the accused, only whether there is enough evidence to satisfy a jury that the accused is guilty. **[6–11]**

In exercising their discretion prosecutors should bear in mind their duty to act honestly, fairly, impartially, objectively, with respect for human rights, to uphold the rule of law, the integrity of the criminal justice system, the right to a fair trial and to remain unaffected by individual or sectional interests, having regard only to the public interest.[24] **[6–12]**

There are three sets of factors which must be considered in reaching the decision: aggravating, mitigating and public interest. Aggravating factors which will increase the likelihood of a prosecution include: the severity of the penalty attaching to the offence, **[6–13]**

---

21 See Office of the Director of Public Prosecutions, *Guidelines for Prosecutors* (Dublin, 2007).

22 See Office of the Director of Public Prosecutions, *Annual Report 1998* (Dublin, 1999), p 14.

23 Above n 21, pp 11-13.

24 Above n 21, p 12.

whether the accused was in a position of trust which was abused, whether he was the ringleader, whether the offence was premeditated, was carried out by a group, involved organised crime or corruption, whether the victim was vulnerable or advantage was taken of difference in actual or mental ages between the accused and the victim, whether previous convictions were relevant to this offence, whether the offence was committed while on bail, probation, suspended sentence, bond of good behaviour etc, and if the offence is likely to be continued or repeated.[25]

[6–14] Mitigating factors which will decrease the likelihood of a prosecution are if the prosecution would result in a small penalty, the loss or harm caused was minor, and if it was a first offence, not serious, and unlikely to be repeated.[26]

[6–15] Public interest factors which must be considered include the age and health of the offender, the possibility of alternatives to prosecution, the need for deterrence from the particular offence, the attitude of the victim or the victim's family, the impact of a decision not to prosecute on the victim, whether the accused has shown genuine remorse, whether the consequences would be disproportionately harsh or if the length and expense of a trial would be disproportionate to the seriousness of the offence and whether it would make a difference if the accused is already being punished.[27]

If, at the end of all of this, the DPP decides to issue a direction to prosecute he will specify the charges. At this point the DPP must believe that the necessary evidence is in his possession or will be for the trial.

Reasons

[6–16] Until 2009 the DPP operated a policy that the reasons for decisions not to prosecute would not be made public in the interest of natural justice due to all parties affected. The reason might be a procedural one and to publicise that might have the result of appearing to declare guilt. The DPP will, however, inform the State Solicitors and the Gardaí of investigatory and procedural reasons for non-prosecution. This position received the support of the Irish courts in *H v DPP*[28] where the Supreme Court ruled that the DPP was under no obligation to give reasons in any case, because if the DPP gave reasons in one he would have to give reasons in all. In *Dunphy v DPP*,[29] the Supreme Court discussed the special protection which the DPP attracts with regard to this decision and stated "his entitlement to that protection is beyond argument."[30] This special protection was discussed further in *Cunningham v DPP*[31] where the applicant sought a motion of discovery against the DPP to assist in judicial review proceedings against the DPP. The Supreme Court found that while she was entitled to this relief, and that the DPP could claim privilege over any document but was required to list every document, "this finding in no way removes, reduces or limits the special position of the Director of Public Prosecutions in relation to giving reasons for his decisions to

[25] *ibid.* p 19.
[26] *ibid.* p 20.
[27] *ibid.*
[28] [1994] 2 IR 589.
[29] [2006] 1 ILRM 241.
[30] *ibid.* at 256.
[31] [2006] 3 IR 541.

prosecute or not to do so."[32] In *Deeley v Information Commissioner*,[33] it was judicially confirmed that the Freedom of Information Act does not apply to the DPP.

However, in 2008 the DPP launched a programme to investigate the possibility of giving reasons for decisions. Following a consultation process he announced that a pilot scheme would be launched whereby reasons would be given in certain cases to certain affected persons, "where it is possible to do so without creating an injustice."[34] The relevant cases are murder, manslaughter, infanticide, fatalities in the workplace and fatal road traffic accidents. Reasons will only be given to parties "closely connected to the deceased" such as members of their family or household, legal or medical advisors or social workers acting on their behalf.[35] The DPP indicated in June 2010 his intention to extend this programme to include sexual offence cases. Reasons will not be given where injustice may be caused, such as where giving reasons would: **[6–17]**

- expose potential witnesses to injustice, e.g. by taking their good names;
- reveal the identity of confidential sources or methods of law enforcement;
- have an adverse affect on law enforcement.[36]

The reasons will be provided in writing on request of the party and "should where possible be sufficiently detailed to enable the interested party to understand why the decision was taken."[37] This does not affect the process of requesting the DPP to review the prosecutorial decision. **[6–18]**

The Decision to Prosecute and Fair Procedures

The above process has been outlined by the DPP must through the guidelines he has issued. However, a number of decisions from the court have clearly signalled that in addition to the above the DPP must also abide by the constitutional principle of fair procedures in making decisions to prosecute. This has arisen through challenges to the decision to or not to prosecute. **[6–19]**

There is no formal right of appeal where an interested party is dissatisfied with the decision of the DPP and in *State (McCormack) v Curran*[38] the Supreme Court indicated that judicial review would only be allowed in some circumstances such as where the decision was reached by "mala fides or influenced by an improper motive or improper policy."[39] To these grounds Denham J has added where the "decision was perverse, or inspired by improper motives, or that he had abdicated his functions."[40] Perversity would appear to widen the window of review, as it implies that a decision which seems out of alignment and character with the facts could be reviewed. **[6–20]**

---

[32] *ibid.* at 547.
[33] [2001] IEHC 91.
[34] See Office of the Director of Public Prosecutions, *Policy on the Giving of Reasons for Decisions not to Prosecute*, para 3.
[35] *ibid.* para 2.
[36] *ibid.* para 3.
[37] *ibid.* para 4.
[38] [1987] ILRM 225.
[39] *ibid.* at 230.
[40] *H v DPP* [1994] 2 ILRM 285 at 293.

[6–21] The Office of the DPP also operates an internal review procedure whereby an interested party can request an internal review of any decision not to prosecute.[41] This process has been the source of some litigation, primarily where the DPP reverses a decision not to prosecute where the accused had not been advised that such a review was possible. This arose in *Eviston v DPP*[42] and the accused challenged the subsequent prosecution. Kearns J in the High Court held that without new evidence to justify a reversal the DPP's decision was "arbitrary and perverse." The Supreme Court upheld this decision. Keane CJ stated that

> "the DPP is not exempt in the performance of his statutory functions from the general constitutional requirements of fairness and fair procedures... his decision is, as a matter of law, prima facie reviewable on the ground that there has been a breach of fair procedures."[43]

[6–22] Stressing that the DPP is permitted to review and alter a previous decision and is not "obliged... to give reasons for his decision", Keane CJ found that in this case the reversal was a breach of the constitutional right to fair procedures given that the DPP had told the applicant she would not be prosecuted "and had not given her the slightest intimation that this was a decision which could be subjected to review."[44] The fact that the procedure was well documented in DPP guidelines was irrelevant; it was not part of the law of the land which all citizens are assumed to know. This decision was reaffirmed in *Q(M) v DPP*[45] where the initial decision not to prosecute was reversed five years after it had been communicated to the defendant with no caveat of review. The applicant had spent over four years believing he would not be prosecuted, without being advised that a review was possible, which when added to the "stress, anxiety and concern suffered" led to an "almost inevitable" conclusion that there had been a breach of fair procedures.[46]

[6–23] The case of *Hobson v DPP*[47] suggested that where new evidence came to light this was a different matter, and further, Peart J in the High Court suggested that since the decision in *Eviston* it had become public knowledge that a review could occur and so:

> "the applicant cannot successfully complain that the respondent failed to indicate when he made his first decision that he was entitled to review and alter that decision."[48]

[6–24] In *LO'N v DPP*,[49] this factor was not mentioned and the jurisprudence of *Eviston* and *Q(M)* was reasserted with mention of the length of time which had passed before the

---

41 Above n 21, Chapter 12.
42 [2002] 3 IR 260.
43 *ibid.* at 279, interpreting and applying the decision in *State (O'Callaghan) v O'hUadhaigh* [1977] IR 42.
44 *ibid.* at 299.
45 [2003] IEHC 88.
46 *ibid.* at para 96.
47 [2006] 4 IR 239.
48 *ibid.* at 250.
49 [2006] IEHC 184.

review (13 years in this case) and the levels of stress and anxiety caused, which were evidenced in this case by an attempted suicide. The prosecution was stayed by the court on the grounds of "the want of fair procedures on the part of the respondent in reversing his decision not to prosecute."

However, in *M v DPP*,[50] the most recent case on this issue, McCarthy J in the High Court reasserted the reasoning in *Hobson* and held that the position in *Eviston*, where the applicant could not have been expected to know that a review was possible, had now changed: **[6–25]**

> "*Eviston* itself articulates a legal rule that a review is possible... I am of the view that the applicant must be deemed to be aware of the fact of the potential for review."

While some uncertainty still surrounds the legal status of the internal review procedure, it is clear that the DPP is required to apply fair procedures in exercising his review powers. **[6–26]**

III. Delay

The matter of delay has become a central factor in the decision to prosecute over the last decade, in particular given the number of cases involving child sexual abuse prosecuted at a later date which have come before the courts. In *McFarlane v DPP*[51] Hardiman J described delay as "the enemy of justice." Article 38.1 of the Constitution provides a right to trial in due course of law. This has been interpreted to provide a right to a fair trial and a speedy trial. In *PC v DPP* Keane J referred to the right to "a reasonably expeditious trial."[52] Article 6 ECHR also guarantees a right to trial within reasonable time.[53] **[6–27]**

The US case of *Barker v Wingo*[54] has been very influential, where three particular interests were deemed to be protected by the right to an expeditious trial: prevention of oppressive pre-trial imprisonment, minimising anxiety and concern to the accused and the limitation of the possibility that the defence will be impaired.[55] The Irish courts have repeatedly stated that the right to have a fair trial in good time takes precedence over the public need to prosecute.[56] Specific concerns as to how delay can interfere with the right to a fair trial which have been identified by the courts include the "fade factor"[57] whereby over time memories of victims and witnesses fade (if witnesses have not died), gathering and testing evidence becomes more difficult (if it has not been lost or destroyed) and the accused may have serious problems remembering the period **[6–28]**

---

[50] [2008] IESC 451.
[51] [2008] 4 IR 117.
[52] [1999] 2 IR 25.
[53] *Yagic v Turkey*, 8 June 1995.
[54] 407 US 514 (1972).
[55] Should an accused opt to remain in prison while awaiting trial this does not bring these interests into play: *JT v DPP* [2008] 1 IR 701.
[56] See *P O'C v DPP* [2000] 3 IR 87; *D v DPP* [1994] 2 IR 465; *Z v DPP* [1994] 2 IR 476; and *JL v DPP* [2000] 3 IR 122.
[57] See *J O'C v DPP* [2000] 3 IR 480.

under examination. Problems which arise in relation to personal rights in ordinary criminal cases are heightened by the passage or elongation of time, including stress,[58] press coverage, stigmatisation, negative consequences for privacy and family life, implications for work as well as legal costs incurred.

[6–29] That said the courts will be very slow to interfere with the DPP's decision to prosecute. In *DC v DPP*[59] the court stressed that applications for prohibition of a trial being sought as a relief for delay

> "may only succeed in exceptional circumstances. The Constitution and the State through legislation have given to the DPP an independent role in determining whether or not a prosecution should be brought on behalf of the people of Ireland. The Director having taken such a decision the courts are slow to intervene... In general such a step is not necessary as the trial judge maintains at all times the duty to ensure due process and a fair trial... The test for this court is whether there is a real risk that by reason of the particular circumstances the applicant could not obtain a fair trial."[60]

[6–30] Successive judgments have emphasised the ability of the trial judge to counter prejudice. In this context Finlay CJ in the Supreme Court in *Z v DPP* stressed that

> "where one speaks of an onus to establish a real risk of an unfair trial it necessarily and inevitably means an unfair trial which cannot be avoided by appropriate rulings and directions on the part of the trial judge. The risk is a real one but the unfairness of trial must be an unavoidable unfairness of trial."[61]

The burden of proving the "unavoidable unfairness" is on the accused[62] and the standard applied is a very high one. Delay can be caused by the State or by the complainant, and these different causes have been treated differently by the courts.

Delay by the State

[6–31] Delay by the State can be caused by gardaí, the DPP, the Courts Service or the judiciary and can involve acts or omissions in the investigation or prosecution of the crime. The courts are highly critical of delay by the State, given the failure to uphold the constitutional rights of the individual. In *DPP v Arthurs*[63] the High Court noted the duty which "rests upon the State... to ensure that all reasonable steps are taken to ensure such a speedy trial is provided."[64]

[6–32] Acknowledging that certain delays may be inevitable in the system, to prohibit a trial the courts will seek to establish 'blameworthy delay' and that the accused "has suffered

58 *PM v District Judge Malone* [2002] 2 IR 560.
59 [2005] 4 IR 281.
60 *ibid.* at 293.
61 [1994] 2 IR 476 at 507.
62 *Connolly v DPP* [2009] IEHC 526.
63 [2000] 2 ILRM 363.
64 *ibid.* at 372.

or is in real danger of suffering some form of prejudice as a consequence of this delay."[65] The court will then enter into a balancing exercise between the rights of the accused and the public interest in securing convictions of those who have committed offences.[66] In *PM v DPP*[67] the Supreme Court stated that an applicant would need to establish that the delay outweighed the public interest in prosecuting serious crimes; establishing blameworthy delay would not itself be sufficient but it would "trigger" an application of the balancing test.[68] Kearns J held that "one or more of the interests protected by the right to expeditious trial must also be shown to have been so interfered with such as would entitle the applicant to relief".[69]

In terms of what constitutes blameworthy delay a number of points can be made. The longer the delay the greater the possibility of it being interpreted as unreasonable and in breach of the accused's rights. In *DPP v Byrne*[70] the Supreme Court emphasised that excessive delay would be determined on the circumstances of each case, but factors like the nature of the offence, the reason for the delay and the impact for the accused would be relevant. Blameworthy delay may arise where gardaí failed to exercise reasonable diligence in the investigation of the offence. In *Cormack v DPP*[71] the Supreme Court held that the "law unambiguously requires Gardaí to execute bench warrants without delay and within a reasonable time frame." Resource constraints do not provide discretion in this area, though where garda efforts were hampered by the accused this will not be blameworthy.[72] **[6–33]**

The obligation placed on the State is high and it will not be a defence to claim overcrowding in the courts as the State should provide sufficient resources to enable the rights of the accused to be protected. Where there is delay in a case coming to the attention of the authorities, they "are under a special obligation to expedite any subsequent investigation and prosecution."[73] This obligation is heightened where the accused is a young person as *per* Geoghegan J in *BF v DPP*,[74] where he described it as "a special duty on the State authorities over and above the normal duty of expedition to ensure a speedy trial."[75] **[6–34]**

---

65 See *PM v DPP* [2006] 2 ILRM 361; *Mc Kenna v Presiding Judge of the Dublin Circuit Criminal Court* unreported, High Court, 14 January 2000; *McNamara v MacGruairc* unreported, Supreme Court, 5 July 2001; and *PM v Malone* [2002] 2 IR 560. In *PP v DPP* [2000] 1 IR 403 and *BF v DPP* [2001] 1 IR 656 the mere existence of blameworthy delay was deemed to merit prohibition of the trial in and of itself.

66 *PM v Malone* [2002] 2 IR 560.

67 [2006] IESC 22.

68 See further on this point, *McFarlane v DPP* [2008] IESC 7 and *JT v DPP* [2008] IESC 20.

69 [2006] 2 ILRM 361 at 374.

70 [1994] 2 IR 236.

71 [2008] IESC 63.

72 *Conway v DPP* [2007] IEHC 434. See also *McDonagh v DPP* [2009] IEHC 7.

73 *PM v DPP* [2006] 2 ILRM 361.

74 [2001] 1 IR 656.

75 *ibid.* at 666. For a discussion of the particular vulnerabilities of young people and the need for a speedy trial see the judgment of Quirke J in *Walsh v DPP* [2004] IEHC 380.

[6–35] In *McFarlane v DPP*,[76] the Supreme Court summarised the following principles which have emerged through Irish jurisprudence on prosecutorial delay:

a. Inordinate, blameworthy or unexplained prosecutorial delay may breach an applicant's constitutional entitlement to a trial with reasonable expedition.
b. Prosecutorial delay may be of such a degree that a court will presume prejudice and uphold the right to an expeditious trial by directing prohibition.
c. Where a period of significant (as opposed to minor) blameworthy prosecutorial delay less than that envisaged at (b) is demonstrated, the court will engage in a balancing exercise between the community's entitlement to see crime prosecuted and the applicant's right to an expeditious trial, but will not direct prohibition unless one or more of the elements referred to in *PM v Malone*[77] and *PM v DPP*[78] are demonstrated.[79]
d. Actual prejudice caused by delay which is such as to preclude a fair trial will always entitle an applicant to prohibition.

[6–36] The court also noted that a state has an obligation under Art 6 ECHR "to organise its legal system so as to allow its courts to comply with the reasonable time requirement."[80] The Supreme Court referred to the ECtHR case of *Barry v Ireland*[81] where it was stated that

> "the reasonableness of the length of the proceedings must be assessed in the light of the circumstances of the case and with reference to the following criteria: the complexity of the case, the conduct of the applicant and the relevant authorities…"[82]

That said, the court was swayed by the argument that these findings in the ECtHR did not mean that a prosecution must be stopped once a breach has been found, as this will not be the impact of such a finding at the ECtHR which will instead award monetary damages.

Delay by the Complainant

[6–37] Summary offences require the complaint to be lodged within six months of the commission of the offence but indictable offences have no such time limit, giving rise to the potential for lengthy periods of delay before a complaint is made. The courts have been willing to find that excessive complainant delay may result in the prohibition of the case given the impact on the accused's right to a fair trial. What constitutes excessive delay will depend on the circumstances of the case. In *P O'C v DPP*[83] a delay

---

76 [2008] 4 IR 117.
77 [2002] 2 IR 560.
78 [2006] 3 IR 172.
79 These being the three factors outlined in *Wingo v Barker* 407 US 514 (1972) of prevention of oppressive pre-trial imprisonment, minimising anxiety and concern to the accused and the limitation of the possibility that the defence will be impaired.
80 [2006] 3 IR 172 at 176.
81 [2005] ECHR 865.
82 *ibid.* at 872.
83 [2000] 3 IR 87.

of 13 years was described as 'inordinate and inexcusable' while in *B v DPP*[84] a delay of nearly 30 years did not prohibit the trial.

For many years the courts believed the first task was to conduct an examination of why the delay occurred and, particularly through child sexual abuse cases which were deemed to form a special category,[85] a number of acceptable grounds for delay were established, including dominion,[86] inhibitions of the complainant,[87] and repressed memories. In 2006 however, the Supreme Court issued the seminal judgment of *H v DPP*[88] where it came to the conclusion that it was, in fact, no longer necessary for courts to consider the reasons for the delay: **[6–38]**

> "At issue in each case is the constitutional right to a fair trial. The Court has found that in reality *the core inquiry is not so much the reason for a delay in making a complaint by a complainant but rather whether the accused will receive a fair trial or whether there is a real or serious risk of an unfair trial.* In practice this has invariably been the essential and ultimate question for the Court. In other words it is the consequences of delay rather than delay itself which has concerned the Court.
> ... In all events, having regard to the Court's knowledge and insight into these cases it considers that *there is no longer a necessity to inquire into the reason for a delay in making a complaint...*" (emphasis added)

The sole question for the court in cases where there has been a delay in a complainant coming forward is whether or not the accused can receive a fair trial in light of that delay. The test to be applied, according to Supreme Court in *H* is **[6–39]**

> "whether there is a real or serious risk that the applicant, by reason of the delay, would not obtain a fair trial, or that a trial would be unfair as a consequence of the delay. The Court does not exclude wholly exceptional circumstances where it would be unfair or unjust to put the accused on trial. The test is to be applied in light of the circumstances of the case."[89]

This provides for two arguments: the delay means the applicant would not obtain a fair trial for evidential or other such reason; or proceeding with a trial, given the delay, would in itself be unfair. Indeed, this test is now applied in circumstances of either complainant or state delay. In *AC (a minor) v DPP*[90] the State was found to have breached its special duty following an eight month delay in proceedings and, while no direct prejudice was found to have resulted from that delay, applying the test of *H*, the court was satisfied that this case fell within the wholly exceptional circumstances, as the young accused was clearly in exceptional levels of distress, culminating in serious **[6–40]**

[84] [1997] 3 IR 140.

[85] See *Hogan v President of the Circuit Court* [1994] 2 IR 513 where it was said that such cases "involve wholly different considerations". See also *B v DPP* [1997] 3 IR 140.

[86] See cases *PC v DPP* [1999] 2 IR 25 and *J O'C v DPP* [2000] 3 IR 478.

[87] *DD v DPP* [2008] IESC 47.

[88] [2006] IESC 55.

[89] [2006] IESC 55.

[90] [2008] 3 IR 398.

self-harming behaviour, as a result of the delay. In *PT v DPP*[91] even where the applicant had not satisfied the court that there was prosecutorial delay or that he had been prejudiced to the extent that there was a real or serious risk of an unfair trial, the court continued to the second test of whether it "would be unfair or unjust to put the applicant on trial." The applicant's age (87) and ill-health were balanced against the public interest and the independence of the DPP and the Court concluded that "a prosecution is not an exercise in vengeance. While a court should give careful regard to the position of victims, it must protect the integrity of the justice system as a whole."[92] In the case at hand the court felt that it would be unfair to proceed with the prosecution, given all the circumstances in the case.

[6–41] In *JM v DPP*[93] McCracken J outlined the omnibus test which can be applied in either scenario:

> "The real question which must be at the heart of all decisions of this nature is whether there is a serious possibility that the accused person will not be able to get a fair trial. In some cases that can be demonstrated very simply, for example, where a vital witness who would have been available had there been a speedy trial, has died or is no longer available for some other reason. There are other cases, such as the present one, which do not depend on a specific prejudice, but rather on a general overview of all the circumstances of the case which could affect the trial."

[6–42] The omnibus principle has been applied in numerous cases but the courts must still bear in mind the capacity of the trial judge to offset any prejudice through directions to the jury.[94] In *P O'C v DPP*[95] despite a 16 year delay and the death of numerous witnesses the Supreme Court ruled that the complainant had "failed to satisfy that there is a real or serious risk of an unfair trial such as cannot be avoided by appropriate rulings and directions on the part of the trial judge." In *JT v DPP*,[96] the alleged offences occurred over 35 years previously but the applicant was just 66 years old, and sufficient medical evidence had not been produced to substantiate claims of acute depression and anxiety. Claims of a poor memory were "vague and ambiguous". Rulings and warnings from the trial judge could mitigate concerns about witnesses who had passed away. [97]

[6–43] On the other hand, in *C v DPP*,[98] the court felt that the death of witnesses, who had lived in the house where the abuse was alleged to have occurred, could not be "ameliorated by appropriate warnings and directions of the trial judge." Hedigan J found that "the loss of evidence in my view has irretrievably damaged the ability of the

---

91 [2008] 1 IR 701.
92 *ibid.* at 715.
93 [2004] IESC 451.
94 See *DD v DPP* [2008] IESC 47.
95 Unreported, Supreme Court, 4 March 2008.
96 [2008] 1 IR 701.
97 See also *JC v DPP* [2009] IEHC 121.
98 [2009] IEHC 400.

applicant to defend himself and must therefore give rise to a real and serious risk of an unfair trial."

Whether a lack of specificity as to the timings of the alleged offences will mean that the accused cannot receive a fair trial will depend on the circumstances. In *DPP v O'Connor*[99] the court felt that it might be unfair to proceed with an allegation relating to one incident on an unspecified date but where, as it was in the case at hand, the allegations were of numerous rapes a week over a period of time it could not be claimed the lack of specificity made it unfair: "In these circumstances the defence is not prejudiced in the sense of being unable to seek out contemporaneous facts to support denial."[100] [6–44]

IV. Pre-Trial Court Jurisdiction

Once the decision to prosecute has been taken, criminal proceedings will be initiated in the courts. Most cases will begin in the District Court, where the accused will be brought either to be charged or soon after being charged. The case will not be ready to proceed at that point and a number of brief legal hearings may be held prior to the trial. A summary offence will be tried in the District Court, while indictable offences will be "sent forward" to another court. [6–45]

Initiating Proceedings in the District Court

There are different ways in which the District Court can become involved in a criminal case. It can be asked to issue either a summons or a warrant for an arrest, it can be asked to issue a summons through a different administrative process under the Courts Act 1986 or it may only be first called upon when the accused is actually charged with the offence. [6–46]

(i) Summons or Warrant

A summons is "a written command issued to a defendant for the purpose of getting him to attend court on a specified date to answer a specified complaint."[101] The summons procedure begins when a person with the authority, usually a garda who has witnessed the offence, makes a complaint that an offence has occurred to a judge of the District Court. This must usually be done within six months of the offence being committed if it is a summary offence,[102] though increasingly statutes afford 12 months for this.[103] There is no official time limit for indictable offences although some may have one specified in the statute. Usually the time limit will be absolute, though the District Court Rules may allow for an extension where the time limit was set by the Rules.[104] [6–47]

---

99 Unreported, Court of Criminal Appeal, 29 July 2002.

100 See further the cases of *McA v DPP*, unreported, High Court, 15 January 2004; *TG v DPP*, unreported, High Court, 10 December 2004; and *N v DPP*, unreported, High Court, 15 June 2005 where the time span of the alleged offences was much shorter than that in *O'Connor* and the courts refused to prohibit proceedings.

101 *DPP v Clein* [1983] ILRM 76 at 77 *per* Henchy J.

102 Petty Sessions (Ireland) Act 1851, s 10(4).

103 For example, the Equal Status Act 2000, s 44(4). See Walsh, *Criminal Procedure* (Round Hall, Dublin, 2002), p 641 for a detailed list.

104 District Court Rules 1997, Ord 12 r 1.

[6–48] A judge has a discretion whether or not to issue a summons and may decide that he does not have jurisdiction to issue it or that the complaint does not warrant it. The form of the summons is regulated by the Petty Sessions (Ireland) Act 1851. This states that the summons should include basic information as to the offence and must be signed by the judge.

[6–49] A summons is served on the person at whom it is directed, and this can be done anywhere in the state. It can be given to him in person, or left at his last known home or place of work.[105] This will usually be done by a garda. If it is a summary jurisdiction case then it can be served by registered post.[106] This must be done within 21 days of the summons being issued by the court.[107]

[6–50] Given the amount of challenges lodged on the basis of defects in the summons, the District Court Rules have issued an order seeking to limit the grounds for appeal on this basis.[108] Incorrect facts will not be fatal. Technical defects will not usually be fatal as the summons is mainly concerned with trying to get the accused to attend court, not proving guilt. Defects may give the accused reason not to attend at the appointed time but will not prevent the case from going ahead if he does attend. In *DPP v Clein*[109] an incorrect date for the original hearing did not prevent the case from going ahead. It seems that there needs to be some "gross violation" of the procedure before the District Court will refuse to proceed with a case once the defendant has appeared on the date specified in the summons. In *DPP v Bradley*[110] there had been an unlawful arrest and detention. This did not prevent the proceedings from going ahead once the accused attended at the time allocated in the summons. The view is that the concerns were matters which could be addressed during the course of the trial. They do not invalidate the summons. A judge also has a discretion to amend a summons if necessary where there has been some omission.[111] This discretion should be exercised properly to ensure that the right offence can be proceeded with.[112]

[6–51] Issuing a summons is quite a passive approach, and is dependent on the accused turning up. If the offence is more serious it may be appropriate to issue a warrant for arrest to allow for that person to be brought before the court as soon as practicable.[113] For a warrant to be issued evidence must be submitted on oath and in writing to the District Court judge charging the individual with the offence.[114] There are no restrictions on who can submit this information, but it usually will be done by a garda.

105 DCR, Ord 10, r 5.
106 DCR, Ord 10, r 13(2).
107 DCR, Ord 10, r 20.
108 DCR, Ord 38, rs 1(1) and (2).
109 [1983] ILRM 76.
110 Unreported, High Court, 9 December 1999.
111 DCR, Ord 12, r 2.
112 DCR, Ord 38, r 1(3).
113 Petty Sessions (Ireland) Act 1851, s 11(1).
114 DCR, Ord 16, r 1(1).

To issue the warrant the offence must have taken place within the judge's district or the accused must live in that district.[115] The judge again has discretion so he must decide if he is satisfied by the evidence that a warrant is justified. Even if a warrant has been applied for, a judge can decide to issue a summons and he probably should do this if of the belief it would be just as effective.[116] There are no time restrictions for indictable offences and the warrant can be issued at any time day or night. The form of the warrant is very similar to that of the summons and must be signed by the judge.[117] The warrant can also include an endorsement for bail, or a statement from the judge that once arrested the individual must be released on bail.[118] If such an endorsement is not included then the accused must be remanded and brought before a District Court judge as soon as practicable. There is no limitation to the warrant; it is effective until it has been utilised. **[6–52]**

(ii) Administrative Procedure

Until the case of *State (Clarke) v Roche*,[119] peace commissioners were permitted to issue a summons under the 1851 Act. In this case, however, the Supreme Court ruled that this was a judicial function, not an administrative one and as peace commissioners are not judges they cannot perform judicial actions. This equally applied to District Court clerks. It had become routine practice for staff of the clerk's office to process applications for summonses and the result of this decision was that this was no longer legal. The court also recommended that government amend the legislation for these to be considered administrative functions which could be performed by officers of the District Court. This was done through the Courts (No 3) Act 1986. **[6–53]**

Summonses can now be issued judicially under the 1851 Act or administratively under the 1986 Act. For the latter an application is made to the District Court (rather than a complaint being made). Applications can be made by gardaí, the DPP, the AG or someone else authorised by legislation. The summons is issued by the clerk. No decision is made on the merits. As long as the form is in order, it is within the time limits and all legal requirements are satisfied, it is issued.[120] Warrants for arrest may only be issued by judges. **[6–54]**

(iii) Charging in Custody

If an individual has been arrested without a warrant and has been charged in custody he will usually be brought before the District Court to be formally charged. A charge sheet is prepared, a copy is given to the accused and one is lodged with the relevant District Court clerk.[121] A formal complaint must then be made to the court, which can decide to formally charge the accused. **[6–55]**

---

115 DCR, Ord 16, r 1(2).
116 DCR, Ord 15, r 10.
117 DCR, Ord 16, r 2(1).
118 Bail Act 1997, s 8.
119 [1987] ILRM 309.
120 DCR, Ord 15, rs 3(1) and 9.
121 DCR, Ord 17, r 1(3).

Fitness to Plead

[6–56] One of the early hearings will involve an arraignment, where the accused is asked how he pleads. There may be a need to determine whether the accused is fit to be tried. Section 4 of the Criminal Law (Insanity) Act 2006 states that

> "an accused person shall be deemed unfit to be tried if he or she is unable by reason of mental disorder to understand the nature or course of the proceedings so as to (a) plead the charge, (b) instruct a legal representative, (c) in the case of an indictable offence which may be tried summarily elect for a trial by jury, (d) make a proper defence, (e) in the case of a trial by jury, challenge a juror to whom he or she might wish to object or, (f) understand the evidence."

The Act permits this decision to be left until the beginning of the defence case if it deems this to be expedient and in the interests of the accused.[122]

Bail

[6–57] An additional key aspect of the initial hearing will be the determination of the issue of bail. Bail is a system which allows for an individual to be released from custody on the basis of an undertaking that he will surrender to garda custody at a certain appointed time. To do this he will usually be asked to enter into what is called a "recognisance": a legally binding commitment to pay a determined set of money if he fails to surrender as agreed. In addition, he may be asked to provide independent sureties – individuals who agree to pay the money to the court if the accused fails to surrender to custody. If bail is lawfully refused, the person can be detained for the duration of the criminal proceedings. Those being tried at the Special Criminal Court require the approval of the DPP to secure bail.[123] Given the right to liberty and the presumption of innocence, the decision to refuse bail should not be taken lightly. Bail can be granted either in the garda station or in court.

(i) Station Bail

[6–58] A person may be released from garda custody on bail by the member in charge (MIC) where it is deemed prudent.[124] The procedures applicable are quite informal. The MIC may take a recognisance, and may require sureties. If a recognisance is taken, it may be substituted by a sum of money paid in lieu of a surety. This can apply to any offence, except for those which the Criminal Procedure Act 1967 states must be dealt with by the High Court. This bail may be granted before or after charge; for instance bail may be granted to appear before the District Court for charging, though as suspects are usually detained until charging, this rarely happens. Station bail can last for up to 30 days.[125] This procedure does not preclude an application for bail once the defendant is taken to court.

---

122 s 7.

123 Offences Against the State Act 1939, s 43(1)(c).

124 Criminal Procedure Act 1967, s 31.

125 Criminal Justice (Miscellaneous Provisions) Act 1997, s 3.

(ii) District Court

The majority of bail applications are heard in the District Court.[126] Bail can be granted here in respect of any offence other than those reserved by s 29 of the Criminal Procedure Act 1967 for the High Court. Once it has been decided by the Court that a person should be sent forward for trial, the judge is obliged to grant bail if it appears that it ought to be allowed. Where bail is granted the accused will have to enter a recognisance that he will attend court at a particular time.[127] This is usually secured by payment of a sum of money which will be forfeited if he does not attend. The amount is at the discretion of the judge. Once the accused fulfils all the conditions of bail the money will be returned. This bail will last until the trial, for the duration of all preliminary hearings. If bail is initially denied further applications can be made at each hearing, or an appeal can be lodged in the High Court.[128] Conditions attached to the bail can also be appealed. **[6–59]**

At the hearing the prosecution will be asked if they have any objections. These will be heard by the court, usually on the testimony of a garda. The defence can cross-examine this witness before presenting their case. The judge then announces his decision. Judges are not obliged to give reasons for their decision though increasingly they do, to assist in appeal applications. **[6–60]**

(iii) High Court

Section 29 of the Criminal Procedure Act 1967 lists a number of offences for which bail hearings must be heard in the High Court: murder, attempted murder, conspiracy to murder, piracy, genocide, treason, an offence under the Offences Against the State Act 1939, and offences under the Official Secrets Act 1963. Further instances where the High Court will hold bail hearings are where an individual applies for a quashing of a conviction from a lower court or where someone is appealing to either the Court of Criminal Appeal or the Supreme Court. The procedure is very similar to that in the District Court.[129] Part of the proceedings can be held *in camera* given the nature of the offences in question.[130] However, the decision on bail must always be given in public. Repeated applications are permitted. **[6–61]**

(iv) At Trial

Where a case is being tried in the Circuit Court or Central Criminal Court the trial court has jurisdiction for any bail matters which arise during the trial or the sentencing of the individual.[131] This can relate to bail for the duration of the trial, for after the conviction but before sentencing, pending appeals or even post-sentencing on a short term basis to allow the individual to make any necessary arrangements. Those offences reserved for the High Court cannot be dealt with here. The procedure is the same as applications before the District Court. The Special Criminal Court deals with bail **[6–62]**

---

[126] Under powers granted by Criminal Procedure Act 1967, s 28, as amended by the Bail Act 1997, s 11.
[127] Criminal Procedure Act 1967, s 23.
[128] s 28(3).
[129] Set out by the Rules of the Superior Courts, Ord 84.
[130] Criminal Procedure Act 1967, s 29(3).
[131] *People (AG) v Kirwan* (1950) Frewen 111.

hearings for individuals charged before that Court or sent there for trial by the District Court.

(v) Court of Criminal Appeal

[6–63] The Court of Criminal Appeal hears bail hearings in cases where a point of law is being addressed in an appeal, it is suggested that the trial was unsatisfactory or there are sufficient grounds to appeal.[132] In these instances, where there will have been a conviction, the court is allowed to release the defendant on bail pending the decision.[133] Given how long the appeals process can take, if an appellant is not granted bail when his verdict looks unsound then he may spend a very lengthy time in prison. The court can also release an individual pending a re-trial following a quashing of the original verdict, though the court appears slow to do this. As stated in *People v Kirwan*,[134] "the fact that the applicants have been convicted by a jury weighs down the scales heavily against them."

[6–64] The procedure for this hearing is set out in the Rules of the Superior Court. Notice must be served and the State Solicitor contacted.[135] In terms of recognisances and sureties the system is the same as in the lower courts. The bail conditions will require attendance at every appeal hearing.[136] This bail can be revoked or altered at any point.[137]

Principles

[6–65] There is a presumption in favour of granting bail due to the punitive nature of imprisonment, particularly where an individual has not yet been convicted. The principles governing bail are found in the Constitution, common law and the Bail Act 1997. The common law indicates that a person should not be unnecessarily detained. In *People (AG) v Gilliland*[138] the Supreme Court stated that a person should be granted bail unless "there is a likelihood that if the prisoner is granted bail he will defeat the ultimate purpose of the imprisonment by absconding."[139]

[6–66] In the *People (AG) v. O'Callaghan*,[140] in 1966, the Supreme Court held that bail could not be denied for an accused who had committed offences while on bail on the basis of concerns that he would commit further offences while on bail. Walsh J declared that this would be "preventative justice which has no place in our legal system and is quite alien to the true purposes of bail."[141] It would be a breach of the right to personal liberty under the Constitution which could only be interfered with where the government legislated for such interference and where public safety and order required it. Following

[132] Criminal Justice Act 1924, s 32 as amended by Criminal Procedure Act 1993, s 3(6).
[133] *ibid.*
[134] [1989] ILTR 120.
[135] RSC, Ord 86, r 19.
[136] RSC, Ord 86, r 19(8).
[137] RSC, Ord 86, r 19(9).
[138] [1986] ILRM 357.
[139] *ibid.* at 363.
[140] [1966] IR 501.
[141] *ibid.* at 507.

substantial disquiet in the wake of the murder of journalist Veronica Guerin, a referendum was held which inserted Art 40.4.7 into the Constitution which provides:

> "Provision may be made by law for the refusal of bail by a court to a person charged with a serious offence where it is reasonably considered necessary to prevent the commission of a serious offence by that person."

The Bail Act 1997 was then introduced to legislate for such circumstances, and it came into effect in May 2000.

The Bail Act 1997

Section 2 of the Bail Act 1997 provides: [6–67]

> "Where an application for bail is made by a person charged with a serious offence, a court may refuse the application if the court is satisfied that such refusal is reasonably considered necessary to prevent the commission of a serious offence by that person."

A serious offence is one scheduled within the Act and meriting a sentence of at least five years.[142] The scheduled offences include murder, manslaughter, rape, serious non-fatal offences, incest, other sexual offences, offences relating to explosives, firearms and weapons, larceny, criminal damage, dangerous driving, offences against the State, riots, forgery, and attempt or conspiracy among others. With some of these offences a basic offence will not merit five years but an aggravated one will: only the latter will fall under these provisions. Remand in custody must be necessary to prevent an offence from occurring. Once satisfied of this the court has the discretion to refuse bail.[143] The Act further stipulates the following range of factors to be taken into account in the decision: [6–68]

- The nature and degree of seriousness of the offence with which the accused person is charged and the sentences likely to be imposed on conviction;
- The nature and degree of seriousness of the offence apprehended and the sentence likely to be imposed on conviction;
- The nature and strength of the evidence in support of the charge;
- Any conviction of the accused person for an offence committed while he or she was on bail;
- Any previous convictions of the accused person including any conviction the subject of an appeal (which has neither been determined nor withdrawn) to a court;
- Any other offence in respect of which the accused person is charged and is awaiting trial. [144]

These incorporate the jurisprudence which had developed through cases such as *O'Callaghan* prior to the introduction of this legislation. In that case Walsh J had [6–69]

142 s 1.
143 s 2(1).
144 s 2(2).

identified three core factors: the seriousness of the charge, the nature of the evidence supporting that charge and the likely sentence on conviction, all of which now find statutory representation. In addition, the court can now take into account whether the applicant is addicted to a controlled drug,[145] though for what purpose is unclear. Fears that the accused would attempt to evade justice or commit a serious offence while on bail are clearly the most influential factors. It should also be noted that the court is not restricted to consideration of the factors listed above. In *Maguire v DPP*[146] the Supreme Court stated that the projected date of the trial and time already served would also be highly relevant. Whatever reason the judge gives for refusing to grant bail must be supported by evidence.[147] In terms of the standard of proof to be applied in making a decision on bail the Supreme Court has opined in *Vickers v DPP*[148] that the Bail Act 1997 confers a wide discretion on the court. It continued to hold:

> "If [the court is] of the view that a real risk of the commission of a further serious offence has been demonstrated the decision of the court must be proportionate to the nature and gravity of the apprehended further offence."

In addition to the presumption of innocence, the need to consider all the evidence and the "prima facie entitlement to bail" must be considered.

[6–70] Case law from the ECtHR also indicates that bail decisions must be made by an independent judicial authority, the accused must be heard and all the relevant factors must be considered, including the public interest and the accused's presumption of innocence.[149] It appears that the ECtHR accepts four reasons for the refusal of bail in domestic courts:

- Risk that the accused will fail to appear for trial;
- Risk that he will interfere with the course of justice;
- Prevention of further offences;
- Preservation of public order.[150]

The grounds for refusing bail in Ireland would, therefore, appear to be compatible with the jurisprudence of the ECtHR.[151]

Conditions

[6–71] As has been shown, recognisances and sureties will invariably be required by the courts where bail is granted. The amount will be decided in relation to the probability of breaches but cannot be so large that it results in an effective denial of bail given the

---

145 s 2(2).

146 [2004] 3 IR 241.

147 *McDonagh v Governor of Cloverhill Prison* [2005] 1 IR 394.

148 [2009] IESC 58.

149 *Caballero v United Kingdom* (2000) 30 EHRR 643.

150 See *Stogmuller v Austria* (1979-80) 1 EHRR 155; *Neumesiter v Austria* (1979-80) 1 EHRR 91; *Wemhoff v Germany* (1979-80) 1 EHRR 55 and *Caballero v UK* (2000) 30 EHRR 643.

151 See O'Malley, *The Criminal Process* (Round Hall, Dublin, 2010), p 448.

circumstances of the accused. This does not mean that it has to be within the accused's means, though these must be considered in the decision.[152]

Under the Bail Act 1997, not committing other offences and being of good behaviour will be conditions, while others can be included as the court sees fit, such as requiring the offender to reside in a particular place, attend a garda station at set times, surrender his passport, refrain from attending specified places or having contact with specified persons.[153] That said, the court cannot impose conditions which are not necessary for the case at hand. For instance, in *Ronan v Coughlan*[154] a condition that the accused remain in his home for 16 hours a day was deemed unnecessary for the purpose of securing his attendance at trial, which is the main purpose of bail. **[6–72]**

A condition which has been legislated for attachment to a bail order, but has not yet come into force, is electronic monitoring.[155] This will be applicable to persons over the age of 18 charged with a serious offence.[156] It will be possible to impose this once one of the additional conditions listed in s 6(1)(b) of the Bail Act, such as requirements to reside at a certain place or attend a garda station regularly, have been imposed.[157] The individual will also have to agree to comply with it for it to be imposed. **[6–73]**

Failure to surrender to bail is an offence under the Criminal Justice Act 1984 leading to 12 months imprisonment as well as proceedings to secure the money set in the bail conditions.[158] Any offences committed while on bail will be an aggravating factor in sentencing and the sentence for those offences is to be served consecutive to the original sentence.[159] **[6–74]**

If the accused is not granted bail he will be remanded in custody in a prison or some other place of detention. If it is going to be for less than four days this can be at a garda station, although the court must be satisfied that there are satisfactory facilities for this.[160] The judge may also order additional hearings prior to the next required hearing, given the punitive nature of the requirement. **[6–75]**

The maximum period of remand detention following the first hearing is eight days and every subsequent remand can be for up to 15 days unless the court feels that this would be unreasonable.[161] This can be extended up to 30 days if both the prosecutor and the accused agree.[162] Remand can be used even where a conviction for the offence would not necessarily involve custodial punishment, though only in exceptional **[6–76]**

---

152 *DPP v Broderick* [2006] 1 IR 629.
153 Bail Act 1997, s 6.
154 [2005] 4 IR 274.
155 Criminal Justice Act 2007, s 11.
156 Bail Act 1997, s 6B(9) as inserted by the Criminal Justice Act 2007, s11.
157 Bail Act 1997, s 6B(1)(b) as inserted by the Criminal Justice Act 2007, s 11.
158 s 13.
159 Criminal Justice Act 2007, s 22.
160 The periods of remand in custody are set out in the Criminal Procedure Act 1967 as amended by Criminal Justice (Miscellaneous Provisions) Act 1997, s 4.
161 Criminal Procedure Act 1967, s 24(2) as amended by Criminal Justice (Miscellaneous Provisions) Act 1997, s 4.
162 *ibid.* s 24(4).

circumstances and where the judge is satisfied that the deprivation of liberty was necessary.[163] If the place of detention is far from the District Court the accused may be remanded to appear in a District Court which is closer to the place of detention.[164] Time served while on remand will be deducted from the period served, if the accused is convicted and sentenced to imprisonment.

V. Conclusion

[6–77] This chapter has covered the procedure which applies following the investigation of an offence by gardaí prior to the trial of the offence in court. We have seen the complexity of considerations involved in the decision to prosecute which continues to be complicated by issues of delay and requirements to adhere to constitutional rights to fair procedures. We have also looked at the initial stages of the prosecution, with a particular emphasis on the decision to grant bail and the way in which the law concerning this has changed in recent years. The conflict between personal rights and the power of the state is particularly stark at this stage of the process, as both prosecutions and the denial of liberty can have serious consequences for an individual. The individual's rights, including the presumption of innocence, must be carefully balanced against public interest in both prosecuting crime and preventing further crime from occurring.

In the next two chapters the different forms of trial which can occur will be considered: summary trial and trial on indictment.

---

[163] *ibid.*

[164] *ibid.* s 24(6)(b).

CHAPTER 7
The Summary Trial

Practically every person prosecuted within the Irish criminal process will begin his journey in the District Court. The vast majority of criminal offences in Ireland are tried in the District Court: in 2008 the Central Criminal Court had 136 new cases, the Special Criminal Court had 10, the Circuit Court processed 2,993 defendants while the District Court dealt with 550,694 offences.[1] Despite this, or perhaps because of the large volume of cases, Walsh notes that proceedings in the court are characterised "by speed and informality", as compared with trial on indictment.[2] **[7–01]**

Proceedings in the court are governed according to the District Court Rules, made under s 92 of the Courts of Justice Act 1924 by the District Court Rules Committee, and we shall be referring to these rules constantly throughout the chapter.

I. Jurisdiction of the District Court

The jurisdiction of the District Court is limited to minor offences. This is clear from Art 34.4 of the Constitution which provides for the establishment of courts of limited and local jurisdiction, and Art 38.2 which provides that minor offences may be tried by courts of summary jurisdiction. The fundamental difference between a trial on indictment and a summary trial is that where the case is heard on indictment, the accused person is entitled to a trial by jury. Where the court is exercising its jurisdiction under Art 38.2, Art 38.5 explicitly removes the right to a jury trial from these proceedings. **[7–02]**

The first question to be determined is what constitutes a minor offence. The case of *Melling v Ó Mathghamhna*[3] is the leading case in this jurisdiction on this matter. The **[7–03]**

---

1 Courts Service, *Annual Report 2008* (Dublin, 2009), pp 60-64.
2 Walsh, *Criminal Procedure* (Thomson Round Hall, Dublin, 2002), p 671.
3 [1962] IR 1.

defendant, accused of smuggling butter, had been charged in the District Court under s 186 of the Customs Consolidation Act 1876. The penalty for the offence was, under s 186, a fine, or in default of such fine, a term of imprisonment for not more than 12 months. The defendant argued that the charges were not minor in nature, and therefore could not be heard in the District Court. The court considered the meaning of the phrase "minor offence", and Lavery J set out the criteria relevant to such a definition:

> "It appears to me that these principles may be stated thus:— first: in the construction of a statute and, at least equally in construing a provision in a constitution as a fundamental law, it is necessary to consider how the law stood when the statute was passed. Second: the severity of the penalty involved. Third: the moral quality of the act. Fourth: its relation to common law crimes."[4]

[7–04] In the case of *State (Rollinson) v Kelly*[5] the court was of the opinion that, due to the moral quality of the particular offences, there were some acts on the statute book that could never be considered minor: treason, murder, rape and genocide being examples of such offences. As Doyle notes, there have been very few cases in recent years on the issue of minor and non-minor offences, largely due to the fact that the legislature have adopted the "severity of punishment" standard as determinative.[6] Thus, once the punishment for the offence is less than 12 months in prison or a fine of less than €5,000, the offence is considered minor and triable summarily.

The District Court Rules

[7–05] The Courts of Justice Act 1924 provided for the District Court to issue rules of practice and procedure. These are drawn up by the District Court Rules Committee, comprised of nine judges, lawyers and representatives of the Minister for Justice.

The Rules deal with sittings and vacations, forms of process, summons, appeals, conditions for making a case stated, and the practice and procedure of the court generally. There are limitations to what can be covered by the rules and in *State (O'Flaherty) v O'Floinn*[7] a rule which extended the statutory period for which an accused could be detained was deemed an excessive use of power. In the *State (Lynch) v Ballagh*[8] a rule which attempted to control the way in which a garda issued station bail was similarly found to be *ultra vires*. The Supreme Court in that case stated that the rules could not be used to regulate the behaviour of gardaí.

II. Independence of District Court Judges

[7–06] Prior to the foundation of the State, the summary jurisdiction was exercised by lay magistrates. However, since the foundation of the State, courts of limited and local jurisdiction have been established through the Constitution, and the current District Court was established by s 5 of the Courts (Establishment and Constitution) Act 1961.[9]

---

[4] *ibid.* at 13.

[5] [1965] IR 411.

[6] Doyle, *Constitutional Law: Text Cases and Materials* (Clarus Press, Dublin, 2008), p 50.

[7] [1954] IR 295.

[8] [1986] IR 203.

[9] s 33 of the Courts (Supplemental Provisions) Act 1961 vests in this District Court all the jurisdiction that had been vested in the previous District Court by the Courts of Justice Act 1924.

O'Malley stresses that as District Court judges are appointed in accordance with the Constitution (rather than a lay magistracy), the superior courts "adopt a sparing approach towards the exercise of a supervisory jurisdiction over the District Court."[10] This position was stressed in the case of *Clune v DPP*[11] where Gannon J stated, in a passage that O'Malley describes as having "canonical status"[12]:

> "The concept of guiding, directing, controlling, supervising or correcting lay magistrates which might have been inferred from proceedings of certiorari and prohibition and mandamus prior to the establishment of the State is not appropriate to courts established under our Constitution. The courts of limited jurisdiction established by legislation pursuant to constitutional authority in that behalf are not in any sense subject to direction, control or supervision by the superior courts established by the Constitution ... Many of the procedures which were appropriate to the circumstances when the inferior courts were administered by lay magistrates have been adapted and adopted in relation to our district courts now administered by fully competent and qualified lawyers, whose independence as judges, not only from the executive but even from their judicial colleagues, must be respected. The Justice sitting in the District Court has the sole and exclusive authority to control and supervise the conduct of proceedings in his own court within the limits of the jurisdiction conferred upon him. His independence and authority is secured in his freedom not only from pressures of political or executive nature but also from purported intervention, direction, or control by any superior court."[13]

Thus, due to the nature of the summary jurisdiction, and the constitutional status of District Court judges, the superior courts are very slow to interfere with a decision made at summary level.

III. The Nature of the Summary Trial

Summary trials are known for being quick and informal. As stated in *Clune v DPP*:[14] **[7–07]**

> "A summary trial is a trial which could be undertaken with some degree of expedition and informality without departing from the principles of justice. The purpose of summary procedures for minor offences is to ensure that such offences are charged and tried as soon as reasonably possible after their alleged commission so that the recollection of witnesses may still be reasonably clear, that the attendance of witnesses and presentation of evidence may be procured and presented without great difficulty or complexity, and that there should be minimal delay in the disposal of the work load of minor offences."[15]

---

10 O'Malley, *The Criminal Process* (Round Hall, Dublin, 2009), p 564.
11 [1981] ILRM 17.
12 O'Malley, above n 10, p 565.
13 *ibid.* pp 19-20.
14 [1981] ILRM 17.
15 *ibid.* at 19.

[7–08] Where a statute defines an offence as a summary one, it must be tried in the District Court.[16] There are limited time frames in which a prosecution may be taken in summary proceedings. Section 10(4) of the Petty Sessions (Ireland) Act 1851 provides that there is a general time limit of six months for the making of a complaint in relation to a summary offence. Where the timing is contested, the onus is on the prosecution to establish that the time limit has been complied with.[17]

[7–09] Summary proceedings are relatively informal. Initially, the court clerk will call out the name of the accused. If the accused is not present, the proceedings will usually be adjourned and a warrant issued, though the court may decide to proceed if the judge is happy that the summons was properly served.[18] If the court believes it would be unfair on the accused in the interests of justice to proceed in his absence then the court must adjourn.[19] If the prosecutor is not present, the court can strike the proceedings out or adjourn.[20] The issue of how the defendant came to be before the court will not be considered — defects in the warrant or summons for arrest will not deprive the court of its jurisdiction so long as the person charged is in court on foot of a valid complaint.[21]

Guilty Plea

[7–10] The procedure is that a complaint is then read out by the clerk and the accused person will be asked how he pleads. Where an individual pleads guilty to an offence once the charge is laid against him, the court may convict or make an order against the individual. In this instance, a conviction will be entered and a sentence imposed.[22]

[7–11] The prosecutor will outline the nature of the offence and the accused will be given an opportunity to enter a plea of mitigation which suggests that some of the circumstances should mean a reduction in sentence. There may be witnesses called to testify at this point as to his good character. The judge will then proceed to impose sentence.

Plea of Not Guilty

[7–12] Where an individual pleads not guilty, the court can proceed to hear and determine the complaint.[23] The court can also adjourn the case, and remand the individual to appear at a later date. Ultimately, there will be a trial and a determination of guilt. This can proceed without the accused being present[24] distinguishing summary proceedings from trial on indictment.

---

16 An example is the Non-Fatal Offences Against the Person Act 1997, as amended by the Fines Act 2010 s 2(4) of which provides, "A person guilty of an offence under this section shall be liable on summary conviction to a fine not exceeding €2500 or to imprisonment for a term not exceeding 6 months or to both."

17 O'Malley, above n 10, p 584. He notes that the date of the alleged offence is excluded from the six month timeframe.

18 District Court Rules, Ord 22.

19 See section VI below for further discussion of this.

20 DCR, Ord 23, rs 2 and 3.

21 Walsh, above n 2, p 662.

22 DCR, Ord 23, r 1. See Chapter Ten for a discussion as to the sentencing jurisdiction of the District Court.

23 DCR, Ord 23, r 1.

24 DCR, Ord 23, r 2.

The prosecution presents its case by calling and examining witnesses. These can be cross-examined by the accused and re-examined by the prosecution if they wish. Once the prosecution has presented its witnesses, the defence can present its case involving witnesses and other evidence. Equally, they can be cross-examined by the prosecution and re-examined by the defence. Both sides can make closing submissions with the prosecution going first. Generally speaking, as O'Malley points out, the prosecution cannot recall witnesses to "mend its hand by furthering evidence in response to defence questions or arguments."[25] That said, the court can allow further prosecution evidence where it relates to formal matters – evidence relating to the merits of the case cannot be put forward after the close of the prosecution case.[26] [7–13]

Adjournments in Summary Proceedings

While on occasion the entire proceedings will take place on first appearance, it is more likely that the case will be adjourned until a later date. Indeed, a case may be adjourned a number of times before the defendant is actually tried for the offence. The statutory justification for this is found in s 21 of the Criminal Procedure Act 1967 which provides, "[w]here an accused person is before the District Court in connection with an offence, the Court may ... remand the accused from time to time as occasion requires."[27] Again, as per *Clune v DPP*[28] the superior courts will be very slow to interfere with this statutory discretion. [7–14]

In *O'Callaghan v Clifford*[29] the accused, charged with failure to make tax returns, was due before the court at 2 pm, at which point defence counsel informed the court that the accused was in Dublin and would not be able to attend the court until 4.30 pm that afternoon. Defence counsel requested an adjournment as he had not had an opportunity to take instructions from his client. The judge refused the request and the applicant was ultimately convicted. The primary reason that the request for adjournment was refused was due to the fact that there were witnesses for the prosecution present in the courtroom to give evidence in relation to sentence. The applicant sought a judicial review of the decision of the District Court judge, on the basis that he had been denied the opportunity to represent himself, and thus denied a trial in due course of law. [7–15]

The case was ultimately heard by the Supreme Court. Denham J, while noting that the appeal courts should be slow to intervene in a matter where the District Court Judge has exercised his constitutional discretion, allowed the application of the applicant. She stated that there were six important factors which led to her decision: [7–16]

1. This was a criminal trial with the consequent possibility of a penalty of imprisonment;
2. This was the first time this case had come before the court;
3. Counsel had not had an opportunity of obtaining instructions from the applicant;

---

[25] O'Malley, above n 10, p 594.

[26] See *Magee v O'Dea* [1994] 1 IR 500 and *Bates v Brady* [2003] 4 IR 111.

[27] See also DCR, Ord 2, r 2.

[28] [1981] ILRM 17.

[29] [1993] 3 IR 603.

4. Because of the nature of the prosecution, by certificate, matters could arise at trial in relation to which, even if the applicant had had an opportunity to instruct counsel prior to the trial, he would not have been able to instruct fully in advance;
5. The applicant was to be in court at 4.30 pm;
6. The witnesses which the State indicated were in court were for sentencing purposes only.[30]

[7–17] Of course, the problem with successive adjournments is that the case can be presented in a very disjointed manner, meaning that prosecutors, defence counsel and most importantly, the judge must try to recall evidence given at an earlier date. This is all the more problematic given the vast caseload of each District Court.

[7–18] Despite this fact, and the right of an accused person to a speedy trial, the superior courts have been slow to interfere with successive adjournments, reasserting the discretion of the trial judge and the view that the superior courts should be very slow to interfere.[31] The approach of the superior courts to this, particularly when an application is made mid-trial, is to refuse an application to prevent prosecution for delay and to defer to the decision of the trial court. As stated by Macken J:

> "the court must accept, unless there is clear evidence to the contrary, that a District Judge during a case such as this will administer justice in the best possible manner, fulfilling all the appropriate functions of a District Judge, including taking into account as appropriate, the fact that there has been a delay, for valid reasons, between the prosecution case and the defence case."[32]

This case was decided on the basis that the more appropriate redress for an applicant is to appeal the final decision of the trial judge rather than to interfere with the decision mid-trial, unless there are truly "exceptional circumstances."

IV. Summary Trial for Indictable Offences

[7–19] There are two instances in which an indictable offence can be tried summarily. The first is in relation to what are referred to as scheduled offences under s 2 of the Criminal Justice Act 1951 which applies to cases where

> "(a) the Court is of opinion that the facts proved or alleged constitute a minor offence fit to be tried summarily,
> (b) the accused, on being informed by the Court of his right to be tried with a jury, does not object to being tried summarily, and
> (c) the Director of Public Prosecutions consents to the accused being tried summarily for such offence."

[7–20] Both the accused person and the DPP must consent to the charge being tried summarily. Importantly, when an individual is being tried summarily in this manner,

---

30 *ibid.* at 611-612.

31 See, for example, *Adams v Reilly* [2005] 3 IR 190 and *Menton v DPP* [1996] IEHC 234.

32 *Adams v Reilly* [2005] 3 IR 190 at 195.

the general limitations on the sentencing jurisdiction of the District Court will apply.[33] Where the District Court judge is considering whether to "send the accused forward" or try him summarily,[34] two issues must be determined: first, whether the facts constitute a minor offence; and second, if it is a minor offence which is fit to be tried summarily.[35] To proceed in this way the trial judge must inform the accused of his right to be tried by a jury and must be satisfied, having heard the facts in support of the charge that it is a minor offence. So satisfied, the judge will accept the accused's plea and try him summarily.[36]

The second type of case where an individual can be tried summarily for indictable offences is in relation to "hybrid offences" or "either way" offences. In recent years, the legislature has included a number of these offences on the statute book, whereby an offence can be tried either summarily or on indictment. An example of this is s 3 of the Non-Fatal Offences Against the Person Act 1997, which allows for assault causing harm to be tried either summarily or on indictment.[37] Importantly, here the decision as to where the offence will be tried is taken by the prosecutor, and the accused person cannot object to the summary jurisdiction being exercised. However, if it appears to the District Court judge that the case is not minor in nature, he must refuse jurisdiction. As O'Malley states, the decision of the DPP to prosecute a case in the District Court "cannot force the District Court to exceed its jurisdiction to a point which would clearly be unconstitutional by proceeding with the trial of a non-minor offence."[38] **[7–21]**

Whatever way the case has found its way to the District Court, where an indictable offence is being tried summarily, the time limits set out in s 10(4) of the Petty Sessions Ireland Act 1851 do not apply, according to the Criminal Justice Act 1951.[39]

In both instances, if the District Court judge comes to the opinion at any stage during the proceedings that the case is not minor in nature, and thus not suitable for a summary hearing, the judge must decline jurisdiction. For the most part, this decision will be made at the initial stages of the hearing, where the evidence is put forward. The procedure was described by Butler J in *State (Nevin) v Tormey*:[40] **[7–22]**

> "[T]he prosecution first gives a general statement of the facts of the case. On this statement the court may form an opinion whether the offence is fit to be tried summarily and, if it so decides, the court may go on to fulfil the second condition by informing the accused of his rights and ascertaining that he has no objection to being tried summarily."[41]

---

33 See Chapter Ten for a discussion of this issue.

34 "Sending forward" means transferring the accused to the Circuit Court for trial.

35 See, for example, *State (O'Hagan) v Delap* [1982] 1 IR 213.

36 DCR, Ord 14, r 1.

37 s 3(2) provides that "A person guilty of an offence under this section shall be liable (a) on summary conviction, to imprisonment for a term not exceeding 12 months or to a fine not exceeding £1,500 or to both, or (b) on conviction on indictment to a fine or to imprisonment for a term not exceeding 5 years or to both."

38 O'Malley, above n 10, p 259.

39 s 7 as amended by s 177 of the Criminal Justice Act 2006.

40 [1976] IR 1.

41 *ibid.* at 6.

[7–23] However, a District Court judge can decide at any stage of the hearing that the case is in fact not minor in nature and relinquish jurisdiction in relation to the case. In *State (O'Hagan) v Delap*[42] the accused man was charged with indecent assault. The prosecutor consented to the offence being tried summarily, and the accused pleaded not guilty. Between the plea and the hearing of the case it was established that the accused had committed the offence while on bail for a similar offence. This, the District Court judge believed, meant the case could no longer be dealt with at a summary level and he sent the accused forward for trial in the Circuit Court. The question for the High Court was whether the District Court judge could change his mind on the issue of jurisdiction between accepting the case and hearing it. O'Hanlon J answered the question in the affirmative, stating:

> "I am of opinion that when a District Justice has elected to try a case summarily, and has embarked on the trial, circumstances may arise which entitle him, or may even make it necessary for him, to reverse his previous decision and allow the case to go forward to the Circuit Court where a higher range of sentence may be imposed."[43]

[7–24] Thus, as long as the case has not been determined, it would appear that the District Court judge can decline jurisdiction on a case at any stage during the proceedings. That said, once a District Court judge has issued a *de facto* conviction, even where this is not formally announced, he cannot then refuse jurisdiction.[44]

Guilty Plea for Indictable Offences

[7–25] The Criminal Procedure Act 1967 allows the District Court to sentence an offender where a guilty plea is lodged with the court.[45] The Act applies to all indictable offences except serious offences such as treason, piracy, terrorist offences, murder and attempted murder. With the consent of the prosecutor, following a guilty plea, the District Court has the power to sentence on a guilty plea for indictable offences.[46] In exercising this power, however, the court is restricted in terms of the sentences it can impose to the general sentencing jurisdiction of the District Court. The accused person must also understand the nature of the offence and the facts alleged.[47] However, if the Court is of the opinion that a more severe sentence is warranted, it can send the individual forward for sentence to the court where the trial would have taken place if a plea of guilty were not made.[48] If the accused is sent forward on this basis for sentencing, he has the option to withdraw the guilty plea after which the case will proceed in the higher court.[49]

---

[42] [1982] IR 213.

[43] *ibid.* at 217.

[44] O'Malley, above n 10, p 263.

[45] Criminal Procedure Act 1967, s 13.

[46] s 13(2).

[47] *ibid.*

[48] *ibid.*

[49] s 13(4)(a).

V. Legal Aid in Summary Proceedings

In *State (Healy) v Donoghue*[50] the Supreme Court held that a constitutional right to legal representation was protected by Art 38.1, which provides for a trial in due course of law. If an accused was not given an opportunity to represent himself it could not be said to be a fair trial. The court stated: [7–26]

> "Where a man's liberty is at stake or where he faces a very severe penalty which may affect his welfare or his livelihood, justice may require more than the application of normal and fair procedures in relation to his trial. Facing, as he does, the power of the State which is his accuser, the person charged may be unable to defend himself adequately because of ignorance, lack of education, youth or other incapacity. In such circumstances his plight may require, if justice is to be done, that he should have legal assistance."[51]

The right to legal representation therefore applies where liberty is at stake, or serious damage to welfare or livelihood may occur. In *Byrne v Judge McDonell*[52] once the court decided a prison sentence *might* be imposed, the right was said to apply even though the offence itself was quite minor. In *Cahill v Reilly*[53] the court was of the opinion that a prison sentence would have to be *probable or likely* before the right came into play; possible was not sufficient. In *Clarke v Kirby*[54] the court opted for a lower threshold of legal aid wherever custody was *possible*. While clearly this means that the right will apply in the vast majority of trials on indictment, it may not always arise in summary trials. [7–27]

As a right to legal representation exists under the Constitution, the State has an associated obligation to provide the defendant with an opportunity to secure legal representation, including providing the impecunious defendant with legal aid. This is also overtly required by Art 6(3)(c) ECHR. The Criminal Justice (Legal Aid) Act 1962 provides for legal aid where the applicant does not have sufficient means himself, where it is in the interests of justice, given the gravity of the offence, that he have legal aid to prepare and conduct his defence.[55] Until recently, the right to legal aid in the District Court extended only to the right to a solicitor – counsel were not provided for. In the case of *Carmody v Minister for Justice, Equality and Law Reform*[56] the question of the extent of the right to legal aid in summary proceedings was examined. Section 2(1) of the Criminal Justice (Legal Aid) Act 1962 provides: [7–28]

> "If it appears to the District Court-
> (a) that the means of a person charged before it with an offence are insufficient to enable him to obtain legal aid, and
> (b) that by reason of the gravity of the charge or of exceptional circumstances it is essential in the interests of justice that he should have legal aid in the preparation and conduct of his defence before it, the Court shall, on

[50] [1976] IR 325.
[51] *ibid.* at 340.
[52] [1997] 1 IR 392.
[53] [1994] 3 IR 547.
[54] [1998] 2 ILRM 30.
[55] s 2(1) as amended by Criminal Justice (Miscellaneous Provisions) Act 1997, s 5(6).
[56] [2009] IESC 71.

> application being made to it in that behalf, grant in respect of him a certificate for free legal aid . . . and thereupon he shall be entitled to such aid and to have a solicitor and (where he is charged with murder and the Court thinks fit) counsel assigned to him for that purpose in such manner as may be prescribed by regulations under section 10 of this Act."

[7–29] The applicant, Carmody, was charged with 42 counts relating to movement of cattle, which were intended to protect cattle from the disease of brucellosis or to prevent the spread of the disease. When he applied for legal aid in the District Court under s 2 it was granted, though limited to the provision of a solicitor. Due to the complex nature of the charges, and the fact that counsel were routinely used to prosecute this type of offence, it was argued in the High Court, and later in the Supreme Court, that Mr Carmody was entitled to counsel in his case. Ultimately, it was argued that "the interests of justice" demanded that Carmody be entitled to counsel to defend his case.[57]

In considering the application, the court noted that the general principle was that

> "the District Court does deal with thousands of relatively trivial cases and that as a general rule the more serious or complex criminal cases requiring legal aid could not, in the Court's view, require more than the services of a professional solicitor to meet the essential requirements of justice."

[7–30] Thus, as a general rule, those accused in the District Court will not be entitled to counsel. However, the court went on to note that the range and complexity of cases heard in the District Court has grown exponentially in recent years, and found that to limit the right to legal aid in certain cases would amount to a violation of the right to a fair trial. The court held:

> "In order to vindicate the constitutional right of an indigent defendant in the District Court to a fair trial he or she must be entitled to legal aid with representation by counsel as well as solicitor where it is established that because of the particular gravity and complexity of the case or other exceptional circumstances such representation is essential in the interests of justice."

[7–31] Not every applicant will be successful in an application for either legal aid, or for representation by counsel. The issue remains to be determined by reference to the two key factors in s 2 of 1962 Act: the gravity of the charge or exceptional circumstances of the case, and whether it is essential in the interests of justice that legal aid be granted. Thus, solicitors will need to establish that the case is truly exceptional to secure representation by counsel.

VI. The Right to a Fair Trial and Summary Proceedings

[7–32] Judges of the District Court, like judges of all courts, are bound by the terms of the Constitution and must respect the right to a fair trial. Given the speed and number of trials that take place in the District Court, the processes afforded to defendants being tried on indictment do not necessarily apply where the individual is being tried

---

57 The case was argued on constitutional grounds, and while the court agreed with the arguments of the applicant, it decided the case without declaring the section of the Act unconstitutional.

summarily. However, this does not mean that the right to a fair trial is not respected at summary level. For example, as noted by the Working Group on the Jurisdiction of the Courts, simply because a general right to advance disclosure of evidence to be adduced by the prosecution does not exist does not mean that the accused is deprived of due process.[58] This was made clear by Denham J when she stated, "while the District Court is a court of limited statutory power it remains at all times a court which must protect the individual constitutional rights of the person."[59] Thus, both the prosecution and the court must ensure that the trial is carried out in a manner which respects principles of constitutional justice.

In terms of the steps which must be taken by the District Court Judge to ensure that the Constitution is protected and respected, *DPP v Gary Doyle*[60] is illustrative. Here, the accused opted for a summary trial in relation to four counts of burglary and attempted burglary, and pleaded not guilty to the charges. The accused, Doyle, had made a confession statement to gardaí, and counsel for the accused had requested that gardaí interview four alleged witnesses but no such statements were provided to the defence. Where offences are tried on indictment, the accused is entitled to a book of evidence under the Criminal Procedure Act 1967,[61] but, as the Supreme Court pointed out, this did not extend to summary trials of indictable offences. Denham J, in the Supreme Court, indicated the question facing the court was whether constitutional justice and fair procedures demanded that the defence see any statements on which the prosecution would rest its case.[62] While noting that such cases were governed by the rules and procedures of the District Court, Denham J went on to state that serious and complex cases may require this information "be furnished in advance of the trial, to inform the accused of the accusation so that he may prepare his defence."[63] She set out the considerations which should guide a District Court Judge in determining whether constitutional justice requires, in particular, documents to be furnished. The considerations which govern the availability of "Gary Doyle orders" are as follows: **[7–33]**

1. The seriousness of the charge;
2. The importance of the statements or documents;
3. The fact that the accused has already been adequately informed of the nature and substance of the accusation;
4. The likelihood that there is no risk of injustice in failing to furnish the statements or documents in issue to the accused.

Principles of constitutional justice and fair procedures clearly, then, apply in the District Court. As O'Higgins CJ stated in *State (Healy) v Donoghue*: **[7–34]**

> "There are thousands of trivial charges prosecuted in the District Courts throughout the State every day. In respect of all these there must be fairness and

---

58 Working Group on the Jurisdiction of the Courts, *The Criminal Jurisdiction of the Courts* (Courts Service, 2003), p 184.

59 *Coughlan v Judge Patwell* [1993] 1 IR 31 at 37.

60 [1994] 2 IR 286.

61 Discussed in Chapter Eight.

62 [1994] 2 IR 286 at 300.

63 *ibid.* at 302.

> fair procedures, but there may be other cases in which more is required and where justice may be a more exacting task-master. The requirements of fairness and of justice must be considered in relation to the seriousness of the charge brought against the person and the consequences involved for him."[64]

Thus, as noted by the Working Group on the Jurisdiction of the Courts, the degree of seriousness of the offence determines the rigour of the procedure to be employed.[65]

VII. Conclusion

[7–35] While the District Court is marked by speed and informality the importance of proceedings in this court should not be underestimated. It deals with the vast majority of criminal prosecutions in this country and is bound by principles of constitutional justice and fair procedures. It has the power to sentence individuals to prison, depriving them of liberty which is the most severe penalty in Ireland. Yet in this court the right to trial by jury does not apply, and, as we have seen, the right to legal aid is restricted. These aspects will become more apparent as we discuss in the next chapter the importance of the jury in trials on indictment.

---

[64] [1976] IR 325 at 350.

[65] Working Group on the Jurisdiction of the Courts, above n 58, p 183.

CHAPTER 8
Trial on Indictment

In this chapter we will focus on the trial on indictment, which can take place in one of three courts: the Circuit Criminal Court, the Central Criminal Court[1] or the Special Criminal Court. The Circuit Criminal Court has the same jurisdiction as the Central Criminal Court for indictable offences except murder, rape, aggravated sexual assault, treason, piracy and related offences, which must be heard in the Central Criminal Court. The Circuit Criminal Court can exercise its jurisdiction in the area where the offence has been committed or where the accused person has been arrested or resides. Trial judges in Circuit Criminal Courts outside Dublin may transfer a trial to the Dublin Circuit Criminal Court on application by the prosecution or the defence and if satisfied that it would be unjust not to do so. The Central Criminal Court previously only sat in Dublin, but more recently has held sittings in Cork, Limerick, Sligo, Ennis and Castlebar. The Special Criminal Court deals exclusively with cases for which it is felt the ordinary courts are unable to secure the effective administration of justice. **[8–01]**

Compared to summary trials, considered in the previous chapter, there are three main differences: the severity of the offence, the formality of proceedings and, save in the Special Criminal Court, the presence of a jury to decide on issues of fact.

[1] The High Court exercising its criminal jurisdiction is called the Central Criminal Court.

I. The Jury

[8–02] The jury is central to the Irish criminal justice system[2] and its role, though not defined by legislation, is to make determinations of issues of fact, primarily on the guilt of the accused. Article 38.5 of the Constitution provides that, save in certain circumstances,[3] no person shall be tried on a criminal charge without a jury. In *O'Callaghan v AG*[4] the court stated:

> "the purpose of trial by jury is to provide that a person shall get a fair trial, in due course of law, and be tried by a reasonable cross section of people acting under the guidance of the judge, bound by his directions on law, but free to make their findings as to the facts."[5]

[8–03] The jury is a group of lay persons who make a determination of guilt based on the facts of the case, unaffected by legal considerations. The use of juries in Ireland is regulated by the Juries Act 1927, which originally restricted jurors to male property owners between the ages of 21 and 65.[6] Women could request to be included on juries.[7] In *DeBúrca v AG*[8] the exclusion of women and the property requirement were held to be unconstitutional, resulting in the Juries Act 1976 which governs eligibility and selection for jury service.

[8–04] Numerous cases have emphasised how a jury should be representative of its community[9] and to this end the 1976 Act states that juries should be called from a panel of jurors who come from the jury district,[10] the area in which the offence was committed. As Henchy J stated in *State (Byrne) v Frawley* "its members will have to live with that verdict."[11]

Who May Sit on a Jury?

[8–05] To be eligible for jury service a person must be a citizen of the State, between the age of 18 and 70, on the electoral register[12] and not disqualified or ineligible on some other grounds.[13] The first schedule of the Act sets out who is ineligible:

- anyone who has held judicial office, or been a coroner;
- the AG or his staff;

---

[2] That said Jackson, Quinn and O'Malley state that in 1997 99.6% of criminal cases were heard in front of a judge without a jury. See "The Jury System in Contemporary Ireland: In the Shadow of a Troubled Past" (1999) 62(2) *Law and Contemporary Problems* 203.

[3] Where the offence tried is minor (see Chapter Seven), or where it is being tried in the Special Criminal Court or by a military tribunal.

[4] [1993] 2 IR 17.

[5] *ibid.* at 25.

[6] Juries Act 1927, s 3.

[7] Sch 1, Pt 1, Persons Exempted but Entitled to Serve on Application.

[8] [1976] IR 38.

[9] *De Búrca v AG, ibid; MacCarthaigh v Éire*, unreported, Supreme Court, 5 July 1998.

[10] As defined by the Juries Act 1976, s 5.

[11] [1978] IR 326 at 347.

[12] Juries Act 1976, s 6.

[13] s 7.

- the DPP or his staff;
- barristers, solicitors, apprentices;
- persons working in the courts;
- gardaí[14];
- prison officers;
- persons working in the Department of Justice or a forensics laboratory;
- a member of the army/army reserve; or
- those who are illiterate or have some enduring impairment which makes it "not practicable for them to perform the duties of a juror."[15]

In 2010 Joan Clarke succeeded in challenging her exclusion from jury service on the grounds of deafness, however the High Court refused to go so far as to allow sign language interpreters to assist during jury deliberations, meaning that deaf persons will not be able to effectively participate in jury service.[16] In 2010 the Law Reform Commission published a *Consultation Paper on Jury Service*, the recommendations of which called for a replacement of exclusion on the basis of physical disability or mental ill-health with a requirement of capacity, as determined by the judge.[17] **[8–06]**

The other grounds for ineligibility are predominantly included to ensure that jury members are in a position to make a decision solely on the facts and are not tainted by their particular expertise. It also ensures that these persons do not have a conflict of interest in terms of making a judgment on a case presented by colleagues. **[8–07]**

Certain persons who may otherwise be eligible can be disqualified from jury service.[18] If a person has been sentenced to at least a five year term of imprisonment following conviction, irrespective of actual time served, he will be barred for life from serving on a jury.[19] A person who has served at least three months in prison in the previous ten years will be barred.[20] This equally applies where the sentence was imposed in Northern Ireland.[21] **[8–08]**

In addition to disqualification, individuals may be excused from jury service where they satisfy certain criteria. A judge must excuse a person from jury service if: **[8–09]**

- he is listed in Part II of the First Schedule of the 1976 Act, which includes TDs, members of the Council of State, the Comptroller and Auditor General, a person in Holy Orders, medical practitioners, heads of government departments, chief

---

[14] s 3 of the Garda Síochána Act 2005 defines "member" in respect of An Garda Síochána as including members of the Garda Reserve. It is presumed that in relation to jury service the term "member of An Garda Síochána" would be given this administrative interpretation so as to include members of the Reserve.

[15] Criminal Law (Miscellaneous Provisions) Act 2008, s 64, amending previous restrictions of persons illiterate, deaf, suffering from mental illness or disability requiring regular medical treatment.

[16] *Clarke v Galway County Registrar*, see "Court Finds in Favour of Deaf Woman" *The Irish Times*, 15 July 2010.

[17] Law Reform Commission, *Consultation Paper on Jury Service* (LRC CP 61-2010), p 211.

[18] Juries Act 1976, s 8.

[19] s 8(a).

[20] s 8(b).

[21] s 8(a) and (b).

officers of local authorities or health services, and full time students, among others;

- he has served on a jury in the last three years;
- he has been excused for a period which has not ended yet.[22]

[8–10] The individual must express a desire to be excused and the registrar must be satisfied as to his position. Other persons who satisfy the registrar that there is good reason may be excused.[23] Individuals caring for children, persons whose business would suffer, or persons who are ill or pregnant are generally excused. The request can be made in writing or orally at the empanelment and the registrar must believe it will impact on the capacity of the individual to give his full attention to the case and to participate in his duties. An excusal will only apply to that summons, not to any future summons. A refusal to excuse can be appealed.[24] During the course of the trial a judge may excuse a juror for good reason[25] and at the end of the trial, may excuse the jurors for as long a period as he thinks appropriate.[26]

Creating the Jury

[8–11] The first stage in the process of 'empanelling' the jury involves the registrar of electors sending a copy of the register to the court registrar, who is charged with the task of empanelment.[27] The number of members of a jury is not provided for by legislation but traditionally there are 12 members. Jurors are selected from the register at random and in a non-discriminatory way,[28] with ineligible or disqualified persons omitted.[29] A written summons, requiring attendance at court on a specified date, is sent to selected individuals.[30] Failure to attend the summons is punishable by way of a fine.[31] The number summonsed will be large enough to ensure that there are sufficient jurors from whom to select a jury as determined by the registrar.

Persons cannot have their pay reduced by employers while serving on a jury.[32] No such provisions are made for self-employed persons who often base an application for excusal on this fact.

[8–12] The selection of the jury from the panel happens on the date specified in the summons, in open court. The judge begins by warning of a penalty for serving while ineligible or disqualified.[33] Any doubts should be communicated to the judge and failing to do so or making false representations to avoid service are offences.[34] A juror should declare

[22] s 9.
[23] s 9(2).
[24] s 9(4).
[25] s 9(7).
[26] s 9(8).
[27] s 10.
[28] s 11.
[29] s 11.
[30] s 12.
[31] s 34.
[32] s 29.
[33] s 15(3).
[34] s 35.

an interest in, or a connection to the parties to the case,[35] which is grounds for a challenge, not exclusion. A juror should inform the judge if he is a victim of the accused.[36] Similarly, having been a victim of a similar crime could mean the juror is unable to bring an impartial mind to bear on the case.[37] Jurors who are unfit for service due to alcohol or drugs may be punished by way of a fine.[38]

Selection is carried out by drawing names from a box, called balloting, by the registrar, who calls the name and asks the individual to step into the jury box.[39] Twenty jurors are normally called forward to allow for challenges. More can be balloted or summonsed[40] if required. The registrar must swear in each juror.[41] Jurors will hold a copy of the New Testament and take this oath: **[8–13]**

> "I swear by Almighty God, that I will well and truly try the issue whether the accused is (or are) guilty or not guilty of the offence (or the several offences) charged in the indictment preferred against him (or her or them) and a true verdict give according to the evidence."

There are different oaths and affirmations for non-Christians[42] and where the issue to be tried is the fitness of the accused to plead. Refusal to be sworn in is a criminal offence and will result in exclusion from the jury.[43]

Challenges to a juror, either pre-emptory or for cause, can be made between the name being called and the oath being taken.[44] Both sides are permitted seven pre-emptory challenges without having to show cause and the individual challenged will be automatically excluded.[45] The basis for this challenge will be a judgment on a subjective issue such as age, sex, appearance, address or employment, which it is believed may influence the candidate juror's decision. If there are several co-accused each will have seven challenges, while the prosecution will always only have seven.[46] Once the jury panel has been summonsed, either party to the proceedings may apply to the county registrar for a copy of the panel list, which will include names, addresses and possibly occupations, which is supplied free of charge.[47] The prosecution may also **[8–14]**

---

35 s 15(3).
36 In *People (AG) v Singer* (1961) 1 Frewen 214 this was grounds for quashing a conviction.
37 *People (DPP) v Tobin* [2001] 3 IR 469.
38 s 34(2).
39 s 15(1).
40 Criminal Procedure Act 1967, s 14(1).
41 Juries Act 1976, s 17.
42 ss 18 and 19.
43 s 37.
44 s 17(4).
45 s 20(1).
46 s 20(2).
47 s 16. Calls for reform of this have been made following the finding of the list of a jury panel, with addresses, in the home of a gangland criminal in April 2010; see "AGS seeks review of supplying jurors' names to defendants" *Irish Times,* 14 April 2010.

check for criminal records of any member of the panel.[48] O'Malley suggests that challenges have been used to exclude minority racial ethnicities from juries.[49]

[8–15] Both the prosecution and the defence can challenge any number of jurors "for cause shown."[50] Cause is not defined in the legislation, which states that it is for the judge to decide "as he shall think proper."[51] Walsh suggests that a challenge would require the ability to function as an impartial juror to be called into question.[52] Some bias will need to be shown.[53] A family member having a criminal conviction is not sufficient.[54] In *People (DPP) v McCarthy*[55] the argument that a juror who worked in a civil capacity in a garda station should be removed failed. The court held he was legally eligible and had taken the oath, which it could not be assumed would be disregarded.[56]

[8–16] Prior knowledge of the case through media reporting is not normally sufficient, as this can be offset by directions from the judge.[57] As Kearns J stated in *Redmond v DPP*,[58]

> "The entire conduct of trials within the jury system proceeds on the assumption that juries will take seriously any directions and guidance given to them by the trial judge. It is wrong... to impute naivety to jurors, and the jury system is a robust and enduring system which has served the community over many hundreds of years."[59]

[8–17] A juror cannot be questioned by counsel during a challenge,[60] though a judge may question a juror to clarify whether or not he is ineligible, or has a conflict of interest in the case.[61] A judge may ask jurors if he feels they have been so exposed to publicity about a case that they would not be able to bring an open mind to the case.[62]

[8–18] Under common law the prosecution or the defence can challenge the whole jury panel on the basis that the person who summonsed the jury acted improperly or was biased.

---

48 In *People (DPP) v McCarthy* [2008] 3 IR 1 it became apparent on challenge that the prosecution had conducted criminal background checks on family members of potential jurors.

49 O'Malley, "A Representative and Impartial Jury" (2003) *Bar Review* 233. See Jeffers, "The Representative and impartial Jury in the Criminal Trial: An Achievable Reality in Ireland Today?" (2008) 18(2) ICLJ 34.

50 Juries Act 1976, s 21(2).

51 s 21(3).

52 Walsh, *Criminal Procedure* (Round Hall, Dublin, 2002), p 835.

53 *R v O'Coigley* (1798) 26 ST TR 1191: an expression of hostility to one side or expressing an early wish as to the outcome of the case would be grounds for exclusion.

54 *People (DPP) v McCarthy* [2008] 3 IR 1.

55 *ibid.*

56 Currently (August 2010) on appeal to the Supreme Court.

57 *R v Kray* (1969) 53 Cr. App. R. 412. Pre-trial publicity in terms of the trial is discussed below at para 8-49.

58 [2002] 4 IR 133.

59 *ibid.* at 144.

60 See *People (AG) v Singer* (1961) 1 Frewen 214 and *People (AG) v Lehman (No 2)* [1947] IR 137.

61 Juries Act 1976, ss 35(3) and 15(3).

62 This question resulted in the exclusion of a number of jurors in the highly publicised trial of Catherine Nevin for the murder of her husband, *People (DPP) v Nevin* [2003] 3 IR 321.

This is known as "challenging the array".[63] English case-law suggests that if the person who did the summonsing had a personal interest in the outcome of the case or if he included people in the panel for certain reasons this can be grounds for challenge.[64] A challenge to the array cannot be permitted on the basis of imbalance due to race, gender or age.

Discharging Jurors

The judge may discharge any member of the jury at any point during the trial, of his own initiative or on an application of either side, if the judge feels it is necessary for the administration of justice.[65] The judge may need to question the juror before so doing. If, through discharges, membership of the jury falls below ten then the jury will no longer be effective and the trial should be abandoned.[66] **[8–19]**

The power to discharge the whole jury exists at common law and can be exercised up until the jury has reached its verdict, resulting in a new trial. In *People (AG) v Heffernan (No 2)*[67] a conviction was quashed because of contact between jury members and a group of tourists despite no suggestion that the trial had been discussed. Walsh outlines that the discretion to discharge the jury can be exercised due to inadvertent prejudice against the accused,[68] misconduct by some members, personal knowledge of the accused or his criminal record,[69] or where they cannot agree on a verdict.[70] **[8–20]**

II. Pre-Trial Matters

When the accused is brought before the District Court, charged with an indictable offence, the court must "send him forward" to the court where he will be tried,[71] unless the offence is triable either way and the accused is being tried summarily,[72] pleads guilty or is unfit to plead.[73] The book of evidence must be served on the accused and his solicitor within 42 days of this first hearing and then submitted to the District Court.[74] Under the Criminal Procedure Act 1967 the book of evidence must contain: **[8–21]**

- a statement of charges;
- copies of any sworn information, in writing, upon which proceedings were initiated;
- a list of witnesses the prosecutor proposes to call at trial;

---

63 Walsh, above n 52, p 841.
64 *R v Dolby* (1823) 2 B &C 104 and *R v O'Doherty* (1848) 6 St Tr NS 831, discussed by Walsh, above n 52, p 841.
65 Juries Act 1976, s 24.
66 s 23.
67 [1951] IR 206.
68 For example, being told negative aspects of the accused's character, including any previous criminal record.
69 *People (DPP) v Conroy* [1986] IR 460. On the other hand see *People (DPP) v Kelly* [2006] 4 IR 273.
70 Walsh, above n 52, p 846.
71 Criminal Procedure Act 1967, s 4(1)(a).
72 See Chapter Seven for a discussion of offences triable either way.
73 Discussed further below.
74 Criminal Procedure Act 1967, s 4B(2).

- a statement of the evidence expected to be given by witnesses;
- a copy of any document containing information proposed to be given as evidence under the Criminal Evidence Act 1992 (the Act refers to records compiled by certain public bodies);
- a copy of a certificate under s 6(1) of that Act, where appropriate (the subsection relates to the information in that record); and
- a list of any exhibits.[75]

[8–22] The accused should see, in certain circumstances, a video-recording of any statement made to gardaí by the alleged victim which is to be given in evidence.[76] Further documents must be submitted by the DPP, including a list of any additional witnesses the DPP decides at a later date to introduce, a statement of the evidence expected to be given by them, a statement of any further evidence to be given by a witness whose name appeared in the original book of evidence and a list of further exhibits.[77] It is important however that these are submitted in good time before the trial out of fairness to the accused.

[8–23] The accused can apply at any point of the trial court proceedings to have one or all of the charges against him dismissed.[78] At a hearing of such an application, of which the prosecution must be given 14 days notice,[79] the accused will be required to prove to the court that there is insufficient evidence to justify a trial. Oral evidence may be presented on permission of the court and the judge may order the serving of relevant documents in the possession of the DPP on the accused.[80] If the court is satisfied that a reasonable jury properly charged could not convict the accused of the charges on the evidence presented, the charge must be dismissed.[81] The prosecution can appeal this decision within 21 days to the Court of Criminal Appeal.[82]

[8–24] These proceedings should be held in open court unless the court believes that it would be desirable in the interests of justice to exclude the public, a section of the public or individuals from the hearings.[83] The press cannot be excluded though limitations can be placed on what can be published or broadcast about the proceedings. If the accused qualifies for legal aid for the trial on indictment, this will apply to any such hearings.[84]

[8–25] Following the decision to send forward, the indictment, the formal document which sets out the offences with which the accused is charged, will be drawn up. The document must be correctly completed or any subsequent trial may be invalid.[85] The

---

[75] DCR, Ord 24, r 7.

[76] Criminal Evidence Act 1992, ss (1) and 16(1)(b). This applies where it involves a sexual offence or an offence involving violence, the alleged victim was under 14 at the time and under 17 when the accused is sent forward to trial.

[77] Criminal Procedure Act 1967, s 4C(1).

[78] s 4E(1).

[79] s 4E(2).

[80] ss 4E(5) and (6).

[81] s 4E(4)

[82] s 4E(8)

[83] DCR, Ord 14, r 3 as amended by the District Court (Criminal Justice) Rules 2000, r 3(b).

[84] Criminal Procedure Act, s 4H(2). Legal aid is discussed below at para 8-28.

[85] The form of the indictment is regulated by the Criminal Justice (Administration) Act 1924.

indictment, compiled by counsel for the prosecution, should identify the prosecutor, the court to which the indictment is to be preferred and the offences charged.[86] Further offences can later be added or substituted. Each offence will be described in a separate paragraph, called a count.[87] A count should only contain one offence otherwise it will be considered "bad for duplicity", meriting a motion to quash the count.[88] Counts should be numbered. Where the offence is contrary to statute law the count should identify the legislation and section.[89] The details of the offence must be outlined in ordinary language and include the name of the accused, the date and location of the offence and the acts or omissions which give rise to the offence.[90] New counts can be 'joined' to the indictment at a later date until an order for a retrial is issued.[91] Two or more defendants can be charged on the same indictment.

The Criminal Justice (Administration) Act 1924 provides that the judge may "sever the indictment", resulting in separate trials for multiple counts or accused[92] on the one indictment, where he feels that "it is desirable".[93] An application for severance can be made at any point following the plea on the indictment, even after the trial has commenced. [8–26]

The final pre-trial matter to be considered is disclosure, which refers to duties placed on the prosecution "to disclose material in its possession to the defence in advance of the trial where that material may be of assistance to the defence."[94] There may be material which is not included in the book of evidence which would be of assistance to the defence, and whether or not this should be disclosed is contentious. The duty to disclose falls within the constitutional right to fair procedures[95] and Art 6 ECHR.[96] The prosecution will be obliged to disclose all relevant evidence in its possession. Failure to do so can result in the quashing of a conviction.[97] This burden of disclosure does not apply to the defence although certain statutory provisions impose obligations to disclose limited pieces of information such as alibis.[98] [8–27]

III. Legal Aid

As discussed in the previous chapter, the Criminal Justice (Legal Aid) Act 1962 provides for legal aid where the applicant does not have sufficient means to fund it, where it is in the interests of justice, given the gravity of the offence, that the applicant [8–28]

---

86 Criminal Procedure Act 1967, s 4M.
87 Criminal Justice (Administration) Act 1924, Sch 1 r 4(1).
88 Walsh, above n 52, p 746. Where this motion is not granted it can serve as a ground for appeal against conviction.
89 Above n 86, Sch 1 r 4(3).
90 reg 9. Sample indictments are provided in the Schedule.
91 *Conlon v His Honour Judge Cyril Kelly*, unreported, High Court, 14 December 1999.
92 Confirmed in *AG v Joyce* [1929] IR 526.
93 Above n 86, s 6(3).
94 Walsh, above n 52, p 715. See also, Fennell, *The Law of Evidence in Ireland* (3rd Edition, Bloomsbury Professional, Hampstead Heath, 2009).
95 *People (DPP) v Tuite* 2 Frewen 175.
96 *Edwards v UK* (1992) 15 EHHR 417.
97 *People (DPP) v Meleady* [1995] 2 IR 517.
98 Criminal Justice Act 1984, s 20(1).

have legal aid to prepare and conduct his defence.[99] Under the legislation, legal aid will be granted for a trial on indictment where:

- an application is made for legal aid;
- the accused has insufficient means to secure representation himself;
- the person is charged with murder or in the circumstances the interests of justice demand that the accused have legal aid in preparing and conducting his defence.[100]

[8–29] Factors beyond these cannot be taken into account by the judge in deciding this matter.[101] The trial judge must inform the accused of his right to legal representation, and, according to *Healy*,[102] the accused must be told of the free legal aid scheme.[103] An accused may of course waive his right to representation but the judge must be satisfied that this has been done "intelligently and understandingly."[104] In such instances the trial may proceed without representation. If it only becomes clear later in the trial that a custodial sentence is likely the court must then again advise the accused of his right to representation.[105]

[8–30] An application can be made by the accused on being charged in the District Court[106] and the court's decision is final.[107] A separate legal aid (trial on indictment) certificate can be applied for in the District Court when the accused has been sent forward for trial or in the court where the accused is to be tried.[108] There is no statement in the legislation that this decision is final.

[8–31] The application can be made orally or in writing. A written statement of means may be required by the court[109] and it is within the discretion of the court to determine whether the means of the accused merit legal aid. Once the court is satisfied as to means it must then consider whether either the gravity of the offence or exceptional circumstances make it essential in the interests of justice for legal aid to be provided. This is automatically satisfied by a charge of murder, but, in line with *Healy*,[110] will presumably be satisfied wherever a custodial sentence is possible.

[8–32] Once a legal aid certificate is granted, it will entitle an applicant to a solicitor and a barrister for trials on indictment. The county registrar and the Minister for Justice maintain a list of all lawyers who opt to participate in the scheme. When legal aid is granted the court will assign a lawyer from the list. An applicant does not have a right

---

99 s 2(1) as amended by Criminal Justice (Miscellaneous Provisions) Act 1997, s 5(6).
100 *ibid.*
101 See *Whelan v Fitzpatrick* [2007] IEHC 213. In that case the judge had a policy of not awarding legal aid in drink driving cases but on appeal it was held that this was not a relevant factor.
102 *State (Healy) v Donoghue* [1976] IR 325.
103 See also *Cahill v Reilly* [1994] 3 IR 547.
104 [1976] IR 325.
105 *Leonard v Garavan* [2003] 4 IR 60.
106 Criminal Justice (Legal Aid) Act 1965, s 2(1).
107 s 2(2).
108 s 3.
109 s 9.
110 [1976] IR 325. See Chapter Seven.

to choose the solicitor[111] although if a preference is stated the courts do not object to this, once it is practically possible. A defendant is not entitled to try and prevent a trial from proceeding if the solicitor he wants is unavailable.[112]

There are accompanying regulations which establish the amounts payable under the scheme.[113] It also allows for payment of expenses for defence witnesses or experts.[114] The scheme does not cover representation while detained in custody, bail applications or habeas corpus applications. [8–33]

IV. Trial Procedure

Proceedings will be conducted in English unless the accused avails of his right to have the proceedings heard in Irish.[115] This does not extend to requiring other witnesses to present evidence in Irish. The court must provide interpreters for this if necessary, as is increasingly the case in a multi-cultural Ireland.[116] An attempt to argue that all jurors should be Irish speakers failed in *MacCarthaigh v Eire*.[117] Article 6 ECHR provides that everyone should have the assistance of an interpreter if he cannot understand or speak the language of the court. The ECtHR has interpreted this so as to give primacy to procedural fairness rather than language rights: interpretation should be provided, free of charge, on the grounds of necessity.[118] [8–34]

The trial on indictment begins with the prosecution presenting its opening statement which summarises the facts intended to be proven against the accused. No mention can be made of inadmissible evidence.[119] The prosecution will then call its witnesses, who will have been summonsed by the court to attend.[120] The general rule is that all evidence must be given orally in court, though there are some documents which may be presented as proof of content. All evidence given by witnesses must be given on oath or solemn affirmation.[121] Prosecuting counsel will then conduct the examination in chief, asking witnesses questions which they are obliged to answer. A leading question, which suggests the answer desired, is not permitted. The evidence may differ from that in pre-trial statements, but, under the Criminal Justice Act 2006, if the evidence given is materially inconsistent with the initial statement or if a witness refuses to testify or denies making a previous statement, that earlier statement can be admitted as evidence.[122] [8–35]

---

[111] *State (Healy) v Donoghue* [1976] IR 325.
[112] *State (Royle) v Kelly* [1974] IR 259.
[113] Criminal Justice (Legal Aid) Regulations 1965.
[114] *ibid.*
[115] Article 8 of the Constitution declares Irish to be the national and first official language which translates to a right to have court proceedings heard in Irish: *Ó Beoláin v Fahy* [2001] 2 IR 279.
[116] *O'Monachain v An Taoiseach* [1986] ILRM 660.
[117] Unreported, Supreme Court, 15 July 1998.
[118] *Cuscani v United Kingdom* (2003) 36 EHRR 2; *Luedicke v Federal Republic of Germany* (1978) 2 EHRR 149.
[119] If evidence was mentioned in this statement which was later ruled inadmissible it could result in a retrial.
[120] Criminal Procedure Act 1967, s 4L.
[121] Oaths Act 1888, ss 1 and 2.
[122] Criminal Justice Act 2006, s 6(1).

[8–36] The evidence of witnesses will be given "live", in front of the jury, though provision is made for vulnerable witnesses to give their evidence via video-link in certain circumstances.[123] Witnesses wait to be called in the courtroom unless an application is made to have some or all of the witnesses excluded from the courtroom.

[8–37] Following the examination in chief of a prosecution witness he can be cross-examined by the defence, primarily to cast doubt on the credibility of the witness. Greater freedom is permitted in this questioning and leading questions are allowed.[124] After this, the prosecution is permitted an opportunity to re-examine the witness to clarify any points which remain unclear. In order to introduce fresh evidence at this stage the permission of the judge is required, and the defence must then be afforded an opportunity to question the witness. Wherever the admissibility of evidence is contested, the jury will be excused from court and a hearing called a *voir dire*,[125] a trial within a trial, will be held. Both parties can call witnesses as necessary in this hearing and cross-examine witnesses called. At the end of the hearing the judge rules on admissibility. The jury will then be recalled to court and the trial will resume, with or without the evidence.

[8–38] At the end of the prosecution case the judge can, of his own volition or on an application from the accused, direct the jury to acquit the accused. This can be based on a determination that the accused is not legally guilty of the crime or the judge may feel that on the basis of the evidence presented no reasonable jury could find the defendant guilty. In the vast majority of cases, however, the trial proceeds to the defence case, the procedure for which will depend on whether he is represented by counsel.

[8–39] If the defence has representation, the judge will ask for any defence evidence to be introduced. If there is none, the trial will proceed to closing statements.[126] If there is evidence, the format will depend on whether or not the defence intends to call witnesses other than the accused as to the facts of the case. If other witnesses are being called then an opening statement by the defence is permitted and the process of examination, cross-examination, re-examination and closing statements by both sides is followed. If no other witnesses are being called, there is no opening statement and the case proceeds to the accused being called as a witness, if he is giving evidence,[127] which can be followed by any witnesses as to the good character of the accused. This is then followed by summations from both prosecution and defence.

[8–40] If the accused does not have legal representation and does not call witnesses the prosecution loses its right to make a closing statement.[128] An accused who opts to

---

[123] See Chapter Twelve para 12-17.

[124] There are some restrictions on what can be asked. For example, a rape victim may not be questioned about previous sexual conduct without leave of the judge, Criminal Law Rape Act 1981, s 3(1).

[125] Literally, to speak the truth.

[126] Criminal Procedure Act 1865, s 2.

[127] The privilege against self-incrimination means that the accused is under no obligation to give evidence.

[128] Criminal Justice Act 1984, s 24.

defend himself has a right to address the jury on his own behalf and the trial judge must make the accused aware of that right.[129] Where the accused is not represented and refuses to participate in proceedings the prosecution has a right to sum up, for the general assistance of the court.[130] Where the accused chooses to give evidence he may be cross-examined though limits are imposed on this by the Criminal Justice Evidence Act 1924.[131] Certain protections are still provided, which are collectively called "the shield". He cannot be asked questions about his bad character or previous offences. The legislation outlines the circumstances when the shield can be lifted: if the questions go to show that the accused is guilty of the offence, if he has given evidence as to his good character, if by his defence he has cast imputation on a witness for the prosecution, or if he has given evidence against a co-accused.[132] Where the accused opts to give evidence, he must do so on oath, can be cross-examined and loses his privilege against self-incrimination.

The judge retains a discretion to permit the prosecution to submit further evidence after the defence case where the defence raises issues which the prosecution could not have anticipated.[133] Additionally, the judge retains a right to call a witness not called by either side.[134] The parties do not have a right to cross-examine such a witness, but should be given leave to do so where the evidence could be considered adverse to the party seeking to cross-examine.[135] **[8–41]**

Following the presentation of evidence by both sides each party makes a closing address which summarises the key evidence and the arguments which the parties wish the jury to draw from the evidence. It should be as short as possible. There are restrictions on what can be said at this point. Neither party can raise any issue which has not been raised and established during the trial procedure. The prosecution cannot say anything about the accused's failure to give evidence or the fact that the accused did not call other witnesses to give evidence.[136] The defence is not allowed to say that the offence was committed by a specific person who is not on trial though it can suggest that it was committed by someone else, non-specific.[137] **[8–42]**

The judge will normally then sum up the case for the jury. The content will differ from case to case but overall it should assist the jury in making their decision, providing an overview of their task and outlining what they may consider in reaching their decision. The wording is important and jury directions have resulted in numerous convictions being quashed due to the wording by the judge.[138] The jury will be told to consider multiple counts and multiple defendants separately, which includes considering the **[8–43]**

---

[129] *State (Healy) v Donoghue* [1976] IR 325.
[130] *People (AG) v Kerins* [1945] IR 339.
[131] s 1(e).
[132] For a more detailed discussion of these evidential issues see Fennell, above n 94.
[133] See, for example, *People (DPP) v Leahy* Unreported, Court of Criminal Appeal, 14 February 2000.
[134] *R v Harris* [1927] 2 KB 587.
[135] *Coulson v Disborough* [1894] 2 QB 316.
[136] Criminal Justice (Evidence) Act 1924, s 1(b).
[137] *AG v O'Leary* [1926] IR 445.
[138] *AG v O'Shea* [1931] IR 713.

evidence for each count or defendant separately.[139] The cases for the prosecution and the defence must be addressed objectively. Any legal rules or principles should be explained clearly to the jury, such as the standard of proof. There is no exact formula for this, but the high level of the standard must be conveyed.[140] Equally where the onus of proof lies must be reiterated and the jury must be advised that the benefit of the doubt must be applied in favour of the accused.[141] The judge can comment on the failure of the accused to testify, but must be balanced and remind the jury that the accused was under no such obligation.[142]

V. Jury Deliberations

[8–44] The jury will then retire to consider their verdict. An officer of the court will be assigned to them with a view to meeting any needs they have and to make sure they do not talk to anyone. At this point the jurors are not permitted to separate without the permission of the court. If deliberations run into multiple days, the jury will be sequestered together.

[8–45] The jury will be given an issue paper which sets out the charges and what they must decide. They can be given access to any exhibits which were admitted as evidence during the trial. They may ask questions of the court, but nothing that could not be asked during the trial.[143] They may ask for a witness to be recalled.[144] If during the deliberations counsel for either party objects to an element of the judge's summation, the judge may if he feels it is necessary, recall the jury and instruct them further. If the jury ask for further assistance/direction this must be done in open court with all counsel present. Juries may not be questioned about their deliberations.

VI. The Verdict

[8–46] The jury must return, at the end of their deliberations, a verdict on each count on the indictment. Possible verdicts are guilty, not guilty or cannot agree. In some circumstances a verdict relating to a different offence, known as an alternative verdict, is permitted by legislation. For instance a verdict of manslaughter may be returned on a murder charge.[145] The jury are also allowed to return a 'special verdict' which involves making a decision on the facts but leaving the legal ramifications of that decision for the court. An example is the verdict of not guilty by reason of insanity under the Criminal Law (Insanity) Act 2006.[146]

[8–47] Traditionally verdicts had to be unanimous but the Criminal Justice Act 1984 introduced the possibility of majority verdicts in certain circumstances, the constitutionality of which has been upheld.[147] Once there are at least 11 jurors and 10 agree on

[139] *People v Wallace* (1982) 2 Frewen 125.
[140] *People v Byrne* [1974] IR 1.
[141] *AG v O'Connor* [1935] Ir Jur Rep 1.
[142] *People (AG) v Travers* [1956] IR 110.
[143] *People (DPP) v Noonan* [1998] 2 IR 439.
[144] *People (AG) v O'Brien* [1963] IR 65.
[145] Criminal Law Act 1997, s 9(4).
[146] s 5.
[147] *O'Callaghan v AG* [1993] 2 IR 17.

the verdict, that is permissible.[148] If there are only 10 members of the jury then the decision must be unanimous. A guilty verdict must be validated by the foreman who must declare in court that it is the verdict of a unanimous jury or a stated majority. This is not required for a verdict of not guilty. At least two hours deliberation are required before a majority verdict can be accepted, longer in cases where the judge feels that is appropriate given the complexity of the issues involved.[149] If they fail to agree on any verdict the judge has the discretion to discharge the jury and order a retrial.[150]

The judge must accept the first unambiguous verdict delivered by the jury and is not allowed to ask them to reconsider. If, however, parts of it are unclear the judge may ask them to reconsider.[151] No amendment can be made to the verdict once the jury have left the jury box. If the accused is found guilty the judge can proceed to a sentencing hearing, which will usually be adjourned for the gathering of necessary reports. If the accused is found not guilty then he should be released immediately. If the accused did not have legal aid, and was found not guilty, he may apply at this point for costs to be ordered against the State. **[8–48]**

VII. Publicity

The Constitution declares that justice is to be administered in public[152] and Art 6 ECHR provides that an accused is entitled to a "fair and public hearing." That said, restrictions can be imposed either on the basis of the accused's right to a fair trial or in the interests of witnesses. **[8–49]**

Legislation can provide for holding cases *in camera*. In an incest case only the parties, legal representatives, the judge, jury and some members of the press can be present during the trial.[153] Witnesses will only be in the courtroom while they are giving evidence. The Children Act 2001 empowers a judge to clear a court of all persons save interested parties to the case and a number of press representatives, wherever a person under the age of 18 is giving evidence as a witness.[154] Similar restrictions can also be imposed for cases concerning official secrets.[155]

Restrictions on the reporting of a case by the press can be imposed by legislation. In sexual offence cases the media will be obliged to report the case in a way which protects the anonymity of the parties.[156] In any case, *voir dire* hearings on the admissibility of evidence cannot be reported until the end of the trial to ensure jury members do not hear of them. In *Irish Times v Murphy*[157] the Supreme Court ruled, in terms of orders to delay the reporting of cases, that where a conflict arose between an individual's right **[8–50]**

---

148 Criminal Justice Act 1984, s 25. This means that a verdict will be lawful if 10/12, 11/12 or 10/11 agree.
149 s 25(3).
150 See *State v M'Mullen*, unreported, Court of Criminal Appeal, 12 July 1999.
151 *R v Carter* [1964] 2 QB 1.
152 Art 34.1.
153 Criminal Law (Incest Proceedings) Act 1995, s 2.
154 s 257.
155 Official Secrets Act 1963, s 12.
156 Criminal Law (Rape) Act 1981, ss 7 and 8.
157 [1998] 2 ILRM 161.

to a fair trial and the need to administer justice in public, the former must prevail. In *Independent Newspapers (Ireland) Ltd v Anderson*[158] it was clarified that restrictions on reporting may not be imposed unless:

- legislation permits it;
- where there is discretion in the legislation, the judge must be satisfied that hearing the case in public would fall short of doing justice; or,
- where there is no statutory provision the court must be satisfied that (a) there is a real risk of an unfair trial and (b) the damage caused by holding it in public could not be remedied by directions of the trial judge.[159]

[8–51] The courts will be slow to go so far as to prohibit the trial on the basis that pre-trial publicity means the accused cannot receive a fair trial, despite the fact that the Supreme Court recognised in *D v DPP*[160] that

> "fair procedures incorporate the requirement of a trial by jury unprejudiced by pre-trial publicity. The applicant is entitled to a jury capable of concluding a fair determination of facts on the facts as presented at trial."[161]

[8–52] In *Rattigan v DPP*[162] the court said that publicity which either strongly points to guilt or innocence or which will impair the accused's ability to conduct his defence could be considered as prejudicial pre-trial publicity. The burden of proof is on the accused to show that the pre-trial publicity represents a real or serious risk of an unfair trial, which could not be averted by directions of the judge. Where satisfied, the court can either prohibit or postpone the trial, or the case can be transferred the Special Criminal Court.

[8–53] However in *D* the Chief Justice felt much potential prejudice can be mitigated by trial judge directions. Prohibition of the trial was not ordered in *Z v DPP*,[163] which involved the prosecution of Z for the rape a fifteen year old who became the centre of the *X case*.[164] The X case was a highly contentious and publicised case on abortion, which had resulted in a divisive referendum. In allowing the prosecution to proceed the Supreme Court stated that the "risk is a real one but the unfairness of trial must be an unavoidable unfairness of trial." The risks could be avoided by the directions of the trial judge. In *Rattigan v DPP*[165] the Supreme Court stated that it would be rare that the directions of the trial judge could not overcome the effects of pre-trial adverse publicity. Again, the court refused the order in that case, despite the court accepting that the details of the gangland murder of which he was convicted were particularly vivid and might be remembered by jurors. Similarly in *Redmond v DPP*[166] the judge

---

[158] [2006] 3 IR 341.
[159] *ibid.* at 347.
[160] [1994] 2 IR 465
[161] *ibid.* at 473.
[162] [2008] IESC 34.
[163] [1994] 2 IR 476.
[164] *AG v X* [1992] 1 IR 1.
[165] [2008] IESC 34
[166] [2002] 4 IR 133.

accepted that it would not be possible to find a panel of jurors who had not been exposed to some of the publicity concerning the case, but that any effects could be overcome by the directions of the judge.

The courts will take alternative measures where necessary. In *People (DPP) v Nevin*[167] the court banned the publication of "colour pieces" in which the appearance of the accused in court was discussed. In *DPP v Haugh (No 2)*[168] the court went a step further and adjourned the trial. **[8–54]**

VIII. The Special Criminal Court

The government may establish special, non-jury courts where they are believed necessary, which usually stems from concerns over jury intimidation. Article 38.3.1° of the Constitution states: **[8–55]**

> "1° Special courts may be established by law for the trial of offences in cases where it may be determined in accordance with such law that the ordinary courts are inadequate to secure the effective administration of justice, and the preservation of public peace and order.
> 2° The constitution, powers, jurisdiction and procedure of such special courts shall be prescribed by law."

While this provision allows for such special courts, legislation is required to establish them. This was done by s 35(2) of the Offences Against the State Act 1939 which provides: **[8–56]**

> "If and whenever and so often as the Government is satisfied that the ordinary courts are inadequate to secure the effective administration of justice and the preservation of public peace and order ... the Government may make and publish a proclamation declaring that the Government is satisfied as aforesaid and ordering that this Part of this Act shall come into force."

As a result of the constitutional and legislative provisions, the government can make a proclamation at any point to establish special courts, a power which has been upheld by the Supreme Court.[169] The government must do this whenever it feels that the ordinary courts are inadequate for achieving justice.[170] This proclamation will remain in force until the Dáil passes a resolution[171] or the government issues a proclamation repealing it.[172] The nature of these courts, including jurisdiction and procedure, is detailed in Part V of the Act. **[8–57]**

---

[167] [2003] 3 IR 321.

[168] [2001] 1 IR 162. A suggestion by the judge that he could survey the jurors to assess their impartiality was rejected by the High Court in *People (DPP) v Haugh* [2000] 1 IR 184.

[169] Constitutional challenges to the Court have been rejected in *Re MacCurtain* [1941] IR 83 and *Kavanagh v Ireland* [1997] 1 ILRM 321.

[170] Offences Against the State Act 1939, s 35(1)(2).

[171] *ibid.* s 35(5).

[172] *ibid.* s 35(4).

[8–58] The government has issued three proclamations bringing the Special Criminal Court into effect: 1939 (lasting until 1946), 1961 (lasting 9 months) and 1972 (to date).[173] The current Court came into being as crime connected to the Northern Irish conflict emerged in this jurisdiction. Since the mid-1990s many organised crime cases have been prosecuted in this Court.[174]

[8–59] The defining feature of the Special Criminal Court is the lack of a jury. Instead, the legislation requires an uneven number of judges with a minimum of three.[175] To serve as a judge of this Court a person must be a judge of the High, Circuit or District Court, a solicitor or barrister of seven years standing or a commandant of the Defence Forces.[176] In practice, however, there is a panel of 11 judges from which three judges are drawn, one from each of the High, Circuit and District Courts. They are appointed and removed "at the will" of the government,[177] making it clear that the ordinary protections for the independence of the judiciary found in Art 35 of the Constitution do not apply to judges of the Special Criminal Court. Arguments that they are not sufficiently independent have failed.[178] Judges are not obliged to sit on the Court and Walsh refers to instances where judges have expressed their unwillingness to do so.[179]

Jurisdiction

[8–60] The jurisdiction of the Court is set out in Part V of the Act. The legislation empowers it to try, convict and acquit people. On conviction, it has the power to sentence individuals, require them to enter a recognisance, detain or direct bail, administer oaths, and punish those guilty of contempt of Court.[180] The jurisdiction of the court has been interpreted strictly. In *Gilligan v Special Criminal Court*[181] it was held that where statute had not expressly provided, the Court did not have the power to make an order of recovery of criminal assets under s 4 of the Criminal Justice Act 1994.

[8–61] Cases can come before the Court for one of two reasons: they are scheduled offences under the Act[182] or the DPP certifies that they should be tried there.[183] Under the Act the government may declare any offence to be scheduled if satisfied that the ordinary courts are inadequate to ensure the administration of justice and the preservation of public peace and order in relation to the offence.[184] A wide range of offences have, since

---

[173] See generally Davis, *History and Development of the Special Criminal Court* (Four Courts Press, Dublin, 2007).

[174] In *People (DPP) v Quilligan* [1986] IR 495 the Supreme Court outlined that the Offences Against the State Act does not exclusively deal with subversive crime and that the Court could be used for any type of crime for which the ordinary courts were inadequate.

[175] s 39(1).

[176] s 39(3).

[177] s 39(2).

[178] *Eccles v Ireland* [1985] IR 545.

[179] Walsh, above n 52, p 971.

[180] s 43.

[181] [2005] IESC 86.

[182] s 36.

[183] s 46(1).

[184] s 36(1).

then, been scheduled[185]: explosive substances,[186] firearms,[187] offences against the State,[188] organised crime,[189] as well as attempts, conspiracy and incitement, aiding and abetting of all of these.[190] Anyone who allegedly commits one of these offences must be tried in the Special Criminal Court unless the DPP directs otherwise.[191] If at any point the government feels that the ordinary courts can try one of these scheduled offences then that offence should be de-scheduled.[192] Beyond scheduled offences, if the DPP decides that the ordinary courts are inadequate to secure the administration of justice and the preservation of public peace in relation to *any* offence he may request that it be sent forward for trial in the Special Criminal Court, a request which must be complied with by the courts.[193]

The Special Criminal Court can sentence just as any other[194] and has all the sentencing options which will be discussed in Chapter Nine available to it, except for community service orders. The Act had provided that if a person was convicted of a scheduled offence by the Court he would have to forfeit any public office held[195] but this was ruled by the Supreme Court to be unconstitutional in *Cox v Ireland*.[196] The provision was more than what was needed to achieve justice and was applied very broadly to one group, but not others. **[8–62]**

Invocation

There are three ways, under the Offences Against the State Act, that a case can come before the Special Criminal Court: where the accused is charged directly before the Court, where the High Court transfers a case pending before the Central Criminal Court or the Circuit Court to the Court, or where the District Court sends it forward to the Court at the time of charging.[197] The legislation specifically states that a person must be brought lawfully before the Court in order to be tried,[198] so if an individual comes before the Court other than through one of these routes the attendance at court will be unlawful.[199] **[8–63]**

---

185 Offences Against the State Act 1939 (Scheduled Offences) Order 1972.
186 Any offence under the Explosives Substances Act 1883.
187 Any offence under the Firearms Acts 1925-2006.
188 Any offence under the Offences Against the State Act 1939 and any offence under ss 6 to 9 and s 12 of the Offences Against the State (Amendment) Act 1998.
189 Any offence under Pt 7 of the Criminal Justice Act 2006.
190 s 37.
191 s 45(2).
192 s 36(3).
193 s 46.
194 s 43(1).
195 s 34.
196 [1992] 2 IR 503.
197 ss 45-48.
198 s 43. Note that in *O'Brien v Special Criminal Court* [2007] IESC 45 the applicant challenged the terms 'lawfully brought' arguing that this implied that an accused should be arrested under the Act to be prosecuted in the Special Criminal Court. The Supreme Court held, however, that any power of arrest, lawfully exercised was permissible.
199 *McElhinney v DPP* [1990] 1 IR 405; *People (DPP) v Pringle* (1981) 2 Frewen 77; *People v Kehoe* [1985] IR 444.

(i) District Court to Special Criminal Court

[8–64] If an individual comes before the District Court charged with a scheduled, indictable offence, and the judge decides to send it forward for trial, it must go to the Special Criminal Court, unless the DPP directs otherwise.[200] The accused will be sent forward in custody unless the DPP consents to bail, though an application can then be made to the High Court for bail.[201] Where the offence can be tried summarily a request from the DPP is necessary in order to send the case forward to the Special Criminal Court.[202] The Special Criminal Court has jurisdiction for guilty pleas to scheduled offences and an accused pleading guilty should be sent forward to that court.[203]

[8–65] For non-scheduled offences the DPP may intervene and have the case sent forward to the Special Criminal Court. The DPP must issue a written certificate that the ordinary courts are inadequate to secure the effective administration of justice and the preservation of public peace and order.[204] Where this certificate is issued by the DPP the Court must comply.[205]

[8–66] The courts have been unwilling to intervene in the DPP's decisions. In *State (Littlejohn) v Governor of Mountjoy Prison*[206] a challenge to this power in relation to a guilty plea for a non-scheduled offence was refused, as the Court could not know the grounds on which the decision to send forward was made. Jury intimidation does not have to be the only ground for such a decision. The case of *Savage and Owen v DPP*[207] confirmed that this power of the DPP was not open to judicial review, given the nature of the crimes and circumstances for which the Court was established. The Court found that if such cases were open to review the DPP might have to reveal serious and sensitive state information.

[8–67] In *Kavanagh v Ireland*[208] the applicant brought his challenge to the use of the Court for organised crime[209] to the UN Human Rights Committee, which held that while trying the accused in the Court itself was not a violation of the right to a fair hearing, the State had an obligation to explain the decision to try the accused in this way. The State was thereby in breach of its obligations under the UN Covenant on Civil and Political Rights. Many organised crime offences have now been scheduled but should the DPP continue to use his discretionary power this could be problematic.

[200] s 45(2).
[201] s 45(3).
[202] s 45(1).
[203] *State (Littlejohn) v Governor of Mountjoy Prison*, unreported, Supreme Court, 18 March 1976.
[204] s 46.
[205] s 46(2).
[206] Unreported, Supreme Court, 18 March 1976.
[207] [1982] ILRM 385.
[208] UN Committee on Human Rights, Communication No.819/1998 (4 April 2001).
[209] Attempts to challenge this domestically had failed: *State (Bollard) v Special Criminal Court,* unreported, High Court, 20 September 1972.

(ii) Transfer to Special Criminal Court

If a case is sent forward for trial to the Central Criminal Court or the Circuit Court the prosecution can transfer it to the Special Criminal Court if the DPP issues a certificate that the ordinary courts are inadequate to secure the effective administration of justice and the preservation of public peace and order.[210] This results in an application to the High Court for a transfer, with which, it appears, the Court must comply.[211] Once the order is made, a garda must serve the transfer order on the accused in writing.[212] Whatever decision has already been made in relation to bail for the accused will remain in place until he appears before the Special Criminal Court. **[8–68]**

(iii) Charged before Special Criminal Court

An individual can be brought before the Special Criminal Court to be charged. If it is a scheduled offence the DPP can direct that he be charged there instead of before the District Court.[213] For a non-scheduled offence the DPP must issue a certificate that the ordinary courts are inadequate.[214] A warrant or a summons can be issued to secure the person's appearance before the Special Criminal Court for charging, if he is not already in custody.[215] **[8–69]**

Procedure

The Court has control over its sittings and its procedure, making its own regulations for practice and procedure, most recently done in 2001.[216] Non-compliance with these rules will not invalidate proceedings. General rules of evidence apply in this Court. The time and venue of the Court is to be determined by the Court,[217] and once decided all relevant parties are alerted by the Court registrar. Hearings may be *in camera*. The Court can instruct gardaí to prevent anyone from attending who it is believed will interfere with proceedings.[218] Identities of witnesses may be concealed for security reasons.[219] Publication of details of witnesses can be prohibited, [220] and an order for separation of witnesses can be given.[221] Witnesses may be summonsed to attend,[222] or a warrant for arrest can be issued if evidence is given on oath that a witness is unlikely to attend.[223] **[8–70]**

Oaths are administered as in other courts. Legal aid can be granted in line with the procedure and grounds of the Central Criminal Court.[224] If an accused before the Special **[8–71]**

---

210 s 48.
211 *State (Coveney) v Special Criminal Court* [1982] ILRM 284.
212 s 48(b).
213 s 47(1).
214 s 47(2).
215 s 47(3).
216 Special Criminal Court Rules 2001.
217 s 41(1).
218 SCCR, r 7(2).
219 SCCR, r 7(4).
220 SCCR, r 5(5).
221 SCCR, r 8.
222 SCCR, r 21(1).
223 SCCR, r 21(1).
224 SCCR, r 30.

Criminal Court refuses to plead, called "standing mute", the Court must hear evidence as to whether he is "mute by malice", in which case a plea of not guilty will be entered, or "mute by visitation of God" which will result in the trial proceeding unless he is found unfit for trial.[225] This was provided for by the Offences Against the State Act as many of those brought before this Court would refuse to recognise the authority of the Court.

[8–72] The trial procedure for the Special Criminal Court is very similar to that adopted by the Central Criminal Court for a trial on indictment. With no jury, the judges will try issues of fact and of law. The Court will therefore hear the arguments concerning evidence deemed inadmissible. In *DPP v McMahon*[226] the Court heard highly prejudicial inadmissible evidence which would in a jury trial have required the jury to be discharged. The Court of Criminal Appeal ruled that Special Criminal Court could continue to hear the case nonetheless. The Special Criminal Court retains a discretion to disqualify itself from hearing the case in such circumstances, as occurred in *DPP v Corrigan*.[227]

[8–73] The court's decision is made by a majority of the Court.[228] A collective judgment, which can assist in later appeals, is given with no dissenting judgments.[229] It will not be known if the decision was unanimous. The Committee to Review the Offences Against the State Acts has recommended a requirement of unanimity to convict in this Court.[230]

IX. Conclusion

[8–74] This chapter has provided an overview of trials on indictment in Ireland. The role of the jury has been examined and problems with the restrictions on eligibility for persons with physical or mental impairments were highlighted. The procedures for creating and discharging juries were reviewed. The trial and related matters have been considered, with particular attention paid to the formality of proceedings, compared to the summary trial, given the potential impact for the accused of a trial on indictment. Issues such as when the accused is entitled to legal aid and what measures can be taken to combat adverse publicity were also considered.

[8–75] Finally the chapter detailed the use of the non-jury, Special Criminal Court for cases where the ordinary courts are deemed inadequate to secure the administration of justice. Numerous problems can be identified with the use of the Special Criminal Court including the denial of the right to trial by jury, the question mark over the independence of judges when in this Court, the stigma for an accused of being brought before this Court as well as the association in the media with paramilitary activity. Worryingly, a high number of cases from this Court have later been over-turned on appeal. The UN Human Rights Committee has questioned the continued need for the Court, given the end of the Northern Irish conflict. Certainly, its continued existence on an emergency basis should be reviewed.

---

[225] Offences Against the State Act 1939, s 51(1).

[226] [1984] ILRM 461.

[227] Unreported case, SCC, cited in *People (DPP) v McMahon* [1984] ILRM 461.

[228] s 40(1).

[229] s 40(1).

[230] *Report of the Committee to Review the Offences Against the State Acts, 1939-1998 and Related Matters* (Stationery Office, Dublin, 2002), paras 13.1–13.4.

CHAPTER 9
Sentencing

Once a person has gone through the trial process and has been convicted, the next stage in the procedure is the sentencing of that person. The term "sentence" does not just mean a term of imprisonment – for our purposes, it includes all the various ways in which the criminal justice system can sanction someone for wrongdoing. Indeed, the **[9–01]**

Law Reform Commission in its *Report on Sentencing*[1] defined the term sentence in a broad manner as "the judicial determination of a legal sanction to be imposed on a person found guilty of an offence."[2]

I. Theories of Sentencing/Purposes of Punishment[3]

[9–02] A sentence is generally considered a punishment for wrongdoing, but there are various theories which justify *why* we punish people for breaching the criminal code. These theories have developed over time and the priority given to one or another changes according to prevalent concepts in criminal justice.

Deterrence

[9–03] The principle of deterrence has two aspects – first, we punish an individual so that he will not commit another crime; secondly, we punish an individual to deter people in society generally from committing crimes. This theory considers that the justification for punishment is that a wrongdoer will learn from the experience of that punishment and not commit another crime. This is then extrapolated into the general population: people will be discouraged from committing offences if they know that they will be punished upon conviction. However, both the specific theory and the general theory of deterrence presuppose a rational actor.[4] While those who plan their crimes and think ahead can amend their behaviour and thus be susceptible to deterrent sentencing strategies,[5] a lot of crime is opportunistic or spontaneous and the deterrent principle will have little effect in that context.

[9–04] Deterrence may be particularly relevant to certain types of offences, however. In *People (DPP) v O'Reilly*,[6] for example, the DPP sought review of an unduly lenient sentence imposed for dangerous driving causing death on the basis, amongst other reasons, that the trial judge did not take account of the need for general deterrence in sentences for such offences. The court admitted that while individual deterrence is seldom needed in such cases "once a tragic outcome has resulted from the driving", general deterrence "should constitute an element of sentencing policy in cases of this nature."[7] As the trial judge had not given due weight to this factor, the suspended sentence initially handed down was replaced by 240 hours of community service.

Retribution (Just Deserts)

[9–05] The principle of retribution states that we punish people because it is deserved. The biblical statement "an eye for an eye and a tooth for a tooth" has retribution as its core, though importantly it is limited to an eye for an eye – not a life for an eye.[8]

---

[1] Law Reform Commission, *Report on Sentencing* (LRC 53-1996, Dublin, 1996).

[2] *ibid.* para 1.1.

[3] For a detailed discussion on the rationales of sentencing, see Ashworth, *Sentencing and Criminal Justice* (Oxford University Press, 2010), pp 76–95 and O'Malley, *Sentencing Law and Practice* (Thomson Round Hall, Dublin, 2006), pp 26–48.

[4] O'Malley, above n 3, p 34.

[5] Above n 3.

[6] [2008] 3 IR 632.

[7] *ibid.* at 641.

[8] O'Malley, above n 3, pp 31–32.

Therefore, retribution places a limit on the amount of punishment imposable for the particular crime: we punish the offender only for that crime he has committed. O'Malley cautions that we must be realistic about the ability of the retribution theory to limit punishment as it is difficult to establish if a sentence is truly reflective of a particular crime, and the theory of retribution does not take into account the circumstances which might have contributed to the offending behaviour.[9]

Incapacitation

The principle of incapacitation justifies punishment on the basis that we punish people to physically prevent them from being able to commit crimes. The most extreme version of this is, of course, the death penalty. The problems with incapacitation as a rationale for punishment are clear: first, it gives rise to disproportionate sentencing, and secondly, it could be viewed as a form of preventative detention. **[9–06]**

The Irish courts have made it clear that preventative detention is not permissible in this jurisdiction. In *People (AG) v O'Callaghan*,[10] Walsh J stated: **[9–07]**

> "... it would be quite contrary to the concept of personal liberty enshrined in the Constitution that any person should be deprived of his liberty ... upon only the belief that he will commit offences if left at liberty, save in the most extraordinary circumstances carefully spelled out by the Oireachtas and then only to secure the preservation of public peace and order or the public safety and preservation of the State in a time of national emergency or in some situation akin to that."[11]

Denunciation (Desert)

Desert, or denunciation, sees the purpose of punishment as a form of censure: punishment is a way by which the state communicates both to the offender and to society that the behaviour in question was wrong. While there is some connection between denunciation and general deterrence, O'Malley explains the difference between the two: general deterrence, he explains, is "explicitly utilitarian with a forward-looking goal" while denunciation is, rather, "motivated by intrinsically moral considerations."[12] **[9–08]**

Rehabilitation

This theory provides that the fundamental purpose of a sentence is to rehabilitate the offender. Thus, an individual will be compelled to take a course of treatment, or engage in a particular type of activity which seeks to curb his propensity for committing crime. Ashworth notes that the types of measures available are generally two-fold: first, those which seek to address the attitude or behaviour of the offender; and secondly, those which provide education or skills.[13] He notes that while this approach reached its **[9–09]**

---

[9] *ibid.*

[10] [1966] IR 501.

[11] *ibid.* at 516–517.

[12] O'Malley, above n 3, p 44.

[13] *ibid.* p 86.

zenith in the 1960s, it began to decline in the 1970s for two reasons: it did not seem to be any more effective than ordinary, non-treatment sentences, and the sentence could be disproportionate to the offence and offender characteristics given the indeterminate nature of the treatment.

Restoration

[9–10] One of the biggest developments in criminal justice internationally in the last quarter of the twentieth century was the victims' movement.[14] In the context of sentencing and punishment, it has had an impact through the development of restorative justice theories. The central aim of this movement, as described by Ashworth is:

> "[A]ll the stakeholders in the offence should become involved in discussion about the appropriate response to the offence. The aim would be to bring about an apology, to ensure that the offender compensates the victim and the wider community for the effects of the crime, and to take steps to ensure that the offence is not repeated."[15]

[9–11] He notes that there are two primary criticisms of the theory: first, it is impossible that all the aims of restorative justice could be achieved, and a focus on one may not enhance others; secondly, the emphasis on community is problematic because the identification of the "community" may not be easily done and it is preferable that decisions are made by an impartial tribunal.[16] Nonetheless, it has had an enthusiastic reception, and in Ireland, the Children Act 2001, in particular, places a strong emphasis on restorative justice.[17]

II. General Issues in Sentencing in the Irish Courts

[9–12] The sentencing hearing is part of the trial process and so the constitutional guarantees, jurisdictional limitations and separation of powers issues which attach to all aspects of the criminal process apply here. The guiding principle in determining the appropriate sentence is proportionality — thus, the critical factors impacting on the sentence will be the circumstances of the offence and the circumstances of the offender. However, in handing down a sentence, the judge must be sure to base his sentencing decision on established facts.

Sentencing and the Separation of Powers

[9–13] In *Deaton v AG*[18] Ó Dálaigh CJ discussed the sentencing power in the context of the constitutional separation of powers. He noted that when the legislature creates an offence, it prescribes what punishment attaches to that offence, which can range from

---

[14] Ashworth, above n 3, p 92. See also Chapter Twelve.

[15] *ibid.* p 93.

[16] *ibid.* p 94.

[17] See Chapter Eleven in relation to restorative justice in the juvenile context. Two restorative justice projects addressing adult crime are currently in operation in Ireland: Tallaght Restorative Justice Services in Dublin and the Nenagh Community Reparation Project in Tipperary. See *Final Report of the National Commission on Restorative Justice* (chaired by Judge Mary Martin) June 2009.

[18] [1963] IR 170.

"a single or fixed penalty, or a maximum penalty, or a minimum penalty, or alternative penalties, or a range of penalties."[19] This, however, the court stated, is the limit of the legislative power in relation to sentencing. Once the range of penalties of a sentence is established by the legislature, the determination of the individual penalty for an individual offender is properly in the judicial domain. The reason for this, the Chief Justice stated, was to safeguard the rights of the citizen:

> "The individual citizen needs the safeguard of the Courts in the assessment of punishment as much as on his trial for the offence. The degree of punishment which a particular citizen is to undergo for an offence is a matter vitally affecting his liberty; and it is inconceivable to my mind that a Constitution which is broadly based on the doctrine of the separation of powers ... could have intended to place in the hands of the Executive the power to select the punishment to be undergone by citizens."[20]

Thus, while the legislature may set out the general scheme and principles regarding the penalties attaching to a particular offence, it is properly the domain of the judiciary to determine the sentence for the individual offender. The courts have repeatedly stated that the Executive cannot interfere with the sentencing decision.[21] **[9–14]**

Theories of Sentencing in Irish Courts

While there is no single established theory to determine sentences in Irish courts, judges will often refer to various principles in justifying or reviewing sentences. Hamilton[22] notes that in the Irish Penal Reform Trust (IPRT) survey of two Dublin District Courts, where judges commented on the reasons for imposing particular sentences,[23] there was an absence of any coherent sentencing policy. Judges committed offenders to prison for the purposes of incapacitation, deterrence, rehabilitation and retribution. **[9–15]**

In *People (DPP) v GK*[24] Finnegan J noted that despite the advantages of basing a sentence on established theories of sentencing, the principle of proportionality cannot be usurped by reference to these theories. Indeed, as Walsh notes, a "bald statement" of the objectives of sentencing will offer little insight into the appropriate sentence for a particular case,[25] proportionality being the dominant principle. Ashworth criticises this approach however, stating: **[9–16]**

> "It is one thing to agree that judges should be left with discretion, so that they may adjust the sentence to fit the particular combination of facts in an individual case. It is quite another to suggest that judges should be free to

[19] *ibid.* at 181.
[20] *ibid.* at 182.
[21] See also *Re Haughey* [1971] IR 217; *State (Sheerin) v Kennedy* [1966] IR 379; *State (O) v O'Brien* [1973] IR 50.
[22] Hamilton, "Sentencing in the District Court: Here be Dragons" (2005) 15(3) ICLJ 9.
[23] Disturbingly, Hamilton states that "reasons were given by judges in respect of a mere 32 per cent of cases, and this number only climbed to 42 per cent for custodial cases." *ibid.* p 9.
[24] [2008] IECCA 110.
[25] Walsh, *Criminal Procedure* (Thomson Round Hall, Dublin, 2002), p 1087.

> choose what rationale of sentence to adopt in particular cases or types of case. Freedom to select from among the various rationales is a freedom to determine policy, not a freedom to respond to unusual combinations of facts. It is more of a licence to judges to pursue their own penal philosophies than an encouragement to respond sensitively to the facts of each case."[26]

That said, the approach of the Irish courts and legislature seems to resemble a "pick 'n' mix" where courts can dip in and out of sentencing theories to justify the particular sentence they propose.

The Requirement of Proportionality

[9–17] The principle of proportionality dictates that a sentence is based on the circumstances of the individual offender and the individual offence. The principle was discussed in the case of *State (Healy) v Donoghue*[27] where the Supreme Court stated that the Constitution necessarily guarantees, "at the very least" that an individual receive a sentence appropriate to his degree of guilt and his relevant personal circumstances.[28] Explaining the principle of proportionality in *People (DPP) v C(W)*[29] Flood J stated that the principle requires that "the imposition of a particular sentence must strike a balance between the particular circumstances of the commission of the relevant offence and the relevant personal circumstances of the person accused."[30]

O'Malley states that

> "[a] proportionate sentence is calculated by first locating the particular offence on the appropriate scale of gravity, and, then applying credit for the relevant mitigating factors to the otherwise proportionate sentence ... It must be recalled that the gravity of an offence is to be assessed not only in accordance with the harm intentionally or recklessly inflicted as a result of the offence, but also having regard to the presence of aggravating factors."[31]

Factors which are considered to aggravate and mitigate sentence will now be examined.

Aggravating and Mitigating Factors in Sentencing

[9–18] In determining a proportionate sentence, the court will assess what sentence is appropriate for the particular crime on the basis of the circumstances and gravity of the offence, usually taking into account the aggravating factors of the offence – such as whether the offence was premeditated, whether a weapon was used or whether particularly vulnerable victims were targeted. The starting point is not the maximum possible sentence imposable for commission of the offence, but rather the appropriate

---

26 Ashworth, above n 3, p 76.
27 [1976] IR 325. See also *People (AG) v O' Driscoll* (1972) 1 Frewen 351.
28 *ibid.* at 353 *per* Walsh J.
29 [1994] ILRM 321.
30 *ibid.* at 324. See also *People (DPP) v M* [1994] 3 IR 306.
31 O'Malley, *The Criminal Process* (Round Hall, Dublin, 2009), p 872.

sentence for the particular offence, having regard to these aggravating factors.[32] Matters relating to the particular offender will be considered thereafter.

(i) Mitigating Factors

In the case of *People (DPP) v M*[33] Denham J stated: **[9–19]**

> "...having assessed what is the appropriate sentence for a particular crime it is the duty of the court to consider then the particular circumstances of the convicted person. It is within this ambit that the mitigating factors fall to be considered."[34]

The most common factor that is taken into account by the courts in mitigation is admission of guilt and cooperation with gardaí. O'Malley states that this is justified for three reasons: first, it saves the criminal justice system time and money; secondly, it may indicate remorse on the part of the offender; and thirdly, it saves the victim and others affected by the crime the experience of being cross-examined.[35] Importantly, in order to get full credit for this factor, an early admission of guilt and an early guilty plea is required. This position now has statutory footing in s 29(1) of the Criminal Justice Act 1999 which provides: **[9–20]**

> "In determining what sentence to pass on a person who has pleaded guilty to an offence, other than an offence for which the sentence is fixed by law, a court, if it considers it appropriate to do so, shall take into account—
> (a) the stage in the proceedings for the offence at which the person indicated an intention to plead guilty, and
> (b) the circumstances in which this indication was given."

However, while the offender will be given credit for pleading guilty and cooperating, he will not be punished for exercising his constitutional right to a trial. Section 29(2) goes on to provide that a court is not precluded from imposing the maximum sentence, even where a plea of guilty is made, where there are exceptional reasons for doing so.[36] This was discussed in *People (DPP) v RMcC and CD*[37] where the court stated: **[9–21]**

> "The presence in a case of exceptional circumstances must now be seen in the light of section 29, as enabling a court, notwithstanding the existence of some mitigating circumstances, to impose a maximum sentence in rare and exceptional cases. That does not mean that the court is relieved of the obligation to consider all mitigating factors and give them due weight, but

---

[32] See *(People) DPP v M* [1994] 3 IR 306; *People (DPP) v Kelly* [2005] 1 ILRM 19; *People (DPP) v Sheedy* [2000] 2 IR 184.

[33] [1994] 3 IR 306.

[34] *ibid.* at 317.

[35] O'Malley, above n 3, p 119.

[36] An example of such exceptional circumstances is found in the case of *People (DPP) v D* unreported, Court of Criminal Appeal, 21 May 2004.

[37] [2007] IESC 47.

> rather that, having done so, the court is not precluded from passing such maximum sentence... Such instances will of necessity be rare and confined to those cases where the offences represent the worst imaginable variation of the offence in question".

[9–22] Another factor which will go to mitigating a sentence is where the offender shows remorse. Whether the remorse is genuine or "tactical" is a matter for the trial judge, but the offender can take steps to show that the remorse on his part is real.[38] A plea of guilty, voluntary surrender to the authorities, an apology, an offer of compensation to the victim, voluntarily seeking treatment or moving to a different environment are all factors which could indicate genuine remorse on the part of the offender.[39]

[9–23] Quite often in the sentencing hearing evidence will be put forward regarding the previous good character of the offender in an effort to mitigate sentence. The absence of previous offending might show that in committing the offence the individual was acting out of character, and this, usually combined with genuine remorse, will more often than not mitigate a sentence.

Other personal factors regarding the accused, such as age (either young[40] or old[41]), illness or disability[42] can also be taken into account in mitigation. Issues such as provocation and duress can also be pleaded in mitigation where there is "reasonable evidential foundation" for them, even if the offender either failed or was precluded from establishing them as a substantive defence.[43]

(ii) Aggravating Factors

[9–24] As already outlined, aggravating factors will generally go towards the characteristics of the offence in determining a proportionate sentence. The absence of a mitigating factor, such as remorse or a guilty plea, will not aggravate the sentence.

[9–25] The standard aggravating factors include premeditation, the use of force or violence where this is not an essential ingredient of the offence and subjecting the victim to degrading or dehumanising treatment.[44] In relation to certain offences, breach of trust or abuse of a vulnerable individual can also aggravate the sentence.[45] Section 11 of the Criminal Justice Act 1984 explicitly provides that where an offence is committed on bail, this must be regarded as an aggravating factor for the purposes of the sentence.

---

38 O'Malley, above n 31, p 880.
39 O'Malley, above n 3, p 134.
40 Children Act 2001, s 96(3).
41 *People (DPP) v M(J)* [2002] 1 IR 363.
42 *People (DPP) v Creighton* unreported, Court of Criminal Appeal, 15 April 2002.
43 O'Malley, above n 31, p 884.
44 *ibid.* p 893.
45 O'Malley notes that breach of trust is so commonly treated as an aggravating factor in relation to sexual or abusive offences committed against children that it is practically "an intrinsic element of them". O'Malley, above n 31, p 893.

While previous good character has been shown to mitigate sentence, the question remained as to what impact a previous "bad" character would have on the sentence – that is, to what extent, if any, evidence of the offender's previous convictions could impact on the sentence. One approach that could be taken to this is that the offender would not benefit from the "previous good character" element in mitigation – or as O'Malley describes it, there would be "progressive loss of mitigation".[46] Another perspective would view previous convictions as positively aggravating the sentence – the viewpoint being that the offender had "not learned" from previous encounters with the criminal justice system and ought to be treated more harshly for this reason. The extent to which this might amount to preventative justice for habitual offenders is obviously problematic.[47] [9–26]

In *People (DPP) v GK*,[48] previous convictions were taken into account as an aggravating factor. Here, the offender pleaded guilty to a count of aggravated sexual assault, and was sentenced to life imprisonment. The offence in question was committed six months after his early release from prison following a conviction of rape. Considering the impact of previous convictions, the Court of Criminal Appeal stated [9–27]

> "... previous convictions are relevant ... in aggravation of the offence. Accordingly in determining an appropriate sentence in this case ... the learned trial judge was entitled to have regard to the two previous convictions of rape, the fact that the offence was committed within six months of having been released from prison for an offence of rape and the matters disclosed in the Probation Service report. These circumstances are relevant not just in terms of their absence in mitigation of sentence but also in terms of assessing an appropriate sentence in terms of the seriousness of the offence, which sentence will be proportionately more severe than would be the case were these circumstances absent."

Rather confusingly, however, in *DPP v S(P)*[49] the Court of Criminal Appeal took the "progressive loss of mitigation" approach. Here, the Court considered the impact of the previous convictions, and clearly stated that as the offender had already been punished for these, he should not be punished again as "previous offending will normally be regarded as an absence of a mitigating factor." This has left the question of relevance of previous convictions in an uncertain state – are they to be treated as an aggravating factor, or simply "progressive loss of mitigation"?[50] The question remains unclear. [9–28]

---

[46] *ibid.* p 890.

[47] See O'Malley, "Sentencing Recidivist Sex Offenders: A Challenge for Proportionality in Criminal Law and Procedure" in *Current Issues and Emerging Trends* (Bacik and Heffernan (eds.), Firstlaw, Dublin, 2009), pp 123–125.

[48] [2008] IECCA 110.

[49] [2009] IECCA 1.

[50] O'Malley, above n 31, p 892.

III. Reform

[9–29] The Law Reform Commission in its *Report on Sentencing*[51] noted that while a statutory scheme of sentencing should not be introduced in Ireland, non-statutory guidelines should be introduced whereby the severity of a sentence to be imposed should be measured in proportion to the seriousness of the offending behaviour considering first, the harm caused or risked by the offender in committing the offence, and second, the culpability of the offender in committing the offence.[52] This is in accord with the current guiding principle in Irish sentencing law: the principle of proportionality. The Commission suggested that sentencing guidelines should outline factors which both aggravate and mitigate a sentence. According to the Commission, factors which should mitigate sentence should include:

1. Whether the offence was committed under circumstances of duress not amounting to a defence to criminal liability;
2. Whether the offender was provoked;
3. Whether the offence was committed on impulse, or the offender showed no sustained motivation to break the law;
4. Whether the offender, through age or ill-health or otherwise, was of reduced mental capacity when committing the offence;
5. Whether the offence was occasioned as a result of strong temptation;
6. Whether the offender was motivated by strong compassion or human sympathy;
7. Whether the offender played only a minor role in the commission of the offence;
8. Whether no serious injury resulted nor was intended;
9. Whether the offender made voluntary attempts to prevent the effects of the offence;
10. Whether there exist excusing circumstances which, although not amounting to a defence to criminal liability, tend to extenuate the offender's culpability, such as ignorance of the law, mistake of fact, or necessity.
11. Any other circumstances which:
    - reduce the harm caused or risked by the offender, or
    - reduce the culpability of the offender for the offence.[53]

[9–30] Factors which would aggravate the sentence, the Commission argued, should include:

1. Whether the offence was planned or premeditated;
2. Whether the offender committed the offence as a member of a group organised for crime;
3. Whether the offence formed part of a campaign of offences;
4. Whether the offender exploited the position of a weak or defenceless victim or exploited the knowledge that the victim's access to justice might have been impeded;
5. Whether the offender exploited a position of confidence or trust, including offences committed by law enforcement officers;

[51] Law Reform Commission *Report on Sentencing* (LRC 53-1996).
[52] *ibid.* p 65.
[53] *ibid.* pp 25–26.

6. Whether the offender threatened to use or actually used violence, or used, threatened to use, or carried, a weapon;
7. Whether the offender caused, threatened to cause, or risked the death or serious injury of another person, or used or threatened to use excessive cruelty;
8. Whether the offender caused or risked substantial economic loss to the victim of the offence;
9. Whether the offence was committed for pleasure or excitement;
10. Whether the offender played a leading role in the commission of the offence, or induced others to participate in the commission of the offence;
11. Whether the offence was committed on a law enforcement officer;
12. Any other circumstances which:
    a. increase the harm caused or risked by the offender, or
    b. increase the culpability of the offender for the offence.[54]

This approach could allow for the structuring of judicial sentencing discretion while respecting the separation of powers. While the courts have already established that some of these factors are to be taken into account in the sentencing decision, the Law Reform Commission's recommendation has the added advantage of providing a coherent and comprehensive approach to the issue. **[9–31]**

IV. Procedure at the Sentencing Hearing

Having established the broad principles which govern decision-making at the sentencing stage in Irish courts, the procedure which governs the manner in which the decision is made will now be examined. **[9–32]**

Disagreement over Facts

Where an individual pleads not guilty to the offence, most of the factual circumstances of the offence will be established through the trial process. Where an individual pleads guilty, however, the facts need to be established for sentencing purposes. This will usually be done by a garda providing the court with the salient facts of the case. The defendant, of course, must have an opportunity to dispute these facts, and where there is a disagreement, a "Newton hearing" takes place. Here, the relevant facts are established to the satisfaction of the court and the defendant has an opportunity to contest facts which the prosecution puts forward.[55] As set out in *People (DPP) v K*[56]: **[9–33]**

> "...there are many cases in which it is of the utmost importance that the factual basis relating to the circumstances in which admitted offences were committed are *established* or *admitted*."[57] (emphasis added)

Regarding the requisite level of proof, it is thought that, as with all other matters in criminal cases, the standard of beyond a reasonable doubt is appropriate here.[58] **[9–34]**

---

[54] *ibid.* pp 26–27.
[55] Called a "Newton hearing" after the leading English case *R v Newton* (1982) 4 Cr App R (S) 388. For further elaboration on this issue, see O'Malley, above n 3, pp 574-577.
[56] [2002] 3 IR 534.
[57] *ibid.* p 538.
[58] Walsh, above n 25, p 1111.

Importantly, as O'Malley notes, there is a fine dividing line between taking account of uncharged criminal conduct, which is prohibited, and taking account of relevant circumstances, which is acceptable.[59] The established facts regarding the circumstances of the offender and the circumstances of the offence will then allow the judge to determine the aggravating and mitigating factors of the case, and determine what sentence is proportionate.

Concurrent and Consecutive Sentences

[9–35] Generally, if a court is sentencing an offender for multiple offences, it can order the sentences to run concurrently or consecutively.[60] There are two general principles which operate to determine whether sentences should run consecutively or concurrently: the one-transaction principle and the totality principle.[61] The one transaction principle essentially provides that where a number of counts can be considered as part of one criminal transaction, the sentences for all counts should run concurrently. Conversely, where the offences are part of separate transactions, the sentences should run consecutively. The totality principle, as described by O'Malley, involves the court selecting an appropriate sentence for each offence, and then standing back to evaluate the cumulative length of sentence against the overall gravity of the offending.[62] Where the cumulative total is disproportionate, the court can then adjust the sentence appropriately. Generally, there is a tendency for courts to order that the sentences run concurrently: as Walsh notes, an exceptionally long cumulative total in any individual case would give rise to an issue of constitutionality due to the absence of proportionality.[63]

Plea Bargaining

[9–36] The issue of judicial plea bargaining, where counsel and the trial judge discuss the possible sentencing implications of a guilty plea in judges' chambers, is a contentious one at Irish law. Writing in 2002, the former DPP, Eamonn Barnes, stated that "plea bargaining does not exist in this country", at least in the form in which it exists in other jurisdictions.[64] Charleton and McDermott consider that judicial plea bargaining is not constitutionally permissible, given the requirement for justice to be administered in public, and the possibility that accused persons might plead guilty, despite their innocence, to avoid a term of imprisonment due to "an unfortunate concatenation of events against them."[65]

---

[59] O'Malley, above n 31, p 885.

[60] There are some statutory exceptions to this position, for example, s 11 of the Criminal Justice Act 1984 relating to offences committed while on bail.

[61] O'Malley, above n 31, pp 887–888.

[62] *ibid.*

[63] Walsh, above n 25, p 1103.

[64] Barnes, "Reflections on Twenty-Five Years as Ireland's First Director of Public Prosecutions" in *Criminal Justice in Ireland* (O'Mahony (ed.), IPA, Dublin 2002), p 99. Mr Barnes stated that he had discovered that the practice of judicial plea bargaining had developed in Irish courts and issued a circular instruction to stop it as, without legislation, he believed, this practice was "thoroughly undesirable."

[65] Charleton and McDermott, "Constitutional Implications of Plea Bargaining" (2000) 5(9) BR 476, pp 480–481.

Prosecutorial plea-bargaining is a separate, though related issue. Here, discussions take place between the prosecutor and the defence regarding the charges which will be proceeded with.[66] The defence may indicate to the prosecution that the defendant is willing to plead guilty to one or more offences in return for more serious charges being dropped. However, Walsh expresses concern that this practice could undermine the notion of justice being done in public and could "render the criminal trial a sham."[67] [9–37]

Thus, while plea bargaining of a sort does exist in Ireland, there are serious constitutional implications for the practice and without clear legislative guidance on how the practice is regulated it should be abandoned.

Victim Impact Statements

Prior to 1993, the role of the victim in the Irish criminal justice system was limited to that of witness for the prosecution, being viewed as largely "irrelevant" in the eyes of the system.[68] Section 5(1) of the Criminal Justice Act 1993, as amended by the Criminal Procedure Act 2010 and discussed further in Chapter Twelve, remedies this, and provides that in determining a sentence for sexual or violent offences, a court shall hear and take into account the evidence of the victim of the offence as to its effect on him. The "victim" is not defined for the purposes of the 1993 Act, but the Criminal Procedure Act 2010 extends the facility to allow an impact statement to be made by families of victims of homicide,[69] or where victims are ill or incapacitated as a result of the offence. Prior to the enactment of the 2010 Act, it had been the practice of courts to allow such family members to submit and read their statements into court, though there was no obligation on the court to do so.[70] [9–38]

There are limits to the impact of the victim's statement on the sentencing decision. While the court is obliged to receive and hear the victim impact statement, as Flood J stated in the case of *People (DPP) v MC*,[71] [9–39]

> "[s]ection 5 cannot, and does not, purport to make any change to the manner in which a court is obliged to carry out its constitutional duty to independently select an appropriate sentence for a particular accused."[72]

The justification for limiting the impact of the victim impact statement, or any report compiled (for example by the probation and welfare service) on the impact of the crime on the victim, is clear: while it may be therapeutic for victims to "have their say" in court in relation to the impact of the crimes on them, as O'Malley notes, "allowing [9–40]

---

[66] Walsh, above n 25, p 801.

[67] *ibid.* p 802.

[68] See McGovern, "The Victim and the Criminal Justice Process" in O'Mahony, above n 64, pp 393–406.

[69] s 4 of the 2010 Act amends s 5 of the 1993 Act. See also Guiry, "Who is the Victim? – The use of Victim Impact Statements in Murder and Manslaughter Cases" (2006) 16 ICLJ 2; Brady, "Death Upon Impact: Family Victim Impact Statements in Irish Law" in Bacik and Heffernan, above n 47, p 134.

[70] Carney, "The Role of the Victim in the Irish Criminal Process" [2007] JSIJ 7, p 8.

[71] Unreported, Court of Criminal Appeal, 16 June 1995.

[72] *ibid.*

victim statements to influence punishment creates, at the very least, a risk of unfairness and inconsistency in sentencing."[73] Finnegan J agreed in the case of *DPP v GK*[74] where he stated, "[t]he Court does not participate in an exercise in vengeance or seek to retaliate against the applicant on behalf of the victim." This issue will be discussed further in Chapter Twelve.

Taking Other Offences into Consideration

[9–41] Section 8 of the Criminal Justice Act 1951 provides:

> "(1) Where a person, on being convicted of an offence, admits himself guilty of any other offence and asks to have it taken into consideration in awarding punishment, the Court may, if the Director of Public Prosecutions consents, take it into consideration accordingly.
> (2) If the Court takes an offence into consideration, a note of that fact shall be made and filed with the record of the sentence, and the accused shall not be prosecuted for that offence, unless his conviction is reversed on appeal."

[9–42] This will arise just before sentence, where the accused will plead guilty in relation to other offences and ask for them to be taken into account when being sentenced.[75] Importantly, the individual cannot be punished for criminal behaviour for which he has not either been charged or convicted, as this would violate the right to a trial in due course of law. Ultimately, the correct position in relation to s 8 is that the court can take account of offences for which the accused was charged but not arraigned, this decision being made on the basis that they would be considered at sentencing stage.[76]

V. Sentencing Options and Ancillary Penalties

[9–43] Courts have a range of sentencing options open to them once an individual has been convicted of a criminal offence. Before examining what these options are, it is important to briefly assess the sentencing jurisdictions of the courts.

Jurisdiction of the Courts

[9–44] The range of sentencing options open to a court will depend on the court in which the conviction was registered. In the District Court, s 5 of the Criminal Justice Act 1951 limits a judge to ordering a term of imprisonment of 12 months. Section 12(1) of the Criminal Justice Act 1984 extended this jurisdiction to two years where consecutive sentences are imposed. The situation regarding the maximum fine available to the District Court is much less clear. Walsh believed in 2002 that the maximum fine in the District Court might be up to €2,500,[77] writing in 2006 O'Malley thought that it might be as much as €3,000[78] while in 2009 he raised this to €5,000.[79]

---

[73] O'Malley, above n 3, p 237.
[74] [2008] IECCA 110.
[75] Walsh, above n 25, p 1107.
[76] *ibid.*
[77] Walsh, above n 25, p 1020.
[78] O'Malley, above n 3, p 545.
[79] O'Malley, above n 31, p 257.

Due to the uncertainty in this area, the Fines Act 2010 provides for an indexation of fines, whereby fines are classed into five categories. Section 3 of the Act provides that the maximum Class A fines are those not exceeding €5,000, with the minimum Class E fines being those not exceeding €500. Sections 4–8 go on to apply this class system of fines to legislation enacted prior to the commencement of the 2010 Act, thus updating all fines in line with the Consumer Price Index. [9–45]

In relation to the Special Criminal Court, s 43(1) of the Offences Against the State Act 1939 provides that, when sentencing, the court can impose any sentence provided for by law, or make an order requiring the individual to enter into a recognisance. However, s 1(1) of the Criminal Justice (Community Service) Act 1983 excludes the Special Criminal Court from the ambit of that Act. [9–46]

Aside from these jurisdictional limits, legislation will generally set out the sentencing options available to the court on conviction for particular offences, reflecting the gravity of the offence itself. An example of this is the range of penalties available for assault under ss 2, 3 and 4 of the Non-Fatal Offences Against the Person Act 1997. This table explains the range of penalties available. Due to the impact of the Fines Act 2010, the amounts imposable under ss 2 and 3 are now classed as "Class C" fines, with the maximum penalty being amended from €1,905 to €2,500. [9–47]

	Summary conviction	Conviction on indictment
Assault (s 2)	Fine not exceeding €2,500; or Imprisonment not exceeding 6 months; or Both	N/A
Assault causing harm (s 3)	Fine not exceeding €2,500; or Imprisonment not exceeding 12 months; or Both	Fine; or Imprisonment not exceeding 5 years; or Both
Causes serious harm (s 4)	N/A	Fine; or Imprisonment for life; or Both

Figure 9.1

Sentencing Options

The sentencing options available to a court range from life in prison to absolute discharge under the Probation of Offenders Act 1907. The way in which these penalties have been developed and imposed will now be assessed. [9–48]

(i) Death Penalty

Until 1964 the death penalty was available as a punishment in Ireland for a limited range of offences, namely treason, murder and piracy. While the Criminal Justice Act 1964 limited the availability of the death penalty to treason, capital murder and some offences committed by a person under military law, in practice if a person was convicted for one of these offences, the penalty would be commuted to life [9–49] imprisonment. Indeed the last hanging in the State, that of Michael Manning, took place in April 1954.[80] Ultimately, the death penalty was abolished statutorily by the Criminal Justice Act 1990, and in 2002 the Constitution was amended by referendum to provide in Article 15.5.2° that "[t]he Oireachtas shall not enact any law providing for the imposition of the death penalty."

(ii) Imprisonment

[9–50] The most severe form of punishment available to an Irish court is imprisonment.[81] Most statutory offences set out the maximum term of imprisonment that can be imposed on conviction for the offence. As Walsh notes, a maximum term of five years imprisonment seems to be the notional benchmark separating serious offences from lesser offences for certain purposes. Indeed, this forms the definition of an "arrestable offence" in various pieces of legislation.[82] Where there is no maximum term explicitly specified in the legislation, the maximum period of imprisonment which the court can impose is two years.[83]

[9–51] Until recently, mandatory minimum sentences were rare: the obvious exception being the mandatory sentence of life imprisonment for murder. Where a person is convicted of treason or murder under s 3 of the Criminal Justice Act 1990 (capital murder), the legislation specifies a mandatory sentence of at least 40 years imprisonment.[84] More recently, the legislature has introduced what are called presumptive sentences for drug offences. Section 15A of the Misuse of Drugs Act 1977 as inserted by s 4 Criminal Justice Act 1999 and amended by s 81 Criminal Justice Act 2006 provides that where an individual is found guilty of certain drug trafficking offences and the drugs in question have a street value of €13,000 or more, the court should impose a sentence of at least 10 years, unless there are exceptional circumstances which demand that the mandatory minimum sentence should not be imposed. Further sections were added to the Act by the Criminal Justice Act 2006 which provide that importing drugs under s 15B carries a presumptive sentence of 10 years, and that a person who has already been convicted of an offence under either s 15A or s 15B must be sentenced to a mandatory minimum of 10 years imprisonment.

(iii) Suspended Sentence

[9–52] Until recently, there was no statutory scheme for suspending sentences in Ireland, though as Walsh notes, in practice, the courts always assumed such a power and it was quite common for courts to impose either the entirety or a part of a sentence.[85]

---

[80] O'Malley, above n 3, p 7.

[81] Sections 11 and 12 of the Criminal Law Act 1997 abolished penal servitude, hard labour and corporal punishment.

[82] Walsh, above n 25, p 1026.

[83] *ibid.*

[84] See McCutcheon and Coffey, *Report into Determination of Life Sentences* (IHRC, 2006) available at http://www.ihrc.ie/_fileupload/banners/Report-into-Determination-of-Life-Sentences.pdf for an assessment of the human rights considerations regarding life sentences in Ireland.

[85] Walsh, above n 25, p 1032.

Section 99 of the Criminal Justice Act 2006 puts the suspended sentence on a statutory footing, stating:

> "Where a person is sentenced to a term of imprisonment (other than a mandatory term of imprisonment) by a court in respect of an offence, that court may make an order suspending the execution of the sentence in whole or in part, subject to the person entering into a recognisance to comply with the conditions of, or imposed in relation to, the order."

Thus, any sentence, except a mandatory sentence, can be suspended in full or in part under the Act. The section goes on to provide that where the sentence is suspended, it is done on the condition that the offender keep the peace and be of good behaviour, and the sentencing court may make further orders in relation to a partially suspended sentence, including, *inter alia*, an order that the offender co-operate with the Probation Service, or undergo treatment for drug or alcohol abuse, a course of education or therapy. Where an individual is convicted of an offence during either the term of his imprisonment or its suspension, the sentence should be reactivated unless the court is of the opinion that it would be unjust to do so. [9–53]

O'Malley notes that there is very little Irish authority on the circumstances in which a sentence could or should be suspended.[86] However, the principles set out in *R v O'Keefe*[87] may well give guidance in this jurisdiction. They are that a suspended sentence should never be imposed, "unless the court is convinced that a custodial sentence is warranted in the first place, and furthermore, the length of the sentence should never be increased merely because it is about to be suspended."[88] [9–54]

(iv) Deferred Sentences

Section 100 of the Criminal Justice Act 2006 introduced a new order referred to as a deferred sentence. The concept is similar to that in England and Wales, the purpose of which Ashworth explains: [9–55]

> "The idea of deferment is to allow the court to test the offender's resolve and intentions, and perhaps also to enable the offender to have a positive influence over the sentence ultimately imposed."[89]

Thus, the purpose of the deferred sentence is to allow the offender to engage in a process of rehabilitation or treatment, and if the offender complies with the order the court will not ultimately impose the sentence. Section 100 provides that where an individual is convicted of an offence for which the statutory penalty is a fine, a term of imprisonment or both, the court may impose the fine and defer the passing of a sentence of imprisonment for the offence while specifying the term of imprisonment that it would propose to impose on the person. Again, where the court imposes such a sentence, it must set out conditions which must be complied with, including a [9–56]

---

[86] O'Malley, above n 31, p 910.
[87] (1969) 53 Cr App R 91.
[88] O'Malley, above n 31, p 910.
[89] Ashworth, above n 3, p 353.

requirement that the person keep the peace and be of good behaviour. The individual sentenced must also agree to the making of the order.

[9–57] When the court issues a deferred sentence, it must specify a date upon which it proposes to pass sentence should the individual fail to comply with the terms of the order. This date must not be more than six months after the making of the order. No later than one month before this specified date, the person must be required to attend a court sitting at which the prison sentence shall be discharged if the individual has complied with the terms of the conditions. Where gardaí have reasonable belief that the individual breached the terms of his conditions in the intervening period, a garda may apply to the court for a hearing at which the original sentence or a shorter sentence can be imposed where the court is satisfied that there has been a contravention. Again, if the court is of the opinion that the justice of the case so requires, it has the discretion to impose a shorter sentence or no sentence at all. O'Malley cautions that courts should be slow to impose a deferred sentence "in circumstances where they would not have been disposed to impose a prison sentence in its absence."[90]

(v) Community Service Order (CSO)

[9–58] The Criminal Justice (Community Service Order) Act 1983 was introduced to provide a community service option to courts (except the Special Criminal Court) as an alternative to a prison sentence. Importantly, this limitation is built into the Act: a court can only order community service as an alternative to a prison sentence. However, Walsh notes that in practice "it seems that community service orders are sometimes perceived as an attractive and appropriate form of punishment for many cases which would never have attracted a custodial sentence."[91] The minimum number of hours under the scheme is 40, and the maximum is 240. The offender must agree to take part in the scheme before the order can be made, and the judge must be satisfied that the defendant is suitable for the scheme.

[9–59] A *Report on Value for Money and Review of the Community Service Scheme* was published in October 2009,[92] and it states that the desire of the Probation Service is to "increase considerably the usage of Community Service Orders" in order to divert more offenders from prison onto community service.[93] This aim is in keeping with the ideal of using imprisonment as a last resort.[94]

(vi) Fine

[9–60] Historically the courts had a general power at common law to impose a fine on conviction for a misdemeanour,[95] and s 10(3) of the Criminal Law Act 1997 grants the

[90] O'Malley, above n 31, p 913.
[91] Walsh, above n 25, p 1036. See also Walsh and Sexton, *An Empirical Study of Community Service Orders in Ireland* (Department of Justice, Equality and Law Reform, 1999).
[92] Probation Service, *Report on Value for Money and Review of the Community Service Scheme* (2009).
[93] *ibid.* p 5.
[94] Irish Penal Reform Trust, *IPRT Position Paper 5: Penal Policy with Imprisonment as a Last Resort* (IPRT, 2009).
[95] Walsh, above n 25, p 1039.

courts a general power to impose a fine where an individual has been convicted on indictment. In terms of the amount of the fine payable, the statute creating the offence will often set out the monetary limitations. Where there is no such limitation, courts are free to impose whatever fine they deem suitable, though in relation to summary offences, they must respect the jurisdictional limits of the District Court.

A controversial aspect of imposing a fine is that, traditionally, if an individual defaulted on payment, a term of imprisonment was automatically imposed. Sections 13 to 17 of the Fines Act 2010 attempt to rectify this, and do three things: first, give the courts power to inquire into the capacity of persons to pay fines in order to implement a policy of equality of impact; secondly, provide for the payment of fines by instalments; and, finally, provide the courts with alternatives to imprisonment for default on payment of fines. The last of these three is provided for in s 17, which provides for the application of a community service order in default of payment of a fine. However, there are a number of problems with this: first, it will be dependent on the defendant consenting to do community service, and some defendants will choose to be imprisoned for a few days rather than commit to a longer term of community service.[96] Secondly, not all defendants will be suitable for community service.[97] A further question on this issue relates to what thresholds will be introduced for fines — CSOs currently equate 40 hours community service to 1–2 months imprisonment. It remains to be seen how the provisions will operate in practice once the relevant sections are commenced. **[9–61]**

(vii) Probation and Entering into a Recognisance

Section 1(1) of the Probation of Offenders Act 1907 provides that where a court of summary jurisdiction "thinks that the charge is proved", but is of opinion that it is inexpedient to inflict any punishment, the court may, without proceeding to conviction, either dismiss the charge or discharge the offender conditionally on his entering into a recognisance. What this means is that the judge will state that he is of the opinion that the case was proven against the defendant, but decline to register a conviction and make an order under the Act instead. In *Duffy v Sutton*,[98] the Supreme Court found that a dismissal under s 1(1) of the 1907 Act amounted to something similar to a conviction, as the District Justice must have been satisfied that the charge against the plaintiff had been proved, and, but for the said Act, he would have been compelled to convict. O'Malley notes that this provision promotes rehabilitation "by allowing minor offenders to be censured without being formally labelled as offenders."[99] **[9–62]**

Section 1(2) of the Probation of Offenders Act 1907 goes on to provide that where an individual has been convicted on indictment, the court can grant a similar order under the Act in relation to the offences charged, though in order for this to occur, there must be a conviction registered against the offender. **[9–63]**

Section 2(1) of the Act provides that where a person enters into a recognisance, he can be ordered to be under the supervision of a named person, usually a member of the **[9–64]**

---

96 Walsh and Sexton, above n 91, p 63.
97 *ibid.* p 76.
98 [1955] IR 248.
99 O'Malley, above n 3, p 472.

Probation Service, and be subject to certain conditions. However, if the offender breaches these conditions, he can be exposed to punishment for the original offence. Section 6 of the Act provides that if a court is satisfied by information on oath that the offender has failed to observe any of the conditions of the recognisance, a warrant or a summons may be issued requiring him to attend court. If the court is satisfied that he has failed to observe the conditions of the recognisance it can "without further proof of his guilt, convict and sentence him for the original offence."[100]

Ancillary Penalties

[9–65] Aside from the formal punishment available to a court, the nature of some offences either requires or gives discretion to the court to impose ancillary penalties on the offender. As Walsh states, "[q]uite often, the object of the ancillary penalty will be to deprive the offender of the fruits of his crime or to render it more difficult or painful for him to repeat the offence..."[101] Importantly, however, these orders are not punishment as defined in the traditional sense of the term. In *Conroy v AG*,[102] in the context of disqualification from holding a driving licence (which the court described as a finding of unfitness to drive), it was considered that "disqualification is not a punishment notwithstanding that the consequence of such finding of unfitness might be both socially and economically serious for the person concerned."[103] This issue was also considered in *Enright v Ireland*[104] where the High Court considered the constitutional validity of the sex offenders register, as introduced by the Sex Offenders Act 2001. The court, while accepting that registering imposed something of a burden on the offender, held that it did not have a punitive effect, and thus could not be considered as part of the sentence. Thus, while an ancillary order might have very far reaching implications for the individual, they are not punishments *per se.* Nonetheless, as Walsh notes in reference to compensation orders, while, strictly speaking, such orders should not be considered part of the punishment, "[i]n practice, they will be perceived as part of the punishment, not least because of the fact that they are ordered by the court immediately upon conviction and in the context of passing sentence."[105]

VI. Structuring Judicial Sentencing Discretion

[9–66] There is at the very least a perception that the unstructured nature of Irish sentencing law and practice leads to inconsistency in sentences imposed on accused individuals in similar circumstances. Hamilton in her assessment of the IPRT study on sentencing practice in the District Court noted that solicitors had "serious concerns" regarding perceived inconsistencies in sentencing by different District Court judges.[106] O'Malley stated in 2000 that it is inevitable that this factor leads to "occasional headline-grabbing inconsistencies."[107] Examples of these headline grabbing inconsistencies

---

[100] Probation of Offenders Act 1907, s 6(5).
[101] Walsh, above n 25, p 1070.
[102] [1965] IR 411
[103] *ibid.* at 442.
[104] [2003] 2 IR 321.
[105] Walsh, above n 25, p 1078.
[106] Hamilton, above n 22, p 10.
[107] O'Malley, above n 3, pp 8–9.

were cited by the Law Reform Commission in their Consultation Paper on the Court Poor Box:[108]

> "[T]wo individuals [were] involved in a rally of four cars travelling at almost 120 miles per hour late at night. One of the drivers had been disqualified from driving for three years and fined £400. Another of the drivers (who had appeared before a different District Court judge) was merely ordered to pay £400 to charity and his case was adjourned for ten months with a view to avoiding the necessity for a conviction. Similarly, in a case involving eight persons charged with the same offence, four were convicted of the offence and each was fined £300 while the other four each contributed £500 to the court poor box and, thus, avoided a conviction."[109]

The question which then requires attention is to what extent, if any, should Irish sentencing law and practice become structured. If we compare our sentencing law with that in other jurisdictions, we see that we are quite unique in that, asides from the statutory minima and maxima, judges have almost absolute discretion in sentencing matters. **[9–67]**

The most extreme form of legislative interference with judicial discretion in sentencing was seen following the introduction of the US Federal Guidelines on Sentencing[110] where the sentence of the offender was determined by reference to a mathematical-type grid system, almost entirely removing judicial discretion in the context of the sentencing decision. However, *Blakely*[111] paved the way for *Booker*[112] where the Supreme Court of the United States found that the Federal Sentencing Guidelines are advisory rather than mandatory. This was taken a step further in *Spears*[113] where the court found that the sentencing court could depart from the sentencing guidelines if it disagreed with the underlying principles on which they were based, a decision which Ashworth states strikes "at the very concept of guidelines, and overextend[s] the proper authority of the sentencing court."[114] That said, it would appear that there is nothing unconstitutional with sentencing guidelines *per* se as long as they allow for latitude for the sentencing court. Ashworth, considering the *Mistretta*[115] decision in the United States and the Australian decision of *Palling v Corfield*,[116] highlights that there is "nothing unconstitutional in a legislature taking back the wide discretion it had left to the courts and then delegating it, within statutorily defined limits, to an independent Sentencing Commission."[117] **[9–68]**

[108] Law Reform Commission *Consultation Paper on the Court Poor Box* (LRC CP21-2004, Dublin, 2004).
[109] *ibid.* p 46.
[110] See http://www.ussc.gov/guidelin.htm .
[111] *Blakely v Washington* 542 US 296 (2004).
[112] *United States v Booker* 543 US 220 (2005).
[113] *Spears v United States* 555 US 606 (2009).
[114] Ashworth, above n 3, p 61.
[115] *Mistretta v United States* 488 US 361 (1989)
[116] (1970) 123 CLR 52.
[117] Ashworth, above n 3, p 60.

[9–69] In Ireland, *Deaton*[118] clearly established that while the legislature was quite justified in establishing the range of penalties which attach to a particular offence, the separation of powers restricts the other two organs of government from interfering with the sentencing of individual offenders. This principle, however, has been used as a justification for resisting statutory guidelines regarding sentences. Having considered the appropriateness of a statutory body which would provide guidelines on sentencing, the Fennelly Working Group[119] noted

> "[t]he remit of such a body... might be more prescriptive in nature, thus possibly encroaching upon judicial discretion, or it might be more flexible, establishing norms from which, having regard to the circumstances, a trial judge could depart."[120]

[9–70] Despite these concerns, it is difficult to argue with O'Malley's statement that whatever the approach taken to structuring sentencing discretion, the objective should be to develop consistency of approach rather than crude uniformity.[121] Possibly due to the uncertain constitutional nature of statutory guidelines on sentencing, the legislature introduced a series of presumptive sentences though the Criminal Justice Acts 2006 and 2007. Commenting on the increasing use of presumptive sentences by the legislature, Campbell[122] opines that this approach "suggests a preference for the mechanical application of generalised standards over the individualised approach which takes the specific characteristics of the accused into account",[123] thus driving the criminal justice system towards a model which has crime control rather than due process as its core value. As she notes, the Court of Criminal Appeal made a clear statement in refusing to impose the mandatory minimum sentence for offences under s 15A of the Misuse of Drugs Act 1977, as amended, thus highlighting the ability of the court to "frustrate the growth of a culture of control".[124] While the capacity of the courts to 'frustrate' the legislature in this context has been diminished somewhat by the presumptive sentences introduced in the 2006 and 2007 Acts, the tension between the legislature and the judiciary in the context of sentencing is no more evident than on this issue.

[9–71] A rather more judicially-palatable solution to sentencing inconsistency in Irish courts was the introduction in 2006 of the Irish Sentencing Information System (ISIS). This database of sentences handed down by the Circuit Courts around the country is run

---

118 [1963] IR 170.

119 Working Group on the Jurisdiction of the Courts, *The Criminal Jurisdiction of the Courts* (Stationery Office, Dublin, 2003).

120 *ibid.* p 172.

121 O'Malley, above n 3, p 66.

122 Campbell, "Decline of Due Process in the Irish Criminal Justice System: Beyond the Culture of Crime Control?" (2006) 6(1) HLJ 125.

123 *ibid.* p 148.

124 *ibid.* p 156. Campbell refers to the Department of Justice Report, McEvoy, *Research for the Department of Justice on the criteria applied by the Courts in sentencing under s. 15A of the Misuse of Drugs Act 1977 (as amended)* (Stationery Office, 2005) which found that out of 55 cases involving s 15A of the Act, the mandatory minimum sentence was only imposed in three cases. That said, the legislation in its form at that time allowed for departure from the mandatory minimum sentences where the defendant pleaded guilty, which they did in all but one case.

through the Courts Service and by 2009 information in relation to 300 concluded "sentencing matters" was available thereon, though this information was not publicly available.[125] As the name would suggest, the aim of the system is to provide a relatively comprehensive database for use by judges when determining the sentence to be imposed in a particular case. The database was further developed and is now publicly available at http://www.irishsentencing.ie. The aim of the website is primarily to assist judges by enabling them to access information regarding sentences imposed for particular offences in previous cases. Further, it also provides a unique and valuable resource to researchers on sentencing practices in Irish courts. Conroy and Gunning note that the information could potentially be used in a number of contexts: where a judge is sentencing for an offence which rarely comes before the courts; for offender characteristics which are unusual; or where a judge wishes to gather information on sentences imposed in a particular offence "with the objective of locating future offences somewhere on the spectrum of sentences previously imposed."[126] That said, it could also be argued that the database will have little utility, as by merely recording sentences without any critical eye, mistakes could be compounded. Equally, judges have no obligation to consult the database. The limited number of cases available on the website is also a drawback. It is expected that the database will grow over time, but this is resource-dependant. Ultimately, ISIS is a valuable tool for judges, researchers and students alike, and it is to be welcomed.

VII. Conclusion

In this chapter, we have discussed the various theories which underpin sentencing decisions of Irish courts and highlighted the importance of the principle of proportionality in the sentencing decision. We also examined the range of sentencing options open to the courts, ranging from dismissal orders under the Probation Act 1907 to terms of imprisonment. Ultimately, it is clear that Irish courts are very protective of their absolute discretion in sentencing decisions, arguing that the principle of proportionality does not sit well with the fettering of their discretion in this regard. That said, given the high profile, headline grabbing cases of sentencing disparity and inconsistency, it would appear that the Courts Service, the legislature, or both must address this issue in the near future to ensure that the general public have faith in the criminal justice system. We will now turn to those occasions where the courts have erred in either the sentencing decision or indeed in the ultimate outcome of the case, and examine the appeals system in Ireland. **[9–72]**

[125] Conroy and Gunning, "The Irish Sentencing Information System (ISIS): A Practical Guide to a Practical Tool" [2009] JSIJ 37.
[126] *ibid.* p 53.

CHAPTER 10
Appeals

This chapter examines the appeals process in the Irish criminal justice system. This issue is entirely regulated by statute, and the manner and circumstances in which an appeal is allowed are clearly set out in legislation. Traditionally, the right of the prosecution to appeal either a sentence or an acquittal was extremely limited. More recently, however, there have been expansions in this regard, most particularly in the Criminal Procedure Act 2010. **[10–01]**

Ashworth and Redmayne note that the appeals process serves many purposes, most importantly, development and clarification of the law and challenging dispositions with which the applicant is unhappy.[1] Having said that, appeal courts are traditionally deferential to the decision of the trial court and, indeed, there is considerable value in a verdict being seen as the authoritative ruling on a disputed issue.[2] **[10–02]**

---

[1] Ashworth and Redmayne, *The Criminal Process* (3rd ed, Oxford University Press, 2005), p 338.
[2] *ibid.* p 345.

I. Jurisdiction of the Court of Criminal Appeal

[10–03] Appeals from the Central, Special and Circuit Criminal Courts are heard in the Court of Criminal Appeal.[3] Although this court has been due for abolition since 1995,[4] and was supposed to have its powers vested in the Supreme Court, the ministerial order required to give effect to such change has never been made. Indeed, a recent report has advocated the establishment of a more permanent court of appeal within the Irish court structure.[5]

[10–04] Section 3 of the Courts (Establishment and Constitution) Act 1961 provides that the Court of Criminal Appeal sits from time to time on the direction of the Chief Justice. There are three members of the court, one of whom must be the Chief Justice or a member of the Supreme Court nominated by him. The other two judges are drawn from the High Court or Supreme Court.

[10–05] The Court of Criminal Appeal has only appellate jurisdiction, meaning that a case cannot be initiated in the Court. The types of cases the Court hears are appeals against conviction or sentence by the convicted person, appeals against unduly lenient sentences by the DPP and applications for declarations of miscarriages of justice.[6] Importantly, when the Court of Criminal Appeal gives judgment on a case, only one judgment is pronounced, with no majority, minority or dissenting judgments.[7]

[10–06] While generally, decisions of the Court of Criminal Appeal are final, s 29 of the Courts of Justice Act 1924[8] provides that an appeal lies to the Supreme Court where the issue involves a "point of law of exceptional public importance and that it is desirable in the public interest" that the appeal is taken. Both the convicted person and either the AG or the DPP can take the appeal. In most situations where an appeal is taken by the AG or DPP following an acquittal, the decision of the Supreme Court will be given on a "without prejudice"[9] basis.[10] This means that the Supreme Court will pronounce on the legal issues, but if it finds in favour of the appellant (either the AG or the DPP), it will not impact on the acquittal of the accused person.

Under s 14 of the Criminal Procedure Act 2010, discussed below, where the Court of Criminal Appeal has considered allowing a retrial following an original acquittal, the acquitted person or the DPP may appeal to the Supreme Court from the decision of the Court of Criminal Appeal on a point of law of exceptional public importance. In this exceptional situation, the Supreme Court decision may prejudice the interests of the

---

[3] Originally established under the Courts of Justice Act 1924, s 8, and again under the Courts (Establishment and Constitution) Act 1961, s 3. Section 14 of the 1961 Act provides that any jurisdiction vested in the 1924 Court is now vested in the 1961 Court.

[4] By virtue of the Courts and Court Officers Act 1995, s 4.

[5] *Report of the Working Group on a Court of Appeal* (chaired by Ms. Justice Susan Denham) (Stationery Office, Dublin, May 2009).

[6] Discussed in Chapter Fourteen.

[7] Courts of Justice Act 1924, s 28.

[8] As amended by the Criminal Justice Act 2006.

[9] A "without prejudice" appeal is one which does not impact on the original disposition; in this context, the acquittal.

[10] Where an appeal is taken under s 2 of the Criminal Justice Act 1993 a further appeal lies to the Supreme Court.

acquitted person. Similarly, where the DPP makes an application to appeal a sentence on the grounds of undue leniency to the Court of Criminal Appeal, a decision by that Court not to interfere with the sentence can also be appealed by the DPP to the Supreme Court under s 3 of the Criminal Justice Act 1993. Again, this appeal can only be taken in circumstances where the DPP or the AG certify that the case involves a point of law of exceptional public importance, and the decision of the Supreme Court can prejudice the interests of the accused, replacing the original sentence with the appropriate one.

II. Appeals by the Convicted Person

Appeals Against Conviction

(i) District Court

Where a person has been convicted of a criminal offence in the District Court he may appeal the conviction to the Circuit Court.[11] Such an appeal is made to the judge of the Circuit Court in whose circuit the District Court lies. Importantly, the decision of the Circuit Court judge on appeal in these circumstances is final and conclusive, and thus not appealable. **[10–07]**

Once the decision is made to appeal, notice must be served on all parties affected by the appeal within 14 days of the decision of the District Court.[12] Within this period, the appellant must also lodge the original notice of the appeal and a statutory declaration with the Clerk for the court area in which the original case was heard.[13] Where the appellant is in custody, the Governor of the prison or the garda Superintendent or Inspector in whose custody the appellant is must provide the appellant with the appropriate forms.[14] When completed, the forms must be given to the Clerk and a garda must serve notice on the relevant parties, as well as ensure that the declaration is made and lodged with the Clerk.[15] The District Court judge must order that a recognisance for the purpose of the appeal be lodged, and the Court has the power to fix the monetary amount, if any, of the recognisance.[16]

An appeal serves as a stay of execution[17] as explained in the case of *Burke v DPP*[18]: **[10–08]**

> "Once the accused person appeals his conviction and enters into a recognisance, the order convicting him, including the imposition of a penalty upon him, is stayed pending the outcome of his appeal to the Circuit Court."[19]

---

[11] Courts of Justice Act 1924, s 18(1). An appeal by a person tried in the District Court against a verdict of not guilty by reason of insanity lies to the Circuit Court also under the Criminal Law (Insanity) Act 2006, s 8.
[12] District Court Rules, Order 101, rule 1.
[13] DCR, Ord 101, r 2.
[14] DCR, Ord 101, r 7.
[15] DCR, Ord 101, r 7.
[16] District Court (Appeals to the Circuit Court) Rules 2003 after by DCR, Ord 101, r 4 as amended by SI No 484 of 2003.
[17] DCR, Ord 101, r 6.
[18] [2007] 2 ILRM 371.
[19] *ibid.* at 376.

In order for the appeal to operate as a stay of execution, however, the recognisance must be entered into within the period of fourteen days.[20] If the appellant is in custody, he will be released when the notice of appeal is given and the recognisance entered into.[21]

[10–09] When such an appeal is made, the Circuit Court conducts a full rehearing of the case on both the facts and the law. This is known as a hearing *de novo* and was described by Palles CB as "a new investigation [of the guilt of the appellant], with an opportunity to both parties to bring forward new evidence, and a decision upon that evidence by an independent tribunal and an independent mind."[22] Thus in this hearing, the entire trial process begins afresh, meaning that new evidence can be admitted. The absolute nature of this position was clearly set out in *State (Aherne) v Cotter*[23] where Walsh J stated that "[t]he retrial commences on an assumption that the accused is innocent until he is proved guilty on the re-trial..."[24] Indeed, in *Burke,* Charleton J stated:

> "Where a District Court conviction is appealed... all of the witnesses must present themselves again before the Circuit Court judge and the case is considered afresh; the only difference from the original hearing being that the Circuit Court judge will be aware that an appeal would not be taking place had a conviction not being previously been recorded against the accused, for that offence, in the District Court."[25]

[10–10] If an appellant is convicted following a guilty plea in the District Court, he may change the plea to one of not guilty on appeal to the Circuit Court. The fact that the accused pleaded guilty in the District Court was described as "irrelevant" by the Supreme Court, though it did concede that the guilty plea may affect "his credit on re-hearing."[26]

[10–11] That said, the fact that a hearing *de novo* takes place in the Circuit Court does not mean that the appellant is afforded the luxuries of a standard Circuit Court trial; for example, the court sits without a jury. Furthermore, if the conviction is upheld on appeal in the Circuit Court, it is open to the Circuit Court judge to increase or decrease the sentence that was originally imposed in the District Court, though it is restricted to the sentencing jurisdiction of the District Court. Again, the case of *State (Aherne) v Cotter*[27] is instructive as Walsh J stated:

> "An appeal by way of retrial enables a totally different case to be made by either side or both. On the re-hearing the case may appear to be a much more aggravated one than it first appeared, or vice versa. All these matters go to the sentence."[28]

---

[20] District Court (Appeals to the Circuit Court) Rules 2003 after by DCR, Ord 101, r 4 as amended by SI No 484 of 2003.
[21] *ibid.*
[22] *Ex parte McFadden, Judgments of the Superior Courts in Ireland,* 1988 ed. at 165, as cited in Walsh, *Criminal Procedure* (Thomson Round Hall, Dublin, 2002), p 1154.
[23] [1982] IR 188.
[24] *ibid.* at 198.
[25] [2007] 2 ILRM 371 at 374.
[26] *AG (Lambe) v Fitzgerald* [1973] IR 195 at 198.
[27] [1982] IR 188.
[28] *ibid.* at 198.

(ii) Indictment

A person convicted on indictment in the Circuit or Central Criminal Court can appeal the conviction and/or the sentence to the Court of Criminal Appeal under s 63 of the Courts of Justice Act 1924. A similar avenue of appeal lies from the Special Criminal Court under the Offences Against the State Act 1939.[29] Also, an appeal by a person tried on indictment against a verdict of not guilty by reason of insanity lies to the Court of Criminal Appeal under s 8 of the Criminal Law (Insanity) Act 2006. [10–12]

The Criminal Procedure Act 1993 provides that where the Court of Criminal Appeal is hearing an appeal against a conviction, it has the power to: [10–13]

a. Affirm the conviction, notwithstanding that it is of the opinion that a point raised in the appeal might be decided in favour of the appellant;
b. Quash the conviction and make no further order;
c. Quash the conviction and order a re-trial; or,
d. Quash the conviction, and if it appears to the Court that the appellant could have been found guilty of some other offence, and that the jury must have been satisfied of the facts which found him guilty of this other offence,
   (i) Substitute for the verdict a verdict of guilty of the other offence, and
   (ii) Impose such sentence in substitution for the sentence imposed at the trial for this other offence, not being a sentence of greater severity.[30]

An appeal against conviction on indictment in the Court of Criminal Appeal is not the same as a hearing *de novo* in the Circuit Court. In *People (DPP) v Madden*,[31] the Court of Criminal Appeal stated that its role was: [10–14]

> "to consider the conduct of the trial as disclosed in the stenographer's report to determine whether or not the trial was satisfactory in the sense of being conducted in a constitutional manner with fairness, to review so far as may be required any rulings on matters of law, to review so far as may be necessary the application of the rules of evidence as applied in the trial, and to consider whether any inferences of fact drawn by the court of trial can properly be supported by the evidence; but otherwise to adopt all findings of fact..."[32]

Walsh advises that the most likely grounds of appeal will concern an error of law or procedure at trial, such as a misdirection on the law to the jury; an error in admitting or refusing to admit evidence; or, witness tampering.[33]

The Court will on occasion be asked to reconsider a verdict in the absence of an error of law, where it is argued that there has been an erroneous finding of fact. However, [10–15]

---

[29] s 44(1).

[30] Criminal Procedure Act 1993, s 3. Prior to the introduction of the Criminal Procedure Act 2010, the convicted person was required to secure leave of the trial judge or the Court of Criminal Appeal to appeal the conviction under s 31 of the Courts of Justice Act 1924. The leave requirement was removed by s 31 of the 2010 Act which amended s 31 of the 1924 Act.

[31] [1977] IR 336.

[32] *ibid.* at 340 *per* O'Higgins CJ.

[33] Walsh, above n 22, p 1194.

appeals courts are generally slow to interfere with a jury verdict. Ashworth and Redmayne give three main reasons for the deference shown to a jury verdict: first, the appeals court is at a disadvantage in relation to the jury who have heard the evidence firsthand; secondly, to overrule a jury decision may undermine their centrality to the system; and finally, appeal courts are reluctant to interfere with decisions of trial courts, due to the necessity of finality in decision making.[34]

[10–16] Generally, Irish courts take a very deferential approach to the factual aspect of verdicts, though they will on occasion quash a conviction where the verdict cannot be supported having regard to the evidence.[35] Importantly, the verdict will not be quashed if the Court of Criminal Appeal would simply have reached a verdict different to that of the jury or the trial court. As the Supreme Court stated in *People (DPP) v Egan*[36]:

> "Save where a verdict may be identified as perverse, if credible evidence supports the verdict, the Court of Criminal Appeal has no power to interfere with it. The concepts of lurking doubt, feel of the case, gut feeling or back of my mind, are foreign to the judicial role... In many instances what may be difficult and obscure to a trial judge is crystal clear to a jury: the converse is also very possible. To permit verdicts on criminal trials to be upset upon such subjective consideration would seem to be a denial of the validity of a trial by jury."[37]

[10–17] Furthermore, as a jury does not give reasons for its decision the appeals court cannot know the precise basis on which the jury found that the defendant was guilty beyond a reasonable doubt.[38] O'Malley suggests that while it is open to an appeals court to review a conviction based on a perverse finding of fact by a jury, the circumstances of the case would be highly unusual.[39]

[10–18] In *DPP v Quinn*,[40] the appellant was convicted of attempted rape and other related charges. The only evidence implicating him at trial was two inconsistent statements that he made at a garda station. There was no medical evidence to corroborate any of the complainant's evidence, no attempt at identification of the appellant, and no samples had been taken. "In a word," the Court of Criminal Appeal stated, "there was no evidence at all aside from the statements." While acknowledging that weighing up evidence is quintessentially a matter for a jury, the court found that given the contradictions that emerged from the complainant's case, as weighed against the totally unreliable confession statements, the conviction could not stand. The Court went so far as to say that this is a case which should have been withdrawn from the jury. The convictions were quashed and there was no retrial ordered.[41]

---

[34] Ashworth and Redmayne, above n 1, p 345.
[35] Walsh, above n 22, p 1194.
[36] [1990] ILRM 780.
[37] *ibid.* at 784.
[38] Ashworth and Redmayne, above n 1, p 345.
[39] O'Malley, *The Criminal Process* (Round Hall, 2009), p 928.
[40] Unreported, Court of Criminal Appeal, 23 March 1998.
[41] See also *DPP v Morrissey* unreported, Court of Criminal Appeal, 10 July 1988, where the Court found that the evidence in the case was so weak that a verdict of guilty on the evidence produced before the jury would have resulted in a miscarriage of justice.

In the main appellants will be limited to raising points which were raised at trial in their appeal to the Court of Criminal Appeal. However, it is open to the Court to admit new evidence at its discretion. Generally, any newly-tendered evidence must be fresh – if the evidence or point of law was not raised at trial for tactical reasons, the Court will be slow to admit it on appeal. The Court will generally only admit newly-tendered evidence where it was not available at trial and may have regard to the credibility of the evidence in coming to its decision to admit it.[42] When considering whether such evidence should be admitted, the courts apply the following criteria: **[10–19]**

1. Given that the public interest requires that a defendant bring forward his entire case at trial, exceptional circumstances must be established before the court should allow further evidence to be called. That onus is particularly heavy in the case of expert testimony, having regard to the availability generally of expertise from multiple sources.
2. The evidence must not have been known at the time of the trial and must be such that it could not reasonably have been known or acquired at the time of the trial.
3. It must be evidence which is credible and which might have a material and important influence on the result of the case.
4. The assessment of credibility or materiality must be conducted by reference to the other evidence at the trial and not in isolation.[43]

When determining whether the conviction should stand on the basis of fresh evidence, a slightly amended test is used. Walsh notes that, rather than asking if the verdict was perverse, the court must conduct an objective evaluation of the evidence to determine whether the conviction was safe: **[10–20]**

> "It cannot reach this conclusion based solely on the course which the defence took at the trial. It must consider the course the defence might have taken had it been aware in advance of the existence of the new evidence and whether a different approach by the defence might have led to an acquittal."[44]

Where an appellant wishes to raise a point of law on appeal, this point of law should also have been raised at the trial stage. The reason for this was made clear in *People (DPP) v Boyce*[45] where the Court stated that it would lean against the admission of points of law identified outside the context of the proceedings, "sometimes by persons who had no connection with the trial, but only after a 'trawl' through the transcript." The exception, as identified by the court in this case, is where the points of law are "substantial and of fundamental importance to the fairness of the trial." O'Malley argues that it would be manifestly unjust if an unsafe conviction were allowed to stand "merely because a lawyer was insufficiently alert or astute to raise an objection or requisition in the course of the trial itself."[46] **[10–21]**

---

[42] Walsh, above n 22, p 1190.
[43] *People (DPP) v O'Regan* [2007] 3 IR 805 at 826, as adopted from *People (DPP) v Willoughby* [2005] IECCA 4.
[44] Walsh, above n 22, p 1191.
[45] [2005] IECCA 143.
[46] O'Malley, above n 39, p 931.

[10–22] Walsh suggests that while the court will overturn convictions on the basis that evidence should not have been admitted, it can be difficult to persuade the court to quash a conviction on the basis of the conduct of the judge during the trial.[47]

The appellant may succeed on one or more grounds of appeal, but still may not necessarily succeed in having the verdict quashed. This is due to what is commonly termed, "the proviso" in s 3(1) of the Criminal Procedure Act 1993 which states that one of the options open to the Court of Criminal Appeal is to "affirm the conviction (and [it] may do so, notwithstanding that it is of opinion that a point raised in the appeal might be decided in favour of the appellant, if it considers that no miscarriage of justice has actually occurred)." The miscarriage of justice standard is a high one, meaning that as long as the court is satisfied that affirming a conviction will not amount to a miscarriage of justice, it can affirm the conviction.[48]

Appeals Against Sentence

(i) From the District Court

[10–23] Where a person has been convicted of a criminal offence in the District Court he may appeal the sentence to the Circuit Court.[49] The rules regarding notices are the same in this context as in an appeal against conviction. The decision of the Circuit Court judge on such appeal is final, conclusive and not appealable.

[10–24] Where such an appeal, against sentence only, is taken, s 50 of the Courts (Supplemental Provisions) Act 1961 provides that "the Circuit Court shall not ... re-hear the case except to such extent as shall be necessary to enable the court to adjudicate on the question of sentence." Thus, the re-hearing will be confined to those matters which would impinge on the severity of the sentence, varying from case to case.[50]

[10–25] When issuing his judgment, the Circuit Court judge is limited to the same sentencing limitations as those in the District Court,[51] though when operating within these limits the Circuit Court judge has the power to increase as well as decrease or approve the sentence imposed in the District Court.[52]

[47] Walsh, above n 22, p 1196. He gives the example of *AG v Hurley* (1937) 71 ILTR 29 in which the Court of Criminal Appeal declined to quash a conviction even though it was satisfied that the trial judge made disparaging remarks regarding a previous acquittal of the accused.

[48] O'Malley does note, however, that the standard is a possibility rather than a probability of a miscarriage of justice. O'Malley, above n 39, p 936.

[49] Courts of Justice Act 1924, s 18(1). While the 1924 Act explicitly excludes "an order returning for trial or binding to the peace or good behaviour or to both the peace and good behaviour", s 16 of the Criminal Justice Act 1951 provides that an applicant may apply under the section to the Circuit Court to be released from this type of order.

[50] Walsh, above n 22, p 1156.

[51] Criminal Justice Act 1951, s 5. Prior to the introduction of the Criminal Procedure Act 2010, the convicted person was required to secure leave of the trial judge or the Court of Criminal Appeal to appeal the sentence under s 63 of the Courts of Justice Act 1924. The leave requirement was removed by s 31 of the 2010 Act which amended s 31 of the 1924 Act.

[52] *State (Aherne) v Cotter* [1982] IR 188.

(ii) On Indictment

Where a person is sentenced in the Circuit Criminal Court, the Special Criminal Court or the Central Criminal Court, he can appeal his sentence.[53] [10–26]

Appeals against sentence can be taken for three primary reasons: the sentence was unlawful, it was imposed in excess of jurisdiction, or it was wrong in principle.[54] It is this final ground that is most commonly utilised. Here, the appellant will argue that the sentence imposed was not proportionate, and that the sentencing court did not take full account of the aggravating and mitigating factors in the case. [10–27]

On appeal, the Court of Criminal Appeal has the jurisdiction to either affirm or alter the sentence imposed by the trial judge. This includes a power to increase as well as decrease the sentence.[55] The appeal court will not interfere with the sentencing decision of the trial judge unless an error of law, jurisdiction or principle is revealed. [10–28]

III. Cases Stated

The case stated procedure is a process by which a judge of the District Court or, less frequently, the Circuit Court, can have an issue of law considered by a superior court. O'Malley explains that the case stated procedure and that of judicial review are similar "to the extent that they furnish an opportunity for a legal point which might not otherwise arise before the superior courts to be argued in some detail before the High Court or Supreme Court."[56] [10–29]

Case Stated from the District Court

A case may be stated to the High Court by a District Court Judge on a point of law at the request of any party to the proceedings heard and determined in the District Court, after the trial has concluded.[57] The judge may refuse to state the case to the High Court if the application is considered frivolous,[58] where there is no doubtful or difficult question of law involved, where the point of law at issue is well settled, or where the point cannot assist the applicant even if it is decided in his favour.[59] Where the judge refuses to state the case, the applicant can appeal to the High Court for an order of [10–30]

---

[53] Courts of Justice Act 1924, s 63. Where a person has pleaded guilty in the District Court, and has been returned for sentencing to the Circuit Court, they can also appeal the sentence handed down to the Court of Criminal Appeal: Criminal Procedure (Amendment) Act 1973, s 1. Prior to the introduction of the Criminal Procedure Act 2010, the convicted person was required to secure leave of the trial judge or the Court of Criminal Appeal to appeal the sentence under s 63 of the Courts of Justice Act 1924. The leave requirement was removed by s 31 of the 2010 Act which amended s 31 of the 1924 Act.

[54] O'Malley, above n 39, p 924.

[55] O'Malley argues that this latter power is one which could usefully be abolished, given the fact that the prosecution now has a power to appeal sentence. O'Malley, above n 39, p 953.

[56] O'Malley, above n 39, p 958.

[57] Summary Jurisdiction Act 1857, s 2, as extended by Courts (Supplemental Provisions) Act 1961, s 51.

[58] Summary Jurisdiction Act 1857, s 4.

[59] Walsh, above n 22, p 1163.

mandamus which would compel the judge to state the case.[60] The case must be stated within 14 days of the determination of the issue by the District Court Judge.[61]

[10–31] Once the case is stated, it has the effect of suspending the proceedings until the outcome of the question has been determined. While the party applying for the case stated (the appellant) drafts the case, usually in consultation with the other party (the respondent), the ultimate responsibility for the statement of the case lies with the judge who signs it.[62] Importantly, the issue to be stated must be one of law, and not go to the credibility or otherwise of evidence.[63]

[10–32] Where the High Court receives a case stated, it must hear and determine the issues before it, and may affirm, reverse or amend the decision of the District Court.[64] Once the case is returned, or remitted, to the District Court, the judge must deal with the case in accordance with the decision of the High Court. The interaction with the case stated procedure and the general right of appeal is interesting. While a person who appeals by way of case stated is taken to have abandoned his right of appeal to the Circuit Court, where a case stated is remitted to the District Court with a direction to convict, that conviction can be appealed to the Circuit Court.

Consultative Cases Stated

(i) Consultative Case Stated from the District Court

[10–33] Section 52 of the Courts (Supplemental Provisions) Act 1961 provides that a question may be referred to the High Court for determination. While the consultative case stated procedure is similar to that of the normal case stated process, it differs in one fundamental way: a consultative case stated is referred to the High Court during the proceedings, before the judge has given his decision in the case. The District Court judge is obliged to refer the case to the High Court where a party requests that he do so unless he considers the matter frivolous.[65] The judge can also state the case on his own volition. Prior to stating the case, the judge should hear all the evidence relating to the point of law in question and make the necessary findings of fact.

(ii) Consultative Case Stated from the Circuit Court

[10–34] Section 16 of the Courts of Justice Act 1947 provides for a consultative case stated procedure from the Circuit Court to the Supreme Court. Here, the Circuit Court judge has a discretion to state the case where requested prior to the determination of the proceedings before him. Unlike the District Court procedure, the judge cannot state the case on his own volition. The test for determining how this discretion should

---

60 *AG v Beirne* [1943] IR 480.

61 Courts (Supplemental Provisions) Act 1961, s 51.

62 O'Malley, above n 39, p 960.

63 See *DPP (Stratford) v O'Neill* [1998] 1 ILRM 221; *DPP v Nangle* [1984] ILRM 171 and *Fitzgerald v DPP* [2003] 3 IR 247.

64 Summary Jurisdiction Act 1857, s 6.

65 Walsh, above n 22, p 1172.

be used was set out in *McKenna v Deery*[66] where the court stated that "if the judge is quite clear in his own mind as to the proper decision in the case, *prima facie* he is entitled to refuse the application and go ahead and decide the case in accordance with his firm and positive views."[67]

Where a criminal case is heard in the Circuit Court, a jury will be empanelled, and in order to preserve the continuity of the trial process, a judge should not refer a question during the course of a jury trial for reasons outlined by Budd J: **[10–35]**

> "Some considerable time must elapse before the decision of the Supreme Court can be given and before the trial can be continued. During that interval it is almost bound to happen that the jury will forget a great deal of the evidence given before them, and the difficulties of recalling the evidence to their minds must be very great, if it can be done satisfactorily at all."[68]

For this reason, it is quite unusual for the Circuit Court to operate the consultative case stated procedure.

IV Appeals by the Prosecution

Prosecution Appeals and the Rule Against Double Jeopardy

The rule against double jeopardy provides that once an individual has been tried in a competent court, and a verdict rendered, he cannot be retried for that same criminal offence. This is true even if "there is fresh evidence of his guilt, even evidence provided by his own admission of guilt."[69] Coffey explains that the rationale for the development of the principle at common law was based on two main principles: the deficiencies in the medieval trial process which tended to favour the prosecution; and the draconian punishments which were imposed on defendants.[70] In modern times, he notes that the principle "prevents the prosecution authorities from convicting an accused solely through persistence by repeated, perhaps inefficient criminal trials."[71] This point was stated clearly in the case of *Green v United States*[72] where Black J explained the importance of the rule: **[10–36]**

> "[T]he State with all its resources and power should not be allowed to make repeated attempts to convict an individual for an alleged offence, thereby subjecting him to embarrassment, expense and ordeal and compelling him to live in a continuing state of anxiety and insecurity, as well as enhancing the possibility that even though innocent he might be found guilty."[73]

---

[66] [1998] 1 IR 62.
[67] *ibid.* at 75.
[68] *People (Attorney General) v McGlynn* [1967] IR 232 at 243.
[69] *People (DPP) v O'Shea* [1982] IR 384 at 432.
[70] Coffey, "Evaluating the Common Law Principle Against Retrials" (2007) 14(1) DULJ 26, p 26.
[71] Coffey, "Post-Acquittal Retrial for Serious Criminal Offences" (2009) 19(3) ICLJ 80, p 81.
[72] 355 US 184 (1957).
[73] *ibid.* at 187–188.

Thus, while the common law has generally provided for appeals by a convicted person against his conviction or sentence, there has traditionally been no reciprocal right of appeal vested in the prosecution though recent legislative developments have changed this position dramatically.

Appeals Against Acquittals

(i) Appeals from the District Court

[10–37] There is no general right for the prosecution to appeal an acquittal or a sentence handed down in the District Court. However, a small number of legislative provisions grant the prosecution power to appeal acquittals from the District Court in relation to specific offences. Section 310(1) of the Fisheries (Consolidation) Act 1959, for example, provides that the prosecutor can appeal to the Circuit Court against an acquittal in the District Court in respect of a complaint brought on a summons under the Act. Similarly, s 52 of the Safety, Health and Welfare at Work Act 1989 empowers the National Authority for Occupational Safety and Health to appeal against acquittals in the District Court. Finally, s 18(2) of the Courts of Justice Act 1928 preserves any right of appeal of a complainant or prosecutor which existed prior to the introduction of the 1928 Act. Woods[74] notes that this right exists in "excise cases, illicit distillation offences and fisheries prosecutions."[75]

[10–38] In *Considine v Shannon Regional Fisheries Board*[76] the plaintiff argued that s 310 of the 1959 Act amounted to a violation of Art 38 of the Constitution as it infringes the common law principle that no appeal shall lie from a decision dismissing a criminal charge, and that a verdict of not guilty on a criminal charge is inviolable in the light of the Constitution. The Supreme Court held that, while there was a common law rule that there should be no appeal from an acquittal, this was subject to the right of the legislature to introduce such an appeal procedure, "provided that it was in clear and unambiguous language".[77] Thus, s 310 was found to be constitutional. Importantly, however, the court stated that this right of appeal was limited to where the court is exercising it summary jurisdiction and would not be appropriate in the context of a conviction reached through a trial by jury.

[10–39] While there are discrete circumstances in which an acquittal can be appealed from the District Court, the same was not historically true for acquittals on indictment. The justification for such this historic position is found in Art 38.5 of the Constitution, which provides that no person shall be tried on any criminal charge without a jury. In this regard, O'Malley noted that, "such is our collective attachment" to a jury trial that a provision which would propose to provide for a "with prejudice" appeal from a jury verdict would be only "reluctantly countenanced", despite the fact that an equivalent appeal lies against a conviction.[78]

---

[74] Woods, *District Court Practice and Procedure in Criminal Cases* (James V Woods, Limerick, 1994).
[75] *ibid.* p 450.
[76] [1997] 2 IR 404.
[77] *ibid.* at 422.
[78] O'Malley, above n 42, p 951.

(ii) Appeals on Indictment

A very limited right to appeal directed acquittals did exist under s 34 of the Criminal Procedure Act 1967, and the Law Reform Commission in their *Report on Prosecution Appeals and Pre-Trial Hearings*[79] noted that, due to the limited nature of the appeal power in question under s 37, it was rarely used. However, the section was amended by the Criminal Justice Act 2006 and now provides for a less limited right of appeal, stating that if an individual is acquitted in a case heard on indictment, the prosecuting authority may, without prejudice to the accused, refer a question of law to the Supreme Court for determination.[80] The Criminal Justice Act 2006 also amended the procedure to allow the acquitted person to be represented at the hearing in the Supreme Court, and to provide that his identity should not be disclosed.[81] **[10–40]**

This is not a general right of appeal – rather the question of law must be clearly stated, and it is only upon this question that the Supreme Court will base its judgment. The court will not enter into a general discussion as to the reliability of the jury verdict but rather determine a specific question, such as whether the trial judge was correct in excluding a particular inculpatory piece of evidence. **[10–41]**

Despite the historic attachment at common law to the rule against double jeopardy, the law relating to appeals against acquittals underwent substantial reform in other jurisdictions. Notably, the Criminal Justice Act 2003[82] in England and Wales allows for the prosecutor to appeal a conviction secured on indictment for an order quashing the conviction for the qualifying offence[83] and an order for retrial on the basis of new and compelling evidence which has emerged.

In its 2006 Report, the Balance in the Criminal Law Review Group[84] recommended the introduction of some new avenues of appeal for the prosecution. These recommendations are partly reflected in the Criminal Procedure Act 2010. This Act provides for exceptions to the rule against double jeopardy and proposes the introduction of two "with prejudice" prosecution appeals to the Court of Criminal Appeal following acquittal. If successful, such appeals would result in a retrial. The first, under s 8, provides that where there is new and compelling evidence in relation to the offence, a retrial may be ordered if it is in the public interest. The second, under s 9, provides that where it is probable that the commission of an offence against the administration of justice by either the person originally acquitted or another person led to that acquittal, and it is in the interests of justice, a re-trial may be ordered. The DPP is allowed only one application for a re-trial order to the court. An appeal on a point of law lies to the Supreme Court by

[79] Law Reform Commission *Report on Prosecution Appeals and Pre-Trial Hearings* (LRC 81-2005), Dublin, 2005.

[80] Criminal Justice Act 2006, s 21.

[81] *ibid.*

[82] ss 75 to 97.

[83] There are 30 qualifying offences in the Act to which the appeal procedure applies.

[84] Balance in the Criminal Law Review Group, *Final Report* (Stationery Office, Dublin, 2007), available at http://www.justice.ie/en/JELR/BalanceRpt.pdf/Files/BalanceRpt.pdf

the acquitted person or the DPP relating to the decision of the Court of Criminal Appeal to grant or refuse a re-trial order. The legislation applies to serious criminal offences, but, importantly does not apply retrospectively.[85] In coming to its decision as to whether it should order a re-trial, s 10 provides that the court should consider four factors:

(i) whether or not it is likely that any re-trial could be conducted fairly,
(ii) the amount of time that has passed since the act or omission that gave rise to the indictment,
(iii) the interests of any victim of the offence concerned, and
(iv) any other matter which the Court considers relevant to the application.

Section 10(4) provides that the Court can order the production of evidence which was admitted in the earlier proceedings, and call any witness who gave evidence in those proceedings to be examined, or call any compellable witness in those proceedings to be examined. Importantly in this regard, s 10(5) provides that evidence may be admitted under the section "whether or not it would have been admissible in earlier proceedings." The meaning of this is unclear, though the explanatory memorandum clarifies the issue somewhat by explaining that the admissibility of evidence "is not dependent on whether the evidence would have been admissible under the laws of evidence pertaining at the time of the original proceedings."

Both the s 8 and the s 9 appeals procedures require the application for appeal to be on notice to the acquitted person, though both provide that the court may proceed to hear the application in the absence of the individual if it is in the interests of justice to do so. Section 11 of the Act allows the acquitted individual to apply for a legal aid certificate. Section 12 provides that, while generally, the proceedings are to heard in open court, where it is in the interests of justice to do so, the public or any person or persons, except for the Press, can be excluded from the court. The court may also order reporting restrictions under this section.

Appeals Against Sentence

[10–42] Where the DPP is of the opinion that a sentence imposed in the Circuit Court, Central Criminal Court or Special Criminal Court is unduly lenient, he can apply for leave to appeal the sentence to the Court of Criminal Appeal.[86] This was described by the Court of Criminal Appeal in *People (DPP) v Egan,*[87] as a "major departure" from the traditional common law position.[88]

---

[85] For arguments for and against the introduction of the legislation, see Coffey, "Post-Acquittal Retrial for Serious Criminal Offences" (2009) 19(3) ICLJ 80 and Duffy "'Balance' in the Criminal Justice System: Misrepresenting the Relationship between the Rights of Victims and Defendants" (2009) 19(1) ICLJ 2.

[86] Criminal Procedure Act 1993, s 2.

[87] [2001] 2 ILRM 299.

[88] *ibid.* at 308.

The court has clarified that simple leniency is not a ground for appeal– there must be undue leniency which amounts to an error in principle in the case. In *People (DPP) v McCormack*,[89] Barron J stated: **[10–43]**

> "In the view of the Court, undue leniency connotes a clear divergence by the Court of trial from the norm, and would, save perhaps in exceptional circumstances, have been caused by an obvious error in principle. Each case must depend on its special circumstances. The appropriate sentence depends not only upon its own facts but also upon the personal circumstances of the accused. The sentence to be imposed is not the appropriate sentence for the crime, but the appropriate sentence for the crime because it has been committed by the accused. The range of possible penalties is dependent upon these two factors. It is only when the penalty is below the range as determined on this basis that the question of undue leniency may be considered."[90]

Thus, simple leniency will not justify amending the original sentence, nor is it appropriate for the Court of Criminal Appeal to ask if it would have imposed a different sentence in the case.[91] What is required is an *unduly* lenient sentence which amounts to a departure in principle. Even if the court finds that a sentence is in fact unduly lenient, it is under no obligation to vary or increase the sentence: the Court of Criminal Appeal retains the power to defer to the sentencing decision of the trial judge and dismiss the appeal.[92] **[10–44]**

Despite the discrete examples which exist whereby a prosecution appeal lies from the District Court, it is unlikely that the legislature will introduce an all-embracing right of appeal from acquittals or unduly lenient sentences handed down in that Court. This was the subject of a Law Reform Commission Consultation Paper and Report.[93] While the Consultation Paper suggested that a right to appeal unduly lenient sentences imposed in the District Court could be introduced, the Commission ultimately came to the conclusion in its Report that this was not appropriate. It stated that while, in principle, sentences imposed in the District Court that are unduly lenient should be subject to review by an appellate court, it was not desirable to introduce such an avenue of appeal. Rather, the Commission felt, it was more appropriate to "enhance the reliability of the sentencing process in the District Court" to address the issue of inconsistent sentencing practices in that jurisdiction.[94] **[10–45]**

---

[89] [2000] 4 IR 356.

[90] *ibid.* at 359.

[91] See *DPP v Byrne* [1994] 2 IR 236.

[92] O'Malley, above n 42, p 954.

[93] Law Reform Commission *Consultation Paper on Unduly Lenient Sentences in the District Court* (LRC CP33-2004, Dublin, 2004) and Law Reform Commission *Report on Prosecution Appeals and Pre-Trial Hearings* (LRC 81-2006, Dublin, 2006).

[94] The Commission was of the opinion that three aspects in particular should be addressed: the role of prosecuting counsel in sentencing, the provision of sentencing information and the provision of reasons by sentencing judges.

V. Conclusion

[10–46] As we have seen, historically, appeals were generally only available to the convicted person, with prosecution appeals only available in the most limited of circumstances and generally on a without prejudice basis. While appeals against sentence by the prosecution were introduced in 1993, it was generally felt that the commitment to the principle of double jeopardy, and the general due process model in operation in Ireland would make a "with prejudice" appeal from an acquittal undesirable. Recent developments in legislation allowing for an appeal against a jury acquittal, albeit in limited circumstances, seem to be driving the Irish criminal justice system away from its due process foundations, towards a "crime control" orientation.

CHAPTER 11
Juvenile Justice

Kilkelly suggests that "[c]hildren in conflict with the law have been a neglected group in Irish law and society for many years",[1] evidenced by a lack of legislative reform in relation to juvenile justice, a dearth of research and data on youth offending, and a lack of political will to implement mounting calls for reform. **[11–01]**

The Children Act 1908, along with the common law, governed juvenile justice in this jurisdiction until 2001. The system created under this regime was, for many years, considered inadequate and unsatisfactory in the context of modern Ireland. The main **[11–02]**

[1] Kilkelly, *Children's Rights in Ireland: Law, Policy and Practice* (Tottel Publishing, Dublin, 2008), p 529.

criticisms levelled were that it emphasised institutionalisation as a remedy for juvenile offenders over community-based alternatives and that there was a distinct lack of co-ordination and communication between differing agencies with overlapping functions in child protection and youth justice.[2] Although many committees had called for reform in this area since the 1970s,[3] it was not until 2001 that new legislation was passed, and not until 2007 that it was fully implemented, with amendments. The Children Act 2001, as amended by the Criminal Justice Act 2006, provided for alterations to the age of criminal responsibility, new potential remedies in the case of juvenile offenders, the principle of imprisonment as last resort and the creation of conferencing opportunities to address child offending outside of a criminal trial.

[11–03] Walsh has observed the need to adopt alternative strategies in dealing with juveniles who come into conflict with the criminal law:

> "The challenge of tackling youth crime in a manner which is sensitive to the circumstances of the youth while at the same time satisfying the law and order demands of adult society is not new. It has long been accepted that subjecting young offenders to the full rigours of the criminal law and the criminal justice system is unjust, inappropriate and counter-productive. They do not have the maturity, foresight and experience of life to appreciate fully the harm caused by their offending both to themselves and to the community around them. It would be unjust, therefore, to subject them to criminal standards which do not take account of these weaknesses. Exposing them to the full rigours of the criminal justice system can also introduce them at a young and impressionable age to a subculture and way of life in which crime is normal....It would seem appropriate, therefore, to have interventions designed to divert young offenders away from an offending lifestyle and to help them appreciate that crime is neither normal nor acceptable."[4]

[11–04] This chapter explores the specifics of the juvenile justice system which operates in Ireland, focusing mainly on the provisions of the 2001 Act, as amended, but looking also to international standards and general objectives of youth justice.

I. Objectives, Principles and International Standards

[11–05] In November 1985, the General Assembly of the United Nations adopted the UN Standard Minimum Rules for the Administration of Juvenile Justice, "the Beijing Rules". Rule 5.1 sets out that:

---

[2] Seymour, "Transition and Reform: Juvenile Justice in the Republic of Ireland" in *International Handbook of Juvenile Justice* (Junger-Tas and Decker (eds.), Springer, Netherlands, 2006), p 118.

[3] *Reformatory and Industrial Schools System Report* ("The Kennedy Report") (Stationery Office, Dublin, 1970); Task Force on Child Care Services *Final Report* (Stationery Office, Dublin, 1980); *Report of the Committee of Inquiry into the Penal System* ("The Whitaker Report") (Stationery Office, Dublin, 1985); Oireachtas Select Committee on Crime *First Report: Juvenile Crime – Its Causes and Its Remedies* (Stationery Office, Dublin, 1992).

[4] Walsh, *Juvenile Justice* (Thomson Round Hall, Dublin, 2005) p vii.

"The juvenile justice system shall emphasize the well-being of the juvenile and shall ensure that any reaction to juvenile offenders shall always be in proportion to the circumstances of both the offenders and the offence."[5]

The Rules provide that fundamental procedural safeguards, such as the presumption of innocence, the right to be notified of charges, the right to remain silent, the right to legal advice, the right to the presence of a parent or guardian, the right to confront and cross-examine witnesses and the right to appeal to a higher court are to be guaranteed to juveniles at all stages of the criminal process.[6] The right to privacy is specifically listed as meriting protection in order to avoid any ill-effects of undue publicity or labelling.[7] In principle, the Rules state, no information which could lead to the identification of a juvenile in the criminal process ought to be published.[8] **[11–06]**

Under the Rules consideration is to be given, wherever possible, to dealing with juvenile offenders outside of formal criminal trial.[9] Where a formal criminal trial is held in relation to a juvenile offender, the Rules state that the proceedings must be: **[11–07]**

"conducive to the best interests of the juvenile and shall be conducted in an atmosphere of understanding, which shall allow the juvenile to participate therein and to express herself or himself freely".[10]

Imprisonment should be a measure of last resort in juvenile cases and restrictions on the liberty of juvenile offenders should be imposed only after careful consideration, should be kept to the minimum possible, and should not be imposed unless the offence involves violence or is of a serious, persistent nature and there is no other appropriate response.[11] This is re-emphasised in the statement that "[t]he placement of a juvenile in an institution shall always be a disposition of last resort and for the minimum necessary period."[12] This is echoed in the UN Rules for the Protection of Juveniles Deprived of their Liberty 1990, Rule 1 of which states: **[11–08]**

"[t]he juvenile justice system should uphold the rights and safety and promote the physical and mental well-being of juveniles. Imprisonment should be used as a last resort."[13]

Although detailed and persuasive, these Rules are soft law only and are not binding. Nonetheless, they provide an informed basis for the development of juvenile justice systems which respect the rights of juveniles and promote their best interests. **[11–09]**

[5] UN Standard Minimum Rules for the Administration of Juvenile Justice 1985, Rule 5.1.
[6] Rule 7.1.
[7] Rule 8.1.
[8] Rule 8.2.
[9] Rule 11.1.
[10] Rule 14.2.
[11] Rule 17.1(c).
[12] Rule 19.1.
[13] UN Rules for the Protection of Juveniles Deprived of their Liberty 1990 ("the Havana Rules"), Rule 1. See also the UN Rules for the Prevention of Juvenile Delinquency 1990 ("the Riyadh Rules").

Other stronger international instruments include the UN Convention on the Rights of the Child (CRC), ratified by Ireland in 1992. Juveniles who have been deprived of their liberty have the right to be treated "with humanity and respect for the inherent dignity of the human person, and in a manner which takes into account the needs of persons of his or her age".[14] Arrest, detention or imprisonment of a juvenile ought to be carried out only as a measure of last resort, for the shortest possible time.[15] Article 40 states that every child within the system should:

> "be treated in a manner consistent with the promotion of the child's sense of dignity and worth, which reinforces the child's respect for the human rights and fundamental freedoms of others and which takes into account the child's age and the desirability of promoting the child's reintegration and the child's assuming a constructive role in society."[16]

[11–10] This Article also provides for the protection of certain basic rights of juveniles within the criminal justice system[17] and for individual state parties to establish laws governing the area of juvenile justice, including a minimum age of criminal responsibility, and alternatives to custody.[18]

[11–11] The ECHR provides for certain legal rights in the context of the criminal process, and these have been interpreted by the ECtHR as applying in the context of juvenile justice. Mainly, the Convention as interpreted provides that children involved in the criminal process should enjoy the right to understand and effectively participate in that process.[19]

II. Age of Criminal Responsibility

[11–12] At common law, a child under seven years of age was presumed to be legally incapable of committing a criminal act; the child was said to be *doli incapax* (incapable of crime). In relation to a child aged between seven and 14 years of age, there was a rebuttable presumption that he was *doli incapax*. This presumption could be rebutted by strong evidence of "mischievous discretion", i.e. the child knew that what he was doing was gravely or seriously wrong.[20] A child above 14 years of age was said to be *doli capax*, i.e. legally capable of committing a crime.

[11–13] The Beijing Rules provide that in setting the age of criminal responsibility, member states ought to ensure that it is not set too low, "bearing in mind the facts of emotional, mental and intellectual maturity."[21] The UN Committee on the Rights of the Child issued General Comment No 10 in 2007 which set 12 as the minimum age of criminal

---

[14] UN CRC, Art 37(c).
[15] Art 37(b).
[16] Art 40.1.
[17] Art 40.2.
[18] Art 40.3.
[19] *T and V v United Kingdom* (2000) 30 EHRR 121 at para 84; and *SC v United Kingdom* (2004) 40 EHRR 10.
[20] *R v Gorrie* (1919) 83 JP 136.
[21] UN Standard Minimum Rules for the Administration of Juvenile Justice 1985, Rule 4.1.

responsibility and promoted the use of a higher age.[22] The General Comment specifically recommended that no exceptions should be made in relation to the minimum age of criminal responsibility in the context of a child who commits a serious offence.[23]

The Children Act 2001 purported to raise the minimum age of criminal responsibility in Ireland from seven to 12. Section 52 of that Act provided that there would be a conclusive presumption that a child under 12 years of age was not capable of committing a criminal act, and a rebuttable presumption of *doli incapax* would operate in relation to children between the ages of 12 and 14. However, this section of the Act was never commenced and was expressly overridden by the Criminal Justice Act 2006, which repealed and substituted s 52.[24] **[11–14]**

The new s 52 provides the general rule that a child under 12 years of age shall not be charged with an offence.[25] However, a child aged 10 or 11 years may be charged with murder, manslaughter, rape, rape under s 4 of the Criminal Law (Rape) (Amendment) Act 1990 or aggravated sexual assault.[26] The section also expressly removed the rebuttable presumption of *doli incapax* in relation to a child between the ages of 7 and 14.[27] Furthermore, the section requires that where a child under 14 is charged with an offence, no further proceedings in the matter are to be taken without the consent of the DPP.[28] **[11–15]**

Where a child under 14 is charged with an offence, **[11–16]**

> "the Court may, of its own motion or the application of any person, dismiss the case on its merits if, having had due regard to the child's age and level of maturity, it determines that the child did not have a full understanding of what was involved in the commission of the offence."[29]

Within the space of five years the legislature changed its position on the age of criminal responsibility for serious offences, and has gone against the CRC by setting up a dual system of juvenile justice: 10 and 11 year old children who commit the most serious offences can be held criminally responsible and tried in the courts. In relation to this, Kilkelly notes that the Committee on the Rights of the Child: **[11–17]**

> "has made it explicit that such a dual approach to the age of criminal responsibility is a matter of serious concern from a children's rights perspective,

---

22 UN Committee on the Rights of the Child *General Comment No 10: Children's Rights in Juvenile Justice*, CRC/C/GC/10 (2007), paras 32–35.
23 *ibid.* para 34.
24 Criminal Justice Act 2006, s 129 inserted a new s 52 into the Children Act 2001.
25 Children Act 2001, s 52(1) as amended.
26 s 52(2) as amended.
27 s 52(3) as amended.
28 s 52(4) as amended.
29 s 76C as inserted by the Criminal Justice Act 2006, s 134.

not least because it means that children in more serious trouble will receive more harsh treatment."[30]

[11–18] Kilkelly also suggests that a "troubled 10 or 11 year old, who commits a violent or sexual crime" may be better served through the social or welfare services of the State as he "deserves more protection and care than punishment."[31] The intervention of such services is provided for in relation to children under 12 (besides 10 and 11 year olds committing the serious offences covered by s 52) where a garda considers that such a child has committed an offence. The garda must endeavour to bring the child to his parent or guardian[32] but if the garda suspects, on reasonable grounds, that the child is not receiving adequate care or protection from his parent or guardian, he must bring the child to the attention of the Health Service Executive (HSE).[33]

III. Treatment of Juvenile Suspects in Garda Síochána Stations

[11–19] Specific provisions apply to the pre-trial detention and questioning of juvenile suspects. A number of these are set out in the Children Act 2001 while others can be found in the general law on pre-trial detention and questioning, including the Criminal Justice Act 1984 (Treatment of Persons in Custody in Garda Síochána Stations) Regulations 1987.[34]

[11–20] Section 55 of the 2001 Act provides that in any investigation into the commission or possible commission of an offence by a child, gardaí must act with due respect for the personal rights of the child and his dignity as a human person. Gardaí should also have respect for the child's vulnerability due to his age and level of maturity.

[11–21] The following more specific rules also apply:

- The member-in-charge (MIC) must, as far as practicable, ensure that a child detained in a garda station does not associate with a detained adult and is not kept in a cell, unless no other suitable accommodation is available[35];
- The MIC must inform the parent or guardian of the child (i) that the child is in custody, (ii) the nature of the relevant offence, (iii) that the child is entitled to legal advice, (iv) and that the presence of the parent or guardian at the garda station is required, without delay[36]; and,
- The MIC must inform the child, in a manner and language that is appropriate to his age and level of understanding, (i) of the offence in connection with which he

[30] Kilkelly, above n 1, p 537 referring to UN Committee on the Rights of the Child *General Comment No 10: Children's Rights in Juvenile Justice*, CRC/C/GC/10 (2007), para 18 and the UN Committee on the Rights of the Child, *Concluding Observations Ireland* CRC/C/CO2/IRL, paras 66–67 which recommended that the provisions of the 2001 Act be reinstated.

[31] Kilkelly, "Reform of Youth Justice in Ireland: The "New" Children Act 2001" Part 2 (2007) 17(1) ICLJ 2, p 2.

[32] Children Act 2001, s 53 as amended by the Criminal Justice Act 2006, s 130.

[33] *ibid.* s 53(2).

[34] See Chapter Two Section IV and Chapter Three Section III.

[35] Children Act 2001, s 56. See also Criminal Justice Act 1984 (Treatment of Persons in Custody in Garda Síochána Stations) Regulations 1987, reg 19(8).

[36] s 58 and reg 9.

has been arrested, (ii) of his right to consult a solicitor and how this might be arranged, and (iii) that his parent or guardian is being informed of the relevant matters outlined above.[37]

If the parent or guardian cannot be contacted, or will not attend at the garda station within a reasonable time, the child should be informed that he is entitled to have an adult relative or other reasonably named adult present.[38] If the MIC has reasonable cause to believe that the child may be in need of care or protection he must inform the local health authorities, and a representative from the health authorities must attend the garda station as soon as practicable.[39] **[11–22]**

Where a solicitor is requested by the child suspect, or by his parent/guardian/adult relative/reasonably-named adult, the MIC must notify a solicitor as soon as practicable.[40] A child is not to be asked to make a written or oral statement until a reasonable time has elapsed for the arrival of a requested solicitor.[41] **[11–23]**

Generally, no questioning of the juvenile suspect ought to take place in the absence of his parent or guardian, or another adult who is not a garda.[42] Questioning in the absence of a parent or guardian can only be sanctioned by the MIC where he has reasonable grounds for believing that a delay in questioning the suspect would involve a risk of death or injury to persons, serious loss of or damage to property, destruction of or interference with evidence, or escape of accomplices.[43] Parents or guardians may be excluded during questioning by the MIC, where they too have been arrested in relation to the offence under investigation, where the MIC has reasonable grounds to suspect that they are complicit in the relevant offence, or, where the MIC suspects they may obstruct the course of justice if present during questioning.[44] **[11–24]**

The strength of these provisions is somewhat undermined by s 66 of the 2001 Act which provides that a failure by a garda to observe any of the rules set out in ss 56 to 63 and s 65 of the Act shall not of itself render that garda liable to any criminal or civil proceedings or of itself affect the lawfulness of the detention of the child or the admissibility in evidence of any statement made by the child.[45] It may result in disciplinary proceedings.[46] **[11–25]**

Specific rules also apply in relation to the taking of fingerprints and bodily samples from persons under 17. These rules require the consent of the child's parent/guardian or other appropriate adult (not a garda) where the child is under 14, and the consent of **[11–26]**

---

[37] Children Act 2001, s 57.
[38] s 58(2).
[39] s 59.
[40] s 60.
[41] s 61(5). This is a stronger protection than that which applies to adult suspects. See Chapter Three paras 3-60 – 3-63.
[42] s 61(1). See also Criminal Justice Act 1984 (Treatment of Persons in Custody in Garda Síochána Stations) Regulations 1987, reg 13.
[43] s 61(2).
[44] s 61(3).
[45] s 66(2).
[46] s 66(3).

both the child and his parent/guardian or other appropriate adult where he is between 14 and 17.[47]

IV. Diversion Programme and Conferencing Options

[11–27] In an effort to avoid bringing children into contact with the courts where possible, a non-statutory juvenile cautioning programme called the "Juvenile Liaison Scheme" has existed in Ireland since 1963. This programme was placed on a statutory footing by the Children Act 2001 and is now known as the "Diversion Programme", the "Juvenile Diversion Programme", or the "Garda Diversion Programme".[48] The Programme aims to divert young people from the criminal justice system and to prevent re-offending. Statistics suggest that it is largely successful in doing so, as almost 88 percent of juveniles cautioned under the Programme reach their 18th birthdays without re-offending,[49] though it is not clear whether the existence of the Programme is the reason for non-offending thereafter, or if the particular juveniles dealt with within the Programme would largely not reoffend in any event.[50]

[11–28] While the Juvenile Diversion Programme is a non-judicial method of dealing with child offenders, the rights of such offenders must still be protected within that process. This is made clear by Art 40(3)(b) of the CRC, which insists that alternatives to judicial proceedings must not undermine the child's human rights and legal safeguards.

Restorative Cautions

[11–29] The Programme allows for persons under the age of 18 who commit criminal offences to be cautioned by gardaí without proceedings being instituted before the courts. In order to be admitted to the programme, a child from the age of 10 to 18 (on the date on which the criminal offence took place[51]), must accept his responsibility for the criminal behaviour and consent to be cautioned and potentially be supervised by a juvenile liaison officer.[52] The Director of the Diversion Programme must be satisfied that admitting the child to the Programme is in the best interests of the child, and is not inconsistent with the interests of the victim of the crime or the interests of society.[53] The consent of the victim is not required but the view of the victim may be taken into consideration when the decision is being made.[54]

[47] See Criminal Justice Act 1984 (Treatment of Persons in Custody in Garda Síochána Stations) Regulations 1987, reg 18; Criminal Justice (Forensic Evidence) Act 1990, s 2(10); and for future plans in this regard see the Criminal Justice (Forensic Evidence and DNA Database System) Bill 2010, s 22. Forensic Evidence is discussed more generally in Chapter Four.

[48] Children Act 2001, Pt 4.

[49] Garda Síochána *Annual Report* (Dublin, 2002), p 106.

[50] This may also be skewed by the fact that statistics do not deal with offending beyond age 18 and 16 to 17 year olds make up over 50% of those admitted to the Programme. They may simply not have time to re-offend before turning 18. See the Annual Reports of the Committee Appointed to Monitor the Effectiveness of the Diversion Programme, available from the Irish Youth Justice Service www.iyjs.ie.

[51] Children Act 2001, s 23(5).

[52] *ibid.* s 23(1) as amended by the Criminal Justice Act 2006, s 125.

[53] s 23(2).

[54] s 23(4).

Once admitted to the Programme, a caution will be administered to the offending child. Two types of caution exist: a formal caution and an informal caution. The Director of the Programme decides which type of caution is appropriate. An informal caution is selected where no previous caution has been administered to the child, or one or more informal cautions have been administered, and the Director of the Programme considers that the child's criminal behaviour was not sufficiently serious to warrant a formal caution.[55] A formal caution is selected where no previous caution has been administered, or one or more informal or formal cautions have been previously administered, and the Director believes that the child's criminal behaviour was of such a serious nature that it could not be adequately dealt with by way of an informal caution.[56] **[11–30]**

An informal caution is usually administered by a juvenile liaison officer (a garda), either in a garda station or at the child's normal residence.[57]

A formal caution is administered in a garda station, by a garda not below the rank of inspector, or by a juvenile liaison officer (JLO) who has been trained in mediation skills.[58] The child's parents or guardian are to be present, along with the child, at the cautioning.[59] The victim of the relevant crime may also be present,[60] in which case it will be described as a "restorative caution" as a discussion is held by the parties present about the child's behaviour,[61] and the victim can make known to the child the effect which his crime has had on the victim's life. The victim may receive an apology and potentially some form of financial or other reparation or "restoration".[62] The presence of the victim may humanise the experience for the child and make it clear to him that his criminal actions have an effect on other people. The presence of the victim and the expression of interest in the child's future may also assist in reintegrating the young person in the community rather than excluding him therefrom.[63] **[11–31]**

Following a formal caution, a child may be placed under the supervision of a JLO for a period of 12 months.[64] In exceptional cases, a child who has received only an informal caution may be supervised by such an officer for six months.[65] The level of supervision which is applied is at the discretion of the relevant JLO, taking into consideration the seriousness of the relevant offence, the level of support and control over the child by his **[11–32]**

---

55 s 25(4).
56 s 25(4).
57 s 25(3).
58 s 25(2).
59 s 25(2).
60 s 26(1).
61 s 26(2).
62 s 26(3).
63 The concept of "restorative cautions" and "restorative conferences" is outlined in the Annual Reports of the Committee Appointed to Monitor the Effectiveness of the Diversion Programme, available from the Irish Youth Justice Service www.iyjs.ie. For more on restorative justice and its application in the Diversion Programme see Griffin, "Restorative justice: A real alternative?" (2005) 15(4) ICLJ 2 and O'Dwyer, "Restorative justice—A response to Diarmuid Griffin" (2006) 16(2) ICLJ 10.
64 Children Act 2001, s 27(1).
65 s 27(3).

parents/guardian, the likelihood of reoffending, and any directions from the Director of the Programme.[66]

Restorative Conferences

[11–33] Where a child has been placed under the supervision of a JLO and he thinks it appropriate, the JLO may provide the Director of the Diversion Programme with a written report recommending that a conference be held in relation to the child.[67] The conference, which is concerned with the welfare of the child, brings together the child, his parents/guardian, other family members or relatives as appropriate, and a facilitator (the JLO or other appointed garda with appropriate training[68]), in order to

- establish why the child has become involved in the behaviour which led to his admission to the Programme;
- discuss how those present could help to prevent the child from becoming involved in further offending;
- where appropriate review the child's behaviour since admission to the Programme;
- potentially mediate between the child and the victim;
- formulate an action plan for the child; and
- uphold the concerns of the victim and have due regard for his interests.[69]

[11–34] Representatives from specific bodies may also be present, for example, the Health Service Executive (HSE), the Probation and Welfare Service, the child's school, and the school attendance service.[70] The child and his parents/guardian must indicate that they will attend the conference.[71] The victim of the relevant offence may also be present. If, in the course of a conference, the facilitator is of the opinion that the continued presence of any person is not in the best interests of the conference or the child, the facilitator may exclude that person from further participation in the conference.[72]

[11–35] The action plan created at this conference must be agreed unanimously by all present, unless the facilitator believes that the disagreement of a particular party is unreasonable.[73] The 2001 Act provides that the action plan may include provision for any one or more of the following:

a. an apology, oral or written or both, by the child to any victim;
b. financial or other reparation to any victim;
c. participation in sporting or recreational activity;
d. attendance at a school or place of work;
e. participation in a training or educational course or a programme that does not interfere with any work or school schedule;
f. being at home at specified times;

66 s 28.
67 s 30(1).
68 s 46(1).
69 s 29.
70 s 32(3).
71 ss 30(2) and 31(3).
72 s 32(6).
73 s 39(2).

g. staying away from specified places or a specified person or both;
h. taking initiatives within the family and community that might help to prevent reoffending; and
i. anything else which in the opinion of those present at the conference would be in the child's best interests or would make the child more aware of the consequences of his criminal behaviour.[74]

A written record of the agreed plan, and the duration of it, is produced by the facilitator in language understandable by the relevant child.[75] It is signed by the child, the chairperson and one other person present.[76] A date within six months is set for reconvening the conference in order to assess compliance with the plan,[77] although it may be reconvened earlier if it appears that the child is not complying with the plan.[78] A report on the conference and the action plan agreed is sent to the Director of the Diversion Programme.[79] [11–36]

No report is to be published or broadcast in relation to the admission of a child to the Diversion Programme or in relation to the proceedings at a conference or in relation to the contents of any action plan.[80] Furthermore, there is to be no reporting which might reveal the identity of the child.[81] Any such publication or broadcast is a criminal offence punishable by fine or imprisonment.[82] [11–37]

Changes under the Criminal Justice Act 2006

The Criminal Justice Act 2006 made a number of significant changes to the Children Act 2001 in relation to the Diversion Programme and Conferencing. The Programme no longer operates only in the context of criminal offences, but may also operate in relation to children found to have been engaged in anti-social behaviour. The second change relates to evidence of involvement in the Diversion Programme being available to the courts in subsequent criminal proceedings. [11–38]

(i) Anti-Social Behaviour

A child who is found to be engaging in anti-social behaviour[83] can first be given a "Behaviour Warning" by a garda[84] which lasts for three months.[85] Following the [11–39]

---

[74] s 39(3).
[75] s 39(4).
[76] s 39(5).
[77] s 39(9) and (10).
[78] s 39(11).
[79] s 41.
[80] s 51.
[81] s 51(1).
[82] s 51(3).
[83] A child engages in anti-social behaviour if he "causes or, in the circumstances, is likely to cause, to one or more persons who are not of the same household as the child— (a) harassment, (b) significant or persistent alarm, distress, fear or intimidation, or (c) significant or persistent impairment of their use or enjoyment of their property." Children Act 2001, s 257A(2) as inserted by the Criminal Justice Act 2006, s 159.
[84] s 257B as inserted by the Criminal Justice Act 2006, s 160.
[85] s 257B(6) as inserted by the Criminal Justice Act 2006, s 160.

issuance of the Behaviour Warning, a meeting may be held to discuss the child's anti-social behaviour.[86] The relevant child, his parents/guardian, the garda who warned the child, and a JLO, (if the child is already within the Diversion Programme) are to be in attendance.[87] At the meeting, the child is asked to acknowledge his behaviour and undertake to stop it. The child's parents are also asked to acknowledge his behaviour and agree to take steps to prevent recurrence. If the child and the parents make these agreements then a "Good Behaviour Contract" is drawn up.[88] This contract lasts for an initial period of six months, which can be extended for an additional three months.[89]

[11–40] If it is felt that a meeting of this nature would be inappropriate, either because it would not help, or because a good behaviour contract could not previously be prepared due to a lack of agreement on the part of the child or parents, or because the child has breached the terms of his good behaviour contract, the child may be admitted to the Diversion Programme.[90] The child must admit his anti-social behaviour and the Diversion Programme then operates in the normal way.

[11–41] The final option in relation to anti-social behaviour is for a "Behaviour Order" to be made by the Children Court.[91] Failure to comply with a Behaviour Order is a criminal offence, punishable by a fine not exceeding €800 or detention in a children detention school for a period not exceeding three months or both.[92]

[11–42] It has been argued that inclusion of children who have been involved in anti-social behaviour within the Diversion Programme constitutes "net-widening" which inappropriately brings children who have committed no criminal offence into contact with the criminal justice system.[93] Kilkelly, pointing to the Beijing Rules, further suggests that

> "This is contrary to international standards, which provide that formal intervention in the lives of young people, who are in conflict with the law, should be kept to a minimum and used only as a measure of last resort in recognition of the fact that youthful behaviour that does not conform to overall social norms and values is often part of the maturation and growth process, and tends to disappear naturally in most individuals with the transition to adulthood."[94]

(ii) Evidence in Criminal Proceedings

[11–43] Section 48 of the 2001 Act, as originally constituted, provided that in any criminal or civil proceedings against a child, the fact that he had previously accepted responsibility for a criminal offence in order to be admitted to the Diversion Programme, evidence of

---

[86] s 257C as inserted by the Criminal Justice Act 2006, s 161.
[87] s 257C(4) as inserted by the Criminal Justice Act 2006, s 161.
[88] s 257C(7) as inserted by the Criminal Justice Act 2006, s 161.
[89] s 257C(9) as inserted by the Criminal Justice Act 2006, s 161.
[90] ss 257C(14) and 257C(15) as inserted by the Criminal Justice Act 2006, s 161.
[91] s 257D as inserted by the Criminal Justice Act 2006, s 162.
[92] s 257F as inserted by the Criminal Justice Act 2006, s 162.
[93] Kilkelly, above n 31, p 6.
[94] *ibid.*

that criminal behaviour, or the fact that a child had been admitted to the Diversion Programme, could not be given in evidence. The 2006 Act alters that position and provides that when a court is determining sentence, post-conviction in a later criminal case, the prosecution may inform the court of any of those matters.[95] Kilkelly expresses concern at the admission of evidence relating to behaviour "for which the child was neither charged nor convicted" and suggests that this may breach Art 6 ECHR and Art 40 CRC. She also argues that "it threatens to undermine an effective part of the Irish youth justice system to pursue an objective that is unclear."[96]

V. The Children Court

The Children Court is the criminal court which deals with children who have not been processed through the Diversion Programme. The Court hears all minor charges against children and young people under 18 and also acts as the clearing house for more serious charges, which it sends to the Circuit and Central Criminal Courts.[97] [11–44]

The Children Court must have regard in each case to the specific level of maturity and understanding of the child and his personal characteristics, while still consistently applying the law and upholding the fundamental rights of the child, in terms of procedural fairness and due process. [11–45]

Operation of the Children Court

The Children Court is in actuality the District Court, operating in the realm of juvenile justice.[98] Although the Children Act 2001 does not specify the role of the Children Court, it outlines the requirements for courts dealing with children charged with criminal offences: (i) the Court must have regard to the principle that children have rights and freedoms before the law equal to those enjoyed by adults, including a right to be heard and a right to participate in any proceedings which can affect them, and (ii) criminal proceedings are not to be used solely to provide assistance or services needed to care for or protect a child.[99] [11–46]

In order to set it aside as a different type of court, and to prevent children charged with criminal offences from coming into contact with adult offenders, the Children Court must sit in a different building or room from other courts, or on different days or at different times from other courts.[100] Waiting times for proceedings ought to be kept to a minimum[101] and any summons requiring a person to attend at the Children Court must state a time at which it is reasonably expected that the proceedings will be heard.[102] The rationale is to avoid having children waiting for long periods of time in the vicinity of the courts, possibly missing school and meeting other offenders.[103] [11–47]

[95] Criminal Justice Act 2006, s 126.
[96] Kilkelly, above n 31, p 7.
[97] Kilkelly, *The Children's Court: A Children's Rights Audit* (IRCHSS, Cork, 2005), p vii.
[98] Children Act 2001, s 71(1)(a).
[99] s 96(1). See also *DG v Ireland* (2002) 35 EHRR 33.
[100] s 71(1)(b).
[101] s 73(1).
[102] Children Act 2001, s 73(2).
[103] McDermott and Robinson, *Children Act 2001* (Round Hall, Dublin, 2003), p 97.

[11–48] As with the Diversion Programme, the Children Court also requires parents/guardians to be present.[104] Failure to attend, without reasonable excuse, may result in proceedings being adjourned and an arrest warrant for the relevant parent/guardian being issued.[105] It may also constitute contempt of court.[106]

[11–49] Provisions to protect the identity and privacy of children before the Children Court are also in place under the 2001 Act. Proceedings in the Court are to be *in camera*, i.e. only certain persons are entitled to be present in the Children Court during the hearing of a case, including, *inter alia*, officers of the Court, the parents/guardians of the child, persons directly concerned in the proceedings, and bona fide representatives of the press.[107] The Act restricts reporting of proceedings in order to protect the identity of child offenders. Any publication or broadcast should not reveal the name, address or school of any child concerned in the proceedings or anything likely to lead to the identification of the child, and no picture of a child before the court should be published or broadcast.[108] The 2001 Act neglected to apply the *in camera* rule to proceedings involving children in courts other than the Children Court. This was rectified by the Criminal Justice Act 2006 which extends the child's right to privacy to proceedings in the Circuit and Central Criminal Courts.[109] However, the 2006 Act also increased the possibilities for a court to dispense with the *in camera* rule in certain circumstances, which now include where this is thought to be "in the public interest".[110]

Family Welfare Conferences and Family Conferences

[11–50] The Children Court has many options at its disposal in dealing with children who come before it, including conferencing. The court may order the HSE to convene a Family Welfare Conference.[111] The purpose of this conference is to determine whether a care order or supervision order under the Child Care Act 1991 ought to be made in relation to the relevant child. It brings together the immediate and extended family of the child and relevant professionals to devise a plan for the child and to resolve issues related to childcare, child welfare or child protection.[112]

[11–51] Alternatively the Children Court can order a Family Conference, administered by the Probation and Welfare Service. The Court may order that such a conference take place where (a) the child accepts responsibility for his or her criminal behaviour, (b) it appears desirable to the Court that an action plan be put together in relation to the child, and (c) the child and his parent/guardian, or members of the child's family or relatives of the

[104] Children Act 2001, s 91(1).
[105] s 91(2).
[106] s 91(3).
[107] s 94.
[108] s 93(1) as inserted by the Criminal Justice Act 2006, s 139.
[109] s 93 as inserted by the Criminal Justice Act 2006, s 139.
[110] s 93(2)(a)(iii) as inserted by the Criminal Justice Act 2006, s 139. The Court may also dispense with the *in camera* rule, allowing for reporting of the child's name in order to avoid injustice to the child, or for the purpose of apprehending the child where he is unlawfully at large: Children Act 2001, s 93(2)(a) as inserted by the Criminal Justice Act 2006, s 139.
[111] s 77.
[112] See further the Children (Family Welfare Conference) Regulations 2004.

child who in the opinion of the Court could make a positive contribution at a family conference, agree to attend such a conference and to participate in its proceedings.[113] The Family Conference is then convened and operates in a manner largely similar to the conference within the Diversion Programme. A report on the conference is made to the Children Court by the Probation and Welfare Service, outlining the action plan which has been formulated, if the conference was successful in that regard, and any difficulties encountered if no action plan could be agreed.[114] If an action plan is submitted to the Children Court, the Court may approve or amend it, and may order that the child comply with it and be supervised by a probation and welfare officer for the duration of the plan.[115] If the Court is informed that no action plan was agreed, the Court may impose such a plan or resume the criminal proceedings in relation to the original offence committed by the child.[116] If an action plan is in place and the child fails to comply with it, the Children Court may resume the original criminal proceedings against the child.[117] The proceedings may be dismissed, on the other hand, if the child has complied with the action plan.[118]

Criminal Proceedings in the Children Court

The Children Court can deal with most indictable offences summarily[119] save for reserved offences (treason, piracy, genocide, murder, conspiracy and attempt to murder, rape and aggravated sexual assault) and manslaughter.[120] The decision to be tried summarily for an indictable offence depends on the age and maturity of the child as well as any other relevant factors.[121] The child must consent to the matter being dealt with summarily.[122] [11–52]

An important principle enshrined in the 2001 Act is that imprisonment should be a last resort in relation to child offenders.[123] Any penalty imposed on a child ought to interfere as little as possible with his education, training or employment and should "take the form most likely to maintain and promote the development of the child".[124] A penalty should not be greater than that which would be imposed on an adult in relation to a similar offence.[125] The child's age and level of maturity may be taken into consideration by the Court in mitigation when deciding on the penalty to be imposed, unless that penalty is set by law.[126] The Act specifically provides that [11–53]

[113] Children Act 2001, s 78(1).
[114] s 81.
[115] s 82(1).
[116] s 82(2).
[117] s 83.
[118] s 84.
[119] s 75(1).
[120] *ibid.*
[121] s 75(2).
[122] s 75(3).
[123] s 96(2).
[124] *ibid.*
[125] s 96(4).
[126] s 96(3).

> "[w]hen dealing with a child charged with an offence, a court shall have due regard to the child's best interests, the interests of the victim of the offence and the protection of society."[127]

Prior to sentencing, the Children Court may order a Probation and Welfare Report or a Victim Impact Report to assist it in choosing the most appropriate sanction for the child.[128]

VI. Sentencing by the Children Court

[11–54] Imprisonment is to be a last resort in sentencing juveniles and, accordingly, the Children Court has many alternative, community-based sanctions at its disposal. If the Court imposes such a community sanction, the child must be informed of the expectations on him in language appropriate to his level of understanding.[129]

Community Sanctions

[11–55] What follows is a brief description of the community sanctions provided for under the Children Act 2001.

(i) Community Service Order

[11–56] This order, under s 3 of the Criminal Justice (Community Service) Act 1983, can only be applied to a child of 16 or 17 years of age. It requires the offender to perform between 40 and 240 hours of unpaid work.[130]

(ii) Day Centre Order

[11–57] Under this order, a child is required to attend a specified centre to participate in activities or training which are likely to be beneficial to him for a period of not more than 90 days.[131] Day centres are operated by the Probation and Welfare Service and a child subject to an order such as this is to be supervised by a probation and welfare officer. A day centre order is not to be made unless the Court is satisfied that the particular day centre is reasonably accessible to the child concerned, having regard to the child's age and sex, the means of access available to him and any other relevant circumstances.[132] Furthermore, the times at which a child is required to attend at a day centre must, as far as practicable, avoid interference with any training he is receiving, any attendance at a school or other educational establishment, or any employment.[133]

(iii) Probation Order

[11–58] This is a traditional probation order under s 2 of the Probation of Offenders Act 1907 whereby the relevant child is placed under the supervision of a probation and welfare officer for a specified period of time.

---

127 s 96(5) as amended by the Criminal Justice Act 2006, s 136.
128 s 99.
129 s 116(2).
130 Criminal Justice (Community Service) Act 1983, s 3(2).
131 Children Act 2001, s 118.
132 s 118(10).
133 s 118(11)(a).

(iv) Probation (Training or Activities) Order

This is a traditional probation order with the additional requirement to complete a programme of training or activities which is recommended to the Court by the probation and welfare officer.[134] The programme must be suitable for the development of the child and likely to help to prevent the child from committing further offences "through the attainment of positive social values."[135] **[11–59]**

(v) Probation (Intensive Supervision) Order

Again, this is a traditional probation order with added value: the child must remain under the intensive supervision of a probation and welfare officer, reside at a specified residence, and undertake and complete an education or training programme, or undergo a course of treatment, recommended to the court by a probation and welfare officer.[136] This order will not last for more than 180 days. **[11–60]**

(vi) Probation (Residential Supervision) Order

Under this order, the Court may require that the child reside in a hostel residence provided by the Probation and Welfare Service or recommended to the Court by that service, as part of the terms of his probation.[137] It should last for no longer than one year. **[11–61]**

(vii) Suitable Person (Care and Supervision) Order

The Court may assign the child to the care of a person, including a relative of the child.[138] The parents/guardian of the child must consent to this in writing. The order provides that the child shall ordinarily reside in the home of the "suitable person" for a period not longer than two years. The child remains under the supervision of the Probation and Welfare Service while this order subsists. **[11–62]**

(viii) Mentor (Family Support) Order

The Court may assign a child to a person (a "mentor"), including a relative of the child, to help, advise and support the child and the child's family in its efforts to prevent the child from re-offending and to monitor the child's behaviour generally.[139] The child is to live with his parents/guardian for the duration of the order, which will not be longer than two years. A probation and welfare officer will supervise the child, and will help and advise the mentor. The child's parents/guardian must consent. **[11–63]**

(ix) Restriction on Movement Order

The Court may order that a child shall be at a specified residence during specified times between 7 pm and 6 am, and/or that the child shall stay away from any specified premises, place or locality during specified days or between specified times.[140] The first of these provisions may last for six months, while the second may last for 12 months. **[11–64]**

---

134 s 124.
135 s 124(3).
136 s 125.
137 s 126.
138 s 129.
139 s 131.
140 s 133.

(x) Dual Order

[11–65] A dual order is where the Court requires that a child be under the supervision of a probation and welfare officer or attend a day centre, which also restricts his movements for a specified period not longer than six months.[141] This order can be made where the Court is of the opinion that neither supervision by a probation and welfare officer nor attendance at a day centre would of itself adequately reduce the likelihood of reoffending.

[11–66] Along with the specifics of any order applied to a juvenile offender, the Court may impose specific conditions including the following:

- requiring the child to attend at school regularly;
- conditions in relation to the employment of the child;
- conditions aimed at preventing further offending;
- conditions related to the child's place of residence;
- requiring the child to undergo medical treatment or counselling;
- limiting or prohibiting the child from associating with particular individuals;
- limiting the child's attendance at specific premises;
- prohibiting the consumption of alcohol by the child; and
- any other conditions which the Court considers appropriate.[142]

A child who fails to comply with a community sanction or any conditions attached thereto should not receive a detention order unless the Court is satisfied that detention is the only suitable way of dealing with the child.[143]

Parental Orders

[11–67] Along with providing innovative community-based sanctions, the Children Act 2001 seeks to involve parents in addressing the criminal behaviour of their children to a significant extent. It does this by providing for a number of orders which may be made against an offending child's parents. One such potential order is a "parental supervision order" which can be made where the court considers that a wilful failure of the child's parents to take care of or control the child contributed to the child's criminal behaviour.[144] The child's parents may be required to

- undergo treatment for alcohol or other substance abuse;
- participate in a course to improve parenting skills;
- adequately and properly control or supervise the child to the best of their ability; and/or
- comply with any other instructions of the Court that would assist in preventing the child from further offending.[145]

[141] s 137.
[142] s 117.
[143] s 116(4).
[144] s 111.
[145] s 111(6).

A probation and welfare officer is appointed to supervise the parents and assist them in complying with the order, which lasts for up to six months. Failure to comply with the order will render the parent in contempt of court.[146]

The Court may also order a child's parent/guardian to pay compensation in a given case, if it is satisfied that a wilful failure of the parent or guardian to take care of or to control the child contributed to the child's criminal behaviour.[147] The Court may bind the parent over to exercise proper and adequate control over the child.[148] In such a scenario, the parent pays a sum of money into the Court, which they forfeit if they fail to control the child. This recognisance lasts for no longer than three years. **[11–68]**

Shannon has suggested that parental control mechanisms "demonstrate a reluctance to acknowledge the social context that contributes to a child's delinquent behaviour, such as poverty, drug addiction and disadvantage."[149]

Detention Orders

When a court is finally faced with no other option but to detain a child, the judge must express his reasons for ordering detention in open court.[150] The Children Act 2001 envisaged the existence of two separate places of potential detention for convicted child offenders: Children Detention Schools which would cater for children under the age of 16, and Children Detention Centres which would cater for children aged between 16 and 18.[151] However, the Criminal Justice Act 2006 altered this plan and provided instead that all children under the age of 18 against whom detention orders were made would be held in Children Detention Schools.[152] As schools appropriate to hold older boys were not in existence at the time, a transitional provision was included such that males aged 16 and 17 who are sentenced to detention may be detained at St. Patrick's Institution or other place of detention until they have completed their period of detention, or suitable places for them become available in Children Detention Schools.[153] **[11–69]**

When a court orders that a child offender be detained in a Children Detention School (or at St. Patrick's Institution at present), any period of detention shall not be longer than that which would be applied to an adult offender in the same circumstances.[154] A court may also make a detention and supervision order, which allows for the first half of the child's sentence to be spent in a Children Detention School, and the second half to entail supervision in the community by a probation and welfare officer.[155] The **[11–70]**

---

[146] s 112(1)(a)(iv).

[147] s 113.

[148] s 114.

[149] Shannon, "A Critical Overview of the Act", Paper from Children Act 2001 Seminar, Faculty of Law, University College Cork, p 25 quoted in Seymour, above n 2, p 132.

[150] Children Act 2001, s 143(2).

[151] s 147.

[152] Criminal Justice Act 2006, s 122 removed the reference to Children Detention Centres in the definition of "detention" within s 3 of the Children Act 2001.

[153] Children Act 2001, s 156A as inserted by the Criminal Justice Act 2006, s 143.

[154] s 149 as inserted by the Criminal Justice Act 2006, s 141.

[155] s 151.

Director of a Children Detention School may also arrange for a child to be placed in the community under the supervision of a probation and welfare officer in certain circumstances.[156]

[11–71] The main objective of the Children Detention Schools is to provide appropriate education and training programmes and facilities for children referred to them by a court, and

> "to promote their reintegration into society and prepare them to take their place in the community as persons who observe the law and are capable of making a positive and productive contribution to society."[157]

The 2006 Act transferred responsibility for running Children Detention Schools from the Department of Education and Science to the Department of Justice and Law Reform.[158]

[11–72] The Irish Youth Justice Service, an executive office of the Department of Justice, administers the Children Detention Schools. There are three such schools in the state at present: Trinity House School and Oberstown Boys' School, catering for boys under the age of 16, and Oberstown Girls' School, catering for girls under the age of 18. All of these schools are located in Lusk, Co. Dublin, which raises concerns in relation to the accessibility of the premises for visiting families of detained children.

[11–73] St. Patrick's Institution, where boys aged 16 and 17 are detained, in fact caters for young men between the ages of 16 and 21. Most of the 16 and 17 years olds are kept separated from the older males, based on the requirements of international law and the reports of the CPT which has visited the Institution on a number of occasions.[159] Some of the younger offenders remain in the main unit on protection, due to fears of harm being caused to them.[160] One of the main criticisms of the ongoing detention of juveniles in St. Patrick's Institution is that it provides a training ground for criminality. The then Inspector of Prisons, Justice Dermot Kinlen, in 2005 suggested that St. Patrick's Institution was being used as "as a warehouse for young people who learnt the finer points of criminality in St. Patrick's which almost certainly guaranteed their progression into the 'university' of Mountjoy."[161]

[11–74] An Expert Group on Children Detention Schools was established in April 2006, to make plans for the redevelopment of residential accommodation for detained child

---

[156] ss 207 and 208.

[157] s 158.

[158] Criminal Justice Act 2006, s 122 altered the reference to the "Minister for Education and Science" within s 3 of the Children Act 2001 to the "Minister", meaning the Minister for Justice, Equality and Law Reform, now the Minister for Justice and Law Reform.

[159] See *Report to the Irish Government on the visit to Ireland carried out by the European Committee for the Prevention of Torture and Inhuman or Degrading Treatment or Punishment (CPT) from 2 to 13 October 2006*, para 28.

[160] Kilkelly, above n 1, p 554.

[161] Inspector of Prisons and Places of Detention *Fourth Annual Report 2004–2005* (Stationery Office, Dublin, 2006), p 17. See also the *Report of the Committee of Inquiry into the Penal System (the Whitaker Report)* (Stationery Office, Dublin, 1985).

offenders up to the age of 18.[162] Members of this Group included representatives of the Irish Youth Justice Service, the Department of Education and Science (at that time responsible for Children Detention Schools), the Irish Prison Service and the Office of Public Works. The Group proposed that a new National Children Detention Facility be built on the Oberstown Campus at Lusk, Co. Dublin to house all child offenders in the state.[163] This does not address concerns about detained children having access to their families on a regular basis. The proposed new facility will not be built before 2012 at the earliest. Until then, 16 and 17 year old boys will remain detained in St. Patrick's Institution, an arrangement which, as noted above, has been widely criticised.

VII. Conclusion

The Children Act 2001 largely revolutionised the system of youth or juvenile justice in Ireland. Difficulties still exist however, and not least among those is the continued detention of 16 and 17 year old boys in St. Patrick's Institution which is entirely inappropriate to their needs. Some of the amendments brought about under the Criminal Justice Act 2006 too have caused new difficulties, particularly in relation to altering the Juvenile Diversion Programme. Kilkelly has stated that **[11–75]**

> "The positive initiatives, including the gradual implementation of the community sanctions under the Children Act 2001 are perhaps overshadowed by the introduction of Behaviour Orders, the trial of children as adults in the higher courts, and the failure to compel the HSE to take full responsibility for the needs of these children. Similarly, despite new buildings being planned with state of the art facilities, it remains unclear what provision is to be made for those young people serving long sentences who continue to be denied the vocational education, therapeutic interventions and range of supports and services that they desperately need."[164]

Certainly things are much improved, but there is still work ahead to ensure that we provide adequately and appropriately for child offenders. Such matters are of utmost importance as it can be said that "[t]he youth justice system is an important test of the State's relationship with its most vulnerable citizens."[165] **[11–76]**

---

[162] See Expert Group on Children Detention Schools, *Final Report 14th December 2007*, available at http://www.iyjs.ie/en/IYJS/Expert%20Group%20Report.pdf/Files/Expert%20Group%20Report.pdf.

[163] Several concerns in relation to this have been raised. See, for example, the views of the Irish Penal Reform Trust in Chapter 1 of *Detention of Children in Ireland: International Standards and Best Practice* (IPRT, 2009) available at www.iprt.ie.

[164] Kilkelly, above n 1, p 569.

[165] Carroll and Meehan, *The Children Court: A National Study* (Association for Criminal Justice Research and Development Ltd., March 2007), p 7.

CHAPTER 12
Victims

Recent years have seen a significant rise in interest in victims of crime within the media, academic study, and the criminal process itself. The academic discipline of Victimology has grown to prominence since its beginnings in the 1940s.[1] Campaign and lobbying groups have impacted too and the emotive, tragic and personal stories of victims and families of victims of homicide have attracted intense media attention. **[12–01]**

The traditional role of the victim of crime has been as a witness in a case taken by the State on behalf of society as a whole. Calls for improvements in the rights of victims and their role in the criminal process have become more insistent in recent years for various reasons, including a recognition of the potentially 'revictimising' nature of the system, the increased media and academic interest, a political desire to be seen to be doing something for victims of crime, the capacity of victims of crime to be catalysts for law reform (e.g. the creation of "Megan's Law" in the United States[2]), and the emergence of an industry built on fear of victimisation (increases in the use of CCTV, private security, burglar alarms etc).[3] **[12–02]**

As a result of calls for change, many accommodations have been made for victims of crime, ranging from the work of voluntary support groups[4] and state-financed **[12–03]**

---

[1] Mawby and Walklate, *Critical Victimology: International Perspectives* (Sage, London, 1994) pp 69-70.

[2] The Violent Crime Control and Law Enforcement Act 1994 (42 USC § 14071) as amended in 1996 allows for members of the public to access information on registered sex offenders and was enacted following the kidnap, rape and murder of seven year old Megan Kanka by a known sex offender.

[3] Rogan, "Victims' Rights: Theory and Practice" Part 1 (2006) 24 ILT 140, pp 140-142.

[4] For example, Victim Support (founded in 1985) and AdVic (Advocates for Victims of Homicide, established in 2005).

compensation schemes[5] to legal protections in relation to giving evidence at trial[6] and court-ordered compensation from offenders.[7] This chapter, in the context of a book on criminal procedure, is primarily concerned with the latter type of accommodations, those which have been made within the criminal process.

I. Victims and the Adversarial Criminal Process

[12–04] Although a number of centuries ago victims were central to the prosecution of crime, having responsibility for the apprehension, charge and prosecution of offenders, the growth of the modern adversarial criminal process has altered that position and to a large extent has side-lined the victim.[8] The modern criminal process which operates in common law jurisdictions has two main actors: the State (representing the interests of the community) and the accused. The victim is little more than an ordinary witness and a source of evidence against the accused. Christie has argued that the State has commandeered the manner of addressing wrongdoing,[9] depriving victims of involvement in seeking justice, retribution or reparation.[10]

[12–05] Walsh puts this in the following terms:

> "Criminal infractions, particularly when they are serious, pose a threat to society which is considered too serious to leave the consequences to be resolved by a private action between the victim and the offender. Accordingly, the State assumes the mantle of victim in the prosecution of the crime. This, in turn, relegates the actual victim to the status of mere witness whose personal situation and interests can be sidelined in the contest between the State and the suspect."[11]

[12–06] Victims often feel lost or, worse, ignored within the criminal justice system and the system itself can cause re-victimisation.[12] Furthermore, the traditional adversarial process metes out punishments for offenders in the form of fines, imprisonment, community service or probation, which do not compensate the victim for pain and suffering, or financial loss, as a result of the offender's criminal behaviour.[13]

[12–07] The counter-argument is that it is better that the State takes responsibility for the prosecution of crime, given the resources available to it. Alternative systems of justice

---

5 The Criminal Justice Compensation Tribunal was established in Ireland in 1974 within the Department of Justice.

6 Within the Criminal Evidence Act 1992 and the Criminal Justice Act 1999, discussed below at paras 12-17–12-23.

7 Provided for under the Criminal Justice Act 1993, discussed below.

8 See Wemmers, "Where do they belong? Giving victims a place in the criminal justice process" (2009) *Criminal Law Forum* 395, pp 395-398.

9 Christie, "Conflicts as Property" (1977) 17 *British Journal of Criminology* 1, pp 7-8.

10 See also Rogan, above n 3, p 141.

11 Walsh, *Criminal Procedure* (Thomson Round Hall, Dublin, 2002), p 9.

12 See Wolhuter, Olley and Denham, *Victimology: Victimisation and Victims' Rights* (Abingdon: Routledge-Cavendish, 2009), pp 47-49 on "secondary victimisation".

13 These traditional remedies can be contrasted with the concept of "restorative justice" which seeks to provide some level of restitution to victims, often by bringing victims and offenders together for discussions. In Ireland, restorative justice has so far been mainly employed in the field of juvenile justice and is discussed in more detail in Chapter Eleven.

would lack the objectivity and consistency of the formalised criminal process and the protection of rights, even of those accused of a crime, could not be assured in more individualised systems.[14]

Indeed, while it seems clear that victims should be provided for within the criminal process and sensitivity to the needs of victims is desirable, there is a danger, while operating in the context of the courts, that asserting victims' rights might interfere with the rights of the accused, for example, the right to a fair trial. O'Malley suggests that any conflict between victims' rights and the rights of the accused would have to be resolved in favour of the accused as "it is upon persons charged with criminal offences, as opposed to those against whom offences were committed, that Art 38.1 of the Constitution confers the right to trial in due course of law."[15] **[12–08]**

II. Victims and Information Rights

Research suggests that victims benefit from being kept informed of the progress of their cases through the criminal process.[16] Failure to keep victims informed leads to greater anxiety and distress. In England and Wales, since the early 1990s, an opt-in system has existed whereby victims of serious crime can choose to be informed of the progress of their cases, even after sentencing. Take-up rates have been quite low on this service.[17] **[12–09]**

In Ireland, under the Victims Charter 2010, a victim may ask the DPP to take the victim's views into account when deciding whether or not to prosecute, and/or to re-examine a decision which the victim does not agree with. Furthermore, where a member of an individual's family or household is the victim in a fatal case the DPP is committed, wherever possible, to providing the reason for a decision not to prosecute. This applies to cases where the death took place after 22 October 2008.[18] **[12–10]**

For victims who are to give evidence at trial, the DPP undertakes in the Victims Charter 2010

- to treat the victim with respect and take account of his personal situation, rights and dignity;
- to work with the Garda Síochána to make sure that the victim is kept up to date on his case, especially if it is about a violent or sexual offence; and
- to arrange a pre-trial meeting for the victim with the prosecution solicitor and barrister, if the victim so wishes. The solicitor and barrister can explain the trial process to the victim, but they cannot discuss the evidence which he will give.

---

[14] Rogan, above n 3, p 141.

[15] O'Malley, *The Criminal Process* (Round Hall, Dublin, 2009), p 18.

[16] See for example, Tudor, "Probation work with victims of crime" in *Reparation and Victim-focused Social Work* (Williams (ed.), Jessica Kingsley, London, 2000), p 132.

[17] See Newton "A study of the policies and procedures implemented by the probation service with respect to victims of serious crime" (2003) 2(1) *British Journal of Criminology* 25. See also Williams, "'Victims'" in *Criminology* (Hale, Hayward, Wahidin and Wincup (eds.), 2nd Edition, OUP, 2009), p 550.

[18] Victims of Crime Office, *Victims Charter and Guide to the Criminal Justice System* (Department of Justice and Law Reform, Dublin, 2010).

[12–11] As noted above, the DPP has undertaken to provide reasons to the families of victims for non-prosecution in fatal cases. This decision was reached following a pilot study and in June 2010, the DPP announced his intention to expand this study and to begin giving reasons for non-prosecution in rape and sexual assault cases.[19] In other cases, reasons for non-prosecution may be provided to the Garda Síochána and not directly to victims. Many jurisdictions, including Australia, Canada, England and Wales, Northern Ireland and Scotland, now operate prosecution systems which provide reasons to victims, or the families of deceased victims, for non-prosecution and it is encouraging to see that the Irish prosecution service is expanding its role in this regard.

[12–12] At the other end of the criminal process, a victim may wish to be kept informed of any post-conviction updates where a custodial sentence has been imposed. The Irish Prison Service has undertaken within the Victims Charter 2010 to inform the victim, if he or a member of his family requests to be so informed, when the offender is to be released from prison, either on temporary release or at the end of his sentence. If the release is court-ordered then the Prison Service will usually inform the victim afterwards. On request the Prison Service will also keep the victim updated on other relevant developments in relation to the offender's sentence, such as transfers between prisons or parole board hearings (for offenders sentenced to eight years or more).[20]

III. Legal Advice and Representation for Victims

[12–13] As a victim is not a party to a criminal trial, he is not usually entitled to legal representation. Specific provision is made, however, for legal advice to be given free of charge to victims under the civil legal aid scheme, in the context of particular offences: rape, aggravated sexual assault, statutory rape, rape under s 4 and incest.[21] Complainants in such cases may be given legal advice, not representation, by the Legal Aid Board without having to satisfy the usual means test or make any financial contribution.

[12–14] There is one exceptional instance in which a victim may be legally represented before a trial court: where, in a sexual offence case, an application is made by the defence to the trial judge to question the complainant about her past sexual history.[22] The offences to which this provision applies are rape, aggravated sexual assault, and related inchoate offences.[23] The application is made in the absence of the jury and the complainant is entitled to be present and to have separate legal representation when the application is being made.[24] The judge will give leave for this line of questioning only if he is satisfied that it would be unfair to the accused not to allow the witness to be questioned about her sexual history, i.e. if the judge believes that if the evidence or question was not allowed

---

[19] Speech entitled "Victims of Crime and the Prosecutor" delivered at the *Accommodating Victims in the Criminal Justice System Conference*, Centre for Criminal Justice and Human Rights, University College Cork, 11 June 2010.

[20] Victims of Crime Office, *Victims Charter and Guide to the Criminal Justice System* (Department of Justice and Law Reform, Dublin, 2010).

[21] Civil Legal Aid Act 1995, s 26(3)(b).

[22] Criminal Law (Rape) Act 1981, s 3 as amended by Sex Offenders Act 2001, s 34.

[23] s 4A.

[24] *ibid.*

the jury might reasonably be satisfied beyond reasonable doubt that the accused person is guilty, and the effect of allowing the evidence or question might reasonably be that they would not be so satisfied.[25] The Legal Aid Board can provide legal representation for complainants at this application hearing, again without requiring satisfaction of the means test or any monetary contribution from the complainant.[26]

In *DPP v McDonagh*,[27] the Court of Criminal Appeal clearly stated that the sole criterion for the granting or refusal of an application for questioning as to past sexual history was that set out in the legislation, i.e. if refusing the application would lead to unfairness to the accused. The same court later seemed to consider other interests also. In *DPP v GK*,[28] Kearns J stated that **[12–15]**

> "[h]aving regard to the severely restrictive terminology of the statutory provision, the court is of the view that, in general, a decision to refuse to allow cross-examination as to past sexual history may more readily be justified in most cases than the converse... Furthermore, the younger the age of a complainant, the less desirable it is to ever allow cross-examination which may well be extremely traumatic for a complainant of tender years. Where a form of questioning is allowed, it should be confined only to what is strictly necessary and should never be utilised as a form of character assassination of a complainant."[29]

In *GK*, the accused was tried three times in relation to the same set of offences, due to retrials being ordered on various grounds. Following conviction in the second trial, a victim impact report, prepared by a clinical psychologist, was tendered on behalf of the complainant. This report alluded to the fact that the complainant had had sexual encounters with other boys prior to the events which grounded the case against GK. This information had not been known to the defence prior to the making of the victim impact report. In the third trial, the defence sought leave to cross-examine the complainant in relation to the information which had been revealed in the victim impact report. Leave was refused by the trial judge, but this decision was deemed incorrect on appeal. The Court of Criminal Appeal held that a limited and carefully monitored cross-examination of the complainant in relation to the relevant matters ought to have been allowed, as failure to do so could lead to unfairness to the accused.[30] **[12–16]**

IV. Victims Giving Evidence at Trial

Departing from the traditional position that an accused person should be able to face his accuser, provision has been made within the Criminal Evidence Act 1992 for certain classes of witnesses, which may include victims of crime, to provide their evidence to a trial court by non-traditional means in order to avoid the trauma of testifying in open court. Part III of that Act applies in the context of sexual offences, offences involving **[12–17]**

[25] s 3(2)(b).

[26] Civil Legal Aid Act 1995, s 28(5A) as amended by the Sex Offenders Act 2001, s 35(3).

[27] Unreported, Court of Criminal Appeal, 24 July 1990.

[28] [2007] 2 IR 92.

[29] *ibid.* at 103-104.

[30] *ibid.* at 105. See also *DPP v TC* [2009] IECCA 63.

violence or the threat of violence, and any attempt, conspiracy, aiding, abetting, counselling, procuring or incitement of such offences.[31] In trials for such offences, evidence may be given by way of live television link by a child under 17 years of age or any other person with the leave of the court.[32] When evidence is being provided in this manner, no wigs or gowns are to be worn by the judge or lawyers in the case.[33]

[12–18] An additional protection exists in this context for children under 17 giving evidence by way of television link: questions may be put to the child by way of an intermediary.[34] This is at the discretion of the trial judge, on application by the prosecution or defence, taking into consideration the age and mental condition of the relevant child and the interests of justice.[35] Video-recordings of evidence may also be admitted in certain limited circumstances, for example, a video-recording of a statement made by a child under 14 years of age during an interview with a garda.[36] The person from whom the recorded statement was initially taken must be available for cross-examination[37] and the court ought not to admit the video-recording if it believes it is not in the interests of justice to do so, considering all the circumstances, including any risk of unfairness to the accused.[38]

[12–19] Further provision for the giving of evidence by way of television link was established under the Criminal Justice Act 1999. Any witness who is in fear or subject to intimidation may give evidence, with the leave of the court, by live television link.[39] The court must be satisfied that the relevant witness is likely to be in fear or subject to intimidation in giving evidence otherwise before granting the required leave.

[12–20] A number of challenges were initially taken to the provision of witness testimony, including victim testimony, in these non-traditional formats. In *White v Ireland*,[40] for example, judicial review was sought of the decision to allow a child victim to give evidence against the accused by way of live television link from a room which was at some distance from the courtroom. The accused sought to assert a constitutional right to confront his accuser in open court (referred to in the case as "eye-ball to eye-ball" confrontation[41]) and claimed that use of the provisions of the Criminal Evidence Act 1992 would lead to a breach of his constitutional right to a fair trial. Kinlen J, in the High Court, held that there is no constitutionally protected right to require a witness giving evidence against an accused person to be physically present in court. In *Donnelly v Ireland*,[42] the Supreme Court came to similar conclusions. While the Court did hold that the right of an accused person to a fair trial is a superior right in the hierarchy of

---

[31] Criminal Evidence Act 1992, s 12.
[32] s 13.
[33] s 13 (3).
[34] s 14 (1).
[35] s 14 (1).
[36] s 16.
[37] s 16(1)(ii).
[38] s 16(2)(a) and (b).
[39] Criminal Justice Act 1999, s 39.
[40] [1995] 2 IR 268.
[41] *ibid.* at 276 and 282.
[42] [1998] 1 IR 321.

constitutional rights,[43] it further held that the provision of alternative methods for vulnerable witnesses to give evidence was not necessarily in breach of that right.

The ECtHR held, in *SN v Sweden*,[44] that the use of special measures in order to protect victims of sexual offences from the ordeal of testifying in open court is not contrary to the accused's right to a fair trial, so long as the accused can adequately and effectively exercise his rights.[45] **[12–21]**

Another provision for victims giving evidence at trial is s 7 of the Criminal Law (Rape) Act 1981,[46] which provides for the anonymity of the complainant in sexual assault and rape offences.[47] It is an offence to publish or broadcast any matter likely to lead the public to identify the complainant, except as authorised by a court direction. On rare occasions victims have waived their right to anonymity in order to tell their stories or challenge the criminal justice system.[48] Section 8 of the Act provides for the anonymity of the accused in a "rape offence" case; however, it lasts only until after he has been convicted.[49] Furthermore, members of the public are not entitled to attend trials in relation to rape and aggravated sexual assault.[50] **[12–22]**

One final measure which could provide protection or support for victims (or other witnesses) who wish to come forward is the Witness Protection Programme, which was set up in the aftermath of the killing of Veronica Guerin in 1996 and is administered by An Garda Síochána. The Programme has no statutory basis[51] or guidelines for operation and it has come in for serious criticism from the courts. In *DPP v Gilligan*,[52] a case which involved testimony from Charles Bowden, the first witness entered into the Programme, McCracken J stated that it was "badly thought out and [had] developed a life of its own." One of the main problems with operating a witness protection programme in Ireland is that, given the size of the country, participation will invariably mean having to move abroad. Both the DPP and the Garda Commissioner have acknowledged that placing such a heavy demand on witnesses diminishes the potential use of the Programme.[53] **[12–23]**

---

43 *ibid.* at 348.

44 (2004) 39 EHRR 13.

45 *ibid.* at para 47. For more on the right to confrontation see Dennis, "The Right to Confront Witnesses: Meanings, Myths and Human Rights" (2010) *Criminal Law Review* 255. See also Ellison, *The Adversarial Process and the Vulnerable Witness* (Oxford Univerity Press, Oxford, 2001).

46 As amended by Criminal Law (Rape)(Amendment) Act 1990, s 17(2).

47 A "rape offence" includes: rape, attempted rape, aiding, abetting, counselling and procuring rape or attempted rape, and incitement to rape. Criminal Law (Rape) Act 1981, s 1.

48 The complainant in *People (DPP) v WC* [1994] 1 ILRM 321, Lavinia Kerwick, waived her anonymity in order to express her view that the suspended sentence handed down to her rapist was overly lenient. See also *Independent Star v O'Connor* [2002] 4 IR 166 which examined the anonymity of the accused.

49 Criminal Law (Rape) Act 1981, s 8.

50 s 6 as inserted by Criminal Law (Rape)(Amendment) Act 1990, s 11.

51 The Labour Party did propose a Witness Protection Programme Bill in 2007, but it was not passed.

52 Unreported, Court of Criminal Appeal, 8 August 2003.

53 "Evidence that puts lives at risk", *Irish Times*, 18 April 2009.

V. Victim Impact Statements (VIS)

[12–24] The concept of victims providing a statement to the court on the effect which the crime has had on them was first established in California in 1974.[54] The aim was to empower victims through participation in the criminal process by creating an opportunity for them to give information about the loss and damage suffered as a result of the offence, and to express feelings about this.[55] It was considered also that invoking the often emotional, personal stories of victims in the formalised criminal process might alter the culture to some extent and make legal professionals more mindful of the sensitivities of the victim and his perspective on the events, which they may view more clinically.[56]

[12–25] Generally, victim impact statements (VIS) are provided at the sentencing stage of the criminal process. McGrath describes the current Irish position in the following terms:

> "An impact statement is typically prepared by the victim and furnished to the court after the offender is found or has pleaded guilty and prior to his sentencing. It affords the victim the opportunity to inform the court, in writing and sometimes verbally, of the physical, psychological, emotional, and financial affects that the crime has had upon him, and should be taken into account, amongst all other relevant considerations, by the trial judge in the sentencing of the offender."[57]

[12–26] Evidence suggests that there is a high degree of satisfaction for victims when a sentencing judge makes reference to their VIS, sometimes even using a specific phrase of theirs.[58] This shows victims that their voices have been heard and that their feelings have been taken into account.

[12–27] VIS are provided for in many systems including in England and Wales,[59] Scotland, Australia, New Zealand, Canada and Ireland. The popularity of these measures may be due to the fact that they are a relatively inexpensive way to be seen to be providing for victims' interests. In this vein, McGrath considers that the introduction of VIS into the Irish criminal justice system was a

> "cursory knee-jerk reaction to public pressure, an exercise in window-dressing that ticked all the boxes for swift action: cheap, visible, politically astute, and relatively benign."[60]

---

[54] See Wemmers, above n 8, p 398.

[55] Williams, above n 17, p 556.

[56] See Brooks & Gewirtz (eds.), *Law Stories–Narrative Rhetoric in the Law; Papke, Narrative and the Legal Discourse: A Reader in Storytelling and the Law* (Deborah Charles, 1991) referred to in Carey, "Victims, Victimology and Victim Impact Statements" (2000) 10(3) ICLJ 8.

[57] McGrath, "Is anybody listening, and why do they hear? The Use of Victim Impact Statements in Ireland" (2008) 15(1) DULJ 71, pp 72-73.

[58] Meredith and Paquette, *Summary Report on Victim Impact Statement Focus Groups* (Policy Centre for Victim Issues, Ottawa Department of Justice, 2001), p 9. See also McGrath, above n 57.

[59] VIS was introduced in England and Wales just after research (Hoyle, Cape, Morgan and Sanders, *Evaluation of the 'One-Stop-Shop' and Victim Statement Pilot Projects* (Home Office Research and Development Directorate, London, 1998)) suggested it should not be.

[60] McGrath, above n 57, p 92.

Whether or not this is a fair assessment of the nature of their introduction, VIS have been a part of the Irish criminal process since 1993.

VIS in Ireland

The Criminal Justice Act 1993, as amended by the Criminal Procedure Act 2010, provides for the giving of a VIS in this jurisdiction in relation to specific types of offences: sexual offences, offences involving violence or the threat of violence, offences under the Non-Fatal Offences Against the Person Act 1997, and related inchoate offences.[61] Section 5(2)(a), as amended, states that **[12–28]**

> "[w]hen imposing sentence on a person for an offence to which this section applies, a court shall take into account, and may, where necessary, receive evidence or submissions concerning, any effect (whether long-term or otherwise) of the offence on the person in respect of whom the offence was committed."

Section 5(3)(a), as amended, provides that where the victim applies to the court to be heard at the sentencing stage of the criminal process, the court shall hear the victim's evidence as to the effect of the offence on him.

The entitlement to provide a VIS was originally extended by the courts, as a matter of discretion, to the family of a deceased victim in homicide cases. This has now been provided for in statute under s 5(2)(b) of the Criminal Justice Act 1993, as amended by s 4 of the Criminal Procedure Act 2010 which states that

> "For the purposes of paragraph (*a*), a 'person in respect of whom the offence was committed' includes, where, as a result of the offence, that person has died, is ill or is otherwise incapacitated, a family member of that person."

Section 5(3)(b), as amended, allows for a VIS to be provided by a parent/guardian of a victim who is under 14 or by the child himself, by a family member of a person with a mental disorder or by the person himself, by a parent/guardian of a child with a mental disorder or by the child himself. Such VIS should refer to the effect of the offence on the victim. The section further provides that a VIS referring to the effect of the relevant offence on the victim and on his family may be provided by a family member of a victim who is ill or otherwise incapacitated as a result of the offence. Where a victim has died as a result of the offence, a family member may give evidence by VIS as to the effect on the victim in any period of time which might have elapsed between the offence and his ultimate death, and on the family members of the deceased.

Where more than one family member of a deceased or incapacitated victim, or child victim or victim with a mental disorder, wishes to give a VIS, the court may order that the family members direct one or more family members to give the VIS. If the family cannot reach agreement on this, the court may nominate one or more family members as it considers appropriate, having regard to the degree of relationship between the relevant family members and the victim.[62] **[12–29]**

[61] Criminal Justice Act 1993, s 5(1) as amended by the Criminal Procedure Act 2010, s 4.

[62] Criminal Justice Act 1993, ss 5(3)(d) and 5(3)(e) as inserted by the Criminal Procedure Act 2010, s 4.

Sections 5 and 6 of the Criminal Procedure Act 2010 insert ss 5A and 5B into the 1993 Act, providing that where a child or a person with a mental disorder is a victim of a crime covered by s 5(2), he may provide a VIS pursuant to s 5(3) through a live television link, unless the court sees good reason to the contrary, and may have questions put to him through an intermediary if the interests of justice so require, having regard to his age or mental condition. Any other victim may also be allowed to provide a VIS through a live television link, with the leave of the court.

The court may order, under s 5(5)(a), that information relating to the giving of a VIS shall not be published or broadcast, in the interests of justice. Publication or broadcasting of the information following the making of such an order is an offence punishable by a term of imprisonment of up to three years, and/or a fine of up to €50,000.

[12–30] Research in the United States and elsewhere suggested that there were low take-up rates in terms of victims giving impact statements.[63] There are no current statistics available on the Irish take-up rates, but such statements as have been made, particularly in homicide cases, have been widely reported in the media and occasionally caused controversy. This has ranged from victims in their statement departing from their prepared statement and referring to evidence not led at trial[64] to a sentencing judge voicing his view on the insincerity of a VIS.[65]

Difficulties in Relation to VIS

[12–31] While allowing the victim to participate in the criminal process by providing an impact statement may be beneficial in some cases, there are concerns in allowing for VIS, both in terms of its benefit to victims and its impact on the criminal process.

[12–32] In relation to victims themselves, it has been suggested that participation by way of VIS at the post-conviction, pre-sentence stage of the criminal process is too little too late in terms of involvement in the criminal process.[66] It could equally place an unwelcome burden on some. A victim may be unwilling to provide a VIS but might fear that without doing so a sentencing judge would be more lenient on the relevant offender than he would otherwise be.[67] It has also been argued that victims' expectations may be

---

[63] Doerner and Lab, *Victimology* (3rd ed, Anderson, Cincinnatti, 2002) and Hoyle, Cape, Morgan and Sanders, above n 59.

[64] Discussed below at paras 12-42 – 12-44.

[65] This occurred in the trial of Ronnie Dunbar for the unlawful homicide of 14 year old Melissa Mahon. The deceased victim had been in the care of the HSE at the time of her death and her family, who lived in England, had been uncooperative with gardaí during the investigation into her disappearance and death. In a VIS prepared by Melissa's mother, Mary Mahon, it was said that Melissa was her baby and that her whole life had been torn apart by what had happened. White J voiced his opinion that the VIS was "disingenuous in the extreme". See "Impact statement criticised by judge" *Irish Times*, 7 July 2009.

[66] Wemmers, above n 8, p 399.

[67] In this regard, the Irish courts have held that the decision of the victim to give or not to give a VIS is not to be treated of itself as either an aggravating or mitigating factor: *People (DPP) v MC*, Unreported, Court of Criminal Appeal, 16 June 1995. This has now been further supplemented by

raised in relation to the likely sentence by providing a VIS, and the handing down of a lesser sentence may then prove quite distressing.[68]

In terms of the operation of the criminal justice system, a number of objections to VIS have been raised. One of these suggests that the use of VIS will lead to harsher sentences generally being handed down by the judiciary. Research from the United States and Australia suggests, however, that this is not the case.[69] Another argument suggests that more articulate victims will be better able to express the effect of an offence on them and thus, offenders in such cases will be more likely to get a harsher sentence than an offender whose victim is not as eloquent.[70] Linked to this is the broader argument in relation to "unequal justice" – if, in two almost identical cases, A and B, Victim A has recovered well but Victim B has suffered serious ongoing stress or anxiety, should Offender A receive a lesser sentence than Offender B? In this regard, Ashworth has queried why the offender's sentence should "vary according to the chance circumstance of whether a particular victim suffers after-effects that are unusually great or unusually small?"[71] **[12–33]**

O'Malley, writing prior to the introduction of VIS in Ireland, made the following observations: **[12–34]**

> "punishment must be proportionate to the blameworthiness of the accused, and ... this blameworthiness must be constructed by reference to the infraction constituting the offence of conviction, the state of mind of the offender at the time of its commission and his or her personal circumstances. Allowing punishment to vary in accordance with the effects suffered by a particular victim would surely conflict with these fundamental principles."[72]

O'Malley suggests that while a victim's wishes or welfare might be one of the reasons for a particular sentence to be issued, it ought not to be the sole reason and matters such as just deserts and deterrence ought to also form part of the sentencing equation.[73] **[12–35]**

---

statute. s 5(4) of the Criminal Justice Act 1993, as inserted by s 4 of the Criminal Procedure Act 2010, states that where no VIS is given "...the court shall not draw an inference that the offence had little or no effect (whether long-term or otherwise)" on the victim or, where appropriate, his family members".

[68] Hoyle, Cape, Morgan and Sanders, above n 59, p 28. McGrath, above n 57, has suggested that the VIS ought to be read *after* sentence has been handed down.

[69] Erez and Tontodonato, "The Effect of Victim Participation in Sentencing on Sentence Outcome" (1990) 28 *Criminology* 451; Davis and Smith, "The Effect of Victim Impact Statements on Sentencing Decisions: A Test in an Urban Setting" (1994) 11 *Justice Quarterly* 453; Erez and Roeger, "Crime Impact v Victim Impact: Victim Impact Statements in South Australia" (1995) 6 *Criminology Australia* 3.

[70] Booth, "The Dead Victim, the Family Victim and Victim Impact Statements in New South Wales" (2000) 11(3) *Current Issues in Criminal Justice* 292, p 303.

[71] Ashworth, *Sentencing and Criminal Justice* (Butterworths, London, 2003), p 319.

[72] O'Malley, "Punishment and moral luck: The role of the victim in sentencing decisions" (1993) 3(1) ICLJ 40, p 55.

[73] *ibid.* p 59.

Effect on Sentencing and "Unequal Justice"

[12–36] The effect of a VIS on the sentencing decision is of interest given the concerns raised by Ashworth and O'Malley in relation to "unequal justice", and this is particularly relevant where a victim actually expresses a view on sentence within the VIS. Guiry has suggested that "judges are expected to treat a VIS with what could be regarded as a genuine but distanced respect."[74] Indeed, the case-law indicates that while the impact of the crime on the victim is a factor to be considered in sentencing it is not the only factor.[75]

[12–37] In *People (DPP) v M*,[76] Denham J, referring to the adversarial criminal process, noted that

> "[t]he nature of the crime, and the personal circumstances of the appellant, are the kernel issues to be considered and applied in accordance with the principles of sentencing, for this is an action between the State and the appellant and not an action between the appellant and the victims."[77]

Nonetheless, the majority of the Supreme Court in that case held that, along with the nature of the crime and the personal circumstances of the offender, the effect of the crime on the victim ought to be taken into account when considering sentence.

[12–38] Some years later Denham J suggested in *People (DPP) v MS*[78] that while the impact of the offence on the victim was not determinant of the court's decision in terms of sentence, it is an important factor.[79] In that case, a rape victim indicated to the court that she would not object to a reduction in the convicted offender's sentence, as long as he did not interfere with her or her children.

[12–39] In *People (DPP) v McCormack*,[80] the victim of a sexual assault and attempted rape told the sentencing judge in her VIS that she did not want the offender to go to jail as she felt that he was very young and would not offend again. Carney J in the Central Criminal Court considered himself bound by precedent to impose a custodial sentence. On appeal, the Court of Criminal Appeal held that there was no obligation to impose a sentence of imprisonment and that sentencing should depend on the individual circumstances of the case. In this case, the Court held that the express wish of the victim ought to have been taken into account, amongst other things. Barron J stated that "[t]he sentence to be imposed is not the appropriate sentence for the crime, but the appropriate sentence for the crime because it has been committed by that accused."[81]

---

[74] Guiry, "Who is the victim?—The use of Victim Impact Statements in murder and manslaughter cases" (2006) 16(3) ICLJ 2, p 3.
[75] See also Chapter Ten.
[76] [1994] 3 IR 306. See also *People (DPP) v Tiernan* [1988] IR 250.
[77] *ibid.* at 317.
[78] [2000] 2 IR 592.
[79] *ibid.* at 601.
[80] [2000] 4 IR 356.
[81] *ibid.* at 359.

A somewhat conflicting statement was made by Geoghegan J in the Court of Criminal Appeal in *People (DPP) v RO'D*,[82] where the accused had pleaded guilty to several counts of sexual assault on his two sisters. Both of the victims requested that a custodial sentence should not be imposed. However, like in *McCormack*, considering himself obliged by precedent to impose a custodial sentence, the trial judge did not acquiesce to the request of the victims. On appeal, it was held that while a court is obliged to take into account the effect of a crime on a victim this did not allow the victim to express a view as to what the appropriate sentence should be. [12–40]

Geoghegan J stated that

> "From time to time victims ... express views as to sentence such as for instance 'he should be locked up for life'. It has never been the practice in this jurisdiction for the victims of an offence to be permitted to express views in that sense as to what a proper sentence might be. In the opinion of the court, s.5 [of the Criminal Justice Act 1993] makes no change in that regard."[83]

In general, it seems that a forgiving attitude by the victim towards the offender can be a factor in sentencing. However, it is not to be the determinative factor, as a crime is an attack on society and not merely an abuse of the individual victim. Thus, sentencing judges maintain their role in imposing an appropriate sentence for a specific offender in the particular circumstances of a specific offence. While this does not entirely allay the concerns raised by Ashworth and O'Malley, it does show a judicial consciousness of the need to insist on proportionate sentencing. [12–41]

New Allegations in VIS

Along with the dangers of "unequal justice" another difficulty which might arise in the context of VIS is that "offenders might be subjected to unfounded or excessive allegations by victims, made from the relative security of a VIS".[84] [12–42]

There have been a number of examples of this in the Irish context. The most controversial involved the VIS provided by Majella Holohan, following the conviction of Wayne O'Donoghue in 2006 for the manslaughter of her 11 year old son. In her oral presentation of the VIS Mrs Holohan strayed significantly from the written version which had been submitted to the court and made reference to alleged evidential material which had not been proffered at trial.[85] This was later indirectly criticised by the trial judge in the case, Mr Justice Paul Carney, in an address at University College Cork and caused significant public and media interest in the issue of victim impact statements.[86]

---

[82] [2000] 4 IR 361.

[83] *ibid.* at 364-365.

[84] Ashworth, "*Victim Impact Statements and Sentencing*" (1993) *Criminal Law Review* 498, p 507.

[85] Guiry, above n 74.

[86] "Majella Holohan criticises comments by trial judge", *Irish Independent*, 11 October 2007. For Mr Justice Carney's views on the role of victims see also "The Role of The Victim in the Irish Criminal Process" (2007) 7(1) JSIJ 7.

[12–43] The inclusion of additional material in the VIS was considered by the Court of Criminal Appeal in the appeal on the leniency of O'Donoghue's sentence.[87] The Court noted that the practice of allowing the families of deceased victims of an unlawful homicide to provide VIS was to be approved of as it might be of assistance to the sentencing judge and provided an opportunity for the family and friends of the victim to express their loss. However, the Court further held that strict conditions should attach to the provision of such a statement and that the statement maker ought to be warned by the sentencing judge that any material departure from the text of the VIS previously submitted to the judge and legal representatives for both sides might lead him to be in contempt of court. Furthermore, if any such departure involved unfounded or scurrilous allegations against the accused, the sentencing judge could take that into account as a mitigating factor in relation to the sentence to be imposed.[88]

[12–44] In a similar case, *People v Magee*,[89] in 1997, the accused had originally been charged with rape and sexual assault. He pleaded guilty to sexual assault and not guilty to rape. The DPP accepted this plea and did not proceed to trial with the rape charge. Evidence of the events in question was provided to the court and the victim in the case made a VIS prior to sentencing. Along with describing the effect of the sexual assault on her, the victim made reference to unlawful sexual intercourse between her and the accused and suggested also that the accused had engaged in an act of oral sex against her will. The sentencing judge imposed a term of imprisonment of four years, the maximum possible for sexual assault being five years. On appeal it was argued that this was excessive. In the Court of Criminal Appeal, O'Flaherty J noted that an "aura" surrounded this case as a result of the statements made by the victim within her VIS and that justice must not only be done but must be seen to be done. Resultantly, the Court of Criminal Appeal reduced the sentence to two years. The Court stated that once a plea of guilty to a lesser charge is accepted, "… it is incumbent on the prosecution that evidence should be marshalled in such a way as to be kept within the four corners of the offence with which the court comes to be concerned." O'Flaherty suggested that in circumstances where the complainant disagrees with a proposal to drop a rape charge it may be wise to take the case to trial and to allow a jury to decide the matter, in order to avoid such circumstances as occurred in this case recurring.

In order to resolve problems in this area, it has been recommended that a booklet be made available to victims intending to produce a VIS in order to outline matters which ought not to be contained therein.[90]

VI. Court-Ordered Compensation for Victims

[12–45] As noted above, compensation for victims is not a natural fit in the context of the adversarial, common law, criminal process. However, s 6 of the Criminal Justice Act 1993 makes provision for compensation to be paid by the offender to the victim for any

---

[87] *People (DPP) v Wayne O'Donoghue* [2006] 2 IR 336.

[88] *ibid.* at 359.

[89] Unreported, Court of Criminal Appeal, 29 July 1997. Discussed in Naidoo, "The Role of the Victim in Certain Sentencing Hearings: A Case Note on the *People v Magee*" (1998) 16 ILT 230.

[90] Recommended in Hanly, Healy and Scriver, *Rape and Justice in Ireland: A National Study of Survivor, Prosecutor and Court Responses to Rape* (The Liffey Press, Dublin, 2009).

personal injury or loss resulting from the offence. Under this provision, a judge may issue a "compensation order" instead of or as part of any sentence for the commission of an offence for an amount which the court considers appropriate, having regard to any evidence or any representations that are made by or on behalf of the convicted offender, the injured party or the prosecutor.[91] The court is also to have regard to the means of the offender and a compensation order may allow for payment in instalments.[92] A directly injured party may be the beneficiary of compensation under this scheme, or, where death has occurred as a result of the offence, a dependent of the deceased victim may receive compensation.[93]

The section does not usually apply in the context of road traffic offences, unless the offender was uninsured at the time of the offence.[94] Compensation orders may be made against the parent or guardian of a juvenile offender in certain circumstances.[95] Recently, a recommendation has been made that s 6 ought to be strengthened such that the DPP would be under an obligation to seek compensation from the offender on behalf of the complainant in all cases.[96] **[12–46]**

The issue of compensation gave rise to a very significant case on the role which the victim should play in the sentencing of offenders: *DPP v McCabe (No 2)*.[97] In the Court of Criminal Appeal, the DPP sought to appeal the leniency of a sentence handed down by Carney J in the Central Criminal Court on a charge of aggravated sexual assault, contrary to s 3 of the Criminal Law (Rape) (Amendment) Act 1990. The learned trial judge had given the convicted offender a four-year suspended sentence, based largely on the fact that he had offered €15,000 in compensation to the victim and she had accepted it. **[12–47]**

The manner in which events unfolded is of particular importance. The offender had pleaded guilty to the charge against him and, at the sentencing hearing, offered €15,000 compensation to the victim. Carney J, addressing counsel for the DPP, stated "[i]t is not my practice to combine payment of monies with imprisonment", and asked if the victim understood this and whether or not counsel wished to consult with her on it. Following a short adjournment counsel for the DPP informed Carney J that the victim was willing to accept the offer of compensation "knowing" the consequences that were attached thereto. **[12–48]**

In imposing sentence, Carney J stated that he had been considering a term of imprisonment of four or five years, but, as he would not combine payment of compensation with custodial detention and the victim having accepted the compensation in the knowledge of that practice, he instead imposed a four-year suspended sentence so long as the accused entered into a bond to keep the peace. He also insisted that the offender be certified as a sex offender under the Sex Offenders Act 2001. **[12–49]**

---

[91] Criminal Justice Act 1993, ss 6(1) and 6(2).
[92] ss 6(5) and 6(6).
[93] s 6(12).
[94] s 6(4).
[95] s 6(5). See also the Children Act 2001, s 113 and Chapter Eleven, para 11-65.
[96] Recommended in Hanly, Healy and Scriver, above n 90.
[97] [2005] IECCA 90.

[12–50] One of the central planks of the DPP's appeal to the Court of Criminal Appeal was that the trial judge had erred in allowing the victim of a crime to play a role in deciding the sentence of the offender and that this was inherently objectionable and contrary to public policy. Furthermore, an argument was raised that significant inequalities would arise within the criminal process between wealthy offenders and impecunious offenders if it was thought to be proper practice to release those who could pay compensation and imprison those who could not. Counsel for the DPP further argued that Carney J's decision was contrary to the wording of s 6 of the 1993 Act, which specifically provided a discretion to the trial judge to order payment of compensation either "instead of or in addition to dealing with [the offender] in any other way".

[12–51] The Court of Criminal Appeal agreed with the argument put forward by counsel for the DPP and Kearns J stated that the Court was

> "strongly of the view that victims in circumstances of this nature should not be drawn into any sort of pro-active role in determining or negotiating the amount of any compensation which an accused person may offer with a view to mitigating sentence. The extent of the victim's involvement should be either to indicate a willingness to accept or refuse any sum of compensation that may be offered. Thereafter, it is entirely a matter for the court to determine the appropriate sentence having regard to all the multiple considerations which must be borne in mind in this context, including any payment of compensation offered or made."

[12–52] On the facts, although the Court was entirely of the opinion that the trial judge had erred in principle in handing down sentence, it did not alter the sentence as it held that there were exceptional circumstances in this case justifying the non-application of a custodial sentence.[98]

McCabe is a significant case, not only in relation to compensation orders and their potential effect on sentence, but more broadly also, in relation to the role which the victim plays in sentencing.

VII. "Justice for Victims" Initiative

[12–53] In June 2008, the Minister for Justice, Dermot Ahern TD, announced a "Justice for Victims" initiative. Along with practical matters such as reconstituting the Commission for the Support of Victims of Crime, creating a Victims of Crime consultative forum and establishing a new executive office of the Department of Justice to focus on the co-ordination of services to victims of crime, the initiative included legislative measures which ultimately became the Criminal Procedure Act 2010.

[12–54] The Act provides for the following changes:

- alterations to the law on VIS, specifically providing for such statements to be made by family members of victims who are deceased or incapacitated as a result

[98] In relation to *McCabe* see Rogan, "The Role of Victims in Sentencing: The Case of Compensation Orders" (2006) 24 ILT 202.

of the relevant crime, where the victim is a child or is suffering from mental incapacity;
- changes in the traditional rule against double jeopardy, allowing for a retrial in cases where new and compelling evidence emerges; and
- allowances for "with prejudice" appeals to be made by the DPP in cases where compelling evidence was erroneously excluded at trial, or a judge's direction to a jury to acquit was wrong in law and there was evidence on which a jury might reasonably have been satisfied of the accused's guilt beyond a reasonable doubt.

Many of these changes stem from the Report of the Balance in the Criminal Law Review Group[99] and while the changes in relation to VIS seem largely uncontroversial, a word of caution seems appropriate in relation to the other alterations. Varying the long-established rule against double jeopardy (discussed in Chapter Ten) under the banner of the "Justice for Victims" initiative is arguably problematic. The terms "victim" or "victim of crime" are emotive phrases and it seems obvious that members of society would be concerned to protect victims and provide for their interests as far as possible. The use of the concept of the "victim" to bring about substantial change in the rules of the criminal process, rather than truly victim-oriented changes, ought to be avoided so that free and open debate on important legal issues can be facilitated. [12–55]

VIII. The EU and Victims of Crime

The European Union has become increasingly interested in providing for victims of crime. In 1999, the European Commission adopted a communication entitled " 'Crime victims in the European Union - standards and action", which sought to improve access to justice for victims of crime within member states of the EU and to protect their rights. In early 2001, the Council of the European Union adopted a Framework Decision on the standing of victims in criminal proceedings,[100] a step towards the harmonisation of the rights of victims across member states. It seeks to provide for the interests of crime victims before, during and after criminal proceedings. [12–56]

The Framework Decision provides for the following: [12–57]

- victims' right to be heard and to furnish evidence in criminal proceedings;
- access to relevant information, such as information about support groups, how to report offences, and access to interpretation and translation services;
- the right to have legal costs refunded when a victim has the status of witness or party in a relevant proceeding;
- a suitable level of protection of victims and their families, including protection of their right to privacy;
- a right to compensation;
- the opportunity to settle disputes by way of mediation; and
- the possibility for victims resident in another member state to participate properly in the criminal procedure (for example through the use of video conferencing).

[99] Balance in the Criminal Law Review Group *Final Report* (Stationery Office, Dublin, 2007).
[100] 2001/220/JHA.

[12–58] The implementation of this Framework Decision has been largely unsatisfactory to date.[101] Nonetheless, the EU remains committed to working on the issue of victims rights across all member states.[102] In July 2010 the European Commission launched a public consultation process, seeking to examine the manner in which victims of crime and violence are protected across member states, the supports that they receive, and what improvements are necessary. The Commission signalled its intention to create a comprehensive package of rules and practical measures in relation to this issue and to issue a Directive on minimum standards for victims of crime in the first half of 2011. This is likely to replace the 2001 Framework Decision on the standing of victims.

IX. Conclusion

[12–59] In the last two decades, at least, there have been significant changes in providing for the needs of victims within the criminal process in Ireland. Victims can now give evidence in non-traditional ways in specific circumstances in order to avoid the ordeal of open-court testimony; victims can be given court-ordered compensation from offenders; victims of "rape offences" can have separate legal representation when an application for questioning on past sexual history is being considered; and victims can express to sentencing judges what effect the relevant crime has had on them. However, there is still more that can be done to facilitate the needs of victims and to avoid any feeling of re-victimisation by the criminal process itself. Such further measures might include, amongst other things, greater legal representation within the pre-trial and trial processes for all victims of crime and more opportunities for mediation between victims and offenders in appropriate cases.[103]

[12–60] In a final note of caution, it is submitted that it is important that the introduction of additional police powers, alterations to well-established rules of the criminal process, or harsher sentencing provisions under the guise of increasing victims' rights should not be tolerated. Such increases in power or alteration of rules seen as favouring offenders do not necessarily improve the position of victims in any way, but their introduction may be legitimised by reliance on the emotive image of a victim of crime.[104] In a similar vein, the Law Reform Commission has suggested that

> "[i]f society is genuinely concerned about improving the lot of victims, more thought should be given to identifying and meeting their specific needs – the need for vindication, for protection, for support, and in some cases for compensation. We should avoid the facile assumption that society's responsibilities to the victim are best discharged through the imposition of heavily retributive sentences."[105]

---

[101] Report from the Commission of 20 April 2009 pursuant to Art 18 of the Council Framework Decision of 15 March 2001 on the standing of victims in criminal proceedings.

[102] See further Groenhuijsen and Pemberton, "The EU framework decision for victims of crime: does hard law make a difference?" (2009) 17(1) *European Journal of Crime, Criminal Law and Criminal Justice* 43.

[103] This exists within the sphere of juvenile justice in Ireland and is discussed in Chapter Eleven.

[104] See further Coen, "The rise of the victim—A path to punitiveness?" (2006) 16(3) ICLJ 10.

[105] Law Reform Commission *Report on Sentencing* (LRC53-1996, Dublin, 1996), Chapter 8 "Victim Impact Statements", p 49 para 8.6.

CHAPTER 13
Prisoners' Rights

Depriving an individual of his right to liberty is one of the biggest intrusions the State can make on the constitutional rights of an individual. For the most part, however, individuals will be committed to prison on foot of a conviction for a criminal offence, and for this reason, the deprivation of their liberty is justified as being in accordance with law and thus compliant with Art 40.4 of the Constitution. **[13–01]**

When we incarcerate an individual on foot of a conviction, the punishment is the deprivation of liberty. The Irish Penal Reform Trust (IPRT) believes that it is "the sentence of deprivation of liberty in itself that is the core punitive sanction in criminal cases; treatment accorded while in prison should not be used as additional punishment."[1] The ECtHR, while noting that there may be restriction on certain rights, stated in *Hirst v United Kingdom (No 2)*[2]: **[13–02]**

[1] Irish Penal Reform Trust, *Position Paper 4: Human Rights in Prison* (IPRT, Dublin, 2009), p 3.
[2] (2006) 42 EHRR 41.

> "...prisoners in general continue to enjoy all the fundamental rights and freedoms guaranteed under the Convention save for the right to liberty ... For example, prisoners may not be ill-treated, subjected to inhuman or degrading punishment ... they continue to enjoy the right to respect for family life ... the right to freedom of expression ... the right to practice their religion ... the right of effective access to a lawyer or to a court ... the right to respect for correspondence ... and the right to marry."[3]

[13–03] This chapter will examine the balance struck between the need of the State to have order in its prisons and the protection of the dignity of prisoners, looking at the protection of prisoners' rights as well as the Prison Rules 2007 which provide for the rules and procedure which govern prison life in Ireland.

I. Prisoners' Rights in Irish Courts

[13–04] International treaties and conventions make it clear that the imprisonment of individuals is punishment, and that prisoners' rights should not be further restricted.[4] Irish courts, however, have stated that while an individual is imprisoned, his rights are suspended, abrogated, or put into a temporary abeyance.[5] This position is used to justify the restriction of prisoners' rights. The IPRT notes that, while international human rights standards insist that restrictions on human rights must be "unavoidable, necessary and proportionate in the context of imprisonment", this principle is not always implemented in Irish prisons.[6] A typical statement is found in the case of *State (McDonagh) v Frawley*[7]:

> "While so held as a prisoner pursuant to a lawful warrant, many of the applicant's normal constitutional rights are abrogated or suspended. He must accept prison discipline and accommodate himself to the reasonable organisation of prison life laid down in the prison regulations."[8]

[13–05] Irish courts are beginning to accept that limitations on constitutional rights while in prison must be proportionate to the objective of incarceration, particularly where constitutional rights are in issue. In *Holland v Governor of Portlaoise Prison*,[9] in the context of a case regarding the applicant's freedom of expression, McKechnie J set out the following principles:

1. When serving a prison sentence, a prisoner must suffer a diminution or compromise on the exercise of certain constitutional rights;

---

[3] *ibid.* para 69.

[4] See for example, Rule 2, European Prison Rules (Council of Europe, 2006) available at http://www.uncjin.org/Laws/prisrul.htm and the UN Human Rights Committee, *General Comment No 21* (1992) available at http://www.unhchr.ch/tbs/doc.nsf/0/3327552b9511fb98c12563ed004cbe59?Opendocument.

[5] See for example, *State (McDonagh) v Frawley* [1978] IR 131; *Murray v Ireland* [1985] IR 532.

[6] IPRT, above n 1, p 4.

[7] [1978] IR 131.

[8] *ibid.* at 135.

[9] [2004] 2 IR 573.

2. The rights affected for the duration of the sentence are primarily the right to liberty but also rights (i) which are affected by the loss of this right and (ii) which are consequential to the serving of the sentence;
3. These "affected rights" are not capable of exhaustive definition but will depend on the circumstances of each case;
4. To be lawful, any limitation on the exercise of these "affected rights" must have as their objective:
   i. The incarceration of the prisoner so as to serve his sentence; and
   ii. The maintenance of security, discipline and good order within the prison;
5. The objective underpinning the restriction must be of such significance or value in a democratic society as to warrant overriding a constitutionally based right;
6. The interference on restriction must:
   i. Be rationally connected to the objective and must not be arbitrary, unfair or based on irrational considerations;
   ii. Be necessary or essential in order to achieve the legitimate aim to which it is addressed;
   iii. Not be more extensive than the minimum required to achieve its intended aim; and
   iv. Otherwise be proportionate to that objective;
7. Each application by a prisoner must be individually considered by the respondent or his deputed officer and must be decided upon by reference to the above criteria;
8. The Governor is vested with a discretion derived from statute which cannot be deprived or fettered by any policy or guidelines.[10]

Before considering issues relating to individual rights in Irish law and considering whether limitations on rights align with the above criteria we will consider the rules which operate to govern prison life.

II. Prison Rules

European Prison Rules

Part 1 of the European Prison Rules sets out three basic principles which are aimed at setting a minimum standard for prisons, and to act as governing principles for the management of prisons. The Rules were adopted by the Council of Europe, and while not binding in an Irish context, provide a statement as to what international best practice is in the area. These principles are: **[13–06]**

> "1. The deprivation of liberty shall be effected in material and moral conditions which ensure respect for human dignity and are in conformity with these rules.
> 2. The rules shall be applied impartially. There shall be no discrimination on grounds of race, colour, sex, language, religion, political or other opinion, national or social origin, birth, economic or other status. The religious beliefs and moral precepts of the group to which a prisoner belongs shall be respected.
> 3. The purposes of the treatment of persons in custody shall be such as to sustain their health and self-respect and, so far as the length of sentence permits, to

[10] *ibid.* at 600.

develop their sense of responsibility and encourage those attitudes and skills that will assist them to return to society with the best chance of leading law-abiding and self-supporting lives after their release."[11]

[13–07] Following the introduction of these European rules new prison rules, the Prison Rules 2007, which came into force on 1 October 2007, were introduced in Ireland and are largely reflective of the European rules. An overview will now be provided.

Irish Prison Rules

(i) Admission to Prison

[13–08] A person cannot be admitted to prison unless there is a valid committal order, warrant, order or certificate of detention.[12] Upon his admission to prison, the prisoner's details, including name, age, nationality, physical measurement, distinctive marks, recent injuries, health, family or guardian, the provision for committal and details of admission shall be recorded by a person designated by the Governor.[13] A family member, or guardian for a prisoner under the age of 18, shall be informed of his committal, readmission to prison, or transfer to another prison.[14] His measurements, photographs, fingerprints and palm prints can be taken on admission or at any time.[15] He shall be physically examined on admission to diagnose any illnesses, physical, mental or contagious, to see if he is fit for work, to note any recent injuries, any medication or anything which might impede integration into the prison or society post-release.[16]

[13–09] A prisoner must be given a hot bath or shower, an explanatory booklet of the rules and be met by the Governor to see that he understands the rules and entitlements.[17] The prisoner must also be informed of his potential release dates and any changes to those arising.[18] A baby may be admitted to remain with its imprisoned mother until the age of 12 months to facilitate breast feeding.[19] Items for the care and maintenance of the child may be brought to the prison at the prisoner's expense.[20] The Governor should meet with long term prisoners every two years to ensure they are aware of the available services and facilities.[21]

(ii) Searches

[13–10] The prisoner may be searched on admission[22] or at any other time where the Governor believes, on reasonable grounds, that it is necessary for the safety and good government

[11] European Prison Rules, above n 4.
[12] Prison Rules 2007, rule 3(1).
[13] r 4.
[14] r 5.
[15] r 10(1).
[16] r 11(1).
[17] rs 13 and 14.
[18] r 15.
[19] r 17.
[20] r 17(6).
[21] r 58(1).
[22] r 6(1).

of the prison, including for the purpose of confiscating prohibited items.[23] This can involve an intimate search of the prisoner's body,[24] but must be conducted with respect for the decency, privacy and dignity of the prisoner[25] and by an officer of the same sex as the prisoner.[26] It must be done in front of another officer but only as many as are necessary for the effective conduct of the search and the maintenance of good order.[27] Reasonable and proportionate force may be used where necessary though this cannot extend to invasive searching of the orifices of a prisoner's body.[28] Anything found during a search which the officer believes relates to the commission of an offence or a disciplinary offence can be seized and retained as evidence.[29] No document relating to legal advice may be seized.[30] A register of anything seized must be kept.[31] A prisoner's property or cell may be searched at any time where considered necessary for the maintenance of good order and safe and secure custody.[32]

(iii) Prisoner Property

An inventory of all articles, including money, brought into the prison by prisoners must be kept by the Governor.[33] The prisoner must be informed if any of these items are being kept in a secure place by the Governor, or given anything which prisoner is permitted to have.[34] If the prisoner has anything in his possession which is not on that list, and which the Governor feels may pose a threat to good order and safety, it may be taken from the prisoner.[35] Any item so taken can later be either given to the prisoner, returned to the person who handed it in (if it came to the prison that way) or sold with the proceeds going to the prisoner or the person who handed it in.[36] **[13–11]**

(iv) Treatment of Prisoners

Cells are to be suitable for the purposes of accommodation, including size, lighting, ventilation and fittings.[37] The Minister is to specify the maximum number of prisoners to be in a cell.[38] Certain cells are to be designated for observation.[39] All cells should have a mechanism for prisoners to attract a prison officer.[40] **[13–12]**

23 r 6(2).
24 r 6(3).
25 r 6(4).
26 r 6(5).
27 r 6(6).
28 r 6(9).
29 r 7(1).
30 r 7(2).
31 r 7(4).
32 r 53.
33 r 8.
34 r 8.
35 r 9(1).
36 r 9(2).
37 r 18(1).
38 r 18(2).
39 r 18(3).
40 r 18(4).

[13–13] A prisoner may wear his own clothing where the Governor permits and it is clean and adequate for health,[41] otherwise the prisoner must be provided with suitable clothing.[42] Facilities must be provided for cleaning clothes.[43] The prisoner must be given appropriate, clean bedding[44] and sufficient nutritious food and water,[45] including special provision for dietary needs. In so far as practicable in-cell sanitary and washing facilities should be provided.[46] Prisoners are to keep clean and shower at least once a week.[47] Hair, including facial hair, shall not be cut without a prisoner's consent.[48] Smoking and drinking alcohol is not permitted without the consent of the Governor.[49] A prisoner may not have a controlled drug or medicinal product unless prescribed by the prison doctor, psychiatrist or dentist.[50] Prison staff must keep a record of any such products.[51] Urine, saliva, oral or hair samples must be given by a prisoner where requested on the authority of the Governor for testing for drugs or alcohol.[52] A refusal to provide the sample is a breach of discipline.[53]

[13–14] Prisoners should be free to spend as much time outside their cell associating with other prisoners as practicable, at the discretion of the Governor.[54] This should include five hours of structured activity, such as work for the maintenance of the prison,[55] rehabilitation or education, five days a week.[56] Prisoners may receive gratuities as decided by the Minister for Justice[57] which can be spent within the prison or given to families.[58] Prisoners can also engage in employment with approved persons outside of the prison.[59] If a prisoner is not engaged in work or activities he is entitled to one hour exercise a day in the open air, as far as is practicable.[60] Indoor exercise equipment should be provided where possible.[61]

[13–15] Prisoners should have access to healthcare while in the prison.[62] Pregnant prisoners should give birth in a hospital outside of the prison.[63] A prisoner should be able to

41 r 21(1).
42 r 21(3).
43 r 21(2).
44 r 22.
45 r 23.
46 r 24. This is discussed further below at para 13–49.
47 r 25.
48 r 25(5).
49 r 26.
50 r 26(2).
51 r 26(3).
52 r 26(5).
53 r 26(6).
54 r 27(1).
55 r 28.
56 r 27(2).
57 r 29.
58 r 29(3).
59 r 30.
60 r 32.
61 r 32(2).
62 r 33(1).
63 r 33(2).

observe his religion as far as practicable.[64] This includes providing access to books and materials[65] and facilitating attendance at services.[66] A request to see a chaplain shall be communicated to the chaplain as soon as may be[67] and any meeting with a chaplain shall be in private.[68]

Prisoners are entitled to at least one visit a week of at least 30 minutes duration.[69] **[13–16]** Prisoners under the age of 18 are entitled to at least two such visits a week.[70] A prisoner held on remand (those individuals detained pending their trial) is entitled to one visit of at least 15 minutes duration between three and six days of a week.[71] The Governor can authorise additional visits where it would be beneficial for the prisoner's rehabilitation.[72] No articles can be exchanged between prisoners and visitors without the Governor's permission.[73] Visitors can be refused permission to visit where the Governor believes it is necessary to control entry of prohibited items, prevent conspiracy to commit an offence or for the good order of the prison.[74] Visitors may be asked for identification and have their clothing searched.[75] If a visitor is unwilling to submit to a search he can be denied the visit.[76]

If a person has been imprisoned for failure to pay a fine he shall be entitled to a visit at **[13–17]** a reasonable time from someone visiting to arrange for payment of the fine.[77] Any prisoner shall be allowed to visit with his legal advisor at any reasonable time, within view but out of hearing of a prison officer.[78] A foreign national, including an asylum seeker, shall be equally entitled to a visit from his consul.[79] Probation officers may visit for reporting purposes[80] and gardaí may visit a prisoner to identify him, or with the prisoner's consent or a court order.[81]

Where practicable the Governor can allow, as he sees fit, prisoners to communicate **[13–18]** with persons outside the prison by a device which transmits both sound and images.[82] Letters may not be written to the victim of the prisoner's crime without the prior consent of the victim.[83] Telephone calls, for which the prisoner is

---

64 r 34(1).
65 r 34(3).
66 r 34(4).
67 r 34 (7).
68 r 37(9).
69 r 35(1).
70 r 35(2).
71 r 35(3).
72 r 35(4).
73 r 36(5).
74 r 36(9).
75 r 36(8) and (10).
76 r 36(16).
77 r 37(1).
78 r 38.
79 r 39.
80 r 40.
81 r 41.
82 r 41.
83 r 45(3).

charged,[84] with friends and family are permitted as determined by the Governor.[85] The amount and rules regarding phone calls to legal advisors replicate the rules on visits.[86]

Where a prisoner is taken out of the prison, for whatever reason, staff must take every effort to ensure his privacy.[87] He shall be moved by suitable transport.[88] Prisoners of different gender should not have access to each other.[89]

[13–19] The Governor shall meet with a prisoner where he has a grievance.[90] Any decision on the complaint must be notified to the prisoner once made.[91] A prisoner can also request to meet with members of the visiting committee or an officer of the Minister, and notification of these requests must be conveyed as soon as possible.[92] If the officer of the Minister for Justice and Law Reform (the Minister), makes a recommendation which is not implemented, following receipt of the complaint, the Director General of the Prison Service may give a direction in relation to the complaint.[93]

[13–20] Prisoners sentenced to more than one month should be able to receive remission of up to a quarter for good behaviour.[94] This can be extended by the Minister to one third of the sentence.[95] This does not apply to prisoners sentenced to life imprisonment or contempt of court.[96]

(v) Control, Discipline and Sanctions

[13–21] Permitted sanctions for a prisoner are prohibitions in engaging in structured activities, communal recreation and association with other prisoners.[97] To impose one of these the Governor must believe on reasonable grounds that allowing the prisoner to engage in such activities would result in a significant threat to the maintenance of good order or safe or secure custody.[98] The period which this direction lasts can be no longer than is necessary to ensure good order.[99] It must be reviewed every seven days.[100] Records must be kept of such a decision, a copy given to the prisoner, and the doctor, chaplain and Director General (where the direction lasts for more than 21 days) shall be informed.[101]

---

84 r 46(10).
85 r 46(1).
86 r 46(4).
87 r 50(1).
88 r 50(2).
89 r 52.
90 r 55(1).
91 r 55(2).
92 rs 56 and 57.
93 r 57(5).
94 r 59(1).
95 r 59(2).
96 r 59(3).
97 r 62(1).
98 r 62(2).
99 r 62(3).
100 r 67(4).
101 r 67.

A prisoner can also be kept separate from other prisoners where he requests it or the Governor believes other prisoners are reasonably likely to cause him significant harm.[102] A record must be maintained of all prisoners kept in this way.[103] Where the Governor believes a prisoner may harm himself or others and other methods would be ineffective, he may be kept in an observation cell for 24 hours.[104] The prisoner must be visited by the doctor as soon as practicable and checked every 15 minutes by a prison officer.[105] Four such periods of 24 hours can be authorised by the Governor in consultation with the doctor.[106] Written authorisation from the Director General is required to extend such detention beyond that time frame.[107] The prisoner may be given special clothing and must be visited by the Governor and a doctor once a day.[108] This form of detention should never be used as a form of punishment.[109] [13–22]

A prisoner may be restrained by a device which restricts his movements without causing him injury where the Governor directs for up to 24 hours.[110] This can be done to prevent injury to the prisoner or others, damage to property and where accommodation without restraint would be inadequate.[111] The Director General, the doctor, the chaplain and the visiting committee must be notified when this is done.[112] The prisoner must be visited by a doctor, released if the doctor so orders and checked every 15 minutes.[113] Extensions can be granted in the same way as for solitary confinement.[114] The Governor and doctor must visit once a day.[115] [13–23]

Schedule 1 of the Rules outlines what are considered to be breaches of discipline. A lengthy list, it includes, among other things: disobeying an order of the Governor or the rules; disrespecting any staff, visitors or prisoners; handling, selling, preparing, buying or using alcohol or controlled drugs; tattooing himself or another prisoner; endangering the health of any person; bullying; obstructing a prison officer from performing his duties; threatening or bribing a prison officer; making false allegations about anyone; failing to comply with a search or a request for a sample for a drug or alcohol test; not being where he is supposed to be; setting fire to, damaging, disfiguring the prison or property therein; failing to work; having a prohibited article in his cell; selling, supplying, receiving prohibited items; escapes; being indecent; offending against good order or discipline; and encouraging another to do any of the above. [13–24]

---

[102] r 63.
[103] r 63(3).
[104] r 64.
[105] rs 64(4) and (5).
[106] r 64(6).
[107] r 64(7).
[108] rs 64(8), (9) and (10).
[109] r 64(13).
[110] rs 65(1) and (2).
[111] r 65(3).
[112] r 65(4).
[113] rs 65(5), (6) and (7).
[114] rs 65(8) and (9).
[115] rs 65(10) and (11).

[13–25] Where a breach is alleged the Governor can decide to hold an inquiry into the breach.[116] The inquiry should be held the day after the prisoner receives written notification if the Governor feels a delay would threaten the good order of the prison, otherwise within seven days, unless the Governor believes more time is necessary.[117] The inquiry shall be conducted by the Governor and the prisoner should be present.[118] The prisoner should be given an opportunity to examine the evidence against him and to reply to allegations.[119] Prior notice must be given if the prisoner wishes to call a witness and the Governor's consent is required for this to occur.[120] Interpreters should be provided if necessary.[121] The prisoner should be informed of the Governor's decision as soon as may be.[122] The Prisons Act 2007 provides the sanctions which may be imposed:

- Caution;
- Reprimand;
- Confinement in cell for no more than 3 days;
- Prohibition for up to 60 days of structured activities, visits (except those of a legal nature), sending and receiving letters, using money, possessing specified articles;
- Forfeiture of a sum of money;
- Forfeiture of up to 14 days remission;
- Postponement of payment of gratuities for up to 60 days; or,
- If the breach concerns an attempt to escape, a requirement to wear prison clothes for up to 60 days.[123]

[13–26] Numerous sanctions are forbidden as forms of punishment: collective or corporal punishment; restraints; sensory deprivation; sleep deprivation; food or drink deprivation; reduction or denial of diet; confinement in a special observation cell; placement in a room with inadequate heat, light or ventilation; a sanction of indefinite duration; or a sanction constituting cruel, inhuman or degrading treatment.[124]

[13–27] The Act also provides for appeal procedures. An appeal must be lodged within seven days to the Minister who can affirm, modify, suspend or revoke the decision of the Governor.[125] Where the sanction has included a forfeiture of remission, the prisoner can appeal to an Appeal Board,[126] established by the Minister which is independent in the performance of its functions.[127] The Appeal Board can uphold or quash the finding of the breach, affirm or quash the sanction, vary the extent of the forfeiture or

[116] r 66(2).
[117] r 67(2).
[118] r 67(3).
[119] rs 67(6) and (7).
[120] r 67(8).
[121] r 67(12).
[122] r 67(13).
[123] Prisons Act 2007, s 13(1).
[124] s 13(7).
[125] s 14.
[126] s 15(2).
[127] s 16.

substitute another sanction.[128] The Appeal Board will be constituted by a solicitor or barrister of seven years standing.[129]

Prison officers are not permitted to use force on a prisoner unless compelled to do so to prevent injury to self or others.[130] If force is used a healthcare professional must be contacted to examine the prisoner as soon as practicable.[131]

(vi) Breach of Prison Rules

While the Prison Act 2007 extensively details the disciplinary procedures where a prisoner is in breach of the Rules, the Act is completely silent as to the consequences where the prison itself is in breach of the Rules. The Rules themselves detail a grievance procedure in rs 55–57 which allow a prisoner to make his grievance known to the Governor,[132] the Visiting Committee[132] or ultimately the Minister. Where the prisoner meets with the Governor, the Governor is obliged to record the details of the complaint,[134] make a decision regarding the complaint and inform the prisoner "as soon as is practicable" following this decision of the outcome.[135] While the prisoner can seek a meeting with the Minister under r 57 in which he can appeal the decision, as the IPRT note, there is no detailed procedure regarding any appeals process, and very little is known about the nature of complaints lodged, or their outcomes.[136] The CPT in its Report highlighted the fact that prisoners had very little faith in the complaints procedure, and recommended that an independent complaints system be put in place,[137] a recommendation which the IPRT supports.[138] **[13–28]**

Having examined the operational rules which govern the workings of a prison, we shall now examine some of the issues which have arisen in Irish courts in the context of prisoners' rights.

III. Prisoners' Rights

Right to Vote

Prior to 2006, an individual imprisoned in Ireland was unlikely to be able to exercise his right to vote, unless he was on temporary release on polling day. The Supreme Court had sanctioned this interference with prisoners' rights in *Breathnach v Ireland* **[13–29]**

---

[128] s 15(6).
[129] s 16(3).
[130] r 93(2).
[131] r 93(3).
[132] r 55.
[133] r 56.
[134] r 55(3).
[135] r 55(2).
[136] Irish Penal Reform Trust, *Position Paper No 7: Complaints, Monitoring and Inspection in Prisons* (IPRT, Dublin, 2009), pp 5–6.
[137] *Report to the Irish Government on the visit to Ireland carried out by the European Committee for the Prevention of Torture and Inhuman or Degrading Treatment or Punishment (CPT) from 2 to 13 October 2006* available at: http://www.cpt.coe.int/documents/irl/2007-40-inf-eng.pdf, para 37.
[138] IPRT, above n 136, p 6.

and the Attorney General,[139] holding that there was nothing unconstitutional in restricting the voting rights of the applicant prisoner, and suggesting that it would impose unreasonable demands on administration to alter that position.

[13–30] Change was required, however, following the European Court of Human Rights (ECtHR) case of *Hirst v United Kingdom (No 2)*[140] wherein the Representation of the People Act 1983 which barred the applicant prisoner from voting in elections[141] was held to be in breach of Art 3 of Protocol 2 European Convention on Human Rights (ECHR), which insists on free elections for freedom of expression of the opinion of the people. Noting that voting is a right rather than a privilege, the ECtHR found that the measure was a blunt instrument and was disproportionate. It highlighted the fact that the provision applied to all prisoners irrespective of the length of their sentences or the nature and gravity of their offences.

[13–31] In the weeks following the *Hirst* decision, the Minister for Justice distinguished, in parliamentary questions, the Irish and British systems as there was no law in Ireland prohibiting prisoners from voting, rather the Government chose not to provide them with the means to vote on election day. This, according to the Minister, was an important legal distinction, and referring to *Breathnach*, he noted that "[t]he Supreme Court …. has held that the State is under no constitutional obligation to facilitate prisoners in the exercise of that franchise."[142]

[13–32] Nonetheless the Electoral (Amendment) Act 2006 was enacted and it now grants prisoners the right to apply for a postal vote. In determining in which constituency the prisoner will be registered, s 2 provides that he is deemed to be ordinarily resident "in the place where he …would have been residing but for his … detention in prison."

Right to Communicate

[13–33] There are two categories of written communication between a prisoner and persons outside of prison. The first is correspondence with the prisoner's legal representative; the second is all other forms of communication.

(i) Correspondence with Legal Representative

[13–34] In *Kearney v Minister for Justice*,[143] Costello J suggested:

> "it is necessary, in the interests of the security of the prison, that *all* letters, incoming and outgoing, between prisoners and their correspondents outside prison be read by the Governor or an officer deputed by him. The danger to security that might arise from unrestricted correspondence between a solicitor and client was … based on actual experience of an abuse by a solicitor of the

---

139 [2001] 3 IR 230.

140 (2006) 42 EHRR 41.

141 s 3 of the Act stated simply, "A convicted person during the time that he is detained in a penal institution in pursuance of his sentence … is legally incapable of voting at any parliamentary or local election."

142 (2006) 583 *Dail Debates* Col 175.

143 [1986] IR 116.

> solicitor-client confidential relationship. ... [T]he restriction on the right to communicate ... requiring letters to and from prisoners to be read, can reasonably be justified and is not therefore unconstitutional."[144]

However, the ECtHR in *Campbell v UK*[145] held that correspondence between a prisoner and his legal representative is privileged and not to be read by prison authorities. Nonetheless, the correspondence may be *opened* by prison officials to check for illicit materials where they have reasonable suspicion to do so, though this should be done in the presence of the prisoner. If this occurs, the principle remains that the correspondence should not be read. **[13–35]**

The *Campbell* principle now has a place in the Prison Rules which, as we discussed above, state that outgoing mail to legal representatives will not be read by prison officials, and that incoming mail will only be opened to determine its authenticity.[146] If this is to happen, the Rules provide that it will be done in the presence of the prisoner. **[13–36]**

(ii) Other Forms of Written Correspondence

While correspondence between a prisoner and his legal representative is protected by the Rules, the same cannot be said for other forms of written communication. As discussed above, where a letter is to be sent by a prisoner, the Governor may open and confiscate it where he believes that if the letter were given to the prisoner it would threaten the maintenance of good order, would facilitate criminal conduct or interfere with the course of justice. Commenting on the Rules in relation to communication, Hamilton and Kilkelly write that the provisions should be strictly interpreted in light of the need for prisoners to maintain contact with the outside world.[147] **[13–37]**

(iii) Telephone Calls

While generally prisoners are permitted to use telephones and devices which transmit both sound and images where practical, we saw above that restrictions can be placed on this. Most notably the Governor may listen to or record telephone calls, once the person with whom the prisoner is communicating has been informed that this may happen. The Governor or a Prison Officer can terminate a call. These interferences may occur in the circumstances outlined above. **[13–38]**

(iv) Communication with the Media

Mobile telephones are not permitted in prisons. Famously, however, in 2007 a prisoner in Portlaoise Maximum Security Prison telephoned the RTE Radio 1 programme *LiveLine* on a smuggled mobile phone from his cell,[148] which led to a crackdown on the possession of mobile phones in prisons. While in *Bamber v UK*[149] the ECtHR upheld a general restriction on prisoners telephoning live radio shows, Dillon-Malone asks **[13–39]**

---

[144] *ibid.* at 119.

[145] (1992) EHRR 137.

[146] This rule also applies to the other legal parties such as the judiciary and the ECtHR as listed above.

[147] Hamilton and Kilkelly, "Human Rights in Irish Prisons" [2008] JSIJ 58, p 80.

[148] "Armed robber phones talkshow" *Irish Times*, 1 May 2007.

[149] European Commission on Human Rights, App No 33742/96, Decision of 11 September 1997.

whether the extent to which rights are necessarily curtailed by imprisonment "extends to access to the media for the purposes of general political debate."[150] He opines that restricting prisoners' rights to access chat shows generally is probably justified within the terms of the ECHR, but individual prisoners may be facilitated on a matter of public importance, such as prisoners' rights or political debate.[151]

[13–40] This exact issue arose in *Holland v Governor of Portlaoise Prison*[152] where the prisoner challenged the prison policy banning communication with the media. He was seeking to highlight what he claimed was a miscarriage of justice in his case. In determining whether the blanket ban on communication was justified, McKechnie J stated that any limitation on the right to communicate "should be strictly construed with the onus of proof being on he who asserts such curtailment."[153] Due to the fact that this was a blanket ban on communication with the media, and that the Governor had given no reasons relating to security to justify the ban, the court found that it was not justified and set aside the decision of the Governor. The new Prison Rules do not address the issue of media communication by prisoners – it seems that this issue is dealt with on a case by case basis, with prison security as the determining factor.

Right to Life and Prisoner Safety

[13–41] The Committee for the Prevention of Torture (CPT) in its 2006 Report on Ireland found that "at least three of the prison establishments visited can be considered unsafe, both for the prisoners and for prison staff (notably, Limerick and Mountjoy Prisons and even St Patrick's Institution)".[154] Article 2 ECHR places a positive duty on the State to protect prisoners in their care, both in relation to acts of violence from prison officers and other prisoners.[155] It is clear that the Irish state is failing in both regards.

(i) Inter-Prisoner Violence

[13–42] Factors such as drug use, gang culture, overcrowding, poor conditions and a failure to adequately assess prisoners on committal have contributed to a growth in inter-prisoner violence in Irish prisons.[156] The CPT, documenting a culture conducive to intimidation and violence, notes that the lack of purposeful activities combined with drug use means that there is a younger, more aggressive prison population "who have little to do beside plotting how to get their next fix."[157]

[13–43] In 2006 a prisoner, Gary Douche, who had expressed concerns for his safety to prison officers, was killed in Mountjoy Prison. He had been placed in a holding cell with seven other prisoners, one of whom, Egan, had just been committed and had not been given

---

[150] Dillone-Malone, "Privacy and Media Law" in *ECHR and Irish Law,* (Kilkelly (ed.), Jordans, Bristol, 2004), p 268.
[151] *ibid.* p 269.
[152] [2004] 2 IR 573.
[153] *ibid.* at 594.
[154] *Report to the Irish Government on the Visit to Ireland carried out by the CPT from 2 to 13 October 2006*) available at http://www.cpt.coe.int/documents/irl/2007-40-inf-eng.pdf, para 38.
[155] Hamilton and Kilkelly, above n 147, p 72. See also *Keenan v UK* (2001) 33 EHRR 38 and *Edwards v UK* (2002) 35 EHRR 19.
[156] Hamilton and Kilkelly, above n 147, p 72.
[157] CPT, above n 154, para 38.

his psychiatric medication, due to a delay in carrying out his individualised risk assessment. Ultimately, he attacked Douche and killed him.[158] The holding cell in which Douche and Egan, along with 5 other inmates, were being held was not designed as accommodation, and certainly not as protective accommodation, which Douche had requested. As noted by the IPRT, the circumstances of the Douche killing mirror those of the case of *Edwards v UK*[159] where the ECtHR concluded that a similar systematic failure by the authorities contributed to the death of the prisoner.[160]

(ii) Officer-Prisoner Violence

The CPT reiterated in 2006 that, despite recommendations in earlier reports, the problem of prison officers using violence against prisoners remains. While it is appropriate to use reasonable force to control prisoners, the CPT recommended: **[13–44]**

> "prison officers must be made fully aware that the force used to control violent and/or recalcitrant prisoners should be no more than is strictly necessary and that once a prisoner has been brought under control there can be no justification for additional use of force."[161]

Indeed, this is the only standard appropriate – if a prison officer uses any more force than is reasonably necessary in the circumstances, this could amount to assault. This position now has a footing the Prison Rules, as noted above, which provide that only necessary and proportionate force should be used. However, even where there is some evidence that an assault took place, the CPT had serious concerns regarding the effectiveness of garda investigations in these circumstances.[162] The CPT has recommended the establishment of an independent complaints system,[163] which could take the form of a Prisoners Ombudsman. Such an office has been suggested in the past but it has not come to fruition to date. **[13–45]**

Right to Family Life

Imprisonment of one or other member of a family can have long lasting implications for family life. If parents are incarcerated, this necessarily limits their ability to exercise Art 42 constitutional rights in relation to their children. If a woman is incarcerated for the entirety of her child-bearing years, this may mean that she is incapable of having children. Despite the very real intrusion into family life which is afforded "inalienable and imprescriptible" protection in the Constitution, the courts justify this as a necessary implication of imprisonment. A prisoner's right to family life is also protected under Art 8 ECHR and this places an obligation on the State to maintain contact between prisoners and their families. Commenting on this issue, the CPT noted **[13–46]**

[158] "Prisoner gets life sentence for killing cellmate" *The Irish Times*, 30 June 2009. Egan was found guilty of manslaughter by reason of diminished responsibility and sentenced to life imprisonment. A Commission has been established to enquire into the killing, though at the time of writing it has not issued its report.
[159] (2002) 35 EHRR 19.
[160] IPRT, above n 1, p 7.
[161] CPT, above n 154, para 33.
[162] *ibid.* para 36.
[163] *ibid.* para 37.

that the "maintenance of prisoners' relationships with their families and friends can be of critical significance for all concerned, particularly in the context of prisoners' social rehabilitation."[164]

[13–47] In *Murray v Ireland*[165] the applicant prisoners, who were married to one another, requested conjugal visits for the purposes of having children as the wife would be unlikely to conceive (because of her age) on release. This request was denied by the Prison Governor. The couple were allowed to visit one another, but these visits were supervised. They applied to the courts for a declaration that such a denial amounted to a violation of their right to family life under Art 41, and their right to procreate, an unenumerated right they established under Art 40.3.1. The question for the court was whether the restrictions on the rights of the plaintiffs, which were a direct result of the exercise of the State's power to imprison, were constitutionally permissible. In the Supreme Court, it was noted by Finlay CJ that were the applicants successful, the ruling would apply to "any married couple one of which was imprisoned for a period of time which would exceed the date on which the wife would reach 40 years of age."[166] The Chief Justice stated

> "[i]t is quite clear that an inevitable practical and legal consequence of imprisonment as a convicted person is that a great many ... constitutional rights arising from the married status are for the period of imprisonment suspended or placed in abeyance."[167]

[13–48] The Court was of the opinion that, of all the rights afforded to the family under the Constitution, the only ones which would survive imprisonment would be "a right of communication, and that without privacy, and a right by communication to take some part in the education of children of the marriage".[168] The rights of the family protected by the Constitution were not, the Court stated, absolute, but qualified and placed in suspense on the imprisonment of one or both spouses. Nonetheless, there is an obligation to respect all other aspects of family life - indeed, in the case of *Dickson v UK*[169] the ECtHR found that the refusal by prison authorities to facilitate testing for artificial insemination breached the obligation on States Parties to respect private and family life under Art 8 ECHR. The ECtHR has also established that there is a state obligation to assist prisoners in maintaining their family life, and contact with those families.[170]

Conditions of Detention — Inhuman and Degrading Treatment: Slopping Out

[13–49] A large number of cells in Limerick and Mountjoy Prisons do not have in-cell sanitation, largely due to the age of the prisons.[171] While locked in their cells, usually during the night, prisoners use a receptacle, called a pot or potty, for urination and

164 CPT, above n 154, para 97.
165 [1985] IR 532.
166 [1991] ILRM 465 at 486.
167 *ibid.* at 487.
168 *ibid.*
169 Application No 44362/04 4 December 2007.
170 See, for example, *X v UK* (1982) 30 DR 113.
171 Limerick prison was built between 1815 and 1821 and Mountjoy prison was opened in 1850.

defecation. The pot is then carried by the prisoner the next morning and emptied down a sluice at the end of each prison corridor, a practice called "slopping-out".

In *Mulligan v Governor of Portlaoise Prison*[172] the applicant argued that the conditions in which he was imprisoned in Portlaoise prison were unconstitutional and in breach of the ECHR as he was obliged to slop out, a process referred to by the court as "archaic". Generally, Mulligan had to use his chamber pot between 8.30pm and 8.30am. For a particular 28 day period of his incarceration, Mulligan was locked up in his cell for 22 hours a day, due to a disciplinary sanction. He ate his meals and slept in the same area, and expressed concern about the unsanitary conditions, particularly the possibility of him contracting TB and Hepatitis A. He also suffered from colorectal disease, which he claimed was exacerbated by the use of the chamber pot. That said, the applicant was the sole occupant of his cell, a factor which the court found was an important feature of the case. **[13–50]**

McMenamin J noted that while imprisonment must give rise to a deprivation of rights, any such deprivation must be proportionate, and "not fall below the standards of human dignity and what is to be expected in a mature society." The Court found that the treatment of Mr Mulligan did not amount to inhuman and degrading treatment as first, there was no evidence that his life or health was put at risk, second, there was no overcrowding, and finally, there was no "evil purpose" behind the regime of slopping out. On the issue of privacy rights, the court again held that because the prisoner had a private cell, his right to privacy was not violated. Due to the fact that Mulligan had not informed prison authorities of his pre-existing medical condition, or sought to remedy his situation, his right to bodily integrity had also not been breached, and, the Court found, even if it had been breached, the lack of information on the part of the Prison Service would constitute a total defence to the claim. Particular emphasis was placed throughout the judgment on the practical implications on the Prison Service of an obligation to install in-cell sanitation, which was estimated at a cost of between €10 and €14 million, with enormous disruption to the prison itself and the service generally. Ultimately, McMenamin J found that given the conditions which governed the slopping out process in Portlaoise Prison, and the fact that Mr Mulligan had failed complain about the process while in Prison, the application was to be dismissed.

In a similar, though not identical case, *Napier v Scottish Ministers*,[173] the Court of Session in Scotland found that the practice of slopping-out combined with overcrowding amounted to an attack on human dignity in violation of Art 3 ECHR. Hamilton and Kilkelly note that the Scottish case was not decided solely on the basis of slopping out, but that other factors also played a part in the decision, including the fact that the applicant shared a cell, had little in the way of structured activity and had eczema which became infected in prison.[174] **[13–51]**

---

172 [2010] IEHC 269.

173 [2005] SC 207. See Clissmann "Degrading Treatment in Prison" (2004) 98 (8) LSG 7.

174 Hamilton and Kilkelly, above n 147, p 74.

[13–52] A similar case arose in Northern Ireland in *Martin v Northern Ireland Prison Service.*[175] Here, however, the case was decided on the basis of Art 8 privacy rights, the High Court finding that the prisoner was not being subjected to inhuman or degrading treatment, but rather that the lack of in-cell sanitation merely caused him annoyance and frustration.[176] While a breach was found, the plaintiff was granted only declaratory relief, as "the financial consequences of even a modest award when seen in the light of the possible implications in relation to the large number of prisoners going through the prison system" was enormous and not in the public interest.[177]

The *Martin* and *Napier* cases were referred to by the Irish High Court in *Mulligan*, but distinguished on their facts. *Napier*, the Court found, was decided on the basis of the cumulative effect of the conditions, rather than the slopping-out issue alone. The Court also noted that in *Napier*, the respondents could have "easily" modernised the sanitation facilities, which was in contrast to the position in Portlaoise Prison. *Martin*, the Court found, could be distinguished on the basis that the regime in operation in that particular prison was "insensitive and uncaring" – again, it was not slopping out *per se* which was deemed inappropriate, but rather the manner in which the practice was managed.

That said, the case does not close the door on a suitable applicant bringing a claim on constitutional and ECHR grounds on the issue of slopping out in the future. If, for example, a prisoner shared a cell which was small, in a prison which generally had low standards of hygiene, and had limited time outside the cell during the day with limited availability for recreation or education, and had to urinate or defecate in the presence of others in conditions of poor ventilation, McMenamin J in his judgment implicitly indicated that such a prisoner may have a case under Arts 3 and 8 ECHR.

IV. Prison Monitoring

[13–53] While individual prisoners have forced changes in prison systems by bringing individual cases, prison monitoring bodies more generally assess prison standards and make recommendations regarding prison conditions. The CPT monitors States Parties' compliance with the European Convention for the Prevention of Torture and Inhuman or Degrading Treatment or Punishment. Article 7 of the Convention provides that the CPT has the power to undertake site visits to assess places of detention. In doing so, it assesses the conditions of the various institutions as well as interviewing prisoners and staff, and consulting with other interested parties.[178] The latest visit of the CPT took place between 25 January and 5 February 2010, though the Report of this visit has yet to be published at the time of writing.

---

[175] [2006] NIQB 1. For a note on the case, see Clissmann "Magilligan, Slopping Out and Art 8 of the ECHR" (2006) 100(3) LSG 11.

[176] [2006] NIQB 1 at paras 11 and 25. This is despite the fact that for a period of time some prisoners used black bags rather than pots as toilet facilities.

[177] *ibid.* at para 42.

[178] For an analysis of the work of the CPT in Ireland, see Hamilton and Kilkelly, above n 147. They note that in particular, one of the main drawbacks of the process is that the States Parties "face little if any censure" on foot of the reporting mechanisms. *ibid.* p 63.

Domestically, there is a Prison Inspectorate which has been in operation since 2002. This position now has a statutory basis in the Prisons Act 2007, and while this was a welcome development, Hamilton and Kilkelly note that there are concerns around the ability of the Minister for Justice to edit or censor the Report of the Inspectorate on grounds of the public interest and security concerns.[179] Another criticism is that the Inspector cannot investigate or adjudicate complaints from prisoners, and it has been noted that the continuing failure of the legislature to establish an independent office of Prison Ombudsman is "highly problematic" in this context.[180] **[13–54]**

Visiting Committees also exist for individual prisons, but as Rogan notes, because the Committees report on individual prisons, "it is difficult to get a sense of the nature of the prison system overall".[181] Ultimately, Rogan argues that an independent Ombudsman for Prisons and Prisoners is vital to shine a "brighter spotlight" on prison conditions today – even if we do not like what is revealed. **[13–55]**

V. Conclusion

At the beginning of this chapter, we examined the European Prison Rules, which set out the basic principles aimed at setting a minimum standard for prisons. As we have seen, many commentators and international bodies are of the opinion that the Irish prison system does not meet these minimum standards. Indeed, Hamilton and Kilkelly go so far as to state that "the treatment of those detained in Irish prisons appears worryingly out of line in a range of areas."[182] Whether Irish policy makers and the Irish prison service will begin to realise that imprisonment *is* punishment rather than *for* punishment remains to be seen. Ultimately, an Ombudsman for Prisons and Prisoners could go some way to address some of the endemic problems in Irish prisons today, as could refurbishment of existing, older prisons. **[13–56]**

---

[179] *ibid.* p 82.

[180] *ibid.* p 84.

[181] Rogan "Visiting Committees and Accountability in the Irish Prison System: Some Proposals for Reform" (2009) 16(1) DULJ 298, p 304.

[182] Hamilton and Kilkelly, above n 147, p 84.

Chapter 14
Miscarriages of Justice

In this final chapter we examine the final stage of the criminal process for a convicted person – an application for a declaration of miscarriage of justice. This involves claims by a convicted individual that he has been convicted in error when the ordinary appeals mechanism[1] has been fully exhausted. **[14–01]**

There have been a number of high profile instances of wrongful convictions in Ireland over the past decades, including the cases of Nicky Kelly,[2] Peter Pringle,[3] Nora Wall (Sr Dominic)[4] and Frank Shortt.[5] There have also been a number of cases where wrongful convictions have been narrowly avoided, including the cases of Dean Lyons,[6] **[14–02]**

1 See Chapter Ten.

2 [1983] IR 1. Nicky Kelly was convicted of the Sallins Mail Train Robbery on the basis of confession evidence, despite continued claims of *inter alia* severe physical abuse during detention. He was ultimately granted a presidential pardon and awarded compensation.

3 2 Frewen 57. Peter Pringle was convicted of murdering a garda despite garda misconduct throughout the investigation and trial. His conviction was ultimately quashed.

4 [2005] IECCA 140. Nora Wall, also known as Sister Dominic, was convicted of rape and imprisoned for life but later was granted a certificate of miscarriage of justice.

5 [2002] 2 IR 696. Frank Shortt was convicted of drugs offences and served three years in prison before being granted a certificate for a miscarriage of justice.

6 Dean Lyons, a heroin addict with borderline mental disability, confessed to murders in Grangegorman in 1997 to which someone else later confessed. Following his death the *Report of the Commission of Investigation into the Dean Lyons Case* (Stationery Office, Dublin, 2006), conducted by Mr Birmingham SC, found that while there was no deliberate breach of his rights, Dean Lyons had been asked inappropriate leading questions during his interrogation.

the Hayes family[7] and Frank McBrearty.[8] These among other cases are leading to a growing body of jurisprudence on the topic with a number of important decisions by the Supreme Court. Alongside the judicial pronouncements, tribunal reports[9] have highlighted inadequacies in this regard in the criminal justice system.

[14–03] This chapter will place the discussion of Irish law within a broader context by considering what the term "miscarriage of justice" means with reference to international literature. It will then review the development of the law in Ireland, analyse the Criminal Procedure Act 1993 which now regulates this area and consider the interpretation of this Act by the courts. Ultimately, the struggle between a desire for finality in the criminal process, and Blackstone's ratio that it is "better that ten guilty persons escape, than that one innocent suffer", will be highlighted.[10]

I. What is a Miscarriage of Justice?

[14–04] After the traditional appeals process has been exhausted, individuals may seek to continue to challenge their convictions. As finality of decisions is central to the legitimacy of the criminal justice system, ordinarily the courts do not permit limitless appeals. In more recent times special procedures have been introduced for cases which may be considered "miscarriages of justice" in which it would be inherently unjust not to permit further appeal or investigation. Determining which cases fall within the term "miscarriage of justice", and who is permitted recourse to any further appeal, is contested.

[14–05] Greer defines the term miscarriage of justice as "occasions upon which the justifications offered for a finding of guilt or a 'non finding of guilt' are seriously defective."[11] Justifications in this context include the evidence upon which the guilty verdict was based, or the way in which the trial process was conducted. The term can include people who are factually innocent; but also those whose rights were violated in such a way in the process of conviction that the conviction should not have occurred and the person should be considered procedurally innocent (though he may be factually guilty of the crime). The inclusion of procedurally, and not necessarily factually, innocent individuals within the term miscarriage of justice is, however,

---

[7] In 1984 Joanne Hayes and her family all falsely confessed to the murder of a baby. The *Report of the Tribunal of Inquiry into the 'Kerry Babies Case'* by Mr Justice Kevin Lynch (Stationery Office, Dublin, 1985), failed to find fault with the conduct of gardaí involved, an outcome which has been heavily criticised; see Inglis, *Truth Power and Lies: Irish Society and the case of the Kerry Babies* (UCD Press, Dublin, 2003).

[8] Frank McBrearty was wrongfully accused of the murder of Richard Barron who died in October 1996, subsequent to a false confession made in custody, considered by the Morris Tribunal. See *Report on the Detention of 'Suspects' Following the Death of the Late Richard Barron on the 14th October 1996 and Related Issues* (Stationery Office, Dublin, 2006).

[9] For example, *Report on the Detention of 'Suspects' Following the Death of the Late Richard Barron on the 14th October 1996 and Related Issues* (Stationery Office, Dublin, 2006); *Report of the Tribunal of Inquiry into the 'Kerry Babies Case'* (Stationery Office, Dublin, 1985), *Report of the Commission of Investigation into the Dean Lyons Case* (Stationery Office, Dublin, 2006).

[10] *Commentaries on the Laws of England* (1769).

[11] Greer, "Miscarriages of Justice Reconsidered" [1994] 57 MLR 58, p 61.

abhorrent to many,[12] though as we shall see the Irish courts have interpreted it in this way.

Why Do Miscarriages of Justice Occur?

Schehr notes six key causes of miscarriages of justice: police and prosecutorial misconduct, often linked to 'tunnel vision'; false eyewitness identification; false confessions; junk science; ineffective assistance of counsel; and snitch, or jailhouse testimony.[13] To this Naughton adds ineffective summing up by the trial judge.[14] Often it is a combination of these causes: police with tunnel vision use oppressive techniques to secure a false confession and ineffective counsel fails to argue this point adequately at trial – this as we will see is certainly true in an Irish context. [14–06]

As to why these problems arise, Zalman *et al* explain that they can occur due to human error or negligence, or more ominously, through corrupt and criminal behaviour.[15] Huff *et al*[16] have suggested that a "crime control" approach may be the reason why false confessions make it to trial, why the police engage in misconduct or why jailhouse testimony is accepted in court: because the drive to secure a conviction outweighs the means by which it is secured. It has been noted by some academics that in periods in which crime control takes prominence over due process models of the criminal justice system, miscarriages of justice are more likely to occur.[17] [14–07]

State Responses to Miscarriages of Justice

Ideally mechanisms to respond to allegations of miscarriages of justice should be provided by states to enable those who wish to make such a claim to have their cases heard or reviewed. States should review any decisions made to identify aspects of the system in need of reform. The manner in which states respond to claims of wrongful convictions can be categorised in a number of ways, from an independent review body, such as the Criminal Case Review Commission (CCRC) in the UK, to a modern form of the power of pardon, as operates in New Zealand. Traditionally, Ireland operated a system of pardon through the President. Today, however, as we will now explore, Ireland is quite unusual in its provision of direct access to the courts after the traditional appeals mechanism has been exhausted. [14–08]

---

[12] See Poveda, "Estimating Wrongful Convictions" (2001) 18 *Justice Quarterly* 689; Naughton, *Rethinking Miscarriages of Justice: Beyond the Tip of the Iceberg* (Palgrave Macmillan, Hampshire, 2007); Walker and Starmer, *Miscarriages of Justice: A Review of Justice in Error* (Blackstone Press, London, 1999); Nobles and Schiff, *Understanding Miscarriages of Justice* (Oxford University Press, Oxford, 2000).

[13] Schehr, "The Criminal Cases Review Commission as a State Strategic Selection Mechanism" (2005) 42 *American Criminal Law Review* 1289.

[14] Naughton, *Rethinking Miscarriages of Justice: Beyond the Tip of the Iceberg* (Palgrave Macmillan, Hampshire, 2007), p 60.

[15] Zalman, Smith and Kiger "Official's Estimates of the Incidence of 'Actual Innocence' Convictions" (2008) 25 *Justice Quarterly* 72, p 73.

[16] Huff, Rattner and Sagarin, "Guilty Until Proven Innocent: Wrongful Conviction and Public Policy (1986) 32 *Crime and Delinquency* 518.

[17] Poveda, "Estimating Wrongful Convictions" (2001) 18 *Justice Quarterly* 689, p 705.

II. Constitutional Power of Pardon in Ireland

[14–09] Prior to 1993, the only avenue for redress was to seek a presidential pardon. The President is granted a power of pardon under Art 13.6 of the Constitution which also provides for commutation and remission of sentences. Unlike the United States President, who has broad discretion to grant pardons,[18] the Irish President grants such pardons "on the advice of the government", a constitutionally polite way of providing that the President can only grant a pardon where instructed to by the Government. Further, under Art 13.6, the power can be conferred by law on other authorities. For example, s 23 of the Criminal Justice Act 1951 states that

> "Except in capital cases, the Government may commute or remit, in whole or in part, any punishment imposed by a Court exercising criminal jurisdiction, subject to such conditions as they may think proper."

[14–10] This power was delegated further to the Minister for Justice and for a considerable period, was used liberally.[19] The exercise of the power was challenged in *Brennan v Minister for Justice*[20] where evidence was established that the Minister routinely granted remission of fines on application to his office, creating what Casey describes as a "parallel or alternative system of justice to that provided for by Article 34."[21] Agreeing with counsel, Geoghegan J stated:

> "Article 13, s. 6 presupposes that the power of remission and commutation may only be exercised in exceptional circumstances such as where there are particular grounds for clemency or where there are other special factors which would justify an interference with the judicial independence guaranteed by the Constitution."[22]

[14–11] The presidential power of pardon, on the other hand, has only been exercised on three occasions in the State: in 1940 for Thomas Quinn, in 1943 for Walter Brady[23] and in the case of Nicky Kelly who was convicted in the early 1980s for the Sallins Mail Train robbery, alongside three other men. Mr Kelly protested his innocence and fled the country when it appeared he was to be convicted.[24] When the other defendants, Breathnach and McNally, were released on appeal he returned to the country and was imprisoned. He went on hunger strike and in 1984 was released on humanitarian grounds. In 1992 he was granted a presidential pardon and awarded over £750,000 in compensation.

---

[18] President Clinton, for example, granted 200 pardons in his last days in office, as did George W. Bush in the same period. Perhaps most controversially, in 1974 President Ford pardoned former President Nixon for his actions which led to the Watergate scandal.

[19] Walsh, *Criminal Procedure* (Round Hall, Dublin, 2002), p 1135.

[20] [1995] 1 IR 612.

[21] Casey, *Constitutional Law in Ireland* (3rd ed., Round Hall, Dublin, 2000), p 248.

[22] *ibid.* p 630.

[23] Both cases cited by O'Donnell, 436 *Dáil Debates* Col 901.

[24] See generally, McGarry, *When Justice Slept: Nicky Kelly and the True Story Behind the Sallins Mail Train Robbery* (Liffey Press, Dublin, 2006).

It is unclear whether the effect of the pardon is to simply relieve the individual of the punishments attaching to the conviction,[25] or whether it replaces a verdict of guilty with not guilty.[26] In 1990 a Committee of Enquiry discussed the scope of the presidential pardon, and assessed the terms of the two earlier pardons in the 1940s. It concluded that the effect is to negative guilt and blame, concluding: "It seems to us that the effect of a pardon in such terms is to clear the person from all infamy."[27] In an earlier report, however, it was argued that the term "pardon" could not be used in the context of a wrongful conviction, as **[14–12]**

> "it suggests that he had done something for which a pardon was needed and that a pardon, unlike a retrial and acquittal, does not conclusively establish the legal innocence of the person concerned nor make the conviction void *ab initio.*"[28]

It would appear that in an Irish context at least, the effect of a pardon is dependent on the terminology of the pardon itself: it may simply discharge the individual of penalties incurred on foot of a conviction,[29] or may go so far as to pronounce that the individual "did not commit and had no part or lot in the commission of the crime with which he was charged."[30] However, McDowell questions whether a free pardon in fact infringes the constitutional doctrine of the separation of powers: **[14–13]**

> "Criminal convictions are not *private* rights: they are adjudications of a public kind. If the Constitution permits the public, through the Executive, to solemnly surrender, or abandon, a court order of a public kind convicting someone of crime, and permits, in so doing, that the convict should thereafter be regarded in public as though he had never been convicted, what affront is there to the courts, the judiciary, or the administration of justice?"[31]

In the case of *Brennan,*[32] while the court held that the commutation of punishment did not amount to a breach of the doctrine of separation of powers, it did not rule on whether the power encompasses a right to restore innocence to the individual.

---

[25] In *R v Foster* [1985] QB 115 the Court held that the power of pardon does not include a power to set aside a conviction.

[26] In the United States case of *ex parte Garland* 71 US 333 (1866) the Supreme Court held that the power of pardon "releases the punishment and blots out of existence the guilt".

[27] *Report of Committee to Enquire into Certain Aspects of Criminal Procedure* (Stationery Office, Dublin, 1990), p 18.

[28] *Report of the Attorney General's Committee on the Constitution* (Stationery Office, Dublin, 1968) as quoted from Hogan and Whyte, *Kelly: The Irish Constitution* (4th ed., Butterworths, Dublin, 2003), p 213.

[29] The language used in the 1943 pardon was "that he shall henceforth stand released and discharged from all penalties, forfeitures, and disqualifications incident to or consequent on his said conviction... as if he had not been so charged or convicted."

[30] These were the terms used in the presidential pardon in 1940 of Thomas Quinn. See *Report of Committee to Enquire into Certain Aspects of Criminal Procedure* (Stationery Office, Dublin, 1990), p 17.

[31] McDowell, "Pardon: An Adequate Response to Injustice?" (1991) 1(1) ICLJ 1, p 6.

[32] [1995] 1 IR 612.

[14–14] While there may be arguments made from the perspective of the separation of powers, if, as in Canada, the power is used sparingly,[33] where considerations of justice, humanity and compassion override the normal administration of justice, the use of the pardon in this way is acceptable. Examples of such occasions might be in relation to a posthumous application, where an individual is terminally ill, or where the evidence of innocence is so overwhelming that a formal apology and pardon from the State is the only means of granting the applicant the absolution he or she deserves.

III. Impetus for Change

[14–15] Up to and including the time of Nicky Kelly's pardon, the presidential pardon remained the only operational procedure for having a miscarriage of justice declared in Ireland. A number of cases prior to this time refer to miscarriages of justice but all resulted in the conviction being overturned on an ordinary appeal.[34] That a miscarriage of justice declaration could only be granted by the President meant it was inaccessible to most individuals. In Nicky Kelly's case it took nearly ten years to be granted. Further, there was no statutory right to compensation attaching to the presidential pardon, although it was granted on a discretionary basis in the Kelly case.

[14–16] In England and Wales the issue of miscarriages of justice came to a head in the late 1980s through the so-called "Irish cases". In 1989 the Guildford Four were released after 15 years in prison, and the following year both the Birmingham Six and the Maguire Seven were also released. The Royal Commission on Criminal Justice set up in their wake reported in 1993[35] which led to the creation of the CCRC in 1997, a body to which individuals who claim wrongful conviction may apply for consideration. The CCRC makes recommendations to the Court of Appeal for reconsideration of the case, where appropriate. In operation for over ten years, the Commission has been lauded internationally as an independent body which assesses claims of miscarriages of justice, despite difficulties with resourcing.[36]

[14–17] From an international perspective, Ireland is bound by the International Covenant on Civil and Political Rights which requires, under Art 14(6):

> "When a person has by a final decision been convicted of a criminal offence and when subsequently his conviction has been reversed or he has been pardoned on the ground that a new or newly discovered fact shows conclusively that there has been a miscarriage of justice, the person who has suffered punishment as a result of such conviction shall be compensated according to

---

[33] Under s 748(3) of the Criminal Code. See further National Parole Board *Factsheet on Clemecy*, available at http://www.npb-cnlc.gc.ca/infocntr/factsh/man_14-eng.shtml#6.

[34] For example, *People (AG) v Grey* [1944] 1 IR 326; *People (AG) v Carney and Mulcahy* [1955] IR 324; *People (AG) v Marshall* [1956] IR 79; *People (AG) v Flynn* [1963] IR 255; *People (AG) v O'Loughlin* [1979] IR 85.

[35] Royal Commission *Report on Criminal Justice* (Cm 2263, HMSO, London, 1993). Also known as the *Runciman Report*.

[36] For an examination of the work of the Commission over its first ten years, see Elks, *Righting Miscarriages of Justice? Ten Years of the Criminal Case Review Commission* (Justice, London, 2008).

> law, unless it is proved that the non-disclosure of the unknown fact in time is wholly or partly attributable to him."

Further, Protocol 7 of the European Convention on Human Rights (ECHR) states under Art 2 that everyone convicted of an offence is entitled to an appeal and, under Art 3, that where a new or newly discovered fact shows that there has been a miscarriage of justice an applicant shall be compensated for any punishment endured. **[14–18]**

In 1989 a Committee was established by the Irish Government to determine the need for an additional appeals procedure, due to concerns emerging domestically following the release in Britain of the Guildford Four as well as the Nicky Kelly and the Kerry Babies cases. The Minister for Justice established a Committee of Inquiry, under Mr Justice Frank Martin, to examine both the need for a system of reviewing alleged miscarriages of justice and the use of inculpatory statements in court. The Martin Report, published in 1990, acknowledged a variety of reasons for the occurrence of miscarriages of justice including mistaken identity, emerging problems with scientific evidence and the emergence of new evidence. The Committee determined that the Irish system did not at that time offer any relief and so: **[14–19]**

> "in consequence, it seems to us that to cater for those rare cases in which substantial doubt as to the correctness of a conviction may arise, the concept of justice calls for a procedure wherein the entire matter, including such new evidence as may have come to light, may be fully and publicly investigated."[37]

The Committee proceeded to examine the options for review systems available to them and rejected a system whereby a case was referred to the courts, as the grounds for review of the case may be based on evidence which would not be admissible in a court of law.[38] The Committee concluded that the establishment of "an independent body with statutory powers of inquiry is by far the most effective manner of dealing with the situation."[39] This body would sit in public, have powers under the Tribunals of Inquiry Act, consist of one or more persons and be in a position to appoint its own counsel if so needed. The Attorney General would be the gatekeeper to the system with applications made to him for consideration as to whether referral to the Inquiry was appropriate. Having considered the evidence, the Board of Inquiry would express an opinion on whether doubt existed "as to the propriety of the conviction" on which the Government could decide what action to take.[40] The Committee also called for statutory compensation for those victims of miscarriages of justice. **[14–20]**

Three years later the Criminal Procedure Bill 1993 was published, the framework of which differed substantially from the Martin Report's recommendations by proposing a court-based remedy. While the Government accepted that there might be some cases in which inadmissible evidence was relied on, it anticipated that in many instances the evidence would be such that a court could deal with the case. For the first time the **[14–21]**

[37] *Report of Committee to Enquire into Certain Aspects of Criminal Procedure* (Stationery Office, Dublin, 1990) p 10.
[38] *ibid.* p 11.
[39] *ibid.* p 12.
[40] *ibid.*

Court of Criminal Appeal was granted the power to reopen a case which it had already decided.

[14–22] There were many benefits to this proposal: it excluded political involvement which remained at that point engrained in the UK system and it allowed anyone with such a claim to make a direct application to the court. The concerns held by the Martin Committee about the use of the courts were addressed through the provision of a number of alternative mechanisms including a petition to the Minister for Justice for a pardon and awarding the government the power to establish a committee of inquiry in such cases. These latter options would cover situations in which the evidence did not meet the standards required by courts. However only the courts retain the power to overturn a conviction under the legislation. The opposition challenged the use of a court procedure during the debates on the legislation, with Deputy McDowell arguing that "the courts, by definition, have a vested interest in upholding their dignity and in upholding their previous decisions".[41] He continued to express substantial concern at the potential impact on the criminal justice system:

> "It will mean that every jury verdict will not be the end of the road; rather, it will be the start of a long battle where people will be furiously trying to establish their innocence by producing new evidence and explaining why they could not produce it before. The Irish Court of Criminal Appeal will be brought into disrepute because it will find itself in the position of either accepting plausible perjury and ordering a retrial or assessing the truthfulness of that evidence, in which case it will substitute itself for the jury."[42]

In spite of these fears, the legislation was passed in late 1993.

IV. Criminal Procedure Act 1993

[14–23] This Act for the first time provides a statutory mechanism for those who wish to claim that they have been wrongfully convicted. It provides a mechanism for review of an alleged miscarriage of justice by the Court of Criminal Appeal and outlines the powers and procedures for such an appeal. It provides a statutory power to petition the Minister for Justice for a pardon and allows for the establishment of a committee of inquiry into such a case. It also regulates the provision of compensation where a miscarriage of justice has been declared.

Review by Court of Criminal Appeal

[14–24] Section 2 of the Criminal Procedure Act 1993 states that a person who has been convicted on indictment or following a guilty plea can, following appeals, apply to the Court of Criminal Appeal to have his sentence quashed where he "alleges that a new or newly-discovered fact shows that there has been a miscarriage of justice in relation to the conviction.".

[14–25] This provides an individual with direct access to the Court of Criminal Appeal where he has evidence of a 'new or newly-discovered fact', discussed below. The court can

[41] 434 *Dáil Debates* Col 447.
[42] *ibid.* at Col 451.

quash the conviction if it is satisfied that this fact shows there has been a miscarriage of justice. The process can be availed of by someone who has been convicted on indictment or who pleaded guilty and was sent forward for trial, so convictions from the District Court are excluded from this process.[43] The fact that a retrial has been held is no bar to this procedure. The sole requirement in terms of other cases is that there must be no criminal proceedings pending in relation to the case.[44]

The procedure followed by the Court on a s 2 application is very similar to an appeal against conviction or sentence. The courts are keen for it to be a co-operative, rather than antagonistic process, encouraging both sides to make full disclosure prior to the hearing: so, for instance, in *People (DPP) v Pringle* the Court made an order for full discovery.[45] The jurisdiction of the Court in s 2 applications is broad: it can affirm the conviction, quash the conviction and make no further order, quash the conviction and order a retrial or quash the conviction and substitute a conviction for some other offence or sentence.[46] In *People (DPP) v Meleady*[47] the Court stated **[14–26]**

> "the Court takes it as clear at the outset that its jurisdiction in a case such as the present is properly invoked when a convicted person who has previously appealed unsuccessfully against his conviction alleges that a new or newly-discovered fact shows that there has been a miscarriage of justice in relation to the conviction and applies to the court for an order quashing the conviction... Thereafter, the application is to be treated 'for all purposes' as an appeal to the court against the conviction. In the result, the Court is empowered to affirm or quash the conviction or to order a re-trial as though it were dealing with an appeal by the well established machinery already in place."[48]

So if an applicant "gets his foot in the door" with a new fact then it is not the case that unless he can show there has been a miscarriage of justice there can be no relief. The jurisprudence of the courts to date indicates that there are three central questions which a court facing such an application asks itself: Is there a new or newly discovered fact? Does this fact make the conviction unsound? Does it go so far as to show a miscarriage of justice? These will now be considered in turn. **[14–27]**

(i) New or Newly Discovered Fact

Under the legislation, a new fact means a fact which was known to the convicted person at the time of the trial or appeal in relation to which he can reasonably explain the lack of evidence. A newly discovered fact is one which was discovered, or came to the notice of, the convicted person after the appeal proceedings. It could also be a fact which he knew at the time but did not appreciate the significance of. The first step taken by the Court of Criminal Appeal when an application is made under s 2 is to **[14–28]**

---

[43] This is not to say that miscarriages of justice cannot occur in the District Court, but they are limited to availing of the other provisions within the Act.

[44] Civil proceedings relating to the case are no bar to an application.

[45] Unreported, Court of Criminal Appeal, 16 May 1995.

[46] Criminal Procedure Act 1993, s 3(1).

[47] [1995] 2 IR 517.

[48] *ibid.* at 541.

determine whether either such fact exists. To assist in these evidential requirements the Court can direct the Gardaí to conduct further investigation.[49]

[14–29] In *People (DPP) v Meleady*[50] evidence relating to the identification of the defendants by the victims and of forensic testing conducted on the crime scene was not disclosed to the defence at trial. The Court of Criminal Appeal ruled that these could be considered newly discovered facts. Equally, in *People (DPP) v Pringle*[51] the non-disclosure of information relating to tests on a blood sample was found by the court to be a newly discovered fact. In *DPP v Michael Joseph Kelly*[52] the Court of Criminal Appeal was satisfied that post-mortem photographs which the pathologist had relied upon in his probative evidence but had previously been undisclosed to the defence constituted newly discovered evidence.

[14–30] In *People (DPP) v McDonagh,*[53] the applicant wished to introduce as a newly discovered fact, a signed statement by his co-accused made to a prison chaplain which exculpated the applicant from all blame in the crime. The Court, however, ruled that it could not consider this a newly discovered fact as evidence of this statement to the chaplain had not been supported, as required, and the co-accused was unwilling to make a statement to this effect.[54] Sufficient evidence to support any alleged new or newly discovered fact is therefore required.

[14–31] The Court of Criminal Appeal in *People (DPP) v Shortt (No 2)*[55] accepted as a newly discovered fact an original statement by a garda, with annotations on it, which proved that the garda had perjured himself at the trial. His evidence had been central to the conviction.

[14–32] In terms of what could be considered new or newly discovered facts, scope exists for development in this area as DNA testing is advanced and individuals may seek to consult privately with forensic testing services. Walsh further raises the point that a decision of the Supreme Court or a European Court, which affects the original conviction, could count as a newly discovered fact.[56]

(ii) Relationship of New/Newly Discovered Fact to the Outcome

[14–33] The presence of a new fact or newly discovered fact is not in itself probative of a miscarriage of justice. In assessing the impact of the new fact the Court has, to date, focused on two potential impacts: on the direction taken at trial and on the decision of the jury.

[14–34] The case of *DPP v Gannon*[57] clarified that the function of the Court in such an application is to evaluate the "new fact" and its relationship to the original conviction.

---

49 Criminal Procedure Act 1993, s 3(3)(a).
50 [1995] 2 IR 517.
51 Unreported, Court of Criminal Appeal, 16 May 1995.
52 (2009) IECCA 56.
53 [1996] 1 IR 305.
54 Such a case, where the courts evidential requirements cannot be met, may instead be suited for the petition for pardon application to the Minister.
55 [2002] 2 IR 696.
56 Walsh, above n 19, p 1216.
57 [1997] IR 40.

That case involved an allegation of a miscarriage of justice in a rape case. The alleged newly discovered fact was the victim's description of her attacker which had been included in documents which had not been shown to the accused at trial. The Court of Appeal dismissed the application, stating that even if the accused had that evidence he could not have chosen to cross-examine the victim and so it did not affect the approach taken at trial. But the Court certified a question of exceptional public importance to be sent to the Supreme Court, questioning whether they should make their decision on the basis of the approach which the defence took at trial or otherwise. In the Supreme Court, Blayney J stated that the obligation of the Court of Criminal Appeal "was to embark on an objective evaluation of the newly-discovered facts to determine whether they were such as to render the conviction unsafe and unsound".[58] The Supreme Court did not accept the approach taken by the Court of Criminal Appeal which considered whether the new fact would have changed the outcome given the approach which the defence took at trial. The Court would have to take into account

> "the course that the defence might have taken had it been aware in advance of the trial of the existence of the newly-discovered fact, and the possibility that a different approach by the defence might have led to an acquittal... The Court cannot have regard solely to the course taken by the defence at trial."[59]

In this case the Supreme Court did not believe that such an analysis led to the conclusion that the conviction was unsafe: "It would not have enabled the defence to present the case to the jury in any different light".[60] **[14–35]**

In *People (DPP) v Pringle*[61] the accused had been convicted in the Special Criminal Court for murdering two gardaí on the basis of confession evidence and sentenced to death. This sentence was later commuted by the President to 40 years penal servitude. His appeal to the Court of Criminal Appeal was unsuccessful. Both at trial and on appeal the defendant challenged the accuracy of the statement on which the prosecution had heavily relied. However, evidence later came to light that raised questions about the credibility of the two gardaí who supposedly took the confession. On his s 2 application the Court of Criminal Appeal, quashing the conviction, stated that had the trial court been aware of this fact then it *may well have* given rise to a reasonable doubt in relation to probative evidence. **[14–36]**

In *DPP v McDonagh*[62] the court stated **[14–37]**

> "What is required is that he establish that if the court of trial had had available to it the new or newly-discovered fact at the time of the trial then there would be reason to believe that the court might have entertained a doubt in relation to the accused's guilt. There is no necessity for the applicant to go so far as to

[58] [1997] 1 IR 40 at 46.
[59] [1997] IR 40 at 47.
[60] *ibid.* at 54.
[61] Unreported, Court of Criminal Appeal, 16 May 1995.
[62] [1996] 1 IR 305.

show that the court would have entertained the doubt. All that is required is that a genuine doubt might have been created."[63]

[14–38] In *Kelly* the Court reinforced that the fact "must be such as would have genuinely enabled the defence to raise a doubt in the minds of a jury. It does not contemplate remote, hypothetical or fanciful propositions".[64]

[14–39] In determining then whether the new or newly discovered fact renders the conviction unsafe the Court is not restricted to assessing the fact in light of the approach taken by the defence and it does not have to be satisfied that the fact would have produced a different result from the jury, just that it was of such probative value that it may have raised a doubt from the jury. If satisfied of that, the court may provide relief, though for a certificate of miscarriage of justice to be granted, the standard will be different. An example of this is the *Pringle* decision in which the court declared the conviction unsound, quashed the conviction but refused to rule that a miscarriage of justice had occurred. Instead the Court ordered a retrial, to which the DPP entered a *nolle prosequi*. A significant consequence of this decision was that compensation could not be awarded.[65]

[14–40] In *People (DPP) v Meleady*,[66] discussed more fully below, the Court of Criminal Appeal ordered the defendants' convictions to be quashed but refused to certify a miscarriage of justice, stating that just because the convictions were unsound it did not mean that a miscarriage of justice had occurred. The Court ruled that the case could not be considered a miscarriage of justice where the jury had not heard the evidence in question. This was appealed to the Supreme Court who ruled that, on the facts, the Court of Criminal Appeal had erred in law in this finding,[67] although a decision to quash a conviction does not necessarily mean that a miscarriage of justice had occurred.

(iii) What is a Miscarriage of Justice?

[14–41] For a certificate of miscarriage of justice to be granted, entitling the applicant to compensation, the court will have to be satisfied that the new or newly discovered fact shows that there was a miscarriage of justice. The legislation does not define this term and assessing what cases should be considered within this term has become a primary focus of the case law to date.

[14–42] The case of *People (DPP) v Meleady*,[68] colloquially known as the case of 'the Tallaght Two', was the first s 2 application to the Court of Criminal Appeal. The case involved the theft of a car by a number of youths from the owner's driveway. Having witnessed

---

[63] *ibid.* at 311.
[64] [2009] IECCA 56.
[65] [1997] 2 IR 225. Mr Pringle is now pursuing a substantial civil claim: *Pringle v Ireland* [1999] 4 IR 10.
[66] [1995] 2 IR 517.
[67] [1997] 1 IR 40. Indeed it would not be possible for the Court to certify that a miscarriage of justice had occurred otherwise – the very fact that it is newly discovered evidence means by definition that the jury never heard it.
[68] [1995] 2 IR 517.

the incident, the owner jumped on the bonnet of the car while it was moving, where he remained until the front seat passenger knocked him off. The owner and his son later identified the two defendants in the District Court. Both defendants were convicted and received five year sentences. A retrial was later ordered subsequent to a third party, who was in the vehicle, claiming that Meleady was not in the front seat of the car during the incident. They were convicted on retrial where the defence lawyer failed to raise this factual issue and did not call the accused to testify in spite of his continued statement that he was not in the car.

Subsequent to public disquiet concerning the case in 1990 a TV documentary revealed fingerprint evidence which had not been disclosed at trial. This confirmed that another passenger in the car had been in the front seat, a fact which that passenger had maintained throughout the trial. The fact that a forensic examination of the car had been conducted was never disclosed to the defence. At this point the Minister for Justice remitted the remainder of the sentences to be served: seven months for Meleady and nothing for Grogan who had by then been released. Following the passing of the 1993 Act both applied to the Court of Criminal Appeal to have their case declared a miscarriage of justice. The Court declared the convictions unsafe and accepted that these two points of non-disclosure could be considered newly-discovered facts. Following an appeal on a point of law to the Supreme Court,[69] the Court of Criminal Appeal found that these new facts were such that had they been available to the trial judge the identification evidence would have been excluded and with no other evidence of guilt the case involved a miscarriage of justice.[70] **[14–43]**

In the original application to the Court of Criminal Appeal in *Meleady*, the court had declined to define a miscarriage of justice, though it did state that the term "is not confined to the question of actual innocence but extends to the administration in a given case of the justice system itself". In *Pringle*, when the decision of the Court of Criminal Appeal not to certify a miscarriage of justice was appealed to the Supreme Court, Lynch J in a minority judgment suggested that the primary meaning of the term was that a certificate should only be issued where an applicant shows that on the balance of probabilities, on the basis of relevant and admissible evidence, he is innocent of the offence.[71] **[14–44]**

When the *Meleady* case was returned to the Court of Criminal Appeal from the Supreme Court, it declined to use the definition of the term suggested by Lynch J in *Pringle* as it would lead to problems of proof for the defence.[72] The Court in that case preferred to say that the applicant had to prove on the balance of probabilities that a miscarriage of justice had occurred. The Court also stated that the term "is not confined to the question of actual innocence but extends to the administration in a given case of the justice system itself."[73] Saying that a jury might have acquitted had they heard the new evidence creates a possibility, not a probability, of a miscarriage. In the *Meleady* case, the judge, had he known the facts, might have excluded the **[14–45]**

[69] [1997] 2 IR 249.
[70] [2001] 4 IR 16.
[71] *People (DPP) v Pringle (No 2)* [1997] 2 IR 225.
[72] [2001] 4 IR 16.
[73] *ibid.*

identification evidence in which case there would have been no evidence of guilt to put to the jury. On this basis the Court ordered that there had been a miscarriage of justice. The conclusion which could be drawn is that for a miscarriage of justice to be found the accused should never have been on trial. The denial of the constitutional rights of the accused in this case could, it was hinted, also have produced the same result. This standard does not require that the accused is factually innocent of the crime. Indeed, in *People (DPP) v Shortt (No 2)*[74] the Court specifically stated that its finding of a miscarriage of justice should not be interpreted as a finding of innocence. In that case, the Court confined its definition of the term to that found in Meleady: innocence or a grave defect in the administration of justice. In *Shortt*, the deliberate concealment of documents by gardaí, the perjury of a garda who was the main prosecution witness and the importance of these documents and this testimony to the conviction was considered "a grave defect in the administration of justice, brought about by agents of the State"[75] which led to a miscarriage of justice within the meaning set out in *Meleady*.

[14–46] The most substantive definition of what is considered a miscarriage of justice was provided in the case of *People (DPP) v Wall*.[76] In 2005 Nora Wall had a conviction for rape certified a miscarriage of justice by the Court of Criminal Appeal. She had been imprisoned in 1999 for life. Six weeks after her conviction the DPP agreed to a retrial after some questions arose regarding non-disclosure of evidence relating to one of the witnesses. Four months later the DPP said he would not be pursuing the retrial, stating that the accused should be considered innocent of all the charges and the Court thereby quashed the conviction. Wall, a nun, sought a certificate of a miscarriage of justice on the basis of newly discovered facts. The DPP agreed at the hearing that a certificate should be granted. The Court, in its decision granting the certificate, clarified a number of the applicable legal principles. It stated that in such an application the burden of proof rests on the accused and that the civil standard of "on the balance of probabilities" is to apply. The Court did not feel it would be helpful to provide an exhaustive definition of the term "miscarriage of justice" but a number of examples, not constituting a complete list, could be provided:

- Where the innocence of the accused can be established;
- Where the prosecution should never have been brought in the first place as there was never any credible evidence implicating the accused;
- Where there has been such a departure from the rules of judicial procedures as to make what happened irreconcilable with judicial or constitutional procedure.
- Where there has been a grave defect in the administration of justice, brought about by agents of the State.

[14–47] In this case, the Court found sufficient newly discovered facts. One of the complainants had a history of making false complaints of assault, both physical and sexual, and had a history of psychiatric problems. It was later revealed that an order had been issued that the key witness should not be called at trial, having been deemed unreliable. That witness later admitted to a friend that she had lied in evidence, in saying that she had

[74] [2002] 2 IR 696.
[75] *ibid.* p 710.
[76] [2005] IECCA 140.

been an eye-witness to the events complained of. The court was satisfied as a result that there had been a serious defect in the administration of justice. There were a variety of factors which led to a conclusion of a miscarriage of justice.

Further elaboration on the meaning of "miscarriage of justice" came in the case of *DPP v Hannon*.[77] Mr Hannon had been convicted of sexual assault in 1997. The conviction was based solely on the testimony of the 10-year-old complainant. Mr Hannon received a four year suspended sentence as the Court did not believe he had a propensity for criminal behaviour and the assault had taken place in the context of a family feud. Nine years later, the complainant, who had since moved to America, returned to Ireland to recant her statement and admit that she had falsified the allegation. Mr Hannon, in the case at hand, sought a declaration of miscarriage of justice. The DPP challenged the declaration, arguing that a miscarriage of justice could only occur where there is some "fault on the part of either the prosecutor or of the Garda investigators or other State agents". No such fault had been established. It was accepted that the case was well investigated and tried but with just the complainant's testimony it was a simple case of the jury believing a false story. Reviewing the Irish and English caselaw, as well as the international commitments Ireland has under the ICCPR and the ECHR, the Court found no requirement of State fault for a miscarriage of justice to have occurred. Hardiman J commented, "It is difficult to know what is more obviously within the ordinary or dictionary meaning of the phrase 'miscarriage of justice' than the conviction of an innocent person". This case reaffirms what may already have been clear from the Wall case, that innocence is sufficient to prove a miscarriage of justice even though the wrongful conviction came about by no fault of the State, and, indeed, where the State acted entirely appropriately at all stages. **[14–48]**

(iv) Further Applications

An application under this procedure does not prevent a further application but the applicant would then have to show that a new fact had come to light after the hearing of the first application, or that there was a fact the significance of which he had not appreciated at the hearing. Indeed there is no reason why an individual cannot continue to make applications indefinitely as long as he can support an application with appropriate evidence. **[14–49]**

Petition for Pardon

Aside from the court procedure provided in the 1993 Act, the Act sets out specific guidelines on the operation of the granting of a pardon. This applies to an individual whose conviction remains following an appeal, and who alleges that a new or newly-discovered fact shows that a miscarriage of justice has occurred in relation to the conviction. Unlike the s 2 procedure, this does not only apply to convictions on indictment though of course those individuals convicted on indictment can also take this route. **[14–50]**

When the Minister for Justice receives the application, he may make enquiries or cause enquiries to be made "as he considers necessary". Naturally, if the Minister does not **[14–51]**

[77] [2009] IECCA 43.

feel it is necessary to make any enquiries, he is under no legislative obligation to do so. Once these initial enquiries are made, the Minister can do one of four things:

1. Advise the petitioner that the matter would be more appropriately dealt with by way of the s 2 application procedure;
2. Find that the facts do not establish that a miscarriage of justice has occurred and that no useful purpose would be served by furthering the investigation;
3. Recommend to Government that the President be advised to grant a pardon in respect of the offence for which the petitioner was convicted;
4. Appoint a Committee of Investigation under s 8.

[14–52] Importantly, the constitutional power of pardon remains separate and apart from the 1993 Act. Section 7(6) further provides that the Minister can be petitioned by someone other than the convicted person – ensuring, for example, that posthumous relief can be sought. According to the Department of Justice, by 2009 no petitions for pardon had been made to the Minister.[78]

Government Committee of Inquiry

[14–53] Section 8 of the 1993 Act also concerns the role of the Government, and its decision-making power in the context of Art 13.6 of the Constitution. Where a petition for pardon has been made, the Government may establish a Committee to enquire into the subject matter of the petition. Again, here, there is no obligation on the Government to set up such an ad hoc Committee every time a petition is made: it is entirely at their discretion. The Committee is a tribunal of inquiry within the meaning of the Tribunals of Inquiry (Evidence) Acts 1921 and 1979.[79] The Committee can comprise of one or more persons. Either the Committee (where it is a single person) or the Chairperson of the Committee must be a judge or former judge, or practicing barrister or solicitor of not less than ten years standing.

[14–54] What is fundamentally different about the s 8 committee, as compared with the courts, is that it is empowered under s 8(5) to receive any evidence or information as it sees fit, even if that evidence would not be admissible in a court of law. Thus, it will not be bound by the usual rules of evidence, a power which is recognised as being crucial to determining whether a miscarriage of justice actually occurred. While the legislation seems to envisage the Committee operating on an *ad hoc* basis, it seems as if there is nothing which would prevent it from having a more permanent existence: that is, there is currently scope for a CCRC-type body to be established in this jurisdiction which would advise the Government on the granting of pardons. Where the Minister is petitioned, it seems that cases are either routinely referred to the Court of Criminal Appeal under s 2 or the Government advises the President to grant a pardon under Art 13.6 without resorting to an independent enquiry. It would appear that there has been no committee of inquiry set up to date.[80]

---

[78] Personal communications with the authors in Spring 2009.

[79] As amended by the Tribunals of Inquiry (Evidence) (Amendment) Act 2002 and Tribunals of Inquiry (Evidence) (Amendment) Act 1997.

[80] The Dean Lyons Inquiry, for example, was set up under the Commission of Investigations Act 2004 rather than this procedure.

Compensation

Section 9 of the Act deals with the issue of compensation and states that in any case where a conviction has been quashed under a s 2 application, where a pardon has been granted under s 7, where the Minister has decided a miscarriage of justice has occurred or where a conviction has been quashed by a court and it is certified that a miscarriage of justice has occurred, the Minister shall pay compensation, unless the miscarriage was due to the non-disclosure of the fact by the convicted person. The amount of compensation to be awarded is at the discretion of the Minister, subsequent to an application to the Minister.[81] An applicant can appeal the amount awarded to the High Court. **[14–55]**

In the case of *Connell v DPP*[82] the applicant had been convicted of murder in 1991, had this conviction quashed in 1995 by way of the initial appeals process and then applied in 1997 for compensation under s 9. On application to the Court of Criminal Appeal it was confirmed that compensation was payable where the conviction had been overturned through ordinary appeal procedures. The argument had been made by the DPP that only individuals whose convictions had been quashed by the s 2 procedure could make an application for compensation to the Minister. The Court clarified however that the procedures under the 1993 Act are open to anyone who has had a conviction overturned, where that court felt a new or newly discovered fact showed that a miscarriage of justice had occurred. If the court which quashed the conviction did not express a view on this issue the applicant "is entitled to have the court enter into an inquiry as to whether he is entitled to a certificate that a newly-discovered fact shows that there has been a miscarriage of justice."[83] Such a certificate must be granted however, before an application for compensation can be submitted. **[14–56]**

In the *Hannon*[84] case the Court considered Ireland's international obligations to make payments of compensation where there has been a miscarriage of justice. Obiter, Hardiman J acknowledged that the question of "whether only a person whose innocence is recognised or incontrovertible is entitled to such a certificate" was likely to arise in the not too distant future. A conflict between national and international requirements could arise here as the 1993 Act states that compensation should be paid where a miscarriage of justice has been certified, which has been established in the Irish courts as not being limited to cases where innocence can be proven. However the ECHR requires compensation to be paid where there has been a miscarriage of justice but the French version of the text, which was consulted in *Hannon*, speaks of a person who is '*reconnu innocent*'. It may therefore be possible to argue that under the ECHR compensation need only be awarded to persons who are clearly innocent. This would be undesirable both for its conflict with established Irish law and the enormous evidential burden it would place on defendants. And while the development of the DNA database in Ireland[85] may expand the cases in which actual innocence can be established, there will remain numerous cases in which innocence is beyond evidential support. **[14–57]**

---

81 Criminal Procedure Act 1993, s 9(3).

82 [1999] 4 IR 1.

83 *ibid.* at 9.

84 *DPP v Hannon* [2009] IECCA 43.

85 See Chapter Four, paras 4-29 – 4-35.

[14–58] In *Shortt v An Garda Commissioner*[86] Mr Shortt, having secured a certificate of a miscarriage of justice from the Court of Criminal Appeal, instituted an action for damages, which is permitted under s 9 as well as applications to the Minister for compensation. As no details are available on whether the Minister has paid compensation to any victims of miscarriages of justice under the 1993 scheme, this case is instructive on the matter. It concerned the owner of a nighclub in Donegal who was convicted on 13 counts of knowing and allowing drugs to be found on his premises, when in fact there had been none. He spent 27 months in prison and his business was burnt down. He suffered serious mental and physical ill-health in prison. On release, aged 63, his business had been destroyed and he was treated like a pariah in the town. Even with the declaration of miscarriage of justice his relationship with the community did not improve. The events also worsened a pre-existing problem of alcohol abuse.

[14–59] The High Court stated that under s 9 the applicant could only claim damages in relation to the impact of the conviction, not the investigation or trial, though there may well be a claim to the latter under separate provisions. The Court accepted that the payment of damages would vindicate the plaintiff in the eyes of his community and it accepted remoteness of damages arguments that the garda actions did lead to the burning of his business. The High Court awarded €1.9 million to the plaintiff, €1.4 million of which was for loss of premises and earnings. €500,000 was awarded as general damages under the 1993 Act for the personal impact of the events on Mr Shortt. The Plaintiff appealed this decision to the Supreme Court which ruled in March 2007.[87] Murray CJ, in that court, felt it necessary to take into account

> "the especially grave features to this case ... the conduct of those two [gardaí] probably constitutes the gravest dereliction of duty and abuse of power that one could fearfully contemplate would be engaged in by servants of the State and officers of law and order."[88]

[14–60] In particular the Supreme Court was keen to award exemplary damages to mark the court's disapproval of this conduct and to have some punitive effect. Given all of this the court awarded €1 million in exemplary damages, which was additional to the High Court's award. Murray CJ also raised the award of general damages from €500,000 to €2.25 million. Hardiman J also gave a detailed judgment in this case and agreed with the monetary findings of the Chief Justice, having paid particular attention to the aggravating factors in the case, including the lack of an apology for what the plaintiff had suffered. This equated to a total of €4.6 million in damages being paid to Mr Shortt.

[14–61] This substantial and merited award is a clear indication of the view taken by the Supreme Court of miscarriages of justice, particularly where agents of the State have so knowingly abused the rights of citizens. In that regard this case is extreme; however in other cases different factors may be present, such as particularly lengthy periods of detention, which could give rise to similar findings.

---

86 [2005] IEHC 311.

87 [2007] 4 IR 587.

88 *ibid.* p 593.

V. Conclusion

The criminal justice system has internal checks and balances to ensure that all convictions are properly made, with due regard to human rights, civil liberties and due process. However, there are occasions when the system breaks down and a miscarriage of justice will occur. Admittedly, this is not often, but the effect it has both on the criminal justice system and society as a whole can be catastrophic. **[14–62]**

Through the operation of the presidential power of pardon and the Criminal Procedure Act 1993, Irish law goes some way in addressing those few cases where the system does not work. Whether this is in line with international best practice is not clear. The issue of payment of compensation has been raised but this legislation could be criticised for failure to provide an opportunity for a person convicted summarily to have the conviction declared a miscarriage of justice. While the sentence might be minor there is no doubt that it can, nonetheless, have serious repercussions for an individual. No doubt, over the coming years, further cases will seek to challenge and expand the provisions of the 1993 Act. **[14–63]**

Throughout this text, we have noted the increasing shift in the Irish criminal justice system from its traditional "due process" underpinnings towards a "crime control" model. This latter model places the centre of gravity of the criminal process in the informal, pre-trial stage and seeks, accordingly, to increase speed and efficiency by circumventing the formal requirements of the trial process to a significant extent. When speed and efficiency are championed over the protection of rights and the satisfaction of rules which exist to protect those rights the risk of miscarriages of justice occurring increases. The Irish courts and legislature must be mindful to ensure that any changes in the criminal justice system which are thought to be necessary do not have this undesirable result.

INDEX